The Human Rights Act and the Assault on Liberty:

Rights and Asylum in the UK

The *Human Rights Act* and the Assault on Liberty: Rights and Asylum in the UK

Parnesh Sharma

Oriel College
University of Oxford

Nottingham
University Press

First published by Nottingham University Press

This reissued original edition published 2023 by 5m Books Ltd www.5mbooks.com

Copyright © Nottingham University Press 2023

British Library Cataloguing in Publication Data
The Human Rights Act the Assault on Liberty:
Rights and Asylum in the UK
Sharma, P.

ISBN 9781789183139

Disclaimer

Every reasonable effort has been made to ensure that the material in this book is true, correct, complete and appropriate at the time of writing. Nevertheless the publishers, the editors and the authors do not accept responsibility for any omission or error, or for any injury, damage, loss or financial consequences arising from the use of the book.

Typeset by Nottingham University Press, Nottingham

EU GPSR Authorised Representative
LOGOS EUROPE, 9 rue Nicolas Poussin, 17000, LA ROCHELLE, France
E-mail: Contact@logoseurope.eu

FOREWORD

A major objective of the *Human Rights Act* (HRA) was to bring about a culture of rights in the UK. Its introduction fore-grounded questions about the use of rights to advance social justice issues and was the impetus for this research. At about the same time as the Act came into effect another law, Section 55, an antithesis of what the HRA promised, was passed which forced thousands of asylum-seekers into destitution. Section 55 became a major battleground pitting non-governmental organisations (NGOs) against the Home Office in a three-year long campaign, characterised by rancour and viciousness, unlike any in recent memory. The NGOs, with the new HRA as a key part of their strategy, defeated the legislation. This book, a bottom-up case study of rights at work, examines the role of rights in the campaign to assess (1) if rights brought about social changes and (2) is a culture of rights developing in the UK? The book first considers the various theoretical frameworks on rights and social change and analyses various case studies of rights at work. Context is important; therefore, it also examines how asylum has come to be framed in present-day discourse, with an overview on the evolution of welfare as a coercive measure. The study, framed against current events of the day, concludes that while test-case challenges eventually defeated Section 55 welfare as a coercive measure continues. In short, the HRA has proven to be ineffective against illiberal policies and the development of a culture of rights, insofar as asylum is concerned, has stalled. And it has happened with deliberation by a government determined to be tough on asylum irrespective of the HRA.

P Sharma

Centre for Socio-Legal Studies

Oxford, 2009

ACKNOWLEDGEMENTS

This research could not have been completed without the patience, kindness, and assistance of countless individuals. I am thankful to all and particularly indebted to the following:

Don Flynn, formerly Senior Policy Director at Joint Council for the Welfare of Immigrants (JCWI), now Director of Migrants Right Network (MRN) and Tauhid Pasha, formerly Legal Director at JCWI, now a globetrotting advisor with the International Organisation for Migration (IOM), were instrumental in so many respects. They provided advice, referrals and guidance, and proved to be a treasure trove of information. They kindly allotted me a work-desk at JCWI for the frequent fieldtrips to London, and put up with incessant emails and telephone calls seeking verification and other information. All this they did with good humour, a great deal of patience, and encyclopaedic knowledge of the issues. I would also like to acknowledge, with gratitude, the gracious assistance of Alex Gask of Liberty, Jonathan, Rhian, and Sameena of JCWI, Kat Lorenz of Refugee Action, Uma Joshi and Clare Shepton of Shelter, Maurice Wren of Asylum Aid, Imran Hussain of the Refugee Council, Sarah Cutler of Bail for Immigration Detainees (BID), Colin Yeo of Immigration Advisory Service, and the many caseworkers and volunteers (at various NGOs) who asked to remain anonymous.

An undertaking of this magnitude requires a supervisor with a sure hand. And for this I am particularly indebted to Denis Galligan, professor of Law in Oxford, who no doubt suffered under the strain of guiding my work from inception to completion. But he did so with good humour, incisive feedback, and liberal use of red ink.

I am grateful to Ximena Cobo Santillan, human rights lawyer and activist, for her unconditional support, encouragement, friendship, and feedback on an earlier version; Insa Koch for her support and friendship and for suggesting much-needed improvements; and Tal Ofek, sports fanatic and athlete, for valuable feedback and rescuing me (more than once) whenever I needed late night access to a rather fortified faculty building.

The dreaming spires, particularly during the long dreary months of winter, can be absent much of its charms. But great friends – Adel Osseiran, Terry Simpson, Carsten Korfmacher, Brad Murray, Elena Christophorou, Christian Glossner, Laura Soverino, Nikola Soukmandjiev, Troels Larsen, Dave Tolley, and Keli Mutiso – were always there and immeasurably enhanced the Oxford experience. We may never meet again but I shall cherish forever a lifetime of memories.

And, finally, a special thanks to Bob Ratner, former graduate supervisor and now Professor Emeritus (University of British Columbia) for his friendship, unending support, encouragement, and advice.

To all I wish to express my most sincere thanks because without you this work would not have been completed. The responsibility for this work, however, and any shortcomings it may contain are mine.

This is especially for my mother
Krishna K. Sharma

TABLE OF CONTENTS

TABLE OF ABBREVIATIONS

ARC	Asylum Rights Campaign
BBC	British Broadcasting Corporation
BIHR	British Institute of Human Rights
BME	black minority ethnic
CAB	(National Association) Citizen's Advice Bureau
CADAS	Coalition Against the Destitution of Asylum-Seekers
ECHR	European Convention on Human Rights
ECRI	European Commission Against Racism and Intolerance
EDM	Early Day Motion
EIN	Electronic Immigration Network
HRA	*Human Rights Act*
IAP	Inter-Agency Partnership
IAS	Immigration Advisory Service
ILPA	Immigration Law Practitioners Association
IND	Immigration and Nationality Directorate
JCHR	Joint Committee on Human Rights
JCWI	Joint Council for the Welfare of Immigrants
LEAF	Women's Legal Education and Action Fund
LJ	Lord Justice
MP	Member of Parliament
MRN	Migrant Rights Network
NACAB	National Association Citizen's Advice Bureau
NASS	National Asylum Support Service
NATO	North Atlantic Treaty Organization
NCADC	National Coalition of Anti-Deportation Campaigns
NGO	Non-Government Organization
NHS	National Health Service
RCO	Refugee community organization
UNHCR	United Nations High Commissioner for Refugees

TABLE OF CASES

Canada

R v Drybones [1970] SCR 282

Singh v Minister of Employment and Immigration [1985] 1 SCR 177 (SC)

European Court of Human Rights (ECHR)

Pretty v United Kingdom (2002) 35 EHRR 1

United Kingdom

R v Secretary of State for Social Security ex parte Joint Council for the Welfare of Immigrants [1997] 1WLR 275, CA (CA)

Saadi & Ors, R (on the application of) v Secretary Of State For Home Department [2001] EWHC Admin 670

Secretary of State for the Home Department ex parte Saadi (FC) and Others (FC) [2002] UKHL 41

R (on the application of Q and Others) v Secretary of State for the Home Department [2003] 2 All ER 905, Admin

R (on the application of S, D, T) v Secretary of State for the Home Department [2003] EWCH 1941 (Admin)

Q and Others v Secretary of State for the Home Department [2003] EWCA Civ 364 (Court of Appeal)

R (on the application of D) v Secretary of State for the Home Department [2003] EWCA Civ 852 (Court of Appeal)

R ('T') v The Secretary of State for the Home Department [2003] EWCA Civ 1285

R (on the application of Q) v Secretary of State for the Home Department [2003] All ER (D) 409

R (on the application of Limbuela) v Secretary of State for the Home Department [2004] EWCH 219 (Admin)

R (on the application of Tesema) v Secretary of State for the Home Department [2004] All ER (D) 247

Adam v Secretary of State for the Home Department [2004] All ER (D) 264

Secretary of State for the Home Department v Limbuela, Tesema & Adam [2004] EWCA Civ 540

Zardasht v Secretary of State [2004] EWHC 91 Admin

R. v. Secretary of State for the Home Department ex parte Limbuela [2005] UKHL 66

Saadi v The United Kingdom [2008] ECHR 80

R v Asfaw [2008] UKHK 31

United States

Brown v Board of Education 347 U.S. 483 (1954)

Roe v Wade 410 U.S. 113 (1973)

TABLE OF STATUTES

Canada

Canadian Bill of Rights, SC 1960, c. 44

Canadian Charter of Rights and Freedoms as Part I of the Constitution Act, 1982, being Schedule B to the Canada Act 1982, ch. 11 (U.K.).

United Kingdom

Asylum and Immigration Appeals Act 1993

Asylum and Immigration Act 1996

Human Rights Act 1998

Immigration and Asylum Act 1999

Nationality, Immigration and Asylum Act 2002

Asylum and Immigration (Treatment of Claimants, etc.) Act 2004

Immigration, Asylum and Nationality Act 2006

United States

The Constitution of the United States (Bill of Rights)

Regional and International Documents

Convention for the Protection of Human Rights and Fundamental Freedoms (European Convention on Human Rights, as amended) (signed 4 November 1950, entered into force 3 September 1953)

Convention Against Torture and Other Cruel, Inhuman or Degrading Treatment or Punishment, 10 December 1984 (United Nations)

Convention Relating to the Status of Refugees, 28 July 1951 (United Nations)

Protocol Relating to the Status of Refugees, 30 January 1967 (United Nations)

Convention against Torture and Other Cruel, Inhuman or Degrading Treatment or Punishment

International Covenant on Civil and Political Rights

Universal Declaration of Human Rights

LIST OF TABLES

1. RESEARCH QUESTION, METHODOLOGY, AND SUMMARY OF FINDINGS

1.1 Introduction

Where is the *Human Rights Act, 1998* (HRA) headed? Is the UK on the cusp of a rights revolution? A major objective of the HRA, entrenching the *European Convention on Human Rights* into domestic law, was to bring about a cultural change or a 'culture of rights'. What was meant by a culture of rights or how it was to be achieved was not clearly defined by the drafters or the government at promulgation and, aside from the articulation of broad and ambitious goals, remains problematic to conceptualize. However it has been generally inferred to mean the pursuit of progressive social goals directed at empowering citizens and providing a real measure of protection for the marginalised and powerless of society.[1] The HRA was introduced during a period of much soul searching about the nature of British society and a perception of a society rife with racism, social exclusion, social malaise, and a deepening chasm between the haves and have-nots.[2] The Act was borne of an ambitious hope that enhancing awareness of human rights would in turn result in a culture of rights, in a more inclusive, more caring Britain.[3]

This chapter outlines the research question, details the methodology, and summarises the findings of a bottom-up study of rights at work – a case study, which examined the role of the HRA in the fight over welfare benefits for asylum-seekers, as a means of assessing if a culture of rights is developing in the UK. The research also examines the larger questions of rights and social change and the rights of asylum-seekers and the right to asylum.

1.2 Research Question: Rights and Social Change

The introduction of the HRA brought to the fore questions about the transformative capacity of law and provided the impetus for this research which is informed by the broader question of rights and social change. What are the possibilities and

---

[1] Joint Committee On Human Rights, *The Human Rights Act: the DCA and Home Office Reviews* (HL Paper 278 2006) 98 (para 140)

[2] William MacPherson and Home Office, *The Stephen Lawrence Inquiry: Report of an Inquiry* (1999)

[3] Home Office, *Rights Brought Home: the Human Rights Bill* (1997)

potential of rights in bringing about social changes for the disadvantaged of society? Can the strategic use of rights be a tool or resource for non-governmental organisations (NGOs) advocating for disadvantaged groups in the UK? Can rights change or improve the social situation for possibly the most disadvantaged and powerless constituency in UK society, the tens of thousands of asylum-seekers seeking sanctuary? Or will it, as some have argued, make no difference; that the existing 'winners and losers' of society will be the same winners and losers under the Act?[4]

To examine rights at work I asked the following questions: (a) how has the Act been received by NGOs which advocate for and work on behalf of asylum-seekers; (b) how are these groups using the HRA to advance social justice issues; (c) how are rights mobilized; and (d) what strategies do these groups employ? This narrowed focus was essential for a contextual and nuanced examination of rights and social change, of the arena in which the NGOs work, and the role of rights in that work.

1.3   Culture of Rights Defined

In a 2003 report, the Joint Committee on Human Rights (JCHR), argued that a 'culture of respect for human rights was a goal worth striving for' and that it would create a 'more humane society, a more responsive government and better public services'. A key to developing such a culture, the Committee continued, was to create a culture in public life where human rights are central to policy, legislation, and public services.[5] Later, in 2006, the Committee, referring to *Rights Brought Home* and paraphrasing the earlier report, further defined what it meant by a culture of rights:

> . . . one that fosters basic respect for human rights and creates
> a climate in which such respect becomes an integral part of our
> way of life and a reference point for our dealing with public
> authorities and each other. Properly understood as a culture in

---

[4]   L Clements (2005) 'Winners and Losers' 32 Journal of Law and Society 1 34-50 (citing Sir Stephen Sedley)

[5]   Joint Committee on Human Rights, *The Case for a Human Rights Commission*, Sixth Report of Session 2002-03 (2003) HL Paper 67-I p. 5

which there is a widely shared sense of entitlement to human rights . . . in which all our institutional policies and practices are influenced by these ideas . . . [6]

The Committee added:

> The building of a human rights culture over time would depend not just on courts awarding remedies for violations of individuals' rights, but on decision-makers in all public services internalizing the requirements of human rights law, integrating those standards into their policy and decision-making processes, and ensuring that the delivery of public services in all fields is fully informed by human rights considerations.

1.4   Section 55: A Case Study

The campaign against Section 55 of the *Nationality, Immigration and Asylum Act 2002*, which limited access to welfare benefits for asylum-seekers, offers an instructive lens to examine the question of rights and social change and ask if a culture of rights is taking root in the UK. Government policy regarding welfare benefits for asylum-seekers has long been and continues to be a fertile ground for conflict.[7] And the fight over Section 55, the most recent in a series of fights over welfare for asylum-seekers, was quite possibly the most acrimonious reaching a level of rancour unlike any in the recent history of asylum.[8] The campaign began in early October 2002, pitting the NGOs against a government intent on limiting the right to asylum *and* rights of asylum-seekers, and ended in November 2005 with a House of Lords ruling which found the government in breach of Convention rights.

Section 55 was introduced as a late amendment to an immigration Bill in October 2002 and set off alarm bells for NGOs who work with and advocate on

---

[6]   Joint Committee On Human Rights, *The Human Rights Act: the DCA and Home Office Reviews* (HL Paper 278 2006) 98 (para 140) referring to *The Case for a Human Rights Commission*, Sixth Report of Session 2002-03 (2003) HL Paper 67-I para. 2

[7]   See Chapter 4 for a review of the recent history of legislating against benefits for asylum-seekers.

[8]   Almost everyone I interviewed, many veterans of past campaigns against the government, reported that they had never experienced such rancour and 'viciousness'.

behalf of asylum-seekers. Almost immediately they commenced a concerted effort, to first amend and then later to repeal the legislation, against a 'tough as boots' Home Office. The campaign was bitter and hard-fought every step of the way and lasted three years.[9] During that period an estimated 10,000 asylum-seekers were deliberately forced into destitution and a 'war' was ignited between the judiciary and the Home Secretary.[10] The campaign was characterised by rancour and heated commentary bordering on incitement; examples include:

- racist and death threats were made against lawyers representing NGOs and asylum-seekers;

- NGOs reported an increase in racist attacks against asylum-seekers;[11]

- a London law firm specialising in asylum was fire-bombed and racist graffiti written on equipment;

- the official Opposition and the media called for the repeal of the HRA;

- there were calls for the UK to withdraw from the *1951 UN Convention Relating to the Status of Refugees;*

- the government promised legislation to limit the reach of the HRA;

- some solicitors received mail from the British National Party urging a 'fight against the influx of asylum-seekers';

- the tabloid media mounted a relentless campaign against the HRA and asylum-seekers calling them 'diseased hordes' and 'cheats'.[12]

Such was the level of rancour that international organisations such as the UN, Amnesty International, and Oxfam felt compelled to call for 'calm' as the 'war against asylum' raged. The Church of England also stepped into the fray rebuking the government for its treatment of asylum-seekers and joined forces with the

---

9   See Chapters 5 to 8.
10   See Chapter 9; BBC, 'Asylum hardships 'are deliberate'' (2007) BBC News <http://news.bbc.co.uk/1/hi/uk_politics/6507961.stm> (29 Jun)
11   BBC, 'Asylum: Attacks and deaths 2001 - 2003' (2003) 22 July BBC News <http://news.bbc.co.uk/2/hi/uk_news/3087569.stm>
12   R Verkaik, 'Immigration lawyers facing campaign of fire-bombing and death threats' *The Independent* (12 April 2004)

NGOs in their campaign against a 'nasty piece' of legislation.[13] And it was a no-holds barred 'bare-knuckle' battle, a classic David v Goliath – the powerful Home Office against a disparate and under-resourced group of NGOs fighting over a policy which an incredulous newspaper editorial described as 'almost beyond belief'; church leaders called it 'grotesque'.[14]

1.5.   Why Asylum (and Asylum-Seekers)?

Asylum-seekers in Britain are an embattled and powerless group and, according to some observers, victims of an undeclared 'war' in a country which does not want them.[15] It is arguable that a true test of rights is the measure of protection they afford to the vulnerable and marginalised of society. And nowhere is the struggle on the ground for social change more apparent than in the fight over asylum waged by a group of dedicated and under-resourced NGOs. Arguably the fight represents a litmus test for rights. The issues concerning asylum are heavily contested; asylum-seekers continue to be vilified in the tabloid press and their rights are under constant attack by the government and conservative organizations in the UK.[16] It has been primarily over asylum that the HRA, in its relatively short period of existence, has achieved prominence, coming under severe and sustained attacks during the campaign.[17] Such was the anger that the official Opposition promised to repeal the HRA if elected. The very government, which implemented the Act, appeared to backtrack with serious consideration given to limiting its reach (and opting out of the 1951 UN Convention).[18] The Home Secretary was reported to be 'spitting blood' and reacting 'with fury' blaming the 'human rights lobby' for defeats (on asylum) in the courts.[19] These are ominous portents for rights and cultural change.

---

[13]   See Chapters 4, 5, and 6 for a fuller discussion on the events covering the period 2002-2005.

[14]   Leader, 'Almost Beyond Belief' *Guardian* (25 November 2003); A Asthana, 'Asylum policy is 'grotesque' ' *The Observer* (27 Feb 2005)

[15]   G Hinsliff and M Bright, 'Labour fuels war on asylum' *The Observer* (06 Feb 2005)

[16]   Joint Committee On Human Rights, *The Treatment of Asylum-Seekers* (HL 81-1 2007); Liberty, *Evidence to the Joint Committee on Human Rights: Treatment of Asylum Seekers* (2006)

[17]   BBC, 'Asylum: Getting tough in 2003 ' (2003) BBC News <http://news.bbc.co.uk/1/hi/uk/3333865.stm>

[18]   S Chakrabarti (2005) 'Rights and Rhetoric: The Politics of Asylum and Human Rights Culture in the UK' 32 Journal of Law and Society 131

[19]   F Gibb, 'Blunkett v the Bench: the battle has begun' *The Times* (04 Mar 2003) 3; A Travis, 'Blunkett fury at asylum camp defeat' *Guardian* (08 Sep 2001)

1.6.   Why Non-Governmental Organisations?

The mere existence of a bill of rights does not automatically bring about social progress or even the playing field. Much more is required to give rights meaning and power. And this is where the everyday struggles on the ground come to the fore. The role of NGOs – as 'watchdogs', pressuring governments, influencing public policy, holding governments accountable, acting as additional checks on governments and other institutions, providing community and other services – have been well-documented and is of central importance in the arena of social justice and social change.[20] Many of these groups, also generally referred to as non-profits, charities, advocacy groups, civil society, voluntary sector, fifth estate, or social movements, have proven to be a thorn in the side of governments, institutions, and multi-national corporations holding them accountable for their actions and bringing about substantive and policy changes. For example Greenpeace and Amnesty International are powerful players in protecting the environment and human rights.[21] Prior to the HRA coming into effect several NGOs in the UK, including Liberty and the Refugee Council, had lobbied for it and supported the then-in-opposition Labour's initiative to 'bring rights home'.[22] These NGOs continue to monitor and challenge government policies on asylum, highlighting egregious abuses, pointing out contradictions, and holding departments and ministries accountable.

Stuart Eizenstat, former senior policy advisor to U.S. Presidents Carter and Clinton, refers to NGOs as the 'Fifth Estate' calling their function 'vitally important for democracies'.[23] According to Charles Epp (1998) it was persistence from below, by committed social movements, which was a key factor in bringing about a 'rights revolution' in the U.S. and Canada.[24] Will rights, then, become part

---

[20]   SE Eizenstat (2004) 'Nongovernmental Organizations as the Fifth Estate' Seton Hall Journal of Diplomacy and International Relations Summer/Fall 15-27; Petr van Tuijl (1999) 'NGOs and Human Rights: Sources of Justice and Democracy' 52 Journal of International Affairs

[21]   P-M Dupuy and L Vierucci, *NGOs in International Law: Efficiency in Flexibility?* (2008); J Nye, 'The Rising Power of NGOs' (2004) Daily Times <http://www.dailytimes.com.pk/default.asp?page=story_27-6-2004_pg3_7>

[22]   R Maiman, 'We've had to raise our game: Liberty's litigation strategy under the Human Rights Act 1998' in S Halliday and PD Schmidt (eds) *Human Rights Brought Home: Socio-Legal Perspectives on Human Rights in the National Context* (2004); Home Office (1997) *Rights Brought Home: the Human Rights Bill*

[23]   SE Eizenstat (2004) 'Nongovernmental Organizations as the Fifth Estate' p15

[24]   CR Epp, *The Rights Revolution: Lawyers, Activists, and Supreme Courts in Comparative Perspective* (1998)

of the social movement landscape in the UK? Much depends on the efforts on the ground and, more importantly, on how NGOs respond to the HRA and whether it is used strategically and effectively to advance social policy agendas.

1.7. Fieldwork

The arena of asylum is a continually changing and dynamic environment, but no one could have envisioned the particular and unique challenges I faced at the commencement of the project. The fieldwork was conducted during a particularly tumultuous period in London, the summer of 2005, a time fraught with unforeseen and tragic events, namely the terrorist bombings of July 7th and 21st which killed several people and brought London to a standstill. These events served to complicate and considerably delay the research and much of the original research plans had to be modified and adapted to this new and changed environment. Another factor which may have affected the findings – and this was particularly pronounced for NGOs serving the asylum-seeker community – was the general election held in May 2005, won by the governing Labour Party. As in previous elections, the topic of asylum-seekers, refugees, and immigration, three legally distinct but inextricably linked and conflated issues, were front and centre as being of major concern for the public and all major political parties.[25] The NGOs maintained a deliberate low profile and wariness fearing that highlighting a rights or any discourse on the subject of asylum would not arouse much sympathy amongst an electorate overwhelmingly opposed to asylum and generally to the HRA. Many felt that it would inflame rather than inform the political debate.[26] And with good reason in view of the general apprehension and suspicion of the Act, the continuing and increasing hostility towards asylum-seekers, and the competing promises of a 'get-tough' approach by both the governing Labour and opposition Conservatives.[27] The NGOs still recalled that not long before the election was announced the Act had come under sustained attack not only in the tabloid press but also by senior government ministers amidst

---

[25]   University of Essex, *The 2005 General Election in Great Britain* (2005); BBC, 'Election issues: Immigration' (2005) April 05 <http://news.bbc.co.uk/1/hi/uk_politics/vote_2005/issues/4352373.stm>

[26]   Interview notes (on file with author)

[27]   M Kettle, 'We hate our politicians, but we've never had it so good: Fear of immigration and crime is driving the parties to outbid each other' *Guardian* (08 Feb 2005)

serious consideration to opting out after high-profile defeats in the courts.[28] The opposition Conservatives had gone farther and promised to repeal the HRA if elected, a promise enthusiastically supported by the *Daily Mail.*[29]

The election factor was, however, mitigated owing to the duration of the fieldwork which concluded late October 2005. The bulk of the interviews were concluded in late August, but clarifications and follow-up interviews in response to new developments continued until November 2005; further follow-up to verify and/or confirm information continued until time of writing (August 2008).

1.8.   Methodology

In view of the extensive body of work on the theoretical and concrete empowerment of rights, case studies of rights at work, the promise of 'rights brought home' to make rights more accessible, the fact that many NGOs (including some who participated in this study) had lobbied for the Act, and the now well-established strategic use of rights by NGOs in various jurisdictions, I reasoned that NGOs in the UK would be receptive to using the HRA as a tool or resource in their work. I also reasoned that a lack of resources, a problem common to many NGOs in the asylum sector, would make them more receptive to using the Act in innovative ways to empower both their vulnerable clients and overworked staff. Furthermore, in view of the promise of the HRA to provide protection for the powerless of society and the theoretical framework underpinning this study, it seemed reasonable to conclude that NGOs, working with some of the most powerless, would look to the Act as important if not fundamental to their work. Many apparently did because, prior to the implementation of the HRA, they were ardent supporters. The nature of that support took various forms but consisted mostly of 'cheering on the sidelines' as many did not know what the Act would look like but instinctively felt that it would be a good thing and potentially useful in their sector.[30]

A case study approach, using multiple sources of data, allows for a detailed and contextual analysis where 'the boundaries between phenomenon and context are not clearly evident'.[31] I adopted Michael McCann's 'broadly interpretive'

---

[28]   J Rozenberg, 'Judges prepare for battle with Blunkett' *Daily Telegraph* (26 Feb 2003)
[29]   Comment, 'Common Sense and Human Rights' *Daily Mail* (05 March 2005)
[30]   Interview notes (on file with author)
[31]   RK Yin, *Case Study Research: Design and Methods* (1984)

framework which he used to good effect in his bottom-up study of rights at work – with the fight over pay equity serving as a case study.[32] This approach allowed for considerable flexibility given the exploratory nature of my research, the 'unknowns' in the field, and the unique circumstances (terrorist bombings in London) of a changed environment. Sources of data included interviews, behind-the-scenes information on campaign and test-case strategy, court decisions, reports by government bodies, independent agencies, and NGOs, and media coverage of the campaign.

During the fieldwork I interviewed a variety of NGO staff members – front-line caseworkers, volunteers, telephone help-line advisors, and managers – who work with asylum-seekers on a daily basis and had seen first-hand the effect of Section 55. I also interviewed several campaigners (solicitors, senior managers, and policy advisors) who, at one time or another, had been directly involved in the campaign. The interviewees also consisted of staff members who, while not directly involved in the campaign, had first-hand knowledge of 'behind-the-scenes' events.

My research, in some respects, breaks new ground for its bottom-up focus on rights and social change in the UK. There has been considerable doctrinal analysis of the HRA but, to date, very little socio-legal research on rights at work on the ground level.[33] This is not surprising in view of the relative 'newness' of the HRA – and undoubtedly it may be argued that it is still early days for 'impact' studies. However, this is not to say that signs should not be emerging as we enter the sixth year (at time of fieldwork) of the Act. The HRA, proclaimed in 1998 with much fanfare and bold predictions, came into effect in 2000; and, during the period beginning in October 2002 and ending in November 2005, played a central role in the campaign against Section 55. It is that period which is the focus of this study.

---

[32] M McCann, *Rights at Work: Pay Equity Reform and the Politics of Legal Mobilization* (1994)

[33] See: T Campbell KD Ewing and A Tomkins, *Sceptical Essays on Human Rights* (2001); S Halliday and PD Schmidt, *Human rights brought home: socio-legal perspectives on human rights in the national context* (2004); S Sedley (2005) 'The Rocks or the Open Sea: Where is the Human Rights Act Heading?' 32 Journal of Law and Society 1 3-17; L Clements and J Young (1999) 'Human Rights: Changing the Culture ' 26 Journal of Law and Society 1 1-5

1.8.1 Sources of Data

1.8.1.1 Test Cases

An important source of data was the three major test-case challenges to Section 55, in particular, the events surrounding the cases. Each decision is examined in-depth. I was provided with 'behind-the-scenes' information on how the cases were selected, and the criteria used to identify them. I was provided access to confidential files, copies of intervenor submissions, notes of meetings, and other materials relating to the strategy; I also interviewed some of the members of the legal team who had devised the strategy and represented the NGOs in the courts. I also examined the government's response to the court decisions and the events on the ground as recalled by those who had been actively involved in the campaign. I reviewed hundreds of press releases, speaking notes, in-house publications, and on-line material. Media coverage (all major newspapers and several websites) of the campaign, the court decisions, and government response were also important sources of data helping to fill in some 'gaps' and provided varying perspectives. Most of the major newspapers have blogs (allowing readers to comment on specific articles) and stories on asylum attract considerable comments, much of it impassioned, much of it clearly racist. I read through hundreds of blogs on the websites of the following: *Guardian, Daily Telegraph, Times, Independent, Sun, Daily Mirror*, and *New Statesman.*

1.8.1.2 Reports and Publications

Of significant value were several reports by independent bodies such as the Joint Committee on Human Rights, Audit Commission, Department of Constitutional Affairs (the ministry formerly responsible for the HRA), Ministry of Justice (the ministry now responsible), and Home Office publications and statistics. Hansard reporting of House of Commons and House of Lords discussions, question period, and debates on Section 55. I reviewed reports, publications, and empirical studies on the effects of Section 55 by the Mayor of London, international organisations such as Amnesty International, Human Rights Watch, and other commissioned studies. I reviewed reports by NGOs and think-tanks opposed to asylum (such as CIVITAS and Migration Watch). Other sources of data included reports by generalist human rights and law organisations such as JUSTICE, Public Law, and the British Institute of Human Rights (BIHR). The Electronic Immigration Network (EIN), a registered charity, allowed free access to their extensive database on immigration and asylum law and proved to be a valuable trove of information.

1.8.1.3 Staff Meetings, Conferences, and Confidential Material

Some NGOs, upon my signing of confidentiality agreements, allowed liberal access; I attended several staff meetings, observed front-line work, and had access to casework files including transcribed notes of various meetings and original copies of written submissions where the NGO had been granted intervenor status by the courts. The Joint Council for the Welfare of Immigrants (JCWI) provided office space and valuable referrals and kept me informed of various events; the Immigration Advisory Service (IAS) offered free admission to their conferences (and reimbursed my travel expenses). The Asylum Rights Campaign (ARC), an umbrella group of asylum-seeker NGOs, allowed me to attend their meetings and access to their membership database. The ARC serves as a clearing house of information and meets monthly to discuss strategy and new developments in asylum law and policy. It is an attempt by member organizations to introduce a semblance of coordination in their varied and relatively isolated approaches to lobbying and campaigning.[34] Their objective is to influence policy-makers and to improve the present system of determining asylum which they view as inefficient, profoundly unfair, and focused almost exclusively on deterrence rather than protection and fulfilling UK's international obligations.

These organizations – JCWI, IAS, and ARC – were crucial to securing the participation of interviewees and an indispensable source of contacts and referrals; many interviewees overcame the initial reluctance to participate once they became aware of their support. Another crucial factor in securing participation had to do with my background – a six-year career at a senior-level position with the Immigration and Refugee Board of Canada, a tribunal much admired by UK NGOs – which opened several doors. Nonetheless, and understandably, it remained difficult to gain access to some NGOs. Many were quite protective of their clients and suspicious of outsiders and would permit only limited access. Some allowed

---

[34]   Interview with Maurice Wren, Policy Officer, Asylum Aid (London May 2005)

only one or two staff members to be interviewed and most refused permission for the interview to be tape-recorded. Some agreed to personal interviews while others insisted on telephone discussions; and, some also complained of 'research fatigue,' of being inundated with far too many requests from too many research students. Most of the frontline caseworkers toil in relative anonymity and deal with what is 'now' and do not see the point of research, the results of which may not be known for months and rarely disseminated back to them.

Most of the interviewees, particularly caseworkers, requested anonymity because almost all had negative things to say about the Home Office, the government department responsible for the Immigration and Nationality Directorate (IND) and National Asylum Support Service (NASS), and feared that such comments would backfire and ultimately impact upon their clients and/or their organization. Whatever the interviewees may feel about the Home Office does not change the fact that they have to deal with it on a regular basis and no one wanted to jeopardise the relationship, no matter its nature. None of them, with the exception of those who had developed personal working relationships with certain Home Office staff, had anything positive to say finding them to be hostile and intransigent. Most interviewees were of the opinion that the Home Office was guided predominately by a 'culture of disbelief' and policy requirements than with complying with the HRA, leave alone UK's international obligations to asylum-seekers.

1.8.1.4 Interviews and Participant NGOs

At the conclusion of the fieldwork I had conducted a total of twenty in-depth and semi-structured interviews; the interviews were recorded (with permission) and all participants were guaranteed anonymity. The interviews were supplemented and complemented by questionnaires (see Appendix) completed by over thirty respondents. The questionnaires were designed for submission via email and asked the same questions that were asked during in-person interviews, though obviously it did not allow for the detailed discussions which often ensued during interviews. The email respondents were persons I had met during the fieldwork and with whom, for various reasons, I was unable to arrange a personal interview; some of the respondents were also unknown to me as they or their organization had been referred by others. The questionnaire served as a bridge – a valuable tool – for gathering data which otherwise would not have been possible via the conventional method of in-person interviews. I did contact several of them via telephone when the information provided required clarification or to seek their permission to ascribe a quote, which most declined preferring to remain anonymous. There were several reasons for requesting anonymity: respondents, generally front-line caseworkers and campaigners, expressed personal views and experiences and feared jeopardising their careers. Many did not wish to be known for voicing views which could be seen as contrary to their organisation's publicly stated position; some also feared antagonising the massive government bureaucracy that they must deal with on an almost daily basis.

The interviewees and email respondents represented a fairly broad spectrum of the asylum-seeker serving NGOs; the common element being that almost all respondents had been involved in or had some knowledge or awareness of the campaign against Section 55. There were also several interviewees who had little knowledge about the campaign but had considerable experience in asylum; their views were important and provided context to the findings. The nature and extent of the interviewees respective involvement varied (i.e. solicitors, case-workers, volunteers, by the very nature of their work, played different roles in the campaign). They were drawn, not in any particular order, from the NGOs listed in Table 1.

Table 1. Participant NGOs

Bail for Immigration Detainees	Shelter
Asylum Welcome	Refugee Arrivals
Asylum Aid	Refugee Legal Centre
Haslar Visitors Group	Churches Commission for Racial Justice
Maternity Alliance	Refugee Council
The Children's Society	Joint Council for the Welfare of Immigrants
Child Poverty Action Group (CPAG)	Jesuit Refugee Service
Dover Detainees Support Group	Immigration Advisory Service
Migrant Helpline	Medical Foundation for the Care of Victims of Torture
Refugee Action	Refugee Housing Association
Religious Society of Friends (Quakers)	Liberty
Gatwick Detainees	Migrant Rights Network

Most of the organizations listed above are also members of the Asylum Rights Campaign (ARC). My visits to the Refugee Council office in Brixton, observations, and interviews with staff members (as well as general discussions with others working in the field) were an important aspect of the fieldwork and crucial for an understanding of the environment in which NGOs work. I also visited the Citizen's Advice Bureau (CAB) which serves a wide variety of constituents; some CAB offices have a large immigration and asylum-seeker caseload. I met with officials from the UNHCR, Oxfam, and various religious orders who provided valuable insight into the situation of asylum-seekers, not only in the UK but worldwide as the West continues to tighten borders in efforts to further restrict access to those seeking asylum.[35]

1.9.   Additional Sources of Data

One source of data was due to fortuitous timing when Refugee Week, an annual information and cultural event held throughout the UK in June, coincided with my fieldwork. The objective of Refugee Week is to highlight the positive impact of refugees to UK society and is an effort by NGOs to dispel public apathy and hostility and the too often negative views and misinformation about their situation. Many of the events were a balance of information sessions and arts exhibitions; I attended several events in Oxford and London, many of which were professionally organized and well attended; some, such as the events in Oxford, had high-profile speakers and celebrities highlighting the positive contributions of refugees. However, and this is primarily anecdotal, it was quite apparent that most of the attendees were 'the converted' or sympathetic towards asylum-seekers and refugees making it difficult to assess the impact of such events.

What these events did offer were missed opportunities because the attendees constituted a receptive audience for a presentation on the potential of the HRA as a tool for substantive changes. Many in the audience seemed eager for information or something tangible with which to 'do something' about the plight of asylum-seekers but very little, aside from condemning current governmental policies, was on offer. To be sure, the audience was encouraged to write letters to newspaper editors, to their MPs, and attend rallies but this is also where rights could have

---

[35]   See Chapter 3 for a fuller discussion on asylum and the mass movement of people around the world.

played a role. It is noteworthy that none of the several events I attended featured anything, peripherally or otherwise, on the HRA, even though the general nature of some of the discussions was how to change the nature of the debate, counter tabloid reporting, and other negative imagery of refugees and asylum-seekers. None of the speakers suggested a rights framework and nor did any of the information booths at the various event feature anything on the HRA. I asked for information about the HRA but the mostly volunteer staff replied that they were not lawyers or did not know much about it. This was true of the several events which I attended; I specifically sought out information on the HRA but none was available.

Another source of data was the publications by ARC-member organizations. I read through hundreds of such publications – brochures, pamphlets, annual reports, press releases, and information kits – in order to assess if the language or discourse of rights was taking root. In this respect, there are emerging signs but most of it is of an ad-hoc nature and very little could be considered a systematic or sustained engagement with rights. There is also an apparent disconnect between official publication and actual practice. Some of the publications of one NGO gave prominence to the HRA and how it could be used to advance social objectives but nowhere was this readily evident in the actual practice of the organization. I queried the writer, a senior policy analyst, who acknowledged the discrepancy and admitted that the plan, while important to the organization's overall strategy, somehow got 'lost' in transition to actual practice. This had more to do with management and demand on limited resources than any attempt to mislead.

What was possibly the most insightful aspect of the fieldwork was meeting committed individuals, some of whom were former asylum-seekers, who have a genuine concern for the plight of this vulnerable and unpopular group. Their views provided nuance to what is a highly-contested and dynamic environment. In my discussions and meetings I came to understand just how desperate the situation is for asylum-seekers pushed to the edge of human endurance: suicides, self-harm, and depression have been documented by mental health specialists.[36] During fieldwork, a failed asylum-seeker, detained and about to be deported committed suicide knowing that it was an option that may allow his thirteen-year old son to remain in the UK.[37] This, and similar examples of desperation, are what many

---

[36]   Oxfam and Refugee Council, *Poverty and asylum in the UK* (2002); Refugee Action, *The Destitution Trap* (2006)

[37]   J Elliott and Z Brennan, 'The ultimate sacrifice' *Sunday Times* (24 Sept 2006)

spoke of and their powerlessness to battle against a government determined to be tough on asylum-seekers. Almost everyone whom I met at various conferences and events or interviewed was unanimous in their condemnation of Labour policy towards asylum-seekers. Many harboured feelings of being betrayed by Labour, a party that they had supported, for implementing the very same policies which they had criticised when in official opposition. Many interviewees singled out the frequent legislative changes, seven in the past decade alone, which means that not only must NGOs devote valuable time training their own staff just to keep abreast of new developments, but deal with the confusion it creates at the Home Office as officers grapple with new laws and policies. An interviewee commented (about the IND): 'it's complete chaos; nobody knows what they are doing'.[38] Many interviewees could barely conceal their anger and frustration. According to Diana Tickell of Asylum Welcome, an Oxford-based NGO, frequent changes in immigration law impact significantly upon her organization's resources with staff barely managing to keep up to date. More fundamentally, this detracts staff from their primary function – helping asylum-seekers and advocating on their behalf.[39]

I also interviewed several asylum-seekers, many of whom have been in the UK for considerable periods of time, and without forming any opinions as to their bona-fides what became apparent was that many were seeking fair and just treatment. Something, they felt, had been denied. Many, without knowing the legal definition of refugee, felt that their particular situation merited the granting of protection. That it could be otherwise seemed inconceivable as they reflected upon why they were seeking asylum in a country seen as affluent and able to accommodate. They spoke of their experiences in the UK as characterised by daily humiliation, but many also spoke of the kindness of strangers and hopes for the future. Many seemed at pains to emphasise that they were not 'cheats' and had genuine reasons for leaving their homelands. Many of the asylum-seekers who agreed to be interviewed were homeless or dependent upon friends or the community for support. During the fieldwork I came across asylum-seekers almost everywhere in London (and elsewhere): sleeping in car-parks, begging outside various transit stations, and camping in green spaces in East London. I observed them being verbally abused by passers-by but also noted many acts of kindness. On the whole, a most deprived and desperate group of individuals.

---

[38]   Interview with anonymous caseworker, Migrant Helpline (London June 2005)

[39]   Diana Tickell (Lecture, Refugee Studies Centre, University of Oxford, May 2005)

1.10   Findings[40]

Is there sufficient evidence to suggest that a culture of rights is emerging or taking root insofar as the asylum-seeker sector is concerned? An answer to such a question must be preceded by a caveat – and it is this: a culture of rights is a work in progress and will remain so for the foreseeable future. However, this is not to say that signs of a rights culture, or at least, its emergence, should not be empirically evident as we enter the sixth year (at time of fieldwork) of the Act. The findings of this research suggest a mixed bag. There are some reasons for optimism because of signs which suggest a cautious yes, but there are also worrying signs which suggest otherwise. Why such ambivalence? This is not to suggest a paradox but to outline the findings of my research which suggest that the development of a culture of rights appears to have bypassed some of the most vulnerable and marginalised people in UK society. And it has happened with deliberation, if not deliberation then with full awareness of the likely impact of its 'get tough' policies, by a government which continues to treat asylum-seekers as if the HRA had never been enacted.

The *Human Rights Act* – the language of rights, rights as leverage, or rights as a catalyst for mobilisation – is not yet an integral part of the work of NGOs serving the asylum-seeker community. And nor is it likely to be in the foreseeable future. A not surprising corollary to these findings is the recent work by the Audit Commission which concluded that the development of a rights culture has stalled and identified asylum as a 'risk area'.[41] The British Institute of Human Rights also concluded that the asylum sector presented reasons for concern and singled out the IND for being less than receptive to human rights issues.[42] The Joint Committee on Human Rights, a parliamentary committee which reports to the House of Lords and House of Commons, has repeatedly criticised the Home Office on asylum. In particular, for its lack of meaningful consultation on HRA issues and not paying enough attention to the HRA in drafting legislation.[43] The Committee also concluded that there are very few signs of a culture of rights taking root in the UK.[44]

---

[40]   See Chapter 9 for a fuller discussion
[41]   Audit Commission, *Human rights: Improving Public Service Delivery* (2003)
[42]   British Institute of Human Rights, *Something for Everyone: The Impact of the Human Rights Act on Disadvantaged Groups* (2002)14
[43]   Joint Committee On Human Rights, *Asylum and Immigration (Treatment of Claimants, etc.) Bill: New Clauses - Fourteenth Report of Session 2003-04* (HL 130 2004)
[44]   Joint Committee On Human Rights, *The Treatment of Asylum-Seekers* (HL 81-1 2007)

1.10.1 How Has the HRA Been Received by NGOs in the Asylum-Seeker Sector?

When the HRA was introduced in 1998, to come into force in 2000, many called it a 'social revolution' and the 'most significant change to British law since the Magna Carta'. Those opposed predicted that it would foster a culture of litigation and serve as a 'burglar's charter' handicapping authorities in the performance of their duties.[45] Such polarised, if exaggerated, views almost ensured that the transition of the Act into British society would disappoint, anger, and excite many. And, now almost ten years into the Act, that has turned out to be the case.

In asylum, one of the most controversial of public policy issues, the Act has disappointed and angered many. The then-Home Secretary, Jack Straw, had assured Britons that the Act would protect 'the weak from the overweening power of the state'. In asylum, however, the Act has failed to protect some of the most vulnerable people from the excesses of the state.[46] Many NGOs in the asylum-seeker sector had welcomed the Act believing that it would be a force for good and something much needed for their constituency. However, the initial enthusiasm has all but disappeared and belief in the Act is at a low point:

> I am not sure if I can say the Act has made much of a difference, at least I haven't noticed. We had discussed the possibility it could be useful before it came into effect. Yes, sure, law students and lawyers get excited and engage in academic debates about its usefulness. But what does such abstract stuff have to do with what happens in life. Has it made any real difference to these people (asylum-seekers)? Not much. We have seen little in the day-to-day lives of these people . . .[47]

1.10.2 How Are NGOs Using the HRA?

The NGOS have utilised the Act in a variety of ways. The most prominent have been in test-case litigation and fundraising drives. The Act has also featured in

---

[45]   BBC, 'Landmark human rights law enforced' (2000) Oct 02 <http://news.bbc.co.uk/2/hi/uk_news/951753.stm>

[46]   See Chapters 5 to 9 for a fuller discussion; see also reviews of other studies on the effects of Section 55.

[47]   Interview with anonymous policy advisor, Immigration Advisory Service (London, Nov 2006)

appeals to MPs and lobbying for changes in law and policy and other campaigns. However, this is not to suggest the existence of an organized, systematic or sustained engagement because most of it has been ad-hoc in nature, with little or no coordination amongst the various NGOs. The efforts to date have not been sustained or consistent and there is a marked absence of creativity and innovation:

> It (the Human Rights Act) could be useful; it is useful in some limited circumstances. There is potential of it being used more imaginatively in this sector (asylum), not just in individual cases but in wider policy considerations. But I really don't see much sign of that happening . . . it's not only the authorities or the courts; it is also us (non-governmental organizations) who haven't really thought about how human rights arguments might actually be used in a more imaginative way.[48]

1.10.3 How Are Rights Mobilized; and What Strategies Do NGOs Employ?

The key finding of this research is simply this: there is no strategy or plan. I found little to suggest that there is an organised, methodical or sustained approach to rights. And more worryingly, the Act does not feature in the future strategy or business plans of the participant NGOs. I observed business meetings of three major NGOs over a period of several weeks. At one NGO a five-year plan was debated and outlined in direct response to the government's five-year plan designed to deal with immigration and asylum matters. In another, future planning took the form of a general discussion; and, in the third, there was no planning. In all cases there was no discussion of how the HRA or rights could be used in any aspect of their work.

1.10.4 Why Have Rights 'Failed' in the Asylum Sector?

One of the key features of NGOs in the asylum-sector is the absence of professional management in its ranks which, in turn, is reflected in a mostly ad-hoc approach to the HRA. And, notwithstanding efforts by the ARC, there appears to be little

---

[48]   Interview with Colin Yeo, Legal Advisor, Immigration Advisory Service (London 03 August 2005)

coordination or strategising amongst the various NGOs insofar as the HRA is concerned. Again, lack of resources is a key factor – professional management costs money, a commodity in scarce supply and something NGOs have difficulty in justifying to the public and funding bodies. While the NGOs may in general have the same objectives there is no apparent consensus on how to achieve them. They also compete for 'clients' and funding sources. During the campaign against Section 55 some NGOs were competing to be first with a hoped-for successful test-case challenge. Many are also ill-equipped in resources and people to sustain their efforts. They are over-subscribed and under-resourced, some operating with one or two paid positions and dependent upon volunteers. With few exceptions most of the offices I visited were cramped and threadbare operations with files piled on floors and hallways. As the chairman of an NGO explained – 'asylum just isn't sexy enough to attract funding'.[49]

If one takes the view that asylum-seekers represent a litmus test for the emergence of a rights culture in the UK – and there are many reasons why it should be so because what good are rights if it fails those who most need it – then whatever hope the HRA may have initially represented to asylum-seeker NGOs seems to have dissipated into a literal throwing up of the hands resignation in the face of a government which has declared war on a powerless and unpopular minority. The culture of rights, while loosely defined, was never meant to yield a culture of human rights litigation. If anything it was the opposite which had been predicted on the assumption that litigation would lessen as respect for rights gained prominence.[50] But in asylum litigation has emerged as the most prominent feature of rights. And this has been primarily because government policy has forced the NGOs into a situation where their options are limited. Sometimes the only alternative has been to seek redress in the courts, an expensive and resource-intensive undertaking (as evidenced by the fight over Section 55). There have been some significant victories – and losses – in the courts, but the overwhelming view of those working in asylum is one of dismay and disappointment at the government's determined and continued hard-line against those least able to challenge the might of the state. In a battle between unevenly matched opponents the HRA has been found wanting.

It is therefore not surprising that a major finding of this research is that many NGOs continue to regard the Act as solely the purview of lawyers and courts, and

---

[49]   Interview with Habib Rahman, Chairperson, JCWI (London 13 June 2005)
[50]   Home Office, *Rights Brought Home: the Human Rights Bill* (1997)

of little use in their day-to-day work even though the very nature of their work is about human rights – the rights of asylum-seekers, a worrying distinction which continues to be made by some NGOs and public-sector agencies.[51] Almost everyone I interviewed expressed dismay and anger at what they view as blatantly contradictory policies of a government extolling the virtues of human rights (for UK citizens) while denying the most fundamental of rights to non-nationals. Many spoke of the steady erosion of existing and hard-won rights via frequent legislative changes; comments such as: 'problem is that the government ignore it (HRA) in pursuit of policy objectives' or 'as long as governments ignore it or find ways around it by legislation it remains ineffective' or 'no one at the Home Office seems to have heard of it (HRA)' were the most common views of those on the front-line.[52]

This resigned view on the usefulness of the HRA, and the relatively powerless position of NGOs, does not bode well for a rights culture. In view of the theoretical approach of this research – a constitutive framework which eschews the traditional top-down approach to the study of law and social change for a bottom-up approach and the central role of NGOs as instigators of change – this finding does not lead to an optimistic conclusion about rights in the UK. While the Labour government must accept most of the responsibility for this morass it cannot be said that the NGOs are entirely blameless. Their outrage and dismay, potentially a catalyst for opposing actions, does not appear to have been translated into efforts at challenging the government position. To be sure, efforts continue but are mostly of a low-profile and ad-hoc nature characterised by wariness rather than strength of conviction.

Early during fieldwork, it became clear that there is an absence of innovation, coordination, and planning in the ranks of the NGOs in the UK, particularly in comparison to how various groups in Canada and the US have harnessed rights.[53] This is something many NGOs acknowledged but have done little to address. The NGOs were slow off the mark in getting ready for the HRA (prior to implementation) and slower still in utilising it upon implementation; a majority of NGO staff claimed to have received no training on the Act prior to it coming into force.[54] Even

---

[51]   A report by the Audit Commission (2003) found that many public-sector agencies have shown little interest in the HRA – see: *Human rights: Improving Public Service Delivery*

[52]   Interview notes (on file with author)

[53]   See: FL Morton, *Law, Politics and the Judicial Process in Canada* (2002)

[54]   British Institute of Human Rights, *Something for Everyone: The Impact of the Human Rights Act on Disadvantaged Groups* (2002) 13

after implementation a small but not insignificant number still had not received any training. Those who had spoke positively of the quality of training received, usually a day-long session, conducted either by Liberty or BIHR. However, such one-off approach to training, no matter its quality, is a poor substitute for a sustained engagement with the Act. And very few NGO staff receive regular training as a matter of course or to update their knowledge in this still developing area of law. A senior caseworker responsible for asylum and traveller issues said he 'rarely uses the HRA . . . in some cases we may mention human rights issues if drawn to our attention by lawyers but normally not'.[55] At time of the fieldwork (almost six years since implementation, eight including the transition period) a significant number of respondents rated their knowledge of the HRA as 'poor'. However, there has been some improvement as an almost equal number rated their knowledge as 'good', and a minority as 'very good.' But that so many should rate their knowledge as 'poor' remains of concern.[56]

Several caseworkers also expressed frustration at what they view as lack of ambition on part of their organization as evidenced by comments such as: 'I feel that we (the organization) are not challenging enough on rights', 'there is more scope of action in using the HRA in day-to-day work but it's not being fully used', 'we could be doing more', and 'we are too timid'. One policy analyst stated that 'management was clueless when it came to the HRA'. This lack of ambition is perhaps explicable by a paucity of resources. This was the primary reason given by one Director, who acknowledged a lack of ambition, and said: 'we have to pick our fights'. He also spoke at length about the possibilities offered by the HRA. But a rights approach requires a long-term strategy, results of which may be not always be readily apparent or may take a considerable time to be seen. According to the Director, NGOs, often by necessity, have to focus their priorities on the immediate needs of their clients, as evidenced in the fight over Section 55 when thousands of asylum-seekers were forced into destitution and had to fed and housed.[57]

Some NGOs, for various reasons, are also nervous about the HRA to the point of downplaying or avoiding the language of rights – from fears the Act will come to be seen as 'something for black people' to its repeal: 'it's making us nervous, all this constant talk of opting-out'. Even legal staff spoke of minimising their work

---

[55]   Interview notes (on file with author)

[56]   Survey notes (on file with author)

[57]   Interview with Habib Rahman, Chairperson, JCWI (London March-Aug 2005)

because of sneering comments of colleagues, such as: 'you're not one of those, are you?' in response to discussions of the Act and its impact on asylum. There is a real concern in the NGO community, a direct response to media and government attacks on the Act, that too much talk of the HRA will lead to it being seen as something for 'others', a charter for unpopular minorities or criminals, and not something for the greater good of society.[58]

In their dealings with Labour the NGOs have found a government generally unreceptive to human rights arguments insofar as asylum is concerned. So unyielding has Labour been that the use of the HRA as leverage or negotiating, for example, have been greeted with a collective shrug, if not an outright challenge, daring the NGOs to proceed with court action. Interviewee after interviewee, from a cross-section of NGOs, spoke of unanswered letters, unreturned telephone calls, and complete silence from the Home Office during the height of the Section 55 crisis as they were left to fend for the thousands of asylum-seekers made destitute by a 'draconian' government policy.

1.11   Reasons for Optimism?

What is it in the findings that, at first glance, suggest a cautious yes regarding the emergence of a rights culture? The signs, few at first glance, are slowing emerging. A British national, fearing the deportation of her asylum-seeker husband, recently started an organization (and petition) for others similarly situated citing her rights (and her husband's) under the HRA. In a newspaper interview Jessica Siavoshy used the language of rights to state her case:

> This is a crucial human rights issue . . . we have written to every member of the House of Lords and House of Commons (explaining) how our rights as British women are being cruelly overlooked due to inhuman immigration rules. We have been denied the right to live freely with our husbands in the UK.[59]

Individual NGO caseworkers, notwithstanding apparent management inertia of their respective organizations, spoke of seeking out training on their own initiative

---

[58]   Ibid.(also with Uma Joshi, solicitor, Shelter (London March 2005)

[59]   E Marais, 'Wives Unite to Fight Against 'Inhumane' System" *Hounslow Guardian* (29 Sep 2005)

and then using the Act on behalf of their clients. Several told me how they had self-trained or sought training not only to better assist their clients but also to gain a measure of confidence in face of an intransigent Home Office, though one interviewee said that 'mentioning the HRA doesn't improve one's popularity'.[60] During the course of the fieldwork, and even after its conclusion, I received emails from several NGOs, including organizations which I had not contacted previously, seeking information on the HRA and asking me to provide training on how to use the Act on behalf of their clients. One organization asked me to travel to Manchester to train a group of asylum-seekers so that they would feel 'more confident' about asserting themselves in the face of rights violations, acts of racism and ill-treatment, not only by the Home Office but by a myriad of other service providers, such as doctors and local authorities. I politely declined but referred these organizations to the BIHR or Liberty, both of which specialise in HRA training.

The BIHR has become a major and reputable player in the field of human rights. The organization is committed to promoting a broader concept of human rights – as a framework for social action and tool for negotiating better or improved services. In its 2002 survey, BIHR concluded that there had been little attempt by any organisation, government or NGOs, to use the HRA to create a human rights culture and has since responded by starting a community outreach program, offering free training to NGOs in sectors viewed as 'high risk,' such as the asylum.[61] Liberty also started an online and telephone service geared specifically to caseworkers and frontline staff. The fact that demand far exceeds what either of these organizations can accommodate speaks of the interest in the HRA as a tool for social action and resource for individual redress.

A more promising example is that of organizations which have seemingly given up on the HRA using it in their fundraising activities. The fundraisers have come to realise that the language of rights carries far more resonance and elicits many more positive responses than the issue of asylum. The interviewees, while unable to readily identify their usage of the HRA in casework, spoke of how the HRA has expanded their options by allowing them, for example, to tailor applications directed at a wider range of funding bodies. More importantly, the Act has acted

---

[60]   Interview with Jonathan, caseworker, JCWI (London July 2005)

[61]   British Institute of Human Rights and Joint Council for the Welfare of Immigrants, 'Workshop - Section 55 and Human Rights' (BIHR/JCWI Conference 2003); *Something for Everyone: The Impact of the Human Rights Act on Disadvantaged Groups* 8

as a reminder that asylum rights are human rights, a fact sometimes overlooked because of persistent stereotypes and negativity associated with asylum-seekers.

1.12   Conclusion

On the whole, the findings suggest a decidedly mixed bag which is not about to change anytime soon. At the time the fieldwork concluded (November 2005) the HRA had been in effect for six years. Much more time is needed for a culture of rights to develop and become part of everyday usage and framework for government policies. And much work remains. A culture of rights will not develop automatically without further input from governments, institutions, and work at the ground level. NGOs would be well advised to engage with rights on a more organised and sustained basis if the UK is to ever experience a rights revolution. And, for the foreseeable future, asylum will continue to present challenges for all concerned – the government, NGOs, and, in particular, those seeking refuge: 'People who have sought asylum are being denied justice in the UK'.[62]

1.13   Outline of Chapters

The thesis is comprised of nine chapters. Chapter 1 outlines the research question, methodology and summarises the findings of my research. Chapter 2 is an overview of the theoretical framework on rights and social change and presents a review of selected case studies of rights at work. In order to understand the challenges faced by NGOs, who work with and advocate on behalf of asylum-seekers in the UK, it is instructive to examine the issue from a 'big picture' perspective which is the focus of the next chapter. Chapter 3 examines asylum in the wider context and how the issue has come to be framed, almost wholly in negative terms, in present-day discourse. Chapter 4 focuses on the battleground – welfare benefits for asylum-seekers – and examines the history of legislative and policy attempts to control welfare, its use as a coercive measure, and efforts to restrict or limit the entry of asylum-seekers to the UK. Chapter 5 presents an overview of the impact of Section 55, the campaign against it, the challenges faced by the NGOs during

---

[62]   Kate Allen, Director, Amnesty International UK, cited in: BBC, 'Asylum detentions 'breaking law'' (2005) BBC News <http://news.bbc.co.uk/1/hi/uk/4109406.stm> (10 Oct 2006)

the peak of the crisis, and the role of the *Human Rights Act* in the lead-up to the first test-case challenge. The first test-case, *Q and Others*, came about at a time of intense interest in asylum and Chapter 6 examines the events surrounding the case. It examines the High Court decision and the furore that the decision created in the media and the political arena. Chapter 7 examines the continuing campaign against Section 55, the set-backs for the NGOs at the Court of Appeal, further test-case challenges which gradually turned the campaign in favour of the NGOs leading to the Court of Appeal decision in *Limbuela*. Chapter 8 examines the events leading up to the House of Lords decision in *Limbuela* and looks at what the fight over Section 55 has meant for the NGOs, asylum-seekers, and the development of a culture of rights. Chapter 9, the conclusion, is an overview of what the case study of the campaign against Section 55 has to say about role of rights in the fight for social change and social justice. The chapter concludes by examining the prospects of using rights to bring about social change in the UK.

2 RIGHTS AND SOCIAL CHANGE

2.1 Introduction

The strategic use of law – specifically rights – by non-governmental organisations advocating to advance social justice issues has long been an established part of the political landscape in the US, Canada, and other jurisdictions.[1] And, with the recent introduction of the *Human Rights Act* (HRA), it has become an emerging field for scholars and a new and untested option for many advocacy groups campaigning on various issues in the UK. While the strategic use of law has long been a component of campaigning tactics in the UK it has not, to date, been as widespread or sustained as it is in Canada or the US or as widely studied by scholars.[2] The movement towards this strategy appears to reflect a growing international phenomenon as seen in the newly emerging democracies of Eastern Europe[3] and other parts of the world.[4] What, then, are the possibilities and potential of law in bringing about social changes for the disadvantaged of society? Can the law, specifically the strategic use of rights, be a resource for social change? Can rights change or improve the social situation for the powerless of society – the poor, minorities, and other disadvantaged groups.[5]

---

[1] SLR Anleu, *Law and Social Change* (2010); D Galligan, *Law in a Modern Society* (2006); H Hershkoff (2009) 'Public Law Litigation: Lessons and Questions' 10 Human Rights Review 2 157-81

[2] C Harlow and R Rawlings, *Pressure through law* (1992); W Friedmann, *Law and Social Change in Contemporary Britain* (1951); For one of the few studies see: T Prosser, *Test cases for the poor: Legal techniques in the politics of social welfare* (1983)

[3] See, for example, T Campbell KD Ewing and A Tomkins, *Sceptical essays on human rights* (2001); A Stone Sweet, *Governing with Judges: Constitutional Politics in Europe* (2000)

[4] See: J Hammond (1999) 'Law and Disorder: The Brazilian Landless Farmworkers' Movement' 18 Bulletin of Latin American Research 4 469-89 (for an examination of rights litigation in Brazil where landless peasants have successfully used the law in expropriating underused farmlands); EA Feldman, *The Ritual of Rights in Japan: Law, Society, and Health Policy* (2000) (for the experiences of Japanese reformers in changing health policy); D Barek-Erez (2002) 'Judicial Review of Politics: The Israeli Case.' 29 Journal of Law and Society 4 611-31 (on the Israeli Supreme Courts continued excursions into areas previously considered non-justicible*);* and CR Epp, *The Rights Revolution: Lawyers, Activists, and Supreme Courts in Comparative Perspective* (1998) on activism by the Indian Supreme Court; see also: Institute of Development Studies (2006) *The Rise of Rights* www.ids.ac.uk/ids/bookshop/briefs/index.html.

5 As defined by the *Guardian/Observer* 'big issues' are, amongst others: asylum-seekers, social exclusion, mental health and homelessness (see http://society.guardian.co.uk/mentalhealth/0,8145,386880,00.html).

2.2   Outline of Chapter

The objective of this chapter is to examine some of the current theoretical issues in the debate, and to consider the possibilities and pitfalls presented by rights. No attempt is made to be exhaustive, an impractical undertaking given the breadth of literature on the subject; rather the objective is to present an overview. The primary focus shall be rights litigation because it is the most salient feature of rights strategies. But rights are much more than that. The focus on litigation is not to diminish the equally important role that rights play in the broader picture, for example, in creating rights consciousness, or as catalyst, which some argue is much more important than litigation.[6] The case studies in the following pages are purposively diverse and selective but cover the major aspects of rights – litigation, consciousness, leverage, and as catalyst for mobilization – the objective is to be expansive and overarching. The chapter is divided into two parts: (a) litigation and rights, and (b) selected case studies.

2.3   Preface

In some respects the introduction of the HRA is part of a greater global movement where the subject of human rights has come to occupy a prominent role in the discourse of the day. This has yielded some uncomfortable truths, which are that many humans remain without rights, not only in authoritarian states but also in western liberal democracies. In efforts to address the widening gap between the haves and have-nots, social advocacy NGOs have turned to the law based on the belief that not only is the law capable of addressing the imbalance, but that it is an efficient and effective means of doing so. Proponents argue that strategic uses of rights law are powerful tools in the battle for social justice. Opponents, on the other hand, argue that the inherent ideological biases of rights serve to constrain and limit social movements, and that rights are costly, ineffectual, and ultimately do little to change the status quo.[7]

---

[6]   P Ewick and SS Silbey, *The Common Place of Law: Stories from Everyday Life* (1998); D Engel, 'How Does Law Matter in the Constitution of Legal Consciousness ' in BG Garth and A Sarat (eds) *How Does Law Matter* (1988); M Hertogh (2004) 'A 'European' Conception of Legal Consciousness: Rediscovering Eugen Ehrlich' 31 Journal of Law and Society 4 457

[7]   For a review of these viewpoints see: BG Garth and A Sarat, *How Does Law Matter?* (1998); BG Garth and A Sarat, *Justice and Power in Sociolegal Studies* (1998)

In view of the divergent positions this paper adopts, as a point of departure, Thompson's (1975) view that law, more precisely the rule of law, must be more than the sham that critical legal or conflict-oriented scholars accuse it of being. According to Thompson 'it may disguise the true realities of power, but, at the same time, may curb that power and check its intrusions'.[8] While some studies have pointed to the law's dearth of successes in addressing matters of social justice, other studies have concluded otherwise because powerless constituents have successfully challenged the status quo. And they have done so with some regularity.[9] There is no question, however, that the results have been decidedly mixed, particularly in certain public policy areas such as, for example, asylum in the UK.[10] This should suggest caution to groups considering rights as a strategy. At the outset, however, the position of this paper is that a strategic deployment of rights holds the potential to advance social justice issues. However, and the evidence is persuasive, it is not a panacea for the various social ills that beset societies.[11] Modern day societies are far too complex and dynamic for a one-solution-fits-all approach, or to expect that any particular approach – for example, rights – can be capable of addressing its myriad of social ills. Barack Obama, former community activist, law professor, and now president of the US, called it an 'imperfect tool for social change'.[12] But it remains the case that, particularly in Canada and the US with its established tradition of rights, disadvantaged groups continually turn to the law to advance social justice agendas.[13]

2.4   Part A: Litigation and Rights

Litigation, as a means of effecting social policy changes or advancing causes generally considered to be consistent with social justice, is a relative newcomer to

---

8   EP Thompson, *Whigs and hunters: the origin of the Black Act* (1975), p. 263

9   For a review of various case studies of rights at work see Part B of this chapter: also see: DA Schultz, *Leveraging the law: using the courts to achieve social change* (1998); B Swedlow (2009); H Hershkoff (2009)

10   See Chapters 1, 6, and 7 to 9 for discussion of my findings on how NGOs used rights to win concessions on behalf of asylum-seekers.

11   K Makin, 'Unions, Most Minorities Have Left the Court Empty-Handed' *Globe and Mail* (11 Apr 2007) A8

12   J Kantor, 'Teaching Law, Testing Ideas, Obama Stood Apart ' *The New York Times* (30 Jul 2008)

13   MM Shapiro and A Stone Sweet, *On Law, Politics, and Judicialisation* (2002)

the field of socio-legal inquiry. A former debate in the sociology of law, on various theoretical arguments, which viewed law as a consensus-based set of norms in a society characterized by social contract, or as conflict-oriented and characterized by class-divisions owing to unequal and disproportionate distribution of wealth and resources, seemingly moved onto other areas. The new concerns were more of an applied and practical nature focusing on, for example, the possibilities of using law to change social relations or to even the playing field, and asking if the law should be used to do so. Until recently, attempts at social engineering in the area of social justice were of a relatively modest but no less ostensibly noble nature; examples include laws implemented to promote racial harmony or to address discrimination in the work-place.[14] How such attempts have turned out are empirical questions. Arguably these early attempts can be seen as seminal to the grand-scale attempts of today as evidenced by the recent flourishing of constitutional protection in the forms of Bills of rights. Perhaps one of the more ambitious has been the recent introduction of the *Human Rights Act* (HRA) in the UK which has been called a 'social revolution' and 'the most significant change to British law since the Magna Carta' in view of its announced objective of bringing about a cultural change or 'culture of rights' in Britain.[15]

While the US has had its Constitution since the 18th century, it has only been the latter half of the twentieth century that has seen the emergence of organised and concerted efforts directed at using constitutional rights to advance social causes, as evidenced by some landmark US Supreme Court decisions addressing compelling issues such as racial segregation and abortion. Rights litigation in Canada was encouraged by a new constitution in 1982, which included the much debated and agonised over *Charter of Rights and Freedoms.*[16] And just like the HRA in the UK, the *Charter* was promoted as fulfilling the needs of minorities for protection and participation in mainstream Canadian society. More poignantly, when the equality provisions of the *Charter* came into effect three years later, there were scenes of celebrations across the nation. Minority groups, euphoric with the promises of constitutional protection, burst into spontaneous and organised celebrations as if

---

14   R Cotterrell, *The Sociology of Law: An Introduction* (2nd edn) (1992) p.44
15   Home Office, *Rights Brought Home: the Human Rights Bill* (1997); BBC, 'Landmark human rights law enforced' (2000) Oct 02 http://news.bbc.co.uk/2/hi/uk_news/951753.stm; C Harvey and British Institute of Human Rights, *Human Rights in the Community: Rights as Agents for Change.* (2005)
16   See: M Mandel, *The Charter of Rights and the Legalization of Politics in Canada* (1994)

somehow their world had suddenly changed for the better.[17] And this was even before any aspect of the equality provisions had been defined, challenged, or litigated. Not many knew what it would look like but assumed it would be better than the status quo. The mere existence of the *Charter* was the cause for celebration demonstrating a consciousness and belief in the power of rights. Even before the equality provisions came into effect some NGOs, such as LEAF (Women's Legal Education and Action Fund), had begun taking an inventory of policies to challenge and have been at the forefront ever since in promoting equality rights.[18] One can now look back at over twenty-five years of life under the *Charter* and ask if the celebrations were prescient or premature. Was it a display of naiveté or perceptive understanding of the possibilities presented by rights? Notwithstanding a fairly mixed-bag of Supreme Court decisions that have mostly favoured powerful interests Canadians 'love their *Charter*'.[19]

2.4.1 Theories of Law and Social Change

Liberal democratic societies with all their promises and guarantees of equality are characterized by immense inequalities and social divides: refugees and new immigrant communities in the UK, for example, are virtually excluded from the mainstream society and live in general deprivation and poverty;[20] indigenous peoples of Canada and Australia live in conditions of despair that rival third-world nations and rank at the bottom of almost all social indices.[21] These are not isolated examples. That such disparities should exist in countries of great wealth and democratic institutions raises profound questions. For the disadvantaged in liberal-democratic societies it has been hypothesized that the law can be a resource for social progress, a tool for bringing about meaningful social change. Notwithstanding the sharp divide in the debate about the role of law in the fight for social causes, it is evident that various NGOs continue to regard the law as an arena where their causes can be effectively advanced. The theoretical suppositions that have given

---

17   See: P Sharma, *Aboriginal Fishing Rights: Laws, Courts, Politics* (1998)
18   FL Morton, *Law, politics and the judicial process in Canada* (2002)
19   D Butler, 'Charting the Impact of the Charter' *Ottawa Citizen* (15 Apr 2007) A6
20   Child Poverty Action Group, *Parallel Lives: Poverty Among Ethnic Minority Groups in Britain* (2003)
21   J Pilger, 'Under cover of racist myth, a new land grab in Australia' *The Guardian* (24 Oct 2008); P Sharma, *Aboriginal Fishing Rights: Laws, Courts, Politics* (1998)

rise to the debate are based on liberal ideals such as, for example, winning legal battles results in social progress. From this premise flow other assumptions: that legal victories serve to legitimatise social struggles; places the issue on the political agenda; and, empowers the litigants. Most prominent is the assumption that the law acts in an even-handed fashion and metes out justice accordingly. While there is considerable research and evidence that have questioned such assumptions and have demonstrated that courts and judges do not act even-handedly, the powerful win most often, the have-nots do not come out ahead, and judges are not immune from political pressures, these beliefs persist.[22]

The opposing views can be subsumed under the critical school banner, which sees society as characterized by conflict and class relations of domination and subordination. Critical theorists see law as an arena where the odds are heavily stacked in favour of the powerful, and ascribe naiveté to those who subscribe to the assumed power of law to change the status quo. More practically, they argue, is that the assumptions overlook one of the greatest source of inequality, the material conditions of disadvantaged litigants who do not have the means to wage protracted legal battles. The critical school takes the view that litigating for rights is a trap because the objective of law is to maintain and perpetuate the status quo. This view ascribes sinister motives to an ill-defined entity, the powerful, because law is seen an instrument that serves the interests of the powerful of society. Therefore, the most that disadvantaged groups can hope for are symbolic formal victories devoid of substantive content. Critical theorists take particular exception to the constitutionalisation of rights arguing that its lofty language and promises serve as an ideological weapon seducing the unwary by promises of what are ultimately unattainable.[23] According to Mandel (1994) it is no accident that the very things that make one equal before the law are precisely the very things that makes one unequal in life. Can the law ever broach such divides and contradictions? The answer, according to Mandel and other critical scholars, is no.[24]

The answers, however, are not that readily apparent. The social world is a gray arena and cannot be demarcated conveniently into 'yes' and 'no' categories. But is

---

[22]   M Lazarus-Black and SF Hirsch, *Contested States: Law, Hegemony, and Resistance* (1994)

[23]   M Mandel, *The Charter of Rights and the Legalization of Politics in Canada* (1994) ; J Fudge, 'The Canadian Charter of Rights: Recognition, Redistribution, and the Imperialism of the Courts' in T CampbellKD Ewing and A Tomkins (eds) *Sceptical Essays on Human Rights* (2001)

[24]   A Hunt, *Explorations in Law and Society: Towards a Constitutive Theory of Law* (1993)

there a middle ground? The Canadian experience with the *Charter* speaks to the ambivalent nature of rights and suggests evidence, which arguably supports both sides of the debate. Instrumentalists have ample evidence in the form of appellate court decisions, which have not only maintained the status quo but have weakened statutory provisions and policies meant to protect minority interests.[25] However, there have also been a significant number of decisions, which have enhanced and promoted minority concerns.[26] Lesser studied has been the impact of the *Charter* in relation to rights consciousness or legal mobilization, but it is clear that the *Charter* has come to occupy a central, and sometimes pivotal, role in Canadian politics and discourse.[27] In a 2002 poll 82% of Canadians agreed that the *Charter* has had a major impact on the protection of rights and freedoms; and, 62% preferred the Supreme Court be the final arbiter on rights compared to 31% for Parliament.[28]

2.4.2   How Does Law Matter?

When rights are deployed by advocacy groups, law becomes an arena where social justice issues are contested. This process has been variously, and sometimes pejoratively, referred to as the legalisation or judicialisation of politics because wide-ranging social issues are filtered through the lens of law. Critics argue that this has the effect of atomising immense social problems into narrow legal issues, which are then disputed in an arena incapable of grasping the nature and complexity of the problems, and of addressing them.[29] But law does matter. The

---

25 See, for example: P McCormick (1993) 'Party Capability Theory and Appellate Successes in the Supreme Court of Canada, 1949-1992. ' 26 Canadian Journal of Political Science 3 523-40; Fudge, 'The Canadian Charter of Rights: Recognition, Redistribution, and the Imperialism of the Courts' in T Campbell KD Ewing and A Tomkins (eds) *Sceptical Essays on Human Rights* (2001)

26 See, for example: R Penner (1996) 'The Canadian Experience with the Charter of Rights: Are there Lessons for the UK' Spring Public Law, 104-25; I Brodie and FL Morton, 'Do the 'Haves' Still Come Out Ahead in Canada' (1998) University of Calgary <http://publish.uwo.ca/~irbrodie/newman.pdf>

27 This is somewhat anecdotal and is based on observing debates in the House of Commons and generalised review of editorials in major newspapers; although rare, it is not unusual for the government to refer major policy issues to the Supreme Court of Canada for assessing its Charter 'worthiness' before legislation is passed; examples include the recent reference regarding gay marriages.

28 www.acs-aec.ca/oldsite/Polls/Poll1.pdf <accessed 10 Dec 2009>

29 M Mandel, *The Charter of Rights and the Legalization of Politics in Canada* (1994); GN Rosenberg, *The Hollow Hope: Can Courts Bring About Social Change?* (1991); A Hunt, *Explorations in Law and Society: Towards a Constitutive Theory of Law* (1993)

contention is, however, does it matter in important ways? Much legal scholarship has explored questions of judicial impact, 'gap' studies, and the ideological biases of law and concluded that law does not matter much in the fight for social progress or that it matters differently and not for the reasons assumed by proponents.[30] But, according to Garth and Sarat (1998a) the law is diffused everywhere and impacts upon almost all facets of the social world, often in immeasurable ways.[31] While the instrumentalist school may minimise or even dismiss the role of law in progressive social changes it is problematic, in this era of globalisation and in view of this continuing debate, to deny its pervasiveness.

It is important to note that rights do not provide limitless options and advocacy groups should exercise caution if emphasising such an approach at the expense of other options. First, liberal-democratic societies are not absent of competing and conflicting interests, and it cannot be expected that advocacy groups will have things their own way, or even that they have unity of purpose. Rights hold power and potential but also limitations and constrains. Scheingold (1974), decades ago, had defined rights as 'political resources of unknown value in the hands of those who want to alter public policy'.[32] However those resources not only hold potential, but also pitfalls. According to Milner and Goldberg-Hiller (2002):

> It is now well understood that rights are not automatic trumps, that the effectiveness of rights often depends on their use in everyday conversations far removed from the legal processes, and that the role of rights is not only contingent but at times also paradoxical and perverse.[33]

---

[30]   See, for example: MLM Hertogh and S Halliday, *Judicial review and bureaucratic impact: international and interdisciplinary perspectives* (2004); S Halliday (2000) 'The Influence of Judicial Review on Bureaucratic Decision-Making' Spring Public Law 110-22; G Richardson and M Sunkin (1996) 'Judicial Review: Questions of Impact' Spring Public Law 79-103; BZ Tamanaha, *Realistic Socio-Legal Theory: Pragmatism and a Social Theory of Law* (1997); G Richardson and D Machin (2000) 'Judicial Review and Tribunal Decision Making: A Study of the Mental Health Review Tribunal' Autumn Public Law 494-514; M Sunkin and K Pick (2001) 'The Changing Impact of Judicial Review: The Independent Review Service of the Social Fund' Winter Public Law 736-62

[31]   Garth and Sarat, *How Does Law Matter?*(1998); also: K Hawkins, *Law as Last Resort: Prosecution Decision-making in a Regulatory Agency* (2002)

[32]   SA Scheingold, *The Politics of Rights: Lawyers, Public Policy, and Political Change* (1974) p. 7

[33]   N Milner and J Goldberg-Hiller (2002) 'Reimagining Rights.' *Law and Social Inquiry* 1-18, p.1

Second, short of an outright revolution, what other options are there but to play by the rules already in place? The courts will not go away, and because rights are almost always contested they may eventually need to be litigated. And even when courts rule on the matter, it rarely settles the question; long-standing disputes, which result in litigation, do not necessarily end with a court's decision although the 'losing' side may be considerably weakened. Often decisions are scrutinized and analysed for future test-case challenges, and, conversely, the losing position may find a renewal of purpose in defeat becoming even more determined in its efforts.[34]

According to Garth and Sarat the current debate about law and society can be generally subsumed, notwithstanding considerable overlap, under the following two analytical frameworks: instrumental and constitutive.[35] The former is grounded in positivism and takes a top-down or court-centred approach to the study of law and its impact, and is dismissive of its ability to transform existing social relations of domination and subordination. The constitutive approach places law at the centre of analysis, but at the same time de-centres formal law by taking a bottom-up approach. This approach argues for the importance of studying law in all its variations because law operates in many arenas outside the formal terrain. Law is continually interpreted and reinterpreted, and 'in the hands of defiant citizens law can be a source of disorder and egalitarian re-ordering'.[36]

2.4.3 Instrumentalism

The instrumentalist framework seeks to understand the direct effects or impact of law by examining what is most tangible, for example, the outcome of litigation, focusing more generally on the courts and major decisions which are evocative of social progress. In other words, a cause and effect approach asking if a decision – generally one considered to be a landmark – did bring about social changes.[37]

---

[34] Garth and Sarat, *How Does Law Matter?* (1998) ; Garth and Sarat, *Justice and Power in Sociolegal Studies* (1998) ; Epp, *The Rights Revolution: Lawyers, Activists, and Supreme Courts in Comparative Perspective* (1998); Hershkoff (2009)

[35] Garth and Sarat, *How Does Law Matter?* (1998) p.2

[36] M McCann, *Rights at Work: Pay Equity Reform and the Politics of Legal Mobilization* (1994) p. ix

[37] For a fuller review of these issues see: Hertogh and Halliday, *Judicial review and bureaucratic impact: international and interdisciplinary perspectives* (2004)

Within this framework falls the work of some prominent scholars: law professor Michael Mandel (1994) and political scientist Gerald Rosenberg (1991) both of whom have come down solidly against rights litigation. Rosenberg, in his much debated study, concluded that the US Supreme Court was nothing more than a 'fly-paper' court. His findings generated immense academic support and praise, with many commentators urging social reformers to abandon the expense and empty promises of rights litigation and to focus on other tactics to advance their causes.[38] Rosenberg's (and Mandel's) conclusions are consistent with the views of critical legal scholars insofar as it pertains to the futility of playing by the rules set out by the powerful of society. One of the central arguments of this school is that ultimately law, even law that is supposed to ameliorate social ills, is an instrument of control that serves powerful interests and keeps subordinates in check. In other words, law perpetuates the status quo and legitimises rather than challenges the existing injustices and therefore cannot be used by the powerless to advance social causes.[39] The concept of hegemony is introduced to explain why it is that the masses acquiesce and play an apparent willing role in their own subjugation.

The problem with the instrumentalist concept of hegemony is the assumption that exploitation readily seen by others is not by those being exploited. Furthermore, it is problematic to seek cause and effect explanations in the social world, and herein is one of the central drawbacks with instrumentalism. It is difficult to isolate law as the variable being the cause of observable social changes. The social world is in a continual state of flux and social changes occur over protracted periods of time. They are incremental in nature, and diffused throughout society making it problematic to ascribe the observed or measured changes to any particular cause. Further complicating the task is the existence of numerous competing explanations. When the instrumentalist framework is contrasted with the constitutive approach, some of the shortcomings of the former become apparent. The latter is holistic in outlook and takes an expansive view of the law in recognition of the complexity of interaction between law and society, and seeks to understand the nature of that interaction. Moreover, the constitutive approach argues against seeking cause and effect explanations because law cannot be properly understood in isolation from the multitude of factors which constantly interact with it.

---

[38] See, for example, reviewers' 'blurbs' on the back cover of Rosenberg's book; see also Mandel (1994) for similar conclusions regarding the Canadian experience with rights litigation.

[39] See M McCann, 'How Does Law Matter for Social Movements? ' in B Garth and A Sarat (eds) *How Does Law Matter* (1998); CE Smith, *Courts and the Poor* (1991)

2.4.4 Constitutive

The law provides a framework through which we understand the world or certain aspects of that world. Whereas instrumentalists see law as an independent variable whose impact, for example, on an already constituted social world can be measured, the constitutive approach sees law from a broader perspective, as more of a pervasive and diffused influence, which does not exist independently of society. Rather than asking, for example, about the impact of certain court decisions, the constitutive approach examines the role of law in bringing about social change.[40] In other words, according to McIntyre (1994) 'to argue that law is constitutive is not only to maintain that law provides categories (of how the world is seen) but also that it can be used to change ideas'.[41]

How does law work as catalyst? What is rights consciousness? What role do rights play in mobilisation? How are rights used as leverage? It is by addressing such questions, rather than examining the impact of policies or court decisions, that a comprehensive picture of the role of law in social change emerges. The constitutive approach is not so much a singular analytical framework as it is a broadly conceived bottom-up, hermeneutic or interpretive approach to the study of law; its fundamental premise being that law is a constitutive element of society. This marks a discernible shift in the theoretical terrain to a broader view of the law, and of rights. Noticeably the shift has been away from examining rights in the formal legal processes to its 'decentred' and 'contingent' nature, in recognition that the power of rights does not always reside in the courts, or in the courts' interpretation, but elsewhere. It is important, however, to note that the power of rights cannot be assumed. It is not automatic and is dependent upon the circumstances and manner in which they are harnessed by activists.[42] According to McCann (1994), to understand how law affects society it is important to pay attention to the myriad of activities or 'indirect law' which occur outside the boundaries of the conventional, an area of inquiry overlooked by positivists. Law is much more than court decisions, lawyers, statutes, and legal norms. Law is a malleable resource, and it is constantly being interpreted and reinterpreted by individuals and organizations that display a sophisticated and critical understanding of its nuances. Further, social

---

[40]   Garth and Sarat, *How Does Law Matter?* (1998) p. 2
[41]   LJ McIntyre, *Law in the Sociological Enterprise: A Reconstruction* (1994) p. 112
[42]   Milner and Goldberg-Hiller (2002) 'Reimagining Rights.'

activists and reformers are not naïve and recognize that with all the possibilities that law presents, it also constrains because law sets the boundaries and defines the parameters by which issues are contested.[43]

That this theoretical shift should occur is not surprising given the limitations of positivism when applied to the social word – something that Eugene Ehrlich recognized in the 1930s when he formulated his views on the 'living law' based on observations that the law was far wider in scope than recognized within its formal terrain.[44] According to Ewick and Sibey (1998) 'the question is not about tracking the causal and instrumental relationship between law and society but towards tracing the presence of law in society'.[45] However this seems a paradoxically vague and ambitious view and raises the criticism that the approach is far too broad to be useful as a framework. How does one, for example, trace the presence of law in society? And furthermore, how does one work around the constraints of rights, particularly of rights litigation, which takes place in a rigid and formal terrain where social issues are distilled into legal categories?

None other than Alan Hunt (1998), an avowedly Marxist critic of law, who has embraced the options offered by a constitutive view of law and society, suggests a way out of this dilemma. According to Hunt actors and institutions exist in relation to one another but not all aspects of that relationship are relevant to the study.[46] Rather the question to explore is the legal dimension of that relationship. In other words, the question is: how is law present in social relations? It is that presence that may be constitutive of a social relationship.[47] However, what is markedly different about Hunt's approach is that he takes on the instrumentalists on their own terms by calling for counter hegemonic measures, which 'reworks' or transcends the very elements that are constitutive of the prevailing hegemony.[48] In other words hegemony also occurs in small groups, or in a particular aspect of social

---

[43]   See Garth and Sarat, 1998a; McIntyre, 1994; McCann, 1994; Cowan, 2003; Hertogh, 2004; Hertogh and Halliday, 2004; Engel, 1998; Burnstein, 1991. Rights tactics have produced relatively uneven results for the aboriginal peoples of Canada; for example, the Supreme Court of Canada, while seemingly expanding some aboriginal rights, has also imported restrictions where none had been envisioned which some critics have said was invented out of 'thin air' (in Sharma, 1998).

[44]   Cotterrell, *The Sociology of Law: An Introduction* (1992) p. 27

[45]   Ewick and Silbey, *The Common Place of Law: Stories from Everyday Life* (1998) p. 35

[46]   Hunt, *Explorations in Law and Society: Towards a Constitutive Theory of Law* (1993) p. 8; also personal/email communication (Summer 2003)

[47]   ibid p.16

[48]   ibid p.232

life, when exceptions are taken to the prevailing views and persistent challenges issued by presenting opposing interpretations. This concept is not dissimilar from rights consciousness, where citizens act on the basis of *their* interpretation and understanding of rights *irrespective* of formal recognition, and sometimes in spite of that recognition if there is a disagreement with the official version.[49] Social activists and organizations can massage the emergence of (rights) consciousness so that it coalesces into a vibrant and powerful force for change.[50]

Implicit in the concept of rights consciousness is a recognition that rights do not necessarily need litigation to hold power or be harnessed by activists, and this view has come to occupy legal consciousness research in the US.[51] From this perspective litigation, then, becomes just one of the tactics to be deployed within the broader range of a rights strategy. To avoid the conflation of rights with litigation, Hunt (1993) suggests disaggregating 'rights' from 'litigation', not because litigation is any less valued but to demarcate its role within a rights strategy.[52] The simplicity and appeal of disaggregating is that the formal terrain may be avoided altogether, which may placate, to some extent, those who regard litigation with concern. However, if the view is that law is constitutive of society, then those seeking redress have the option of negotiating through all its mechanisms, both formal and informal, including litigation. Litigation is not necessarily viewed as a handicap by the constitutive approach because law is not viewed as hostile or as an instrument of control. To be sure, there is recognition that law is also a mechanism of regulation and control, but control is not its only function; law is also facilitative.[53] In modern-day societies, characterized by immense complexity and different or competing objectives, law serves many and varied purposes.

Can it then be said that rights are not empty vessels requiring judicial interpretation or litigation to imbue them with power? Do rights intrinsically hold power, which can be applied in creative and innovative or counter-hegemonic tactics by social movements or advocacy groups? If so, how is it that rights acquire this

---

[49] For a review of legal consciousness see: L Edelman and M Cahill, ' How Does Law Matter in Disputing and Dispute Processing' in BG Garth and A Sarat (eds) *How Does Law Matter* (1998); Engel, 'How Does Law Matter in the Constitution of Legal Consciousness ' in ibid

[50] See, for example, MacKinnon's (1989) study on the emergence of the women's movement in the US: C MacKinnon, *Towards a Feminist Theory of the State* (1989)

[51] M Hertogh (2004) 'A 'European' Conception of Legal Consciousness: Rediscovering Eugen Ehrlich' 31 Journal of Law and Society 4 457

[52] Hunt, *Explorations in Law and Society: Towards a Constitutive Theory of Law* (1993) 237

[53] See McCann, 1998; Hunt, 1993; McIntyre, 1994; Schultz, 1997; Ewick and Sibey, 1998.

power because mere existence of rights is nothing more than words on paper? In Canada, for example, a bill of rights predated the *Charter* by at least two decades, and it is almost unanimously agreed that it was a meaningless document ignored by the courts and the general public.[54] Similarly, the US Supreme Court consistently ignored constitutional rights for almost 150 years insofar as they concerned civil rights and liberties.[55] And it was not long ago that a bill of rights was considered unnecessary for the UK – under the assumption that common law, with its foundation in protecting the propertied classes, provided sufficient protection.[56] What are the reasons for the emergence and prominence of rights not only in the US and Canada, but also the UK, a nation noted for a conservative judiciary and, until recently, an absence of a formal 'made in Britain' rights document?[57] According to Epp (1998) the reason for the dramatic changes are several: judicial leadership, constitutional guarantees, rights consciousness, and, most importantly, a persistent push from below, consisting of deliberate and strategic organising by advocacy groups persistent in having their vision heard.[58] While Epp's arguments are not without shortcomings or detractors critical of some of his conclusions and scant attention to activism outside the courts, his arguments and research on ground-level advocacy holds considerable merit.[59] In his comparative analysis of the 'rights revolution' in the US, UK, and Canada, Epp concludes that the development of a support structure – consisting of rights lawyers, organisations, and funding – was central to bringing about a cultural change.

It is worth noting that when activists engage with rights, notwithstanding its conceptual separation from litigation, the decision to litigate remains an option that is not always within their control. The party being challenged may wish to litigate for various tactical reasons of their own, including a conviction in the 'rightness'

---

54   Some observers have wryly noted that one of the few decisions of note under the Bill, *R v. Drybones* [1970] SCR 282, accorded an aboriginal Canadian the 'right' to be intoxicated off reserve (prior to the decision it was illegal for an 'Indian' to be drunk when not within the boundaries of an Indian reservation). See: P Sharma, *Aboriginal Fishing Rights: Law, Courts, Politics* (1998)

55   Epp, *The Rights Revolution: Lawyers, Activists, and Supreme Courts in Comparative Perspective* (1998)

56   Harvey, Colin J. and the British Institute of Human Rights, *Human Rights in the Community: Rights as Agents for Change* (2005)

57   Home Office, *Rights Brought Home: the Human Rights Bill* (1997)

58   ibid p. 3

59   For a critique of Epp's research see: A Southworth (2000) 'The Rights Revolution and Support Structure for Rights Advocacy' 34 Law and Society Review 4 1203-19

of their position, to seek clarification of a vague area of law, cause delays, or call the challenger's 'bluff' leaving little option but to go to court. Is litigation, then, something to be feared?

2.4.5 Criticisms of Litigation and Rights

The opposition to rights has to do with more than just theoretical differences. Some of these criticisms are: rights litigation is undemocratic; litigation ties up valuable resources; legal battles take far too long; litigation produces hollow victories; and, other (and presumably more effective) options for social progress are ignored or accorded less attention.[60]

The central problem with litigation is one that is shared by both parties to a dispute: litigation can be a gamble and the outcome, while in many cases predictable, is never assured. For example, even the best argued cases can be thwarted by an unreceptive judiciary, and this applies to both parties. While the risks are not shared equally, and the disadvantaged remain at a disadvantage, the outcome is something that neither party can take as a given. For example, the government, for which the law is presumably an instrument of control, cannot always be certain of winning irrespective of the resources at its disposal as evidenced by several high profile cases in the UK, US, and in Canada dealing with, for example, indigenous rights, gay rights, pay equity, and asylum rights.[61] Canada, in particular, has had to contend with aboriginal Canadians asserting constitutional rights with considerable vigour not only in the courts but also in direct negotiations with the government. And the victories have been significant – particularly a recent out-of-court class-action settlement in excess of one billion dollars in compensation for historical wrongs;[62] there have also been several land-claims settlements – each exceeding $100 million.[63] Pay equity battles, as documented by McCann (1994), resulted in

---

[60] For an in-depth review see: SA Scheingold, *The Politics of Rights: Lawyers, Public Policy, and Political Change* (2nd edn) (2004); see also Hershkoff (2009) for a concise summary.

[61] See case studies (next section)

[62] JJ Llewellyn (2002) 'Dealing with the Legacy of Native Residential School Abuse in Canada: Litigation, ADR, and Restorative Justice' 52 The University of Toronto Law Journal 3 253-300; A McIlroy, 'Severance payments' *The Guardian* (03 Jan 2006)

[63] There are various types of claims being negotiated by the Canadian government; some address historic grievances and others involve modern-day treaties addressing unresolved issues over resources and lands. See http://www.ainc-inac.gc.ca/al/ldc/index-eng.asp for details.

settlements in the hundreds of millions of dollars in the US and Canada. Critics, however, argue that such victories are exceptions because the government is the overwhelming victor – and, to be sure, such is the case in the courts of Canada, UK, and the US.[64] But notwithstanding the fact that the odds favour governments, the losses suffered have not been insignificant. However, the problem with a win-lose dichotomy is the equation that winning is everything; in other words, litigation has to succeed for there to be gains by social movements. This is far too hasty a conclusion because even when a case is lost it does not necessarily follow that gains, such as publicity for the cause, other (concurrent) settlements, rights consciousness, or empowerment, have not occurred; for example, as documented by McCann (1994) in his case-studies of pay equity battles.[65]

When social movements engage in litigation it is judicial policy-making which is sought. Often it is because the political door is inaccessible or has been closed. Many critics, however, regard judicial policymaking or forays into areas of social policy as anathema to democracy, and argue that such matters should best be left to elected bodies, which are presumably more accountable. The normative view is that judges should interpret and apply the law to the matter before them, and avoid policy making.[66] It is argued that judges violate the principles of democracy because they are unelected and not accountable to the general public.[67]

This view, however, is not without problems, the least of which is that it is an idealistic view of democracy and a simplistic view of the complex interplay between the various branches of government, governmental institutions, including the courts, and the public in democratic societies. This criticism does not take into consideration the overlap and difficulties in oftentimes separating policy issues from a strict interpretation of the letter of the law. And even when the judgments are strictly interpretation, that interpretation, presumably, must be applied by bureaucrats or policy-makers who seek guidance from decisions to make policy, or issue directions for departments or institutions. In other words, there are both

---

[64]   Both Mandel (1994) and McCormick (1993), in their review of Charter litigation in Canada, concluded that the State is the overwhelming victor in the courts of Canada, including the Supreme Court, just as it had been before the Charter; Rosenberg (1991) also concluded the same for litigation in the US Supreme Court.

[65]   McCann, *Rights at Work: Pay Equity Reform and the Politics of Legal Mobilization* (1994)

[66]   M Feeley and EL Rubin, *Judicial Policy Making and the Modern State: How the Courts Reformed America's Prisons* (1998)

[67]   Cotterrell, *The Sociology of Law: An Introduction* (1992)

direct and indirect ways in which the courts either make or affect social policy. It is also important to be clear about what is meant by judicial policy-making. For some, it means (illegal or unprincipled) excursions into areas of social policy; and, for others, it means judicial activism or judicial policy-making aimed at producing socially desirable results.[68] It is one thing for the judiciary to seek guidance from social policy but quite another when they actively engage in making policy, areas considered to be sacrosanct of the elected; judges readily acknowledge the former but rarely the latter.[69] However, when social activists litigate it is the latter that they seek. Horowitz cites several examples of judicial intervention in various social policy areas, and concludes that judges have always engaged in 'policy-making not only in areas where there is vague guidance, but also in areas where there is a plethora of statutes and regulations'.[70]

The phenomenon of judicial policy-making had been remarkably absent in the Canadian courts prior to the introduction of the *Charter*, and relatively inconsequential in the UK courts (see Prosser, 1983). It has been argued that the presence of constitutional rights encourages and is conducive to judicial policy making; Epp (1998) argues that a persistent push from below, by advocacy groups, is also necessary; Shapiro and Stone-Sweet (2002) argue that federalism is another necessary ingredient. Another view is that the public at large demand and expect robust protection of rights that are accorded constitutional status.[71] In some instances, this expectation extends to the state itself as in the case of the UK where the HRA was promoted on this very basis in the government's White Paper *Bringing Rights Home*.[72] Similarly, in Canada, during the early days of the *Charter*, a special government fund was established to assist groups in initiating legal challenges against actual or perceived excesses of the state.[73]

In view of the above it is then naive to suggest that advocacy groups should avoid the (assumed) undemocratic process of litigation for the (supposed) democratic process of politics for several reasons. What is it that makes rights

---

[68] Feeley and Rubin, *Judicial Policy Making and the Modern State: How the Courts Reformed America's Prisons* (1998) p.5

[69] DL Horowitz, *The Courts and Social policy* (1977) p.14

[70] ibid p.5

[71] See also H Hershkoff (2009) 'Public Law Litigation: Lessons and Questions' 10 Human Rights Review 2 157-81

[72] See, for example, various statements by the Chief Justice of England and Wales, Lord Woolf.

[73] FL Morton, *Law, Politics and the Judicial Process in Canada* (2002)

litigation so apparently undemocratic? First, it is problematic to assume that there is a demarcation point where processes, be they democratic or undemocratic, are readily apparent.[74] Rather it is more a question of degree, and this would suggest a possible empirical query rather than assuming that judicial policy-making is inherently undemocratic. Second, it is noteworthy that elected officials appoint judges. In many jurisdictions, there is also a lengthy vetting process before judges are entrusted to such elevated positions. If one of the major functions of the judiciary is to act as a check on other branches of the government, how can it be said that when its decision goes against the state, the court is acting undemocratically when it is doing precisely what it is supposed to. How else are the courts to give substance to the liberal ideal of 'protecting minorities from the tyranny of the majority'? It cannot be expected that the legislature or executive will always get it right.

Third, the ability of minority interests to effectively use the electoral process raises several questions? Are MPs any better (or less) informed about social issues than the judiciary? Are they sympathetic or hostile to non-majoritarian causes? Do they take time to study and understand the issues? Does the parliamentary system allow for informed debate particularly where the governing party has a large majority? Do those agitating for social change have access to their respective MPs? Are MPs open to minority viewpoints if they have been elected by the majority to presumably serve them? Are MPs influenced by professional lobbyists who are financed by powerful interests? To assume that the majority would want protection for the minority particularly at their expense, or because it is for the greater good, is just fanciful thinking. It is precisely because disadvantaged groups do not have political clout or access to political institutions that they seek redress from the courts. Oftentimes, it is the only accessible option.[75] And, as Hershkoff (2009) argues, an engagement with rights is a form of politics, a challenge to the status quo.[76]

2.5   Part B: Rights at Work (Selected Case Studies)

By far the most extensive work that has been done on the subject, both theoretical and empirical, has been in the US. NGOs comprising social movements as diverse

---

[74]   See also Horowitz, 1977: p.17, for a similar discussion.

[75]   M Malik, 'Minority Protection and Human Rights' in T CampbellKD Ewing and A Tomkins (eds) *Sceptical Essays on Human Rights* (2001) p. 277

[76]   p. 159-160

as the civil rights movement of the 1950s, environmental groups, women's groups, and gay-rights activists have used the US Bill of Rights to mobilise and challenge state and federal governments. Some of these movements, particularly the various environmental groups, have made impressive gains, while some have not had as much success, for example, gay-rights activists litigating for recognition of same-sex marriages. In this section, I shall focus on the works of Gerald Rosenberg (1991) and Michael McCann (1994)

2.5.1   Rosenberg's Impact Study of the U.S. Supreme Court

Amongst the decisions most often cited by advocates of rights (litigation) as an example of the effectiveness of law in challenging the status quo, and advancing the causes of oppressed or powerless minorities, are the landmark US Supreme Court decisions on racial segregation in schools and abortion rights: *Brown v Board of Education* and *Roe v Wade.*[77] Until recently, it was a commonly accepted view that *Brown* had had a significant impact not only on the (eventual) desegregation of schools and other public institutions but also on race relations.[78] While *Brown* and *Wade* were decided several decades ago, these landmark decisions continue to feature prominently in general discussions and scholarly discourse on law and its ability and potential to bring about social change.

In 1991 Professor Rosenberg asked if such views had an empirical basis. He analysed several landmark decisions of the US Supreme Court including *Brown* and *Roe v Wade* and concluded that Court is a 'fly-paper court'. Asking if the Supreme Court can bring about social change, Rosenberg's positivist approach is a search for direct linkage between the decision and its assumed effects. Rosenberg is dismissive of the Court's ability to transform existing relations of domination and subordination, and he concludes that social movements, law reformers, and supporters alike have been misled into ascribing to the Court successes it cannot rightly claim. The findings by Rosenberg created a great deal of controversy; to be sure, some of his criticisms are valid but his study is not without flaws – the key problem being a positivist approach to a fluid and dynamic subject matter.

---

[77] *Brown v Board of Education* 347 U.S. 483 (1954); *Roe v. Wade*, 410 U.S. 113 (1973)
[78] Schultz, *Leveraging the law: using the courts to achieve social change* (1998)

2.5.2   Critique of Rosenberg and Positivism

Rosenberg's in-depth analysis focuses on areas where it has been popularly assumed that the US Supreme Court has had the greatest impact: civil rights and abortion and, to a lesser extent, the environment. Rosenberg's argument is thought-provoking, but in setting out to test his hypothesis, he sets up some very stringent conditions that most institutions, leave alone courts, could not possibly meet. The first hurdle the Supreme Court would have to overcome is definitional. Rosenberg wants to see social change as 'significant social change' – meaning that the changes would have to have nation-wide impact and affect a large group of people, such as black Americans or women as a group. In other words, groups constituting a wide variety of differently situated individuals are seen as homogenous with uniform objectives, a most problematic, if not fatal, conceptualisation. Arguably *Brown* did not mean as much for black Americans living in the Northern states as it perhaps did for those in the South. And most likely *Roe v Wade* did not have much impact for urban middle or upper-class women, or those living in liberal or progressive states. In any event, the conceptualisation of women and black Americans in such a broad-brush manner renders the analysis of questionable value. Rosenberg further clarifies significant social change to mean that litigation which simply sought to change the way a single bureaucracy functions would not meet his criteria, but litigation to 'change the functioning of a whole set of bureaucracies or institutions nation-wide would'. In both instances it is difficult to imagine a situation where both definitional conditions would be satisfied. First and foremost Rosenberg fails to consider the structure of government in the US, particularly the Federal/State division and overlap in jurisdiction over laws and institutions. Further, in view of the incremental nature of social changes, it is improbable that nation-wide institutional changes, which affected large groups of people, would occur that would satisfy the definition – even more so in such a large and diverse nation. In other words, Rosenberg's is an easy argument to make in hindsight because history is devoid of any particular court decisions that have resulted in such wide-scale changes. Even if there was such a decision the intervening number of years that it would take for nation-wide changes to occur, and the confounding variables of history, would make it problematic, in a positivistic framework, to link those changes to the decision.

There are also methodological and theoretical issues in Rosenberg's study that merit criticism. Rosenberg outlines the theoretical underpinnings into two distinct camps: the dynamic court view and the constrained court view. The former views the courts as 'powerful, vigorous, and potent proponents of change' and the latter as 'weak, ineffective, and powerless to affect the types of social changes desired by reformers'.[79] However, the views are so polarized that it presents as caricatures rather than analytical concepts. The theories outlined by Rosenberg, which are subsumed under the constrained and dynamic views, are patently outdated and very few, if any, scholars are making such claims today. At least they were not during the time that Rosenberg undertook his study. Many of the references are dated, and with a few exceptions, all citations in this section are pre-1982; many are in the 1970s. The dynamic court view is unrealistically positive and the constrained court is hopelessly negative; and, in spite of his insistence that he is not setting up a 'straw-man', that is precisely what he does.

Rosenberg approvingly cites Scheingold (1974) throughout his study with particular emphasis on Scheingold's theorising on what he labelled the 'myth of rights'.[80] However Scheingold's theoretical arguments appear to have been accorded empirical validity in Rosenberg's study who seems to have ignored Scheingold's argument that law is far too complex, requiring a comprehensive approach to analysing issues such as its role in social change. To be sure, Rosenberg does consider to the indirect effects of litigation but the analysis is perfunctory, consisting of analysis of newspaper citations (not content) and public polls, neither of which are sufficiently explored.[81] In this respect, there is a contradiction between Rosenberg's positivistic approach, and Scheingold's theoretical position that sees law as a potent tool for social change when combined with other tactics, such as political mobilization. Scheingold also cautions that determining when circumstances most conducive to legal tactics leading to social changes occur remain elusive. The problem is not so much in the approach itself, Scheingold argues, but in the 'impenetrable uncertainties of the politics of change'.[82] Nevertheless Scheingold, in contrast to Rosenberg, concludes that there are distinct advantages

---

[79]   Rosenberg, *The Hollow Hope: Can Courts Bring About Social Change?* (1991) p.2

[80]   See: Scheingold, *The Politics of Rights: Lawyers, Public Policy, and Political Change* (1974)

[81]   See: BC Cannon, 'The Supreme Court and Policy Reform: The Hollow Hope Revisited ' in DA Schultz (ed) *Leveraging the Law* (1998) for a constitutive analysis of how *Brown* served to raise consciousness and as catalyst for mobilization as increasing numbers of activists joined the ranks of NAACP and other civil rights organizations.

[82]   Scheingold, *The Politics of Rights: Lawyers, Public Policy, and Political Change* (1974) p. 213

to working towards political change by legal means, and urges activists to explore its possibilities.

Rosenberg's work is important not only for its ambitious scope and generating much needed debate on the subject, but also for the sheer number of commentary and rebuttal that it has invited. However, it is also difficult to overlook the impression that Rosenberg seems to have worked backwards, from an already articulated conclusion and then to a development of hypothesis. The conditions upon which he argues the Supreme Court will produce significant social changes reduces the court to a 'rubber stamp' formality. If that is indeed the case then the Supreme Court has managed to fool a great number of people, including countless social activists, who have invested immense efforts in attempts to improve the situation for the disadvantaged and have apparently failed to see how the Court has failed them.[83] However, as demonstrated in studies by McCann and others, social movements are not that naïve and the nature of rights not that impotent.

2.5.3   Pay Equity and Rights: A Constitutive Analysis

Whereas Rosenberg focused on the Supreme Court as the centre of analysis, Michael McCann's (1994) bottom-up approach focused on the activists involved in the fight for pay equity and on legal mobilisation, which is described as a situation when a 'desire or want is asserted as a right, and law is seen as capable of addressing those desires or wants'. McCann's self-defined, loosely-interpretive approach combines the conventional analysis of law, as represented by court decisions with an expansive view, centring it firmly on how ordinary activists understand the law, and their interpretation of rights. McCann examines how social activists viewed and interpreted the law, and used rights counter-hegemonically (strategically) to reframe their objectives as social justice issues; how rights were employed to organise and mobilise over certain issues; how it was used as leverage in bargaining, particularly in avoiding lengthy and costly court battles and encouraging employers to negotiate settlements; how law served as a catalyst, for example, in organizing protests and uniting workers; and, how it gave rise to a rights consciousness.

---

[83]   See, also, Swedlow's (2009) case study on how US Ninth Circuit courts acted to protect eco-systems in the Pacific Northwest; Swedlow argues that the case study 'invalidates' Rosenberg's theory. He also suggests a 'reformulation' of Rosenberg's theory by broadening what are fatally narrow, and as argued above, self-serving, definitional shortcomings in The Hollow Hope (1991).

In examining how women's groups across the US used rights and mobilised in their battles over pay equity reform, McCann concludes that 'legal norms shaped the terrain of the struggle' and, in turn, 'litigation and other tactics provided activists with an important resource for advancing their cause' as news of court victories or negotiated settlements were widely trumpeted across the country. As extensively documented by McCann using standardized surveys, in-person interviews with 140 union and feminist activists across the US, content-analysis of newspapers, and case studies of specific pay-equity battles, the fight was not easy. Not only did the women's groups battle all levels of government and various private and public institutions, but also gender stereotypes and labour unions. The fight, which had been building momentum, started in earnest in 1981 following the US Supreme Court's decision that rejected a county government's wage policy where female prison-guards, doing essentially the same job, were paid significantly lower wages than their male counterparts. As McCann documents, activists found considerable strength in the court's affirmation of their position. The decision served as a catalyst for women's groups as they mobilized across the US, rejuvenated by a new found ally in the form of the US Supreme Court.

In the following years, however, many other battles were fought in and out of courtrooms. While many such battles were lost, particularly in the waning years of the movement, many were won resulting in significant changes in the economic status of large groups of people. During the peak of the wage-equity reform battles, many large-scale employers and organizations fearing lawsuits and witnessing court victories for pay-reform and having to contend with agitating employees, settled for hundreds of millions of dollars. And many were compelled to do so by activists unafraid to use the leverage afforded by law. McCann provides several examples: one of the most interesting was the campaign by Washington State public employees who had nothing to show for years of lobbying until the filing of a lawsuit, which resulted in legislative action by the state promising to redress pay equity issues. However, the lawsuit proceeded to judgment where the court ordered the state to pay $377 million in back wages; on appeal the state won. But the union continued to pressure the state; to avoid further legal action the state agreed to a $100 million settlement in pay-raises. According to the activists, the lawsuit, even though unsuccessful in the courts, was the key in resolving the matter.[84]

---

[84] McCann, *Rights at Work: Pay Equity Reform and the Politics of Legal Mobilization* (1994) p. 154-55. The battle for pay equity has also been waged in Canada; while the fight is far from over, there have been some settlements. The Federal government settled with some of its clerical workers at a cost of over $3billion, or about $30,000 per employee (http://www.slis.ualberta.ca/cap03/regan/canada.htm). In the private sector Bell Canada settled for $56million with its employees after unsuccessfully pursuing legal remedies to avoid pay equity (http://www.payequityreview.gc.ca/4432-e.html).

McCann's case studies are thorough, and his methodological approach rigorous, as he looks beyond the courts to demonstrate the malleability of law and the potent resource that it represents in the form of rights. It is McCann's argument that because judicial victories produce uneven results, it is in the strategic uses, such as leverage in bargaining and negotiating, or as rights consciousness, that the power and potential of law in addressing questions of social justice lies. McCann's work challenges Rosenberg because he takes a more expansive approach rather than Rosenberg's narrowly focused positivistic framework. For those who define law in a narrow sense and seek to determine the direct impact or cause-and-effect of litigation the approach by Rosenberg has much to offer. However, in this respect, the conclusion or findings, while easily predictable, provide a rather limited understanding of how law operates in the larger world, outside official forums, which McCann argues is far too important to neglect.

2.5.4   A Constitutive Analysis of School Underfunding

The study by McMahon and Paris (1998) examined a highly complex chain of events dealing with underfunding of poorer school districts in the state of New Jersey. The authors utilised McCann's framework in an attempt to demonstrate the potential and effectiveness of law in mobilising and empowering reformers.[85] The study focused on a succession of court battles brought about by activists during the period of 1970 to 1997 aimed at increasing funding for schools catering to mostly Hispanic and Black Americans. For the activists, many of whom had never been involved in social policy challenges, the objectives leading up the decision of the New Jersey Supreme Court were modest. Their organisation was skeletal at best and focused initially on a legal interpretation of certain provisions of the state constitution. However, when the Court (to their surprise) ruled in their favour the activists found a renewed sense of purpose. And they responded with vigour by mobilising, organising, and re-organising in response to successive and continuing court battles. While there were many setbacks the activists were successful in redefining the frame of reference to the degree that school funding issues are now almost entirely debated according to those terms. For example, the issues of race and poverty must now be factored into school funding decisions whereas prior to

---

[85]   KJ McMahon and M Paris, 'The Politics of Rights Revisited: Rosenberg, McCann, and the New Institutionalism' in DA Schultz (ed) *Leveraging the Law* (1998)

the court battles, these were non-issues. However, the degree to which either the courts or local governments actually consider such issues remains an empirical question.

As documented by McMahon and Paris the ever-changing political climate in the state, from cooperative to oppositional, and counter mobilisation efforts by opposing groups presented the activists with few other options but to seek changes through the courts. And during that period the courts were a relatively constant ally. It was in the courts that the activists succeeded in having their vision realised and having it translated into policy imperatives insofar as such issues (race and poverty) had to be considered in funding decisions. According to McMahon and Paris the immediate results of the court battles were disappointing because the state effectively thwarted the activists by legislation and other dilatory tactics. But the activists persisted and turned to the courts. They used successive court victories to build upon their vision by introducing issues of equality, race, and poverty not only in funding matters, but also on the subject of educational reform. However, the fight is far from over as there continues to be determined opposition, by both the richer school districts and the political leaders of the state. While the poorer districts have managed to make significant gains in budgetary allocations, an immense divide remains.

If anything the above study serves as a reminder that law and rights are not without peril. A determined opposition and the changing tides of political will, combined with counter-tactics, can do much to stifle activists seeking to bring about social changes.

2.5.5 Role of Rights in Litigation: Prison Reform, the Environment, and Gay Rights

The case studies of prison-reform litigation by Feeley and Rubin (1999) presents an argument for the legitimacy of judicial policy-making.[86] Notwithstanding differences of opinion on what is considered their proper role judges do engage in policy-making. And Feeley and Rubin set out to demonstrate just how it is that they do so. Their analysis examines how rights brought about significant changes in an area long neglected by government and the courts. Feeley and Rubin argue that

---

[86]   Feeley and Rubin, *Judicial Policy Making and the Modern State: How the Courts Reformed America's Prisons* (1998)

notwithstanding the claims of various judges that their intervention in reforming American prisons was merely an interpretation of the Eighth Amendment, prohibiting 'cruel and unusual punishment', it was anything but. And this, according to the authors, was policy-making because the degree and extent of judicial intervention, the nature of orders that were imposed, could not have been derived from the narrow scope of the Eighth Amendment.[87] How is it, the authors ask, that so many separate and uncoordinated federal courts, without guidance from the Supreme Court or the government, moved in the same direction towards reforming American prisons: 'where one would have expected uncertainty, retrenchment, and disagreement, there was only relentless unanimity'.[88]

According to Feeley and Rubin prisoners had been complaining to the courts since the 1930s about the conditions of their confinement; and, almost all such lawsuits were routinely dismissed notwithstanding the Eighth Amendment. However, starting in 1965, federal courts began to incrementally place prisons under court orders or injunctions ordering changes and restructuring various institutions. By 1995 prisons in 41 states and the entire correctional systems of 10 states were under comprehensive court orders. Not only did the judges impose a comprehensive set of judicially enforceable rules but ensured that the orders were implemented by delegating that duty to other agencies. According to the authors, the judges 'derived these rules from their own perceptions of morality, sociology, and existing literature on correctional issues'.[89] As explained by the authors the inhumane conditions in American prisons cried out for reform. However, once major restructuring had been completed, the movement naturally waned and the courts seemingly lost interest in prisoner's rights once the worst abuses had been effectively dealt with.

2.6   A Rights Strategy for the Environment

A complementary view of rights litigation holds that social policy issues can be made much more palatable if framed as being for the greater good, in the best interests of society. The assumption being that wide public support will reduce opposition making it easier to implement policy changes. Perhaps the most successful of

---

[87]   ibid p 14
[88]   ibid p 145
[89]   ibid p 14

all social movements, in terms of sustained public support and mobilisation, has been the environmental movement in the US which succeeded in bringing to the forefront protection of the environment. Notwithstanding Rosenberg's analytical framework, it is also one of the few areas in which both a positivist and interpretive framework leads to the conclusion that rights significantly altered the landscape in the battle over the environment. Gary Coglianese's (2001) examination of how the environmental movement, which had long existed as a fringe player, transformed itself during the 1960s and 70s and became an important player in American politics, is a case study on pushing the boundaries, which the movement did so via a sustained engagement with rights combined with grassroots organising, public information events, protests, and political lobbying.[90]

What gave impetus to the movement were a series of major ecological disasters, oil spills, gas blowouts, and wild fires, and the apparent immunity of those responsible. According to Coglianese rights tactics, similar to that practiced by the civil rights movement, were adopted by environmentalists leading to some significant legal victories. While the movement's objective of gaining constitutional protection for the environment failed, the initial victories in court served as a springboard for increased legal activity as the movement focused primarily on a legislative agenda. Under pressure the US Congress responded and a plethora of laws and statutes were created; the Environmental Protection Agency (EPA) was also created to oversee enforcement of the laws. As Coglianese explains the movement did not neglect other venues and worked diligently to inform the public and garner their support; in the process the movement gained both governmental and industrial allies. When during the Reagan Administration the environment took a backseat to economic issues, the movement turned to the laws it had helped create to maintain what had already been achieved and to keep the spotlight on the issue. The movement also filed numerous lawsuits resulting in penalties against corporations; lawsuits were also filed against the EPA when it was felt that the agency was being less than diligent or not proactive in fulfilling its mandate. The movement transformed the legal landscape and, according to Coglianese, the planet and its inhabitants are better for it; arguably, the results of such efforts have resulted in cleaner air, cleaner water, and preservation of other natural resources.[91]

---

[90] G Coglianese (2001) 'Social Movements, Law, and Society: The Institutionalization of the Environmental Movement' 150 University of Pennsylvania Law Review 85-118

[91] ibid p 93-99

Coglianese cites several reports and data attesting to measurable reductions in toxic waste and pollution but acknowledges that contrary conclusions are also possible using the same data. For example, it remains open to argue that the environment continues to suffer from degradation and the advances or changes achieved have fallen far short of what is necessary. In other words, the movement's tactical focus on legislating protection and litigation possibly distracted it from considering the potential of or pursuing other tactics. And this is the position that Rosenberg (1991) presents in his analysis about the ineffectiveness of litigation.[92] However, Rosenberg's conclusions also suffer from what Coglianese acknowledges in his assessment of the environmental movement – that different conclusions are possible using the same data. Nevertheless, some measure of success must be granted to the movement's strategy for transforming the manner in which the environment is now regarded by industry, government, and the public. This is not to say that the movement can rest on its laurels or be satisfied with its successes – environmental issues continue to be highly contested and much work remains. However this case study does offer valuable lessons to social reformers in how a formerly fringe movement was able to reframe issues, legally and otherwise, so that it became everyone's concern. One of the possibilities this suggests for activists is how to transform minority issues into majority issues so that promotion of minority issues is not only seen as not contrary, but as beneficial to the interests of the majority, and for the greater good.

2.7   Gay and Lesbian Rights

The battle for gay rights, in the US in particular, has also been framed as one involving issues of fundamental rights but the activists have been thwarted by a coalition of powerful conservative forces.[93] For many in same-sex relations what is missing is legal recognition, which carries with it several other rights that those in conventional marriages take for granted. However, the attempts by the gay rights movement to gain legal recognition of same-sex marriages backfired in Hawaii, where the battle had culminated after the movement failed to win legal recognition

---

[92]   Rosenberg, *The Hollow Hope: Can Courts Bring About Social Change?* (1991) p 271
[93]   See JP Heinz A Southworth and A Paik (2003) 'Lawyers for Conservative Causes: Clients, Ideology, and Social Distance' 37 Law and Society Review 1 5-50 on how conservative organizations use the law to advocate for their vision of rights.

in other states. This was not a court battle but, nonetheless, a battle involving rights as citizens were asked to vote on a constitutional amendment seeking to block same-sex marriages. As documented by Hull (2001), the movement's attempts faced stiff resistance from opponents, who in turn sought the constitutional amendment.[94] The failure of the gay rights movement resulted in the passage of the federal *Defense of Marriage Act* and similar legislation in over thirty other states. According to Hull the movement worked hard to persuade voters that they had a stake in the issue and that a constitutional amendment was a slippery path that could result in the derogation of the rights for other segments of society. However the opponents countered with moral arguments and framed the issue as protecting the institution of marriage, and not about denying civil rights. Hull's study suggests that the force of a determined and organised majority, opposed to minority concerns, places severe limitations on rights for advancing social issues. And by most measures the battle in the US is a losing one for activists.[95]

Same-sex marriage in Canada is a non-issue. But it was not always so. The battle over same-sex marriages effectively ended in Canada when events culminated in three different provincial judges ordering a reluctant federal government to amend the *Marriage Act*. The highest courts in Ontario and British Columbia ruled that prohibitions against same-sex unions violated the equality rights of the *Charter*; the BC Court of Appeal gave the federal government until July of 2004 to amend the Act accordingly. However the Ontario Court of Appeal in June of 2003 went farther; the Court refused to allow a grace-period and ordered that couples seeking same-sex unions be issued marriage licenses with immediate effect. The Ontario government complied but marriage laws are the jurisdiction of the federal government, which gave uncertain signals but did suggest that the law would be changed in the face of various provincial court decisions.[96] During that period, however, gay marriages became legal in Ontario; in other parts of the country, activism continued in the form of public gay wedding ceremonies.[97] In addition

94   K Hull (2001) 'The Political Limits of the Rights Frame: The Case of Same-Sex Marriage in Hawaii' 44 Sociological Perspectives 2 207-32

95   R Archibold and A Goodnough, 'California Voters Ban Gay Marriage' *The New York Times* (05 Nov 2008)

96   C Clark, 'Government steers vote on accepting same-sex ruling' *The Globe and Mail* (13 June 2003)

97   Canadian Press, 'Ontario Appeal Court rules in favour of same-sex marriage' Ibid.(in *The Globe and Mail* 10 June 2003)

to its intangible and human elements, such as respect for different lifestyles, legal recognition of gay unions carries with it a multitude of substantive rights in the form of pension, taxation, and other benefits. In Canada, the battle has been long and hard, but recent evidence in the form of successive high court rulings indicates the successes of rights in transforming the situation of gays and lesbians.[98] In 2002 the government of Canada, pushed by the provincial courts, enacted legislation legalising gay unions.

2.8   Conclusion

What becomes apparent, following a review of the case studies by McCann, McMahon and Paris, and Coglianese, is that in the hands of committed, organized, and persistent groups, rights hold potential for improving the life situation of the disadvantaged and for bringing about social change. What is also clear is that the battlegrounds for social changes are heavily contested, and that social changes take many forms, and are subtle, incremental, and manifests itself over varying periods of time. Sometimes, the results are tangible as in pay equity settlements or the measurable decline in toxic emissions, and sometimes the changes are intangible, such as the worth of human dignity in the recognition of gay rights.

The strategic deployment of rights presents possibilities and pitfalls for social movements; rights have resonance, power, and potential. However rights are not a panacea for the many social problems that are an inherent part of modern societies. But clearly many NGOs believe in the potential and power of rights – that a guarantee of rights must mean something, and when there are actual or perceived shortcomings or breaches, governments must be held accountable. This belief is not without substance. NGO advocacy groups engage with rights in a deliberate, strategic, and organized manner to bring about social changes; furthermore, they are not naïve and have more than just an intuitive understanding of law. In the case studies examined what stands out is the level of sophistication demonstrated by non-legal actors, the ordinary people who are constantly structuring and restructuring their relationship with law determined to have their vision of their rights realised.

---

[98]   See Fudge, 'The Canadian Charter of Rights: Recognition, Redistribution, and the Imperialism of the Courts' in T Campbell KD Ewing and A Tomkins (eds) *Sceptical Essays on Human Rights* (2001)

One of the key strengths of rights is that they can be deployed to challenge the prevailing hegemony.[99] To apply an analogy consistent with instrumentalism, it would as if an ally of the powerful is turned against them, engaging them using their own language and terms to point out injustices making the wrongs difficult to avoid or ignore. What is also clear is that law and society (including social movements in that society) interact in a more dynamic and bi-directional fashion than has been generally recognized by those seeking direct cause and effect relationship. The relationship is complex, constantly changing, but it is not inherently exploitative because law serves many functions; law is regulatory but also facilitative. The objective of the case studies was to illustrate not only the range of possibilities offered by rights, but also the pitfalls that the strategy presents. Asking if rights can be an effective resource for bringing about social change, presents theoretical and methodological problems such as, for example, how to measure success. The positivist focus on cause and effect or 'win or lose' dichotomy tends to understate the role of rights and offers an incomplete picture – but the constitutive is not without shortcomings. How, then, can successes be measured; how is it be defined? And what must have transpired for it to fall within the ambit of progressive social changes? These seemingly simple questions belie the complexity at the heart of the matter because of the problematic in measuring efficacy or success. What constitutes effectiveness or success differs amongst advocacy groups, and is dependent on the objective(s) of the group seeking changes. Further, and crucially, social movements rarely have things their own way; important issues are continually contested in an environment that can be unpredictable and hostile, particularly where the status quo or long-held beliefs are challenged. Those issues, and the environment in which they are contested, do not remain static; they continually change and evolve.

The experiences of both American and Canadian activists offer valuable lessons for those seeking to harness rights in the UK. While Rosenberg's conclusion, that activists should devote limited resources to other channels to advance social issues, is well taken, it does not necessarily follow that those other options, such as the political process, would be more effective or receptive to the interests of disadvantaged groups. Rights are important and they are global and everywhere.[100]

---

[99]   Hunt, *Explorations in Law and Society: Towards a Constitutive Theory of Law* (1993)

[100]   See: Hammond (1999) 'Law and Disorder: The Brazilian Landless Farmworkers' Movement'; Milner and Goldberg-Hiller (2002) 'Reimagining Rights'; Feldman, *The Ritual of Rights in Japan: Law, Society, and Health Policy* (2000)

And, as demonstrated by the case studies in the preceding pages, rights do not always require the courts, or other official forums, to bring them to 'life'. In the hands of activists, working at the ground level, rights have the potential to change the paradigm of engagement in positive and powerful ways. While the possibilities are not limitless rights do have potency and provide activists with the means to affect or bring about change. As McCann argued, rights, in defiant hands, can be a source of power. However, as demonstrated by McMahon and Paris in their study of school funding in New Jersey, it is no easy matter particularly when faced by powerful opposing forces which can also counter with the currency of rights. Such was also the case in the prison-reform study by Feeley and Rubin. In this instance, however a determined judiciary recognized the cruelties of America's prisons and effectively reined in the excesses.

What lessons can be drawn from the preceding case studies for future research? First and foremost, success is relative; social change is incremental and engagement with rights is a long process, taking decades for measurable variables to become apparent. Further, rights cannot be taken for granted because what may have worked in one situation may not in another. It also requires a determined judiciary and a social issue that cries out for reform.[101] The case studies by McCann, Epp, and Coglianese make clear that possibly the most important element is sustained engagement with rights by determined activists committed to their vision of social justice. In almost all the case studies there is an apparent common ground in the debate regarding the usefulness and efficacy of using law to advance social causes? And it is this: it is not in the direct effects that one will find or realise the potential and power that rights presents for social progress, but in its many and varied indirect possibilities such as: using law as leverage, for example, threats of lawsuits. What is also apparent, from the diverse range of case studies examined, is that rights are not a panacea for addressing the myriad of social justice issues confronting society.

---

[101]   Feeley and Rubin, *Judicial Policy Making and the Modern State: How the Courts Reformed America's Prisons* (1998)

3   ASYLUM IN THE WIDER CONTEXT

3.1   Introduction

At its most fundamental level asylum matters because often it is potentially a matter of life and death. But it is a concept under sustained attack by governments across the West unwilling and/or unable to deal with the influx of tens of thousands of migrants. What has happened to the concept and principle of providing sanctuary to humans feeling persecution, wars, and other misfortune? In order to understand asylum and the challenges faced by NGOs, which work with and advocate on behalf of asylum-seekers, it is important to first examine asylum in the wider context. This chapter presents an overview of the international law on refugees, considers asylum in the global context, and examines how the UK has attempted to deal with the phenomena. The chapter also examines why it is that asylum and asylum-seekers excite so much controversy and how it has become a major public policy issue. And what is it that compels asylum-seekers to continue to seek to enter the UK and Europe notwithstanding formidable barriers, both legal and physical, designed to stop them?[1]

3.2   A Global View

It is not for the weak of heart. Even on a day punctuated by tranquillity the waters of the North Atlantic can be unforgiving, coursing up this narrow strip of rock and sand to smash against the seawall, spraying the air with the stench of untreated sewage. I am standing on the Malecón, along Havana's decrepit shoreline, looking towards the distant horizon, towards the shores of the land of dreams – America, the state of Florida – just over 170 kilometres away across shark-infested waters, and unattainable. But for so many in this impoverished island nation those shores represent freedom, endless opportunities, and riches beyond imagination. And, so

---

[1]   GS Goodwin-Gill and J McAdam, *The Refugee in International Law* (3rd edn) (2007); AC Helton, *The Price of Indifference: Refugees and Humanitarian Action in the New Century* (2002); G Loescher A Betts and J Milner, *The United Nations High Commissioner for Refugees (UNHCR): The Politics and Practice of Refugee Protection into the Twenty-first Century* (2008); C Dauvergne (2004) 'Sovereignty, Migration and the Rule of Law in Global Times' 67 Modern Law Review 4 588

in the dark of night following in the footsteps of tens of thousands who preceded them, Cubans risk it all to make that perilous crossing, often in rickety home-made crafts. Some make it and some don't, but still they come.

In detention centres on the West coast of Canada, Chinese boatpeople, so-called because of their mode of travel, bang their heads against metal-bars out of frustration and fear.[2] Unable to speak the language or understand their predicament, many just sit or pace their cells. They see a 'Canada' badge on my shirt and plead for release, many confused by their reception in a nation seen as tolerant and welcoming.[3] Even weeks after the dispersal of its cargo, the stench of humans packed like sardines, of vomit and urine, hangs heavy as I walk inside the hulking rust-buckets on which they travelled and wonder again at how terrible and frightening the journey must have been. But I also wonder how terrible were the lives they left behind? Many had sold their worldly possessions, used their life-savings, borrowed monies, and/ or indebted themselves or families to a lifetime of bondage to travel to Canada. The rusting vessels, barely sea-worthy, sailed across the vast Pacific and dumped its load of passengers along the remote and rugged coastline of British Columbia, forcing them to swim the ice-cold waters to the shore. Unknown numbers were swept out to sea but hundreds made it to land, turning up bedraggled in remote little towns where bemused locals initially welcomed them. But as more and more 'boatpeople' turned up that welcome turned to anger as people gathered and angrily demanded the migrants – cheats, illegals, and queue-jumpers as they were called – be sent back. Some of those calling for 'them' to be sent back were members of the Chinese-Canadian community, some of whom had once entered Canada as refugees.[4] There were even calls for the Constitution to be amended when blame fell on the *Canadian Charter of Rights and Freedoms* for restricting the ability of the state to deport the migrants without due process.

---

[2]   In 1999 four boats, carrying about 600 Chinese migrants, were seized by the Canadian navy; however, many have speculated that there were other boats, which were undetected by the under-resourced navy.

[3]   In interviews with several immigration adjudicators (independent immigration judges) many reported pressure – indirect and direct – to detain the arrivals notwithstanding tenuous legal basis for continuing the detention. Similar reports have also emerged in the UK where tribunal members, responding to other pressures, have taken to disparaging eminently qualified expert witnesses, in order to justify negative decisions. See: A Hirsch, 'Asylum tribunal apologises for questioning academic's evidence' *Guardian* (27 Oct 2008)

[4]   A Tizon, 'Waves of boat people divide Chinese-Canadians in B.C.' *Seattle Times* (19 Sep 1999)

The world over, the scene is repeated countless times, the human face of suffering often lost in the compilation of statistics and fatigue-inducing litany of misery: of migrant ships circling various first-world ports and denied permission to dock by governments, often with overwhelming support from the public convinced they are being 'swamped' by 'queue-jumpers';[5] armed vigilantes, with night-vision scopes, patrol the US/Mexico border against the 'menace of tens of millions of invading illegal aliens';[6] boatloads of Haitian refugees intercepted at sea by the US Navy and forcibly returned to their imploding homeland, an action deemed legal yet paradoxically condemned by the US Supreme Court seemingly unable to comprehend 'why any nation would gather fleeing refugees and return them to one country they had desperately sought to escape';[7] border officials in Thailand stand accused of binding the hands of migrants seeking port and setting them adrift in the open sea.[8] Tens of thousands, if not millions, risk their lives in attempts to reach the borders of the rich nations, the industrialised powers of Western Europe, Australia, and North America. And, en route, thousands die: suffocating in the backs of lorries, electrocuted on border fences, thrown overboard from ships, duped and exploited by traffickers, raped, beaten and/or killed. So common is the sight of dead asylum-seekers that tourists on a Spanish beach were photographed ignoring drowned victims as they continued playing ball-games and sunbathing.[9] In a period of three months (November 2005 to February 2006) at least 1,200 African migrants from just one transit point drowned in their attempts to reach Europe.[10] But still they come, responding to a basic human instinct to better their lives, to flee a terrible existence whether it is political turmoil, environmental degradation, wars, and/or economic hardship.[11] Most often it is a complex interplay of factors because rarely does misfortune have a singular cause or effect: political turmoil begets economic hardship, wars beget oppression, and so it continues in an almost

---

[5]   United Nations High Commission for Refugees, 'UNHCR criticises Australia for turning boat people away' *UNHCR News Stories* (2003)

[6]   L Smith-Spark, ''Vigilantes' set for Mexico border patrol' (2005) March 28 BBC News

[7]   UNHCR (2003) 'The Wall Behind Which Refugees Can Shelter' Refugees Magazine 123

[8]   I MacKinnon, 'Thailand accused of setting migrants adrift at sea' *Guardian* (19 Jan 2009)

[9]   KE Tunstall, *Displacement, Asylum, Migration: the Oxford Amnesty Lectures 2004* (Oxford University Press, Oxford 2006); Information Centre about Asylum and Refugees, 'Dead migrant photo: truth worse than fiction?' (2006) Nov 9 <www.icar.org.uk/?lid=7773>

[10]   BBC, 'Dozens drown off Mauritania coast ' (2006) March 6 BBC <http://news.bbc.co.uk/1/hi/world/africa/4780734.stm>

[11]   S Kirchner (2007) 'Hell on Earth - Systematic Rape in Eastern Congo' Journal of Humanitarian Assistance

never-ending cycle. Richard Holbrooke, former US representative to the United Nations, is succinct:

> Refugees matter because they are there. How can the world turn away from people made homeless by political evil? Apart from the dead, they are the most obvious victims of political disasters, which the world simply cannot ignore.[12]

3.3   International Protection of Refugees

In addition to domestic laws of host countries, there are several international conventions which refugees can turn for protection, but unless those conventions have been incorporated into domestic legislation, the protection offered can be patchy, inaccessible or non-existent. The *International Covenant on Civil and Political Rights,* for example, has proven itself unable to provide effective protection in signatory countries, whether First World or Third World; similarly, the *Convention Against Torture* and a myriad of other such instruments have been found wanting and ineffective in time of need.[13] The *1951 UN Convention relating to the Status of Refugees* and the *1967 Protocol Relating to the Status of Refugees* are the primary international instruments dealing with refugees, which a majority of UN member-states have signed; also on the list of signatories, however, are many nations with poor human rights records and major refugee-producing nations.[14] Many industrialised nations, including the UK and Canada, have given force to the 1951 Convention via incorporation in domestic legislation.[15] The companion book to the Convention is a fairly commonsensical approach to the application of the Convention. It outlines parameters for treatment and assessment of claims but leaves to individual states to decide on procedures pertaining to reception (including matters pertaining to welfare

---

[12]   cited in AC Helton *The Price of Indifference* (2002) 1
[13]   CA MacKinnon, 'Crimes of War, Crimes of Peace' in S Shute and SL Hurley (eds) *On Human Rights: the Oxford Amnesty lectures 1993* (1993); SSontag, 'Regarding the Torture of Others' *New York Times* (2004)
[14]   A Edwards (2005) 'Human Rights, Refugees, and The Right 'To Enjoy' Asylum ' 17 International Journal of Refugee Law 2 293-330
[15]   The *Asylum and Immigration Appeals Act 1993* incorporated the Convention into UK domestic law. The UN Convention, in part, defines 'refugee' as any person who owing to well-founded fear of being persecuted for reasons of race, religion, nationality, membership of a particular social group or political opinion, is outside the country of his nationality and is unable, or owing to such fear, is unwilling to avail himself of the protection of that country.

and employment) and determination.[16] The result, however, has been a patchwork and inconsistent approach across various jurisdictions, creating an impression, not without justification, that the granting of refugee status sometimes has more to do with politics then the merits of a particular claim.[17]

Notwithstanding the Convention guidelines its application varies widely across jurisdictions. This has created additional problems for both the host country and those seeking refuge as some states come to be seen as (and are) more restrictive and some more generous. Some, for example, have refused to recognize persecution arising from non-state actors (such as militias or rebel forces) or 'non-traditional' grounds of persecution, such as sexual orientation or gender-based persecution. This has resulted in widely-varying rates of successful applications of similarly situated asylum-seekers, the by-product of which has been 'asylum-shopping' where claimants seek out jurisdictions which are considered to have a more favourable approach to their individual circumstances.[18] An example illustrates: Sri Lanka, strife-torn for the past two decades, has produced thousands of refugees;[19] between 1989 and 1998 Canada accepted 80% of Sri Lankan refugee claimants, France 74%, and the UK 1%.[20] When measured against what is at stake, quite literally a matter of life and death, then 'shopping' must be seen as a pragmatic choice amongst severely limited options. Instead this further opens 'asylum-shoppers' to criticism and accusations that their claim lacks merit without any consideration given to why such individuals 'shop'. This is not to deny the existence of fraud and misrepresentation but to point out other factors which compel would-be refugees to play the roulette wheel of present-day asylum determination. An asylum-seeker with the stigma of a rejected claim in one jurisdiction generally faces greater hurdles (i.e. overcoming an existing negative decision rather than just the evidentiary requirements to do with the substance of his/her claim) in trying to persuade another jurisdiction to grant protection.[21]

---

[16]   UNHCR Handbook on Procedures and Criteria for Determining Refugee Status under the 1951 Convention and the 1967 Protocol relating to the Status of Refugees

[17]   G Clayton, *Textbook on Immigration and Asylum Law* (1st edn) (2004) 349

[18]   Tunstall, *Displacement, Asylum, Migration: the Oxford Amnesty Lectures 2004*; JC Hathaway, *The Law of Refugee Status* (1991)

[19]   Human Rights Watch, *Sri Lanka: Human Rights and the Peace Process* (2002)

[20]   Clayton, *Textbook on Immigration and Asylum Law* (2004)

[21]   In Canada, for example, asylum-seekers are routinely challenged to explain why a refusal in Europe or elsewhere should not also result in a refusal in Canada; often claimants will not admit to having made claims elsewhere (which further impugns their credibility if investigations reveal that other claims were made) (personal observations during a ten-year career with the Immigration Directorate in Canada).

Since its inception, millions of people have turned to the 1951 UN Convention for help, and millions have been helped. But the Convention continues to come under repeated attacks, notably by some signatory states, the UK in particular, for being too broad with idealistic notions of citizenship and protection, unachievable for its own citizens.[22] The UK has been at the forefront in seeking changes to the Convention; Tony Blair, former Prime Minister and fierce critic, has said that it is time 'to stand back and consider its application in today's world'.[23] Many NGOs, on the other hand, have urged an expansion of the Convention so that the realities of present-day refugee movement are recognized.[24] The Convention, drafted in 1951, was never meant to be permanent and was designed to deal with European refugees created by World War II.[25] It was assumed by the drafters and the signatories that the need for the Convention would cease once all the refugees had been settled.[26] The drafters made a conscious effort to avoid issuing a 'blank cheque' for the future refugees of the world.[27] And, most certainly, it was never envisioned that the world would see such massive movements of refugees or that Third-world refugees would one day claim the protections offered by the Convention; or that NGOs would contest and persist in pushing its boundaries to include previously excluded groups (with equally compelling grounds of persecution), such as homosexuals, or to recognize the unique challenges faced by female and child refugees; of forced abortions, sexual violence, and conscription.[28]

Herein is one of the major problems: An instrument which was never meant to deal with such massive movements of people remains today the only one that does. And it has proven to be hopelessly outdated and inadequate in the face of present-day conflicts. In many ways, however, it is not so much the adequacy of the Convention as it is the unwillingness of receiving countries to accept asylum-seekers, most of whom are ethnically (and visibly) different from the host population. In many instances other, often unspoken, issues of 'outsiders', race,

---

[22]   G Hinsliff, 'Blair savages critics over threat to civil liberties' *The Observer* (23 Apr 2006)

[23]   UNHCR (2003) 'The Wall Behind Which Refugees Can Shelter' 2

[24]   Asylum Rights Campaign, *Providing Protection in the 21st Century* (2004)

[25]   The 1967 Protocol removed the temporal and geographical limitations of the 1951 Convention but did not address substantive issues, leaving the definition of refugee unchanged as drafted in 1951.

[26]   The 1967 Protocol removed the time and geographical constraints of the 1951 Convention

[27]   UNHCR (2003) 'The Wall Behind Which Refugees Can Shelter' 2

[28]   GS Goodwin-Gill, *The Refugee in International Law* (2nd edn) (1996)

and racism serves to add further layers of complexity.[29] There is also the matter of an inability on part of the international community to intervene in (developing) humanitarian crisis. No matter the cause or reason, these various factors can combine to produce deadly consequences: for example a majority of present-day refugees, created by imploding states (Democratic Republic of Congo, Sudan) or failed states (Somalia), do not easily fall within the current definition because many remain trapped within the borders of their nations and are 'not outside the country of nationality' as required by the 1951 UN Convention or have not been singled out for persecution (some states do not recognise persecution which is widespread and indiscriminate calling it 'generalised treatment', no matter the degree or level of atrocities and violence).[30] In effect, a legal formality not only absolves an international community all too willing to be so absolved, but confines masses of humanity to a hellish existence – trapped and subjected to atrocities and violence outside the reach of the Convention and the global community.[31]

3.4 Asylum in the 21ˢᵗ Century

At the turn of the century there remains no apparent end to the suffering inflicted upon humans by humans. So how has it come to pass that the noble concept of providing a safe haven to those fleeing persecution has slowly been dismantled to the point where most governments of the First World have turned their backs to the suffering and despair of fellow humans? And it has happened with deliberation by a global community seemingly indifferent to the plight of others. This is not a recent or unknown phenomenon. The flight of refugees has almost always excited xenophobic reactions, one of the more egregious examples being the refusal of asylum to Jews fleeing Nazi Germany by many in the West. Notwithstanding lessons of history, refugees and asylum-seekers continue to be met with indifference,

---

[29]   R Sales (2002) 'The deserving and the undeserving? Refugees, asylum seekers and welfare in Britain ' 22 Critical Social Policy 3 456-478; L Smith, 'Britain: Government steps up attacks on asylum seekers' (2004) World Socialist Web Site <http://www.wsws.org/articles/2004/jan2004.bak/asyl-j05.shtml> (16 Oct 2006); Leader, 'Strangers at our gates' *Guardian* (20 April 2006)

[30]   GS Goodwin-Gill, *The Determination of Refugee Status: Problems of Access to Procedures and the Standard of Proof* (1985)

[31]   L Polman and RL Bland, *We Did Nothing* (2004); R Dallaire and B Beardsley, *Shake Hands with the Devil: The Failure of Humanity in Rwanda* (2005)

apathy, and extreme hostility not only in the UK, but in almost every major First-world nation.[32]

Asylum is a complex matter and there are various explanations of the causes of present day upheavals in the world; arguably, however, some of the blame rests on First-world governments for its sometimes relentless pursuit of self-interest at the expense and/or exploitation of poorer regions. And many of the explanations – such as the legacy of colonialism, the ramifications of past and present-day foreign policies, exploitation of resources, and the £500billion arms trade – are beyond the scope of this study.[33] But these issues play a significant role in creating and perpetuating instability For example, during the 2002 flashpoint in Kashmir, with India and Pakistan poised for war, the-then Prime Minister, Tony Blair, while ostensibly pushing for peace was also involved in promoting the sale of British fighter jets to India.[34] The central issue, however, insofar as asylum is concerned is not so much where the blame lies but rather what is the world to do about the seemingly innumerable humanitarian crises facing it today? And, assuming that the global community is able and/or willing, how is it to deal with the complex and logistically challenging situations such as found in the continuing crisis in the Darfur region of Sudan, the Democratic Republic of Congo, or the lawless state of Somalia?[35]

In this era of globalisation there is awareness that many things, even seemingly diverse and unrelated events, are directly or indirectly connected. Events in one part of the world can have ramifications far beyond its borders. Nowhere is this better illustrated than in the present-day movement of refugees because never before in human history has the world seen such a mass movement of peoples from all corners of the globe.[36] And by any measure the numbers are staggering: statistics

---

[32]   Human Rights Watch, *Defending the Human Rights of Migrants and Asylum Seekers in Western Europe* (2006); Loescher Betts and Milner, *The United Nations High Commissioner for Refugees (UNHCR): The Politics and Practice of Refugee Protection into the Twenty-first Century* (2008)

[33]   R Norton-Taylor, 'Arms sales record as firms duck controls with 'flat-pack' weapons' *Guardian* (03 Oct 2006); Campaign Against Arms Trade, 'Fanning the Flames: How UK Arms Sales Fuel Conflict' (2006)

[34]   BBC, 'Blair sold jets at Kashmir talks' (2002) 21 Oct <http://news.bbc.co.uk/2/hi/uk_news/politics/2345127.stm>

[35]   Human Rights Watch *Defending the Human Rights of Migrants and Asylum Seekers in Western Europe* (2006)

[36]   S Castles and MJ Miller, *The Age of Migration: International Population Movements in the Modern World* (4th edn) (2009)

on refugees, those whom the United Nations consider to be refugees or in refugee-like situations, are inexact and subject to variations but according to informed estimates there are approximately 11 to 15 million refugees on the move around the world.[37] This figure does not include the approximately 25 million internally-displaced – those considered to be in refugee-like situations except that they are not 'outside their country of nationality or residence' as defined in the Convention.[38] It is important to note that the movement of refugees is happening at a time of unprecedented movement and migration of humans in general. According to estimates there were approximately 185 million to 192 million people on the move in 2005.[39] Most of the movement is legal migration, an important component of economic activity and human endeavour, but an increasing percentage is unwanted and undesirable. And these are the world's refugees. Notwithstanding the lessons of history, the world community continues to overlook or ignore suffering, the most egregious of recent examples being the genocide in Rwanda and the continuing crisis in the Darfur, a crisis fifty years in the making and anaemically attended to by regional and international organisations.[40]

While the rapid and mass movement of people to advanced economics is a relatively recent phenomenon the movement has been almost entirely a South to North migration; from the poorer countries to the developed and richer. The reasons for migration, where people uproot established lives or lives interrupted, are varied; but generally humans flee natural and human-made disasters, wars, famine, poverty, and the countless other ills in search of a better and/or safer life.[41] However, for the overwhelming majority of the world's refugees, the borders to the West and safety are closed and tightly controlled.[42] The array of control measures and punitive action used by the West against refugees seeking safety has been

---

[37]   U.S. Committee for Refugees and Immigrants, *World Refugee Survey* (2005); (the International Organization for Migration puts the figure at 17 million).

[38]   United Nations High Commissioner for Refugees *Internally-displaced Persons: Questions and Answers* (2007).

[39]   International Organization for Migration, *World Migration: Costs and Benefits of International Migration* (2005)

[40]   BBC, 'How many have died in Darfur?' (2005) 16 Feb BBC <http://news.bbc.co.uk/1/hi/world/africa/4268733.stm> ; Dallaire and Beardsley, *Shake Hands with the Devil: The Failure of Humanity in Rwanda* (2005); Human Rights Watch *Targeting the Fur: Mass Killings in Darfur* (2005)

[41]   J Huysmans, *The Politics of Insecurity: Fear, Migration, and Asylum in the EU* (2006)

[42]   Human Rights Watch, *Commentary on the United Kingdom Home Office White Paper: Secure Borders, Safe Haven: Integration with Diversity in Modern Europe* (2002)

dubbed 'Fortress Europe' by Amnesty International.[43] Those who are able to leave their country (and hence are no longer internally-displaced) often remain caught in a no-man's land of refugee camps or virtual non-existence – undocumented, unwanted, and unwelcome. A vast majority of the world's refugees remain trapped in situations of violence or turmoil, unable to escape and end up leading lives of oppression, poverty, and desperation. For the millions of internally-displaced the situation is even more perilous because they fall into a legal limbo where they are considered to be in refugee-like situations but are not legally refugees (because they remain trapped within the borders of their country of nationality). Some critics have argued that the clause, a meaningless dichotomy because the situation is no less dire, serves to provide a convenient escape clause for a generally reluctant world community unwilling and sometimes unable to intervene.[44] Of those who do manage to leave their country (often it is to the nearest bordering state) most find refuge in some of the world's poorest nations, which are the least able to host them. Iran and Pakistan, for example, host twice as many refugees as does all of Western Europe.[45] It is estimated that about 7.8 million refugees remain confined in camps or situations where they are deprived of basic human rights for periods lasting five years or more.[46] And the suffering can be extreme. In one camp, recounted by eye-witnesses, thousands of refugees (including the dying) were forced to stand cheek-by-jowl, sleeping, urinating and defecating where they stood, unable to move and surrounded by guards all too ready to shoot stragglers.[47]

3.4.1   The West and Asylum

The increasing number of refugees, particularly the movement of refugees to the West, has made asylum a contentious and a major political and public policy issue. And most in the West have responded by shutting the gates. What this has created is a huge and unmanageable influx of peoples trying to enter states unable and/or unwilling to accommodate them.[48] In the poorer regions of the world such

---

[43]   Amnesty International, *Ten years of EUROMED: Time to end the human rights deficit* (2005)

[44]   Edwards (2005) 'Human Rights, Refugees, and The Right 'To Enjoy' Asylum '; R Verkaik, 'Asylum-seekers put at risk by law, warns top judge' *The Independent* (02 Jul 2008)

[45]   UNHCR (2003) 'The Wall Behind Which Refugees Can Shelter'

[46]   US Committee for Refugees and Immigrants *World Refugee Survey* (2005) p 20

[47]   Polman and Bland, *We Did Nothing*

[48]   See Chapter 4 for a fuller discussion

mass movements have the effect of destabilising already weak or impoverished states, some of which are barely able to look after its own population. The route onwards, to the West, is generally an arduous and dangerous journey involving people traffickers, fraudulent documents, and clandestine border crossings. In the West, this has created a bottleneck of refugees seeking to enter tightly-controlled borders only to be denied by concrete walls, razor-wired fences, armed border guards, and an array of other control measures such as visa requirements or off-shore immigration control.[49] For those who succeed in entering, a reception policy based not on humanitarian grounds or international obligations but deliberated on deterrence awaits them: a repressive and punitive regime of detention, below-subsistence levels of support, consigned to an invisible existence and forced repatriation in violation of international law. This is the cornerstone of UK asylum policy, a system in continual flux, in search of better and more efficient methods of shutting the gates.[50] A major drawback of deterrence-based policies, notwithstanding its attractiveness in domestic politics, is that it does little to address the root causes of why people flee. No matter how repressive or punitive a regime of reception it is almost always better than what is left behind whether it is persecution or impoverishment. The former head of the UNHCR, Ruud Lubbers, is succinct: 'no wall will be high enough to prevent people from coming'.[51]

According to the UN voluntary repatriation is the preferred solution for dealing with the majority of refugees while re-settlement in a third-country, for many reasons, remains the least desirable and an option of last resort.[52] But a problem which requires an international response is instead left to the domestic policies of unwelcoming host countries unwilling to compromise on self-interest or unable to agree on a common approach.[53] In 2000, for example, the world's richest nations contributed less than US$1 billion to fund the UNHCR's protection-related work, while spending approximately $10 billion on domestic asylum procedures.[54] The gap between the rhetoric and promises and practice of working to address the problem is rarely matched in practical terms; the UNHCR is highly critical:

---

[49]   United Nations High Commissioner for Refugees, *The State of the World's Refugees* (2006)

[50]   BBC, 'Asylum: Getting tough in 2003 ' (2003) BBC News <http://news.bbc.co.uk/1/hi/uk/3333865.stm> ; Huysmans, *The Politics of Insecurity: Fear, Migration, and Asylum in the EU*

[51]   UNHCR (2003) 'The Wall Behind Which Refugees Can Shelter' 7

[52]   See: www.unhcr.org.uk

[53]   Human Rights Watch, *Human Rights Overview: European Union* (2004)

[54]   UNHCR (2003) 'The Wall Behind Which Refugees Can Shelter' 23

> Many prosperous countries complain about large number of
> asylum-seekers, but offer too little to prevent refugee crises . . .
> it is a real problem that Europeans try to lessen obligations to
> refugees.[55]

While this apparent contradiction may be a result of various competing priorities
and/or political expediency, it remains difficult to achieve consensus in the EU,
particularly when it is only a few member-states that host a majority of asylum-
seekers leaving others not as affected wanting no part of the crisis.[56] This is
particularly true of Western countries which serve as transit points; there are
persistent reports of border officials encouraging asylum-seekers to continue their
journey onwards lest they make a claim where they are first detected.[57]

3.4.2   Race and Racism

In seeking to understand Western opposition to asylum it is instructive to look
beyond the salient issues (i.e. statistics of arrivals, the ability to cope with
or absorb asylum-seekers, and costs) to issues of race and racism made all the
more conspicuous by its relative absence in public discourse, unspoken and
unacknowledged by most policy-makers or politicians. The sensitivity of the issue
appears to preclude reasoned debate with discussion sometimes degenerating into
accusations of racism. But, whether admitted or unspoken, racism is a major factor;
and, often it is there beneath the surface and underpins not only immigration but
asylum policy.[58] While the questions of race and racism are not the primary focus
of this research they should not be seen as less important. The undercurrent of
racism are diffused throughout UK society and provides an important framework

---

[55]   ibid 7 (citing Ruud Lubbers)

[56]   Human Rights Watch *Defending the Human Rights of Migrants and Asylum Seekers in
Western Europe* (2006); Amnesty International *Ten years of EUROMED: Time to end the
human rights deficit* (2005)

[57]   In my ten-year career with the immigration service in Canada it was not uncommon to
encounter asylum-seekers who had been 'helped' by US officials to enter Canada; similarly,
it was not unknown for Canadian immigration officials to turn a blind-eye to transiting
asylum-seekers bound for the US.

[58]   Oxfam, *Asylum: The Truth Behind the Headlines* (2001); P Waugh, 'Think-Tank Distorts
Asylum Facts, says Former Minister' *The Independent* (19 Nov 2003) 9; R Verkaik, 'Race-
hate crimes reach record levels - and experts say asylum policy may be to blame' *The
Independent* (07 April 2004) 12; L Pirouet, *Whatever Happened to Asylum in Britain* (2001)

to understanding the background and general morass within which asylum and immigration policy is engulfed.[59] The European Commission against Racism and Intolerance (ECRI) has been highly critical of UK policies on asylum (and minorities), saying that much needs to be done to tone down the climate of hostility.[60] It is evident that a vast majority of asylum-seekers are ethnically and culturally of backgrounds which are different from and seen as inferior by the host country. For many nations in the West, which have historically curtailed non-white immigration, asylum is the wrench in the spoke of immigration policy.[61] Race, for example, long a factor in UK immigration policy and controlled by various means is played out almost without such controls in the asylum process. In other words, asylum compromises the ability of receiving nations to control and manage migration; specifically, non-white migration.

3.4.3 Conclusion

In addition to a scholarly interest in asylum, my previous career, spanning over ten years at a senior-level, was with the immigration service in Canada (including a position as advisor to the Immigration and Refugee Board of Canada, a tribunal responsible for adjudicating claims for refugee status). The experience of investigating and interviewing (including conducting cross-examinations before administrative tribunals) hundreds of asylum-seekers attunes one to seeing the invisible and the outsider. And they are almost everywhere and visible to the discerning eye: cleaning toilets, sweeping streets, and serving your morning coffee.[62] It is on behalf of this ill-treated and ill-regarded constituency that NGOs in the asylum-sector have continually challenged laws and government policies. But, in many ways, it is a losing fight.[63]

---

59   R Norton-Taylor, *The Colour of Justice* (1999); A Travis, 'Asylum centres plagued by racism and abuse, says report ' *Guardian* (22 July 2005)

60   Council of Europe: European Commission Against Racism and Intolerance (ECRI), *Third Report on the United Kingdom* (2005)

61   J Hampshire, *Citizenship and Belonging: Immigration and the Politics of Demographic Governance in post-war Britain* (2005); C Joppke, *Immigration and the Nation-State* (1999)

62   D Casciani, 'Secret Life of the Office Cleaner ' (2005) 19 Sep BBC

63   See Chapters 1 and 9 for a fuller discussion; M Lipman, 'In the hysteria over illegal asylum seekers, refugees like my Nepalese friend Tham are being let down by the system' *Guardian* (London 24 March, 2006)

3.5   Asylum in the UK

Asylum in the UK is mired in controversy and has often been conflated, sometimes deliberately, with a range of major public policy issues further complicating an already complex matter. Issues such as immigration, race, the changing face of Britain, terrorism, crime, Islamphobia, and abuse of benefits have at one time or another been linked or continue to be linked with asylum.[64] Its link with immigration is inescapable even though each represents a distinct route/source of entry, the first grudgingly wanted, particularly in areas of labour shortage, and the latter, resolutely unwanted.[65] The terms asylum and immigration are often used synonymously in public discourse, with both acquiring a pejorative tone, though 'asylum' has become imbued with particular venom.[66] The terms have also been legally combined in various Acts of Parliament representing the government's continuing battle against asylum; the recent introduction of the *Borders, Immigration and Citizenship Bill* in December 2008 marks the seventh legislative overhaul since 1993. In other words, there have been major legislative changes in asylum law averaging every two years. These recent legislative efforts should not be seen in isolation but as logical extensions consistent with the history of immigration and asylum policies in the UK, which has been primarily about restricting migration; more precisely, it has been about stopping non-white migration, 'the unwashed masses, scroungers, disease carriers' attracted to the UK for its supposedly generous welfare system.[67]

One of the key factors that make asylum a major policy issue is that it takes away from the receiving state its ability to manage the orderly flow of migration. The regularised route to migration has generally been via a lengthy and complicated process whereby would-be migrants are vetted for such things as level of education, skills, language, and ability to settle in the UK. These factors are, in turn, measured against what is best for the needs of the receiving country (such as labour market

---

[64]   Ipsos MORI *British Views On Immigration* (2003); R Winnett and D Leppard, 'Shires buckle under migrant tension' *Sunday Times* (29 Aug 2004); A Kundnani, 'Britain gripped by populist campaigns against immigrants' (2003) Institute of Race Relations <http://www.irr.org.uk/2003/january/ak000017.html> (May 27); Verkaik, 'Race-hate crimes reach record levels - and experts say asylum policy may be to blame'

[65]   Joppke, *Immigration and the Nation-State* (2004); Clayton, *Textbook on Immigration and Asylum Law* (2004) 1-16

[66]   Article 19, *What's the Story: Results from Research into Media Coverage of Refugees and Asylum-Seekers in the UK* (2003); Oxfam, *Asylum: The Truth Behind the Headlines* (2001)

[67]   S Chakrabarti (2005) 'Rights and Rhetoric: The Politics of Asylum and Human Rights Culture in the UK' 32 Journal of Law and Society 131

requirements); built into the process are allowances for other types of migrants, for instance, recent immigrants are allowed to bring immediate family members or to fulfil international obligations, such as resettlement of UN mandated refugees (usually from camps where third-country resettlement is the only viable option). Historically, immigration to the UK (and many other immigrant-settled/colonised countries such as Australia, New Zealand, and Canada, member-states of the Commonwealth) was explicitly whites-only. When such blatantly racist policies became unpalatable other means were instituted which allowed receiving states to continue as before, albeit with minor concessions.[68] Non-white immigration to the UK (particularly from the Commonwealth), starting in earnest in the 1950s, came about as a result of a hard-fought campaigns and the growing need for primarily low-skill labour. Within this framework control of migration followed a more or less orderly flow, with severe restrictions on who could enter the UK; and it was generally on a temporary basis with the expectation that the migrant would return to his/her home country.[69] The key to all this, however, was that immigration policy was generally governed by the discretionary exercise of almost unfettered powers by government officials with virtually no judicial oversight. And even then the judiciary generally deferred to government policy.[70] With asylum, however, the state has almost no control over who accesses the asylum-determination system. Any person entering the UK can make an asylum-claim. However, those making claims are generally not those whom the UK wants and, most probably, almost none would qualify to enter via the regular immigration processes. This raises certain questions: to whom do we offer protection from persecution or accord compassion? Is it to those who are ethnically or culturally similar? Is it to those whom we like? Is it to those who will bring benefits or contribute to society? While such questions can be addressed or controlled by immigration policy, it is not possible to do so when it comes to asylum.[71]

While the state had been effective in curtailing non-white migration a new route of migration opened up in the late 1980s, early 1990s and continuing today, with the

---

68   C Joppke, *Immigration and the Nation-State* (1999); L Pirouet, *Whatever Happened to Asylum in Britain?* (2001)

69   BBC, 'Short History of Immigration' (2002) <news.bbc.co.uk/hi/english/static/in_depth/uk/2002/race/short_history_of_immigration.stm> accessed 10 Dec 2009; also: Hampshire, *Citizenship and Belonging: Immigration and the Politics of Demographic Governance in post-war Britain*

70   Pirouet, *Whatever Happened to Asylum in Britain* (2001); Joppke, *Immigration and the Nation-State* (2004)

71   Joint Committee On Human Rights, *The Treatment of Asylum-Seekers* (HL 81-1 2007)

advent of 'mass asylum-seeking' heralded in by Tamil refugees fleeing Sri Lanka, a then strife-torn homeland.[72] From an annual average of about 5,000 asylum-seekers in the early 1980s to an almost tenfold increase in the 90s (44,840 in 1991) to almost 90,000 in 2002; stricter border controls and off-shore interdiction methods reduced the number of arrivals to just under 30,000 in 2005 and 24,000 in 2007.[73] While these numbers are relatively small (compared to, for example, the millions of refugees worldwide or refugees hosted by other nations such as Pakistan; or in relation to the population of the UK) the increase in numbers, from 5,000 to 92,000 served to create a 'siege mentality' and of a crisis in asylum; such statistics, without context, provides fodder for the tabloid media which have been relentless in its attack on asylum and asylum policies.[74] Asylum has climbed to rank among the top of list of issues which most concern the British public; a public, along with its ruling elite, historically and demonstrably uncomfortable with and hostile to immigration, most particularly, non-white migration.[75] In surveys, conducted by various polling organisations, immigration and asylum consistently place in the top three lists of issues of concern to the public.[76]And consistently the polls indicate a public overwhelmingly in favour of a more punitive and restrictive approach to asylum and immigration respectively: 77% of respondents agree that all asylum-seekers should be detained upon arrival; 78% feel that government policies are not working; 80% say the government is not tough enough. Such is the opposition to asylum that 49% believe even genuine asylum-seekers (who arrive illegally) should not be allowed into the UK. Even arguments which purport to demonstrate the positive impact of immigration (and asylum) finds few takers as a large majority remain convinced that the UK is too crowded (75%) and does not need more immigration.[77]

In short asylum has been, since the early 1990s, and continues to be a key policy challenge for all major political parties, a crucial issue for think-tanks, and

---

[72] Clayton, *Textbook on Immigration and Asylum Law* (2004)

[73] BBC, 'Asylum applications continue fall ' (2006) 28 Feb <http://news.bbc.co.uk/1/hi/uk/4758144.stm>

[74] Economic and Social Research Council *Negative Press Gives Asylum-seekers a Bad Name* (2006)

[75] A Stanley (2004) 'A knee-jerk immigration policy' 154 New Law Journal 7127 673

[76] See various surveys conducted by YouGov and MORI Social Research Institute between 2004 and 2006 at: www.YouGov.com and www.mori.com

[77] YOUGOV/Mail on Sunday, *Survey* (2004); A Green, 'Opinion: This influx 'must stop' ' (2005) 07 Sep BBC <http://news.bbc.co.uk/1/hi/uk/4222362.stm>

fodder for the tabloid media. When measured against other polls which indicate a large majority of Britons want less immigration or want it stopped altogether it becomes apparent that the UK is an anti-immigrant and anti-asylum nation. Moreover, Britons are more than willing to support stricter measures to control it irrespective of human rights or civil liberties issues.[78] This is evidenced by the increasingly repressive and harsh policies implemented by a government attuned to the public and electoral mood. The passage of illiberal laws is further facilitated by negative imagery and stereotyping; media attacks on asylum, for example during the campaign against Section 55, were of such a virulent nature that they earned the UK international condemnation.[79]

The mass arrivals of asylum-seekers are seen as affecting the quality of life for citizens of the host country in the form of increased taxes, increased crime rates, and a host of other ills. There is little evidence to support such linkages but that does not often restrain the tabloid media, for example, of making precisely such linkages and creating a siege mentality.[80] Many observers blame governments for contributing to the morass and doing little to combat it.[81]

Another factor which adds to the complexity of the issue is that among the arrivals there are undoubtedly many who do not fit the UN Convention criteria but may have equally compelling reasons for migration. And they come from all corners of the globe, many from oppressive regimes with genuine fears of persecution; but also many without such fears who see the asylum system as a means out of an impoverished existence. The most visible face of asylum (and immigration), notwithstanding the arrivals of refugees from the Balkans during the NATO-led war in the former Yugoslavia, has been predominantly non-white. Herein is the nub: from this mass of humanity, how does one differentiate the persecuted from

---

78   Green (2005) 'Opinion: This influx 'must stop' ' cited by BBC News
79   UNHCR, 'UN Refugee agency has grave concerns over tabloid reporting of asylum'
      (2003) <http://www.unhcr.org.uk/press/press_releases2003/pr23Oct03.htm> ; R Dunston,
      'Blunkett's uncivilised act' *New Statesman* (11 Aug 2003); Council of Europe, *Report by
      the Commissioner of Human Rights on his visit to the United Kingdom 2004* (2005); M
      Townsend and G Hinsliff, 'Truth about Calais 'immigrant menace'' *The Observer* (17 Apr
      2005); UNCHR (2003) 'The Wall Behind Which Refugees Can Shelter' Refugees Magazine
      123; BBC, 'Media linked to asylum violence ' (2004) BBC News <http://news.bbc.co.uk/1/
      hi/uk/3890963.stm> (09 October 2006)
80   Institute for Public Policy Research, *Seeking Scapegoats: The Coverage of Asylum in the UK
      Press* (2005)
81   C Marsden, 'Britain: Labour government steps up persecution of asylum seekers' (2001)
      World Socialist Web Site <http://www.wsws.org/articles/2001/apr2001/asyl-a28.shtml> (20
      Oct 2006); Smith, 'Britain: Government steps up attacks on asylum seekers'

the impoverished; the deserving from the fraudulent? And is impoverishment not a human rights issue? What if that impoverishment is a result of some persecutory action? It is worth noting that an asylum-seeker may not even know that s/he is being persecuted – international law posits no such requirement.[82] Oftentimes there is no evidence except that of oral statements by the asylum-seeker, a notion that does not fit well with western concepts of evidence. Further exacerbating the situation is the persistence of broad-brush assumptions, of asylum-seekers as 'playing the system' and taking advantage of a 'soft-touch' Britain.

3.5.1   Conclusion

In general the UK approach to asylum is most characterised by what is politically expedient at the expense of what is just and humanitarian; of reducing the complex to the simple. It also has been and continues to be in contravention of its international obligations (i.e. prosecution of asylum-seekers for being without documents, detention, including detention of children).[83] It is in this the arena that the fight between NGOs and the government takes place. The fight is a contest between highly polarised positions, the most notable being the entrenched positions of the Labour government (including previous Conservative governments), which views most asylum-seekers as economic migrants, and the various NGOs which work with asylum-seeker and view them as needing protection from persecution.

3.6   Asylum in the UK: Getting Tougher

Several attempts have been made to redefine or change the Convention with many receiving states, the UK among the most prominent, wanting to further limit its ambit, but, so far, with mixed success. But the government has been persistent and having failed in the international arena has turned to the domestic arena to achieve what it could not elsewhere.[84] The result has been a plethora of legislation which has effectively

---

[82]   GS Goodwin-Gill, *The Refugee in International Law* (2nd edn) (1996)

[83]   BBC, 'Jailing asylum seekers 'must end'' (2004) BBC News <http://news.bbc.co.uk/1/hi/uk/3564968.stm> (10 June 2006); E Allison, 'Asylum seekers still held in jail' *Guardian* (01 Sep 2004); A Travis, 'Asylum operation racist, say law lords' *Guardian* (10 Dec 2004); Ekklesia, 'World churches criticise UK policies on asylum and immigration' (2005) Ekklesia <http://www.ekklesia.co.uk/content/news_syndication/article_050222asylum.shtml> (10 Oct 2006)

[84]   Human Rights Watch, 'UK Asylum Proposal Denounced' (2001)

undermined the spirit of the Convention; moreover, there have been deliberate violations of the Convention, such as forcible deportation to unsafe areas, criminal prosecution of those arriving without proper documents, and the detention of minors.[85] Not content with making life as difficult as possible for asylum-seekers once in the UK, the government has also deployed a variety of enforcement measures, including extra-territorial actions such as interdiction, in attempts to reduce if not eliminate the flow of migrants.[86]

Faced with increasing numbers of asylum-seekers, the primary objective of many receiving states is to reduce the number of arrivals – stopping asylum-seekers from gaining entry to its borders and access to the determination process. In the UK, the Labour government's stated objective to 'halve the numbers and increase removals' forms the cornerstone of its policies but much remains opaque. For example, little is known about what levels would be considered acceptable.[87] Many NGOs working with asylum-seekers have criticised this as a 'bare minimum' approach and a breach of UK's international obligations.[88] One of the effects of tighter border controls or 'get tough' laws is that it drives the movement further underground and creates an environment ripe for exploitation by human-traffickers. What all these enforcement measures mean is that asylum-seekers have no easy or legal means of entering a host country and are forced to resort to clandestine means which opens them to accusations as 'cheats' or 'illegal migrants'. And being illegal – particularly when circumventing border controls, often seen as a challenge to a state's sovereignty – invites and justifies a host of other enforcement measures with states emphasising an imperative to control its borders.[89] This wide array of policies and objectives has the effect of creating an untenable position for many asylum-seekers and driving them further to the margins of society.[90] The *Daily Mail*, for example, in regular 'attack' articles has little doubt about the bona-fides of the migrants: 'Bogus asylum-seekers, and why enough is enough'.[91]

---

[85] See Chapter 4 for a fuller discussion

[86] A Asthana, 'Asylum policy is 'grotesque' ' *The Observer* (27 Feb 2005)

[87] D Bamber and C Brown, 'Blunkett says Blair's pledge on asylum-seekers 'undeliverable'' *Sunday Telegraph* (09 Feb 2003) 1

[88] Leader, 'Asylum rights evaporate ' *Guardian* (10 Feb 2003); H O'Nions (2006) 'The Erosion Of The Right To Seek Asylum' 2 Web Journal of Current Legal Issues ; D Stevens (2001) 'The Asylum and Immigration Act 1996: Erosion of the Right to Seek Asylum' 61 Modern Law Review 2 207-222

[89] U Rippert, 'EU summit steps up attack on refugees and foreigners' (2002) World Socialist Web Site <http://www.wsws.org/articles/2002/jul2002/eu-j05.shtml> (16 Oct 2006)

[90] L Fekete (2005) 'The Deportation Machine: Europe, Asylum and Human Rights' 47 Race & Class 1 64-91; Leader, 'Asylum rights evaporate' *Guardian* (10 Feb 2003)

[91] *Daily Mail* cited in Article 19 *'What's the story: A case study of media coverage of asylum and refugee issues'* (2003)

Of the millions of impoverished, displaced, and/or persecuted on the move around the world a few thousand succeed in entering the UK.[92] And once in the UK an equally arduous and obstacle-filled journey begins: of navigating through a maze of bureaucracy, adapting to a new and often hostile environment, often alone and unable to speak the language, settling in a country which does not want them, and hoping that they are one of the lucky few granted the right to stay. While waiting for the outcome of their application to be recognised as refugees, which may take anywhere from a few weeks to years, asylum-seekers are legally prohibited from working or attending school and must depend on the state for benefits which are deliberately kept at below the subsistence level.[93] Thousands, including children, are detained but many remain invisible, pushed to the margins of society and leading lives of isolation and desperation.[94] There are other obstacles: cuts to legal-aid impact upon the ability to exercise rights and have the effect of curtailing access to the determination process;[95] lack of welfare support and legal prohibition to employment means that many are left homeless and without the means to properly pursue their claims.[96] While the UK (or any receiving state) may to a large extent be handicapped by what happens abroad there is no such handicap as to how asylum-seekers are treated once within its borders. And it is this reception and treatment which has opened the UK to vigorous criticism and earned it reprimands from the courts and domestic and international NGOs.[97]

3.7   Conclusion

Asylum-seekers in the UK have become the latest demons.[98]Vilified and marginalised, they have been blamed for various social ills such as the increase

---

[92]   B McMahon, 'Asylum seekers' voyages of hell' *The Observer* (17 July 2005)

[93]   F Bodi, 'Fear and loathing ' *Guardian* (21 Jan 2003)

[94]   Amnesty International, *Seeking asylum is not a crime: Detention of people who have sought asylum* (2005)

[95]   C Dyer, 'MPs attack legal aid cuts ' *Guardian* (23 Oct 2003)

[96]   Refugee Council, *Hungry and Homeless: The Impact of the Withdrawal of State Support on Asylum Seekers, Refugee Communities and the Voluntary Sector* (2004) 1-38

[97]   M Pickett, 'On the asylum frontline ' *Guardian* (02 Feb 2003); Joint Committee on Human Rights *The Treatment of Asylum-Seekers* (2007); Oxfam and Refugee Council, *Poverty and asylum in the UK* (2002); R Verkaik, 'UN criticises Home Office over refugees' *Independent* (28 June 2006) 4

[98]   R Yarde, 'Demon of the Day' *Guardian* (12 Nov 2001)

in crimes, unemployment, and abuse of the welfare system.[99] They have been hounded, assaulted, subjected to racist attacks, forced to flee from council housing, firebombed, and some even murdered.[100] They are a constant subject of vitriolic media attacks, politicians use the issue to gain political capital by promising to be tougher than their opposition, and the state continues to impose increasingly restrictive laws and policies, ignoring some of the most fundamental of rights in the process.[101] They are detained in 'appalling' conditions and subjected to violence, ill-treatment, and racism by institutional officials.[102] For countless asylum-seekers in the UK life is characterised by desperation, suffering, and compelling accounts of humanity and inhumanity.[103] And countless others are subjected to abuse and extreme exploitation, some to death. In 2004, for example, twenty-three asylum-seekers working illegally as cockle-pickers (earning 11p an hour) were swept out to sea and left to die.[104] According to Tim Finch of the Refugee Council:

> The government has perceived there's been a crisis of asylum seeker numbers and the press and public opinion has been whipped up…and the government feels it has to respond politically by introducing tougher legislation. It's now got to a situation where it's incredibly difficult to get to this country and claim asylum and if successful, the chances of getting a place of sanctuary are very, very small.[105]

---

[99]   N Cohen, 'How we scape-goated asylum-seekers' *New Statesman* (17 Apr 2000)

[100] BBC, 'Extremists 'must not drive out' refugees' (2002) Sep 27 <http://news.bbc.co.uk/1/hi/england/2284800.stm>

[101] P Waugh, 'Crackdown on asylum leaving genuine refugees homeless and destitute, MPs say' *The Independent* (26 Jan 2004) 4; BBC, 'Asylum laws under fresh attack' (2004) BBC News <http://news.bbc.co.uk/1/hi/uk_politics/3501702.stm> (10 June 2006); Travis, 'Asylum operation racist, say law lords' (2004); BBC, 'Asylum seekers 'denied justice'' (2005) BBC News <http://news.bbc.co.uk/1/hi/uk/4552523.stm> (10 Oct 2006)

[102] J Burns, 'Abuse of detainees puts asylum policy in the spotlight' *Financial Times* (03 March 2005); Travis, 'Asylum centres plagued by racism and abuse, says report ' (2003); M McFadyean, 'Centres of barbarism' *Guardian* (02 Dec 2006); Birnberg Peirce & Partners, Medical Justice and NCADC *Outsourcing Abuse: The use and misuse of state-sanctioned force during the detention and removal of asylum seekers* (2008); R Verkaik, 'Investigation into claims of abuse on asylum-seekers' *The Independent* (30 Sept 2008); R Verkaik, 'How 'Independent' story was denied – then accepted' *The Independent* (30 Sept 2008)

[103] Anonymous, 'Driven underground' *Guardian* (06 April 2005)

[104] I Johnston, 'Worked to death' *The Scotsman* (08 Feb 2004)

[105] cited in: Colorful, 'Life of an asylum seeker in Britain' (2006) 26 Feb <www.iamcolourful.com/news/details/2031/politics/>

It is in this contentious and volatile milieu that NGOs serving asylum-seekers continue to fight for the rights of a powerless and unpopular minority. And those rights, according to the *Guardian* newspaper, have 'evaporated'.[106] Often the plight and desperation of individual asylum-seeker loses its potency when considered in the context of tens of millions on the move and seeking sanctuary. But it does not make it any less compelling.

---

[106]   Leader, 'Asylum rights evaporate' *Guardian* (10 Feb 2003)

4   ASYLUM AND WELFARE BENEFITS: A REVIEW

4.1   Introduction

Government policies concerning welfare benefits for asylum-seekers have long been a fertile ground for conflict often pitting the Home Office against the NGO community. Beginning in the mid-1990s successive governments, alarmed at both the increasing costs of welfare and exponential increase in asylum-seekers, implemented various laws and policies based on the assumption that restricting access to and reducing benefits would deter asylum-seekers from coming to the UK.[1] Section 55, the most recent and considered by many observers to be the most draconian, follows on the heels of an established pattern of legislation aimed at achieving the twin objectives of cost-savings and deterrence.[2] To understand the role of welfare in asylum policies and the NGO campaign against Section 55, it is instructive to briefly review previous battles over the same issue. This chapter is an overview of campaigns and court challenges from 1993 to 2005, with particular focus on how welfare has evolved as a coercive measure in asylum policy. The chapter will also examine how Section 55 became law, its human rights implications and impact on NGOs and asylum-seekers, and the initial stages of the NGO campaign against it.

4.2   The Battle Over Benefits: A Brief Background

The battle over benefits began well before 1996, the year which marked the first legislative attempt to restrict access to benefits for asylum-seekers previously allowed benefits under the same scheme as British nationals or on an ad-hoc basis by local authorities. And the stakes in the battle are considerable. For the government it is the estimated costs in excess of £3 billion and increasing.[3] Even

---

1   A Bloch and L Schuster (2002) 'Asylum and welfare: contemporary debates ' 22 Critical Social Policy 3 393-414

2   P Dwyer (2005) 'Governance, forced migration and welfare' 39 Social Policy & Administration 6 622-639; P Johnston, 'Tough New Asylum Laws 'Too Draconian'' Daily Telegraph (09 Jan 2003)

3   P Johnston, '£2bn Bill for Flood of Asylum Seekers' Daily Telegraph (01 March 2003); J Pollock, 'Opinion on asylum seeker integration remains mixed' Guardian (27 June 2001)

more fundamentally it is also about control over borders, who to allow into the country, and the changing face of Britain.[4] For the NGOs it is no less than the very nature of what it means to seek (and provide) asylum and the human rights of a powerless and unpopular minority.[5]

The policy of limiting benefits presumes that asylum-seekers seek to enter the UK, or select it as a destination, because of its 'soft touch' accessibility to generous welfare benefits. This is a view shared by a large majority of Britons (almost 80%; the same poll also found 63% think that too much is being done to help asylum-seekers).[6] In other words, the policy takes a populist rather than empirical view that most asylum-seekers are economic migrants fleeing poverty and economic hardship rather than fear of persecution for any of the grounds in the 1951 UN Convention.[7] To be sure there is fraud and abuse – and according to some sources it is at significant levels[8] – but the evidence to support such a broad-brush presumption, that denying benefits is effective in combating fraud, reducing costs, and reducing the number of arrivals is far from persuasive.[9] As the NGOs point out it is no accident that the top-ten refugee producing countries are the very same countries which number in the top-ten of asylum-seeker arrivals in the UK.[10]

Nonetheless, the 'soft touch' presumption continues to prefigure major aspects of policy-making as it has since the mid-1990s when the then-Conservative government became alarmed, along with the British public, at the almost exponential increase in asylum-seeker arrivals – from a few thousand in the late

---

[4]   R Sales (2002) 'The deserving and the undeserving? Refugees, asylum seekers and welfare in Britain ' 22 Critical Social Policy 3 456-478

[5]   Justice, 'Refugees: Renewing the Vision' (2004) <http://www.justice.org.uk/ourwork/asylum/index.html>

[6]   MORI/Reader's Digest Survey October 2002

[7]   See the 1951 UN Convention Relating to the Status of Refugees

[8]   Institute for the Study of Civil Society (Civitas), *Tomorrow is Another Country: What is wrong with UK's asylum policy?* (2003); D Barrett, 'How Migrant Crackdown Opened the Floodgates' *Daily Telegraph* (06 Dec 2009) p. 19

[9]   R Verkaik, 'Asylum system flawed, rules High Court' *The Independent* (20 Feb 2003); Asylum Rights Campaign, *Providing Protection in the 21st Century* (2004); Independent Asylum Commission, *Deserving Dignity – A Nationwide Review of the UK Asylum System* (2008); Oxfam, *Asylum: The Truth Behind the Headlines* (2001); J Johnstson, 'Most Asylum-Seekers 'come to the UK because lives are in danger'' *Sunday Herald* (13 June 2004)

[10]   In 2002, according to Home Office statistics, the top ten countries were: Iraq, Zimbabwe, Afghanistan, Somalia, China, Sri Lanka, Turkey, Iran, FRY, and the DRC (www.homeoffice.gov.uk/rds/pdfs04/hosb1104.pdf)

1980s to almost 110,000 in 2002.[11] In addition to increasingly strict border controls the government has devoted its attention to eliminating what it considers major reasons or 'pull-factors' that have made the UK an apparent destination of choice for those seeking asylum. In short, a complex global problem where distinctions are characterised by blurring rather than clarity, and generally agreed by many to be insoluble, is assigned a response based on a belief that restricting welfare will deter and reduce arrivals.[12] And it is this belief that has dominated asylum policy irrespective of political ideology since the 'panic' over asylum-seekers began in the late 1980s.[13] The fact that this should dominate policy irrespective of increasing global instability and turmoil, the primary factors responsible for the mass movement of people, means a system in a constant state of flux and in constant search for a quick fix.[14]

4.3   Welfare and the 1993 Act[15]

No one from the present staff at the Joint Council for the Welfare of Immigrants (JCWI) recalls much of the events preceding 1996 when the organisation challenged the government regulations limiting welfare benefits, and won at the Court of Appeal. In the decision it was apparent that the Court had difficulty in coming to terms with the government's approach so extreme were the measures when it ruled:

> *The regulations necessarily contemplate for some a life so destitute that to my mind no civilised nation can tolerate it.* So basic are the human rights here at issue that it cannot be necessary to resort to the European Convention on Human Rights to take note of their violation . . . some basic provision should be made, sufficient for genuine claimants to survive and pursue their claims . . . *Parliament cannot have intended a significant number of genuine asylum-seekers to be impaled on the horns*

---

11   House of Commons, *Asylum Applications* (2004) 22; also see Chapter 3
12   Comment, 'A Shameful Asylum Policy' *The Independent* (30 Nov 2003)
13   L Pirouet, *Whatever Happened to Asylum in Britain* (2001)
14   H Crawley, 'Tackling the Causes of Asylum' *Guardian* (11 May 2003); D Stevens (2004) 'The Nationality, Immigration and Asylum Act 2002: Secure Borders, Safe Haven?' 67 Modern Law Review 4 616-631
15   *Asylum and Immigration Appeals Act 1993*

of so intolerable a dilemma: the need to either abandon their
claims to refugee status or alternatively to maintain them as best
they can but in a state of utter destitution.[16] (emphasis added)

The Court, however, provided an opening for the Home Secretary when it added that had such measures been introduced via primary legislation, they would have been upheld (the impugned regulations were ultra vires in relation to the rights conferred in the 1993 Act). It was therefore no surprise to the NGOs when the Conservative government responded by doing exactly that and introduced the *Asylum and Immigration Act 1996* (coming less than three years after the 1993 Act) which reduced benefits to those asylum-seekers claiming at a port of entry, and expressly eliminated all benefits for those who claimed after having entered the UK. This dichotomy was based on the assumption that asylum-seekers who initiate a claim at the first opportunity, usually a port-of-entry, are more likely to be credible than those who do so later. It is assumed that those fleeing persecution and seeking sanctuary would declare so at the first opportunity when at the borders of a country where they intend to seek refuge.[17] While such notions may appeal to a commonsensical view of the world, it overlooks a specific provision in the 1951 UN Convention, Article 31, which recognises that while asylum-seekers are expected to file claims without delay, they may have good reasons for failing to comply.[18]

The preceding also overlooks other factors: for example, border controls and other measures which are constantly fine-tuned make it almost impossible for asylum-seekers to enter the UK legally. Many therefore have little option but to use clandestine means, human traffickers, and/or fraudulent documents that necessitates avoiding official contact until safely in the country of refuge. This creates a host of difficulties further along the process compounding the problems for both asylum-seekers and the Home Office. Often there is no tangible proof of entry and/or

---

[16]   *R v Secretary of State for Social Security ex parte Joint Council for the Welfare of Immigrants* [1997] 1WLR 275 (CA) 292-3

[17]   Interview with anonymous immigration officers, Immigration and Nationality Directorate (Heathrow and Gatwick Airports January 2005)

[18]   The House of Lords, like the Court of Appeal below, examined this issue at length in *R v Asfaw* [2008] UKHK 31(also [2006] EWCA Crim 707) finding reasons for delays in filing claims 'reasonable' and 'consistent with Article 31' of the 1951 UN Convention. The Lordships also admonished the Home Office for prosecuting asylum-seekers rather than complying with international obligations.

citizenship (such as passports or other documents) making it difficult for the Home Office to assess credibility and for the asylum-seeker to establish credibility. The NGOs blame the Home Office for this conundrum, for creating a catch-22 situation where legal entry is virtually impossible. However in defence of the Home Office there is not much evidence to suggest that legal entry would ease such problems (of fraud) but it remains a major concern that hundreds of asylum-seekers are being prosecuted (convicted and imprisoned) for illegal entry in contravention of the UN Convention.[19] There is supposed to be a theoretical and actual separation between administrative and criminal court proceedings, but asylum-seekers encouraged to plead guilty or found guilty realise too late the ramifications; often that plea or finding is used to challenge the credibility of their asylum claims. And not only do they end up being denied asylum they have also acquired a criminal conviction and added untold long-term consequences in the process.[20]

4.4   Welfare and the 1996 Act[21]

The 1996 Act, which closed the loophole identified above, was the first to use direct legislation (as opposed to regulations) to restrict welfare benefits and further reduced the right to asylum.[22] The legislation, while ostensibly intended to change behaviour (i.e. encouraging early applications), failed to consider or ignored the clandestine nature via which most asylum-seekers enter. The effect of these legislative changes forced many into destitution; and, once again, the NGOs were faced with destitute asylum-seekers and left with no apparent options with which to challenge the policy. But creative activists discovered a loophole in the form of a long forgotten statute, the *National Assistance Act 1948*, which placed upon local authorities an obligation to provide for those in need of care and attention and

19   BBC, 'Jailing asylum seekers 'must end'' (2004) BBC News <//news.bbc.co.uk/1/hi/ uk/3564968.stm> (10 June 2006); BBC, 'Asylum: Getting tough in 2003 ' (2003) BBC News <//news.bbc.co.uk/1/hi/uk/3333865.stm> ; A Travis, 'Asylum operation racist, say law lords' *Guardian* (10 Dec 2004); Amnesty International, *Seeking asylum is not a crime: Detention of people who have sought asylum* (2005); Independent Asylum Commission, *Deserving Dignity - A Nationwide Review of the UK Asylum System* (2008)

20   Presentation by the Immigration Advisory Service (Conference in London, Summer 2005); Bail for Immigration Detainees (BID) and Asylum Aid, *Justice Denied* (2005)

21   *Asylum and Immigration Act 1996*

22   D Stevens (2001) 'The Asylum and Immigration Act 1996: Erosion of the Right to Seek Asylum' 61 Modern Law Review 2 207-222

without means of supporting themselves.[23] Again the NGO challenge took the form of a lengthy and expensive court battle; Lord Woolf MR (as he was then) ruled:

> The destitute condition to which asylum-seekers can be reduced as a result of the 1996 Act coupled with the period of time which, despite the Secretary of State's best efforts, elapses before their applications are disposed means inevitably that they (will become destitute) . . . the longer (the duration of destitution) the more compelling their case.[24]

The decision, however, offered a temporary respite. Its effect was nullified by the passage of yet another legislative overhaul, the *Immigration and Asylum Act 1999*, the third in six years which repealed most of the 1993 and 1996 Act.[25]

4.5   Welfare, the 1999 Act, and NASS

For many in the NGO community the 1999 Act was a 'betrayal' by a newly-elected Labour government, a party traditionally aligned with the Left, who had been highly critical of the Conservative's asylum policy when in opposition.[26] In a 1998 White Paper, and to the relief of NGOs at that time, Labour made clear their position that 'no asylum-seeker (will be) left destitute while waiting for their application or appeal to be determined'.[27] The NGOs found strength in the statement feeling that it reflected a more humane approach. Labour, during that time, had also sought input from various NGOs on its asylum policy and raised hopes and expectations of a new and positive era for asylum rights. The Conservatives had never engaged in consultations with NGOs and Labour's approach was eagerly welcomed.[28] But when the NGOs reviewed the new legislation they realised the consultation had been a farce. Nowhere in the legislation did they find an expression of their input. Much to their dismay, the NGOs found themselves almost exactly where they had

---

[23]   Interview with Clare Shepton, Solicitor, Shelter (London April 2005)

[24]   R v. Westminster City Council ex parte M (1997) 1 CCLR 85, 94

[25]   Information Centre about Asylum and Refugees, *Key Issues: UK Asylum Law and Process* (2006)

[26]   Asylum Rights Campaign, *Providing Protection in the 21st Century* (2004)

[27]   Home Office, *Fairer, Faster and Firmer - A Modern Approach to Immigration and Asylum* (1998) para 8.5

[28]   Interview notes (on file with author)

been when the Conservatives were in power.[29] Not only that but little did they know that the right to asylum and rights of asylum-seekers would face further attacks with Labour in government.[30]

In addition to introducing several measures aimed at deterrence, such as the increased use of detention, the 1999 Act was notable for the creation of an entirely new bureaucracy, the National Asylum Support Service (NASS), at a start-up cost of £300m with a specific mandate to deal with asylum-seeker benefits and housing.[31] Many in the NGO community questioned the need for yet another level of bureaucracy unable to understand why the existing benefits infrastructure could not manage a relatively small client group. To the NGOs this separation had an ominous ring. They feared its effect would further isolate asylum-seekers from the mainstream social services system while at the same time perpetuating an image of asylum-seekers as a drain on the public purse. Of concern was that benefits would be paid in the form of vouchers, redeemable only in certain shops, for which no change would be offered should the purchase be less than the value of the voucher. Again the NGOs, with remarkable prescience, complained that the vouchers would further humiliate and stigmatise asylum-seekers making them readily identifiable to xenophobic elements of society. But not many at the Home Office paid much attention. Many NGOs felt that the creation of NASS played into the hands of the right and far right and, more effectively than any tabloid, conveyed a message that asylum-seekers had become such a drain on public finances that a new infrastructure was required to manage them.[32]

It was then no surprise to the NGOs when the NASS proved to be as equally intransigent and unwieldy as the IND. The 'culture of disbelief' which, according to many NGO caseworkers, dominates the ethos at the Home Office came also to prefigure NASS decision-making. For many caseworkers, NASS proved to be a 'nightmare' to deal with. According to the Citizen's Advice Bureau (CAB), an organisation experienced in dealing with all levels of bureaucracy, NASS holds the distinction as being the worst.[33] The Bureau went even further and condemned the

---

[29]   Asylum Rights Campaign, *Providing Protection in the 21st Century* (2004) 4

[30]   See: Comment, 'A Shameful Asylum Policy' (30 Nov 2003); L Smith, 'Britain: Government steps up attacks on asylum seekers' (2004) World Socialist Web Site <http://www.wsws.org/articles/2004/jan2004.bak/asyl-j05.shtml> (16 Oct 2006)

[31]   EUROPA, *Mid-Term Evaluation Report – United Kingdom* (2003)

[32]   Asylum Rights Campaign, *Providing Protection in the 21st Century* (2004) 4

[33]   Mayor of London, 'Destitution by Design' (2004) 22

NASS for having 'comprehensively failed both asylum-seekers and taxpayers'.[34] During the course of the fieldwork almost all interviewees spoke of being frustrated and bewildered by the incompetence at NASS; lost files, indifferent and hostile staffers, by rote and inconsistent decision-making, unreturned telephone calls, and unanswered queries were the order of the day. In other words, a progeny acting very much like its progenitor.[35] A government ordered independent review of the NASS (in March 2003) was so critical that it was never published, not even when requested by a Home Affairs Committee.[36] Even worse, the bureaucratic inefficiency meant that hundreds of asylum-seekers were caught in limbo or waiting decision without access to benefits. The situation for asylum-seekers who should have been helped by NASS deteriorated; without benefits many became clients of the NGOs adding considerably to their workload. This caused a great deal of resentment on part of the NGOs who knew that the NASS, while uncooperative and hostile, was relying on them to make up for their own systemic shortcomings.[37]

4.6   Welfare, the 2002 Act and Section 55

By now the pattern of increasingly stricter controls on welfare benefits for asylum-seekers had become clearly established. But even stricter was to come. And it came in the shape of another legislative reform, the fourth in less than nine years, the *Nationality, Immigration and Asylum Act, 2002* which introduced Section 55. The irony, for the NGOs, concerning the 1999 and 2002 Acts, particularly the 1999 Act, was that they were drafted, debated, and passed into law during the very same period as the *Human Rights Act* was being drafted, debated, and passed (with considerably much more fanfare) into law. Not many in the NGO community were blind to so obvious an irony, but neither were they surprised because Labour was turning out to be just as impervious to criticism on asylum policy as the Conservatives had been during their reign.[38]

The introduction of Section 55 caught many off guard and set off immediate alarm bells. The NGOs knew they faced a tough fight. And even at this early stage in

---

[34]   BBC, 'Asylum system 'failing' refugees' (2002) 20 Feb <http://news.bbc.co.uk/1/hi/uk/1830886.stm>

[35]   Citizens Advice Bureau, *Distant Voices* (2002)

[36]   House of Commons, *Asylum Applications* (2004) 58

[37]   Citizens Advice Bureau, *Distant Voices* (2002)

[38]   Asylum Rights Campaign, *Providing Protection in the 21st Century* (2004)

the life of the HRA long-serving NGO caseworkers, experienced in battles with the government, instinctively knew that principled arguments with or without the HRA as a framework would not be effective against a 'get-tough' government, and that drawn-out court battles offered the only real alternative for achieving their objective – a repeal of Section 55.[39] During this period some of the more experienced NGO campaigners, particularly the legal staff, were also contemplating how the HRA could be used in test-case litigation.[40] Liberty, a veteran of many battles and in full expectation of an obstinate response by the Home Office, had already put out 'feelers' seeking suitable Section 55 cases for test-case challenges, an enterprise in which Liberty was now being joined by other NGOs curious about how the new HRA could serve their constituency and their respective agendas.[41]

While the courts in previous battles over welfare had ruled in their favour many in the NGO community viewed them as a 'reluctant ally'. During the campaign against Section 55 some of the legal campaigners at Liberty, Shelter, and the JCWI voiced frustration that the courts seemed unsure about how to approach the HRA and were being too conservative, slow, and piecemeal in interpreting Convention rights.[42] But notwithstanding such frustrations it has been in the courts where the HRA has shown some promise. The Court of Appeal and House of Lords decisions, concerning successive challenges to Section 55 were crucial to its eventual defeat and during the campaign served to mitigate some of the harsher elements of the policy. According to many interviewees the courts were instrumental in saving hundreds of asylum-seekers from destitution and other ill-effects of Section 55.[43] In doing so the courts raised the ire of the government and ignited a very public and unseemly feud; particularly combative was the-then Home Secretary, David Blunkett, who attacked the judiciary in intemperate language.[44] Faced with repeated challenges and defeats on asylum policy Blunkett declared: 'frankly I am fed up with having to deal with a situation where Parliament debates issues and judges overturn them'.[45]

---

[39]   Interview with Tauhid Pasha, Legal Director, JCWI (London April 2005)

[40]   Interview with Don Flynn, Policy Director, JCWI (London May 2005)

[41]   R Maiman, 'We've had to raise our game: Liberty's litigation strategy under the Human Rights Act 1998' in S Halliday and PD Schmidt (eds) *Human Rights Brought Home: Socio-Legal Perspectives on Human Rights in the National Context* (2004)

[42]   Interview notes (on file with author)

[43]   See Chapters 5 and 6 for a fuller discussion; Leader, 'Judges v ministers: Courts step in where MPs fear to tread' *Guardian* (24 Feb 2003)

[44]   A Bradley (2003) 'Judicial Independence Under Attack' Public Law Aut 397-405

[45]   J Rozenberg, 'Judges prepare for battle with Blunkett' *Daily Telegraph* (26 Feb 2003)

4.6.1   Section 55: Destitution by Design (Overview)

As later noted by the High Court in *Zardasht* Section 55 was not intended to be a 'benevolent piece of legislation', with Liberty calling it a 'cruel' law.[46] And, at first glance, it is a curiously designed piece of legislation.[47] Section 55 of the 2002 Act, in part, reads:

> (1)   The Secretary of State may not provide or arrange for the provision of support to a person under a provision mentioned in subsection (2) if –
>
> a.   the person makes a claim for asylum which is recorded by the Secretary of State, and
>
> b.   the Secretary of State is not satisfied that the claim was made as soon as reasonably practicable after the person's arrival in the United Kingdom.
>
> (5)   This section shall not prevent –
>
> a.   the exercise of a power by the Secretary of State for the purpose of avoiding a breach of a person's Convention rights (within the meaning of the Human Rights Act 1998) . . .

Subsection 55(5) mandates that the Secretary of State shall not provide benefits to asylum-seekers unless it is to avoid a breach of Convention rights. Clearly, then, there was an implicit anticipation that the legislation may result in a breach, or verge on a breach, notwithstanding the Secretary of State's statutory declaration that the legislation was compatible with the HRA. It is instructive that the declaration was made in the face of direct warnings (of the likelihood of human rights violations) by a parliamentary body, the Joint Committee on Human Rights (JCHR), and vigorous lobbying by the NGOs who reminded the Home Office of the harsh effects of previous such policies.[48] Another important factor in the design of Section 55

---

[46]   Interview with Alex Gask, Solicitor, Liberty (London Nov 2005)

[47]   *Zardasht v Secretary of State* [2004] EWHC 91 Admin (para 9-10); Alex Gask, Solicitor, Liberty (interview notes November 2005)

[48]   See Chapter 5 for a fuller discussion on how Section 55 became law.

was that it deliberately provided no right of appeal by which to challenge NASS decisions. The only recourse was the common law right of review by a superior tribunal; in this instance, judicial review in the administrative courts. In retrospect this lack of appeal rights may have turned the tide in favour of NGOs because it raised the ire of the judiciary which suddenly found itself inundated with hundreds of judicial review applications. The judiciary repeatedly warned the Home Office of pressures on the courts and urged that something be done but received little in response.[49]

4.7   Welfare as a Coercive Measure

In general the policy of restricting welfare benefits is often couched in palatable language and supported by the articulation of reasonable objectives, such as the imperative to control costs, change asylum-seeker behaviour, and encourage compliance in their removal should they fail their claims.[50] However there can be no denying the severity of the effects of Section 55 on asylum-seekers.[51] Significantly, there is much to infer that the Home Office was aware (or should reasonably be expected to have known) that Section 55 would bring about destitution and suffering, but pushed ahead.[52]It was an approach characterised by a relentless determination on part of the government and drew strong criticism from international organisations such as Amnesty International and Oxfam. That such organizations, more accustomed to battling repressive regimes than governments of liberal western democracies, should be compelled to comment on UK policies provides a measure of the suffering brought about by Section 55 on vulnerable peoples.[53]

---

[49]   C Dyer, 'Asylum cases 'clogging the courts'' *Guardian* (16 Oct 2003); see Chapters 5 and 6 for a fuller discussion on the judiciary's response to Section 55

[50]   See, for example, various White Papers preceding legislative reform/changes: Home Office, *Building Trust and Confidence - Home Secretary Tackles Asylum Abuse* (2002); *Fairer, Faster and Firmer - A Modern Approach to Immigration and Asylum*; Home Office, *Secure Borders, Safe Haven: Integration with Diversity in Modern Britain* (2002)

[51]   R Dunston, 'Blunkett's uncivilised act' *New Statesman* (11 Aug 2003)

[52]   Leader, 'Asylum rights evaporate ' *Guardian* (10 Feb 2003); Leader, 'Almost Beyond Belief' *Guardian* (25 Nov 2003)

[53]   Amnesty International, *Human Rights: A Broken Promise* (2006); Human Rights Watch, 'UK Asylum Proposal Denounced' (2001) HRW (20 Oct 2006); Human Rights Watch, *Commentary on the United Kingdom Home Office White Paper: Secure Borders, Safe Haven: Integration with Diversity in Modern Europe* (2002); Oxfam and Refugee Council, *Poverty and asylum in the UK* (2002); UN, *Sofia Judicial Round Table on Refugee Protection* (2003)

The denial of welfare under Section 55 served to further marginalise a constituency already relegated to the margins. It brought about homelessness, suffering, and hunger for thousands exercising an internationally recognised right to seek asylum.[54] The deprivation also caused problems in other related and crucial processes of the asylum system, such as the ability to meet and instruct counsel, complete lengthy and complex application forms within strict time-limits, or maintain contact with the Home Office (difficult to do, for example, without a residential address).[55] Add to this array of obstacles the well-documented inefficiency and inflexibility of the Home Office, criticised as 'not fit for the purpose', it then becomes apparent that the new arrivals, unversed and unfamiliar with the country and its bureaucracy and more than likely unable to communicate in English, faced significant challenges.[56] At that time, compounding the situation even further, many asylum-seekers were not legally represented; continuing cuts to legal aid having resulted in fewer and fewer lawyers doing asylum work. In some areas the cuts have been so severe that entire regions are without firms or lawyers doing asylum work.[57]

The situation today remains relatively unchanged. In view of these obstacles it is not surprising that many asylum-seekers are all but doomed to fail. And many do, not because of substantive shortcomings but rather an inability to comply with procedural and technical requirements (i.e. such as completing forms on time, failing to maintain contact with the Home Office). In January 2001, for example, 1 in 3 asylum claims were refused on non-compliance grounds.[58] And, notwithstanding government statements to the contrary, an inference can be drawn

---

[54]   Inter-Agency Partnership, *The impact of section 55 on the Inter-Agency Partnership of leading UK refugee agencies and the asylum seekers it supports* (2004); Refugee Council, *Hungry and Homeless: The Impact of the Withdrawal of State Support on Asylum Seekers, Refugee Communities and the Voluntary Sector* (2004) 1-38 (Note: It is sometimes claimed that the UK violates Article 14 (right to seek asylum) of the Universal Declaration of Human Rights when it places obstacles in the path of those seeking to enter the UK for such purposes. It should, however, be noted that the instrument is not binding on any signatory state).

[55]   Shelter, *Briefing: Section 55 of the Nationality, Immigration and Asylum Act 2002. Independent Review* (2004)

[56]   G Younge, 'The Waiting Game' *Guardian* (22 May 2001); R Verkaik, 'UN criticises Home Office over refugees' *Independent* (28 June 2006) 4

[57]   Refugee Council, *The Refugee Council's submission to the Campaign Against Legal Aid Cuts (CALAC) about the impact of changes to legal aid* (2005)

[58]   Home Office, *Bridging the Information Gaps: A Conference of Research on Asylum and Immigration in the UK* (2001)

that that is exactly the objective of its 'get tough' policy albeit in arcane language and innocuously worded legislation, to drive home a message to asylum-seekers already in the UK (and those contemplating entering the UK) that they are not wanted. Such policies have the effect of making life so difficult that abandoning claims and returning home becomes the more attractive of options, a situation criticised as 'intolerable' by the courts.[59]

The government, however, has shown little sign of retreating from such policies. In many ways these are policy objectives based on populist notions than empirical evidence because countless do not return to their home countries.[60] There are no official statistics but it is apparent that after undertaking such an arduous journey to enter the UK, many do not return and simply vanish; thousands are effectively absorbed into the underground economy creating a huge swathe of an underclass.[61] The Home Office has no record of the 'vanished' or even how to track or manage this underclass.[62] Recently the Home Office was forced to admit that it has no idea of the actual numbers and its estimates of approximately 310,000 to 570,000 vanished, a meaningless statistic.[63] Meanwhile thousands keep arriving because whatever it is that they fled, persecution or poverty or both, is much worse than life in the UK, even if unwanted and forced into destitution.[64]

An effect of restrictive welfare policies has been the creation of large swathes of the listless and idle who are legally prohibited from employment and are forced to play a waiting game, humiliating in its impact.[65] It is this group of asylum-seekers that is usually photographed (and the photographs are often of able-bodied young men) by the tabloid media and labelled 'benefits cheats' and 'scroungers'.[66] The numbers of this 'idle' group keeps increasing because of the inefficiency that characterises the massive bureaucracy that is the Home Office means there is a

---

[59]   See: *R v Secretary of State for Social Security ex parte JCWI* p. 292-3

[60]   Oxfam, *Asylum: The Truth Behind the Headlines* (2001)

[61]   BBC, 'Watchdog criticises asylum decisions' (2004) 23 June <http://news.bbc.co.uk/1/hi/uk_politics/3831163.stm>

[62]   House of Commons, *Returning Failed Asylum Applicants* (2006)

[63]   S Jenkins, 'Not too round, not too precise: that's why 11,000 is a magic number' *Guardian* (19 May 2006) 38

[64]   B McMahon, 'Asylum seekers' voyages of hell' *The Observer* (17 July 2005)

[65]   L Smith, 'Britain: New government attack on asylum seekers' (2003) World Socialist Web Site <http://www.wsws.org/articles/2003/nov2003/asyl-n15.shtml>

[66]   Article 19, *What's the Story: Results from Research into Media Coverage of Refugees and Asylum-Seekers in the UK* (2003); BBC, 'Media linked to asylum violence ' (2004) BBC News <http://news.bbc.co.uk/1/hi/uk/3890963.stm> (09 October 2006)

huge backlog of cases waiting determination. The Home Office is so unwieldy that it rarely surprises when it fails to meet its objectives. And there is persuasive evidence to suggest that it is not in effective control over asylum (and immigration) matters.[67] One interviewee, with considerable experience in dealing with the Home Office, said 'it is utter chaos. I don't think they know what they are doing. And it's very cruel to everyone'.[68]

4.7.1   The Impact of Section 55

When the Joint Committee on Human Rights first examined the Bill introducing Section 55 it remarked, in anticipation of its probable effects, that:

> We consider that the way a State treats powerless and vulnerable
> people is an important indicator of the vitality of its human rights
> culture.[69]

The announced attention behind Section 55 was to specifically target those clearly seen as abusing the asylum system – the 'overstayers' and others who delay making a claim (after being in the UK for long periods of time) and only do so to circumvent enforcement action. In this respect the legislation mandated that asylum-seekers make their claim as 'soon as reasonably practicable'. And if not, the Home Secretary would not provide welfare support unless that lack of support resulted in a breach of Convention rights.

On paper the legislation seemed fairly straightforward and its objectives, to 'change behaviour' of asylum-seekers and encourage timely claims (generally at a port-of-entry), not unreasonable.[70] In general, port-of-entry claims make it easier to identify date of entry, mode of travel, country of origin, and other issues central to establishing identity and credibility whereas in-country claims leaves such issues more open to fraud.[71] However, as stated elsewhere, such assumptions fail to consider that legal entry remains virtually impossible and those seeking asylum

---

67   S Moxon, 'Ineptitude and Political Correctness Gone Mad ' *Daily Mail* (28 April 2006);
       BBC, 'Blair 'rattled' over immigration' (2006) 17 May <http://news.bbc.co.uk/1/hi/uk_
       politics/4988816.stm> ; P Johnston, 'Reid Blasts Failures at Home Office' *Daily Telegraph*
       (24 May 2006) 2

68   Interview notes (on file with author)

69   Joint Committee on Human Rights, *Nationality, Immigration and Asylum Bill: Seventeenth
       Report of Session 2001-02* (HL 132 2002)

70   House of Commons, *Asylum Applications* (2004) 63

71   Interview notes (on file with author)

generally avoid contact with officialdom until in the country.[72] Notwithstanding such complexities Section 55, in the hands of the Home Office, became a tool, a broad brush, which indiscriminately targeted almost all in-country asylum-seekers and pushed thousands into homelessness and destitution.[73] The provision 'as soon as reasonably practicable' was interpreted by officials to mean 'immediately upon arrival' and those not claiming immediately were assumed to have been within the borders of the UK for extended periods. Decisions which had profound implications for asylum-seekers were made on the basis that claims not filed at a port-of-entry were generally without merit. A report by the Mayor of London called Section 55 a 'grave threat' and estimated that from January 2003 to December 2003 approximately 10-15,000 asylum-seekers (at a rate of roughly 200 per week) were forced into destitution in London alone, a figure seen by some as conservative.[74]

4.7.2   Human Rights Concerns about Section 55

When Section 55 came into effect in January of 2003, the Home Office, then under the guidance of Home Secretary David Blunkett, sat back and waited knowing full well the likely impact that the legislation was going to have during one of the coldest winters on record.[75] That is unless the Home Secretary was unaware of repeated and public warnings from various sources. If anything, Section 55 represented the latest in the government's continuing battle against asylum-seekers and the erosion of asylum rights.[76] The clause, with welfare as a coercive measure, that became Section 55 more or less blind-sided the NGOs because there had been no mention of it in the White Paper preceding the Bill first introduced in Parliament in February 2002.[77] During the consultation period preceding the Bill, a process

---

[72]   Many asylum-seekers are accompanied by smuggling agents and advised on surreptitious entry lest they be caught. Many have paid for the services of smugglers but then are expected, by the Home Office, to disregard the advice of persons who have facilitated their entry and declare their intentions at a port-of-entry – a notion described as 'absurd' by immigration lawyers (interview notes). See also: *R v Asfaw* [2008] UKHK 31

[73]   Interview notes (on file with author); M Taylor, 'Asylum policies 'make 10,000 people destitute a year' ' *Guardian* (09 Feb 2004); Smith (2003) 'Britain: New government attack on asylum seekers' ; R Verkaik, 'Asylum system flawed, rules High Court' (20 Feb 2003)

[74]   Mayor of London, 'Destitution by Design' (2004) p 3-5

[75]   Interview with Uma Joshi, Solicitor, Shelter (London May 2005)

[76]   D Stevens (2004) 'The Nationality, Immigration and Asylum Act 2002: Secure Borders, Safe Haven?'

[77]   Home Office, *Secure Borders, Safe Haven: Integration with Diversity in Modern Britain* (2002)

described by NGOs as frustrating, there had been no indication that such a measure was being considered.[78] There is much to infer that the Home Secretary was aware of the human rights implications of the clause given the manner of its (under-handed) introduction as a last-minute amendment to a Bill already being debated in Parliament (and unmistakeably timed for just before the final stage in the House of Lords).[79] And if he had not known when his officials drafted the amendment he would have become aware when it was scrutinised by JCHR, which expressed serious concerns and warned that the clause was potentially in violation of the HRA.[80] The Committee, albeit restrained in language by parliamentary decorum, also seemed displeased at the manner of its introduction (without proper explanatory notes) and the apparent confusion it caused during debate in both Houses. To cynics, and veteran observers, of the process it was apparent that the government was trying to hide something. The JCHR expressed concerns that Section 55 test of 'as soon as reasonably practicable' was too imprecise and lacking in objectivity; and, further, it placed too undue a burden on asylum-seekers to satisfy the Home Secretary rather than being given an opportunity to provide a 'credible explanation' for the late application. The Committee concluded:

> . . . [I]t is difficult to envisage a case where a person could be destitute without there being a threat of a violation of Articles 3 and/or 8 of the ECHR. We reiterate that the Secretary of State has a duty . . . under the *Human Rights Act* to avoid that risk.[81]

And even prior to the introduction of the amendment (which became Section 55) the Committee had other concerns about the human rights implications of the Bill and wrote to the Secretary of State seeking answers. To the consternation of the Committee no answers were provided by the deadline:

> We draw attention to the fact that this made it impossible for us to report on the Bill in time for our conclusions to be useful to the House of Commons. It is essential for Departments to comply

---

[78]   Asylum Rights Campaign, *Providing Protection in the 21st Century* (2004) 4; interview notes (on file with author)

[79]   A Bradley (2003) 'Judicial Independence Under Attack'

[80]   Joint Committee On Human Rights, *Nationality, Immigration and Asylum Bill: Further Report* Twenty-third Report of Session 2001-02 (HL 176 2001)

[81]   ibid para 15

with deadlines . . . This is particularly important when a Bill has substantial human rights implications . . .[82]

But even for so decorum-bound a committee as the JCHR the government's tactics, of effectively limiting debate by (deliberate) late amendments, went beyond the pale as it commented (in another report on yet another immigration Bill in 2003):

> The Committee repeats its previously stated view that it regards as unacceptable that amendments having obvious implications for human rights should be introduced at such a late stage in a Bill's passage . . . without adequate warning and without a clear explanation of the Government's view of the human rights implications . . .[83]

> . . . [W]e find it particularly regrettable that we find ourselves once again in the very same position so soon after having made clear that such a practice undermines parliamentary scrutiny of legislation for compatibility with human rights . . .[84] (emphasis added)

4.7.3   NGO Reaction to Section 55

If a Parliamentary committee seemed concerned about both the human rights implications and behaviour of the Home Secretary it was nothing compared to the alarm felt by the NGOs. For them it was the worst days of 1996 revisited when the then Conservative government had introduced similar measures.[85] The NGOs, all too experienced with Home Office treatment of asylum-seekers, anticipated the worst and complained about the clause; in particular, the nature of its introduction as a last-minute amendment which effectively limited substantive debate (to 15 minutes, most of it devoted to introducing the amendment) as it progressed through both the House of Commons and House of Lords. And even then there was little

---

[82]   Joint Committee On Human Rights, *Nationality, Immigration and Asylum Bill: Seventeenth Report of Session 2001-02* (2002)

[83]   Joint Committee On Human Rights, *Asylum and Immigration (Treatment of Claimants, etc.) Bill: New Clauses - Fourteenth Report of Session 2003-04* (HL 130 2004) 3

[84]   ibid 5

[85]   Interview with Tauhid Pasha, Senior Policy and Legal Analyst, JCWI (London April 2005)

debate as the Home Secretary used a guillotine motion to push the legislation through the Houses.[86] The NGOs, in response, flooded the inboxes of sympathetic Labour MPs, who, in private meetings with the Home Secretary, were reassured that the fears expressed by the NGOs would not come to pass. The Home Secretary also assured both Houses that Section 55 would be implemented with due consideration to human rights issues in that it was specifically designed to target those clearly abusing the asylum system.[87] It is likely the Home Secretary sincerely believed that the Home Office, which to date had been repeatedly and with justification criticised by NGOs and the courts for its culture of disbelief and treatment of asylum-seekers, would be even-handed in its approach.[88] It is also likely the Home Secretary understood full well that his 'get tough' approach to asylum, of which Section 55 represented further escalation in a long line of increasingly stringent measures, had many supporters in the Home Office concerned almost solely with stopping asylum-seekers. In other words, fighting the liars, cheats, and economic migrants, which to them represent the face of the present-day asylum-seeker.[89]

Many in the NGO community knew what the likely effects of Section 55 would be. Such were the concerns about the impending implementation they refused to concede a fight clearly lost. Even days before the coming into effect of Section 55 the NGOs worked hard to get the government to change its mind. Many of the experienced staffers knew too-well that they would end up picking the pieces once Section 55 took effect. They knew also that they would be unable to do so and that resources would be stretched to the breaking point.[90] On the day before Section 55 was to take effect the Refugee Council, JCWI, Shelter, Maternity Alliance, and others issued a joint statement (Amnesty International and the Jewish Council for Racial Equality also added their voices):

> The concerns we share are in part informed by the collective
> experiences of our organisations in 1996 . . . (when) we witnessed
> chaos, hardship and despair . . . all we could do was offer plastic
> sheeting for shelter. Although voluntary organisations mobilised

---

[86] A Bradley (2003) 'Judicial Independence Under Attack'

[87] Refugee Council, *Hungry and Homeless* (2004) 9

[88] R Verkaik, 'UN criticises Home Office over refugees' (28 Jun 2006); P Johnston, 'Reid Blasts Failures at Home Office' (24 May 2006); B Leapman and M Kite, 'Hundreds of corruption inquiries at Immigration' *Daily Telegraph* (27 July 2006).

[89] Interview with Tauhid Pasha, Solicitor, JCWI (London May 2005)

[90] Interview notes (on file with author)

to do the best they could, the truth is that only the intervention
of the courts prevented a greater tragedy . . . withdrawing food
and shelter from in-country asylum applicants will at a stroke
show that nothing has been learnt from two of the biggest public
policy failures in recent years – the voucher system and the
implementation of a similar measure in 1996. We call on the
Government to consider the concerns raised in this statement, to
think again . . .[91]

4.8   Conclusion

In the end, however, the NGOs lobbying efforts and pleas, insofar as changing
the government's mind and halting Section 55 came to nought. And this came as
no surprise. The NGOs, given their history of battles over asylum with the Home
Office, knew that Section 55 would become law. The government, concerned
with spiralling costs – in the billions – and having to contend with fierce public
opposition to asylum, had no intention of conceding on the issue. But the NGOs
were also determined and not unprepared. On the day before Section 55 was to take
effect Liberty made clear its plans:

We are absolutely appalled by these new government measures
which will throw thousands of asylum-seekers into destitution
and add to the chaos in the asylum system . . . we are prepared to
take this issue to the courts.[92]

And from January 2003 the campaign against Section 55 shifted to another level.

---

[91]   Refugee Council, 'A Joint Statement on the Withdrawal of Asylum Support for In-country
Applicants' <www.refugeecouncil.org.uk/infocentre/nia_act2002/joint_sment_ics.htm
> accessed 25 April 2006

[92]   Liberty (Press Release), 'Asylum Destitution Law: Liberty Challenge' (London 07
January 2003) <www.liberty-human-rights.org.uk/press/press-releases-2003/asylum-
destitution-law-liberty-challenge.shtml >

5   THE CAMPAIGN AGAINST SECTION 55

5.1   Introduction

The campaign against Section 55 began in earnest from almost the moment it was introduced on 7th October 2002, as a late amendment to a Bill already before the House of Commons, and effectively ended with the House of Lords decision on 3rd November 2005. By the time the campaign ended a disparate and determined group of NGOs – comprised of anti-poverty, homelessness, human rights, refugee advocacy, and faith groups – had come together and fought against a government unwilling to concede on its get-tough policy on asylum. This chapter is divided into two parts. The first is an overview of how Section 55 became law and describes the overall campaign against it, with particular focus on the crisis brought about by Section 55 and its impact on asylum-seekers and NGOs. The second part examines the campaign, the challenges faced by the NGOs, media coverage, overview of the legal strategy, and the role of the nascent *Human Rights Act* in the lead-up to the first test-case challenge against a 'draconian' law.[1]

5.2   Part I

5.2.1   Section 55 (Nationality, Immigration and Asylum Act 2002)

When Section 55 was first introduced the NGOs recognised that it represented an escalation of the government's continuing battle against asylum.[2] It was yet another measure, quite possibly the harshest, in a long line of increasingly stringent measures by successive governments focused on the view that most asylum-seekers seek to enter the UK, not for reasons of fleeing persecution but are economic migrants exploiting 'soft-touch' Britain for welfare and social benefits.[3] Although there is scant empirical evidence in support it is this premise that has underpinned

---

[1]   P Johnston, 'Tough New Asylum Laws 'Too Draconian" *Daily Telegraph* (09 Jan 2003)
[2]   Interview with Don Flynn, Policy Analyst, JCWI (London May 2005) (this view was expressed by almost all interviewees).
[3]   L Brooks, '5 tough questions about asylum ' *Guardian* (01 May 2003); A Kundnani, 'Britain gripped by populist campaigns against immigrants' (2003) Institute of Race Relations <http://www.irr.org.uk/2003/january/ak000017.html> (May 27)

major aspects of modern-day asylum policy.[4] This presumption, irrespective of the political stripe of government, has been a driving force in asylum policy since the early 1990s, and continues to define present-day approach as governments struggle to control costs and appease a public overwhelmingly opposed to both asylum and immigration, two distinct but often conflated issues.[5]

Prior to coming into effect Section 55 had been promoted as a necessary measure to curb what is viewed, by the Home Office, as widespread abuses of the asylum system, including 'over-stayers' who make last-minute claims as a means of avoiding/delaying enforcement action. Section 55 was also designed to encourage early claims (at a port of entry) rather than in-country (after entering the country) where crucial information such as date of arrival, embarkation points, or identity becomes much more difficult to ascertain. And, on the whole, these are not unreasonable requirements of a government strategy seeking to manage the intake of asylum-seekers, control costs, and curb abuses. The NGOs do not disagree that abuses and costs must be addressed and that such issues are central to the credibility of the system, but disagree with the broad-brush approach. Herein, according to the NGOs, is one of the key problems: the Home Office mentality which appears to view most asylum-seekers as economic migrants and a 'culture of disbelief' which permeates its vast bureaucracy.[6] Add to that mix the interplay of factors such as racism and xenophobia and a perception of the UK overrun with asylum-seekers, an image promoted by the tabloid media, then one gets some understanding of the complexity of the issue and just what the politicians, bureaucrats, and the public perceive the battle to be.[7]

---

[4]   Some veteran observers (see Webber (2004)) hold the view that immigration and asylum policy in the UK is driven largely by the tabloid media, which, in its vitriolic, has promoted and perpetuated the image of asylum-seekers as 'welfare cheats' and 'scroungers'. The combined readership of the various tabloids exceeds 20 million – far exceeding that of the broadsheets – a fact ignored by politicians at their own peril. Not by coincidence the tabloids are overwhelmingly opposed to the HRA and attack it at every opportunity (see Chapter 6); also: Article 19, 'What's the Story' (2003) at: www.article19.org/pdfs/publications/refugees-what-s-the-story-.pdf#search=%22article%2019%2C%20what's%20the%20story%22 accessed 11 August 2006

[5]   L Pirouet, *Whatever Happened to Asylum in Britain* (2001); S Cohen B Humphries and E Mynott, *From immigration controls to welfare controls* (2002); S Cohen (2002) 'The local state of immigration controls' 22 Critical Social Policy 3 518-543; N Cohen, 'How we scape-goated asylum-seekers' *New Statesman* (17 Apr 2000)

[6]   Asylum Rights Campaign, 'Providing Protection in the 21st Century' (2004) 4

[7]   Oxfam, *Asylum: The Truth Behind the Headlines* (2001)

5.2.2 Overview of the Campaign

The degree of deprivation and suffering caused by Section 55 was severe in the extreme.[8] So severe that the High Court, in a succession of cases in 2003, decided that Article 3 of the *European Convention on Human Rights* (ECHR) prohibition against 'inhumane or degrading treatment' had been breached (or there existed a 'real risk' that breach was imminent).[9] The decisions were appealed by the Home Office but much remained unclear in the subsequent rulings leading to confusion in the lower courts and uncertainty amongst NGOs and others about the status of Section 55. During this period, however, there was no apparent confusion at the Home Office which continued to reject applications at roughly the same rate during the various court challenges and subsequent decisions.[10]

Article 3 is an absolute right and no derogation is permitted. So what were the government's objectives in implementing a policy knowing that there was a potential breach of Article 3? The government had been repeatedly warned by the JCHR of serious human rights concerns about Section 55 but choose to go ahead. They were also warned by the campaigning NGOs and several MPs.[11] Presumably the government must have been assured that Section 55 was compatible with the HRA having made a mandated declaration to that effect. However, when examined in light of how the clause, which became Section 55, had been initially introduced and rushed through the legislative process, it raises serious questions. For example: did the government mislead Parliament? Did it act deliberately, knowing the likely effects or human rights implications, in legislating Section 55? The government had repeatedly assured Parliament, in responses to questions raised in the House of Commons, that Section 55 would be applied to stem abuses of the system and not indiscriminately as feared by the NGO.[12] However, as experienced by NGOs and asylum-seekers and noted by observers, its application was indiscriminate

---

[8] M Taylor, 'Asylum policies 'make 10,000 people destitute a year' ' *Guardian* (09 Feb 2004)
[9] *R (on the application of Q and Others) v Secretary of State for the Home Department* [2003] 2 All ER 905 (Admin); *R (on the application of S, D, T) v Secretary of State for the Home Department* [2003] EWCH 1941 (Admin)
[10] Inter-Agency Partnership, *The impact of section 55 on the Inter-Agency Partnership of leading UK refugee agencies and the asylum seekers it supports* (2004)
[11] See Chapter 4 for a review of the events preceding the implementation of Section 55
[12] Hansard HC Column 235WH (04 March 2003) (referring to initial debate on Section 55):www.publications.parliament.uk/pa/cm200203/cmhansrd/vo030304/halltext/30304h04.htm accessed 11 July 2006

and deliberate. This was acknowledged five years later, in 2007, when the JCHR examined the events concerning Section 55 and concluded that 'forced destitution' was deliberate.[13] Many experienced NGO staff believed that direction (to refuse support) 'came from above'.[14] Frances Webber, a long-time critic, is adamant that officers were following direct orders from the Home Office to refuse all unmarried in-country applicants (which constitute the vast majority of asylum-seekers).[15] For a western-liberal democracy to impose a regime where Article 3 is breached (or is about to be breached) alarmed the NGOs and they questioned Labour's commitment to human rights in general and the HRA in particular. The crisis also brought to the fore questions about the treatment of a vulnerable minority and disregard of international obligations in a quest to be tough on those powerless to fight back and in need of protection.[16]

However, what remains most notable about that the campaign, particularly during the early months when the first test-case challenge was decided by the courts (*Q and Others*), was not that it caused controversy (because of a breach of an absolute right and the court's finding that the treatment of asylum-seekers was inhumane) but because of the anger expressed by the then-Home Secretary, David Blunkett, towards the courts for defeat of his policies.[17] Instead of celebrating what the *Guardian* called a 'victory for humanity' the decision became a major news event because of the vitriolic unleashed by the tabloids on the HRA and the courts for upholding Convention rights.[18] Justice Collins, who first ruled against Section 55, was 'out-ed' by the tabloid media as a 'serial offender' and subjected to vituperative attacks.[19] The conduct by both the Home Office and segments of the media 'ignited a war' and lowered to new depths the tone of debate on the HRA and, with constant talk of opting-out, seemingly ended the government's commitment to

---

[13]   BBC, 'Asylum hardships 'are deliberate'' (2007) BBC News <http://news.bbc.co.uk/1/hi/uk_politics/6507961.stm> (29 Jun); Joint Committee On Human Rights, *The Treatment of Asylum-Seekers* (HL 81-1 2007)

[14]   Interview with Claire Sephton, Managing Solicitor, Shelter (London 13 June 2005)

[15]   F Webber, 'NASS: Chronicle of Failure' (2003) Institute of Race Relations <http://www.irr.org.uk/2003/july/ak000010.html> ; also personal email communication (April 2005)

[16]   S Chakrabarti, 'So much freedom lost and on my watch' *Daily Telegraph* (20 May 2007)

[17]   R Sylvester, 'Blunkett accuses judges of damaging democracy' *Daily Telegraph* (21 Feb 2003)

[18]   Article 19, *What's the Story: Results from Research into Media Coverage of Refugees and Asylum-Seekers in the UK* (2003)

[19]   See Chapter 6 for a fuller discussion on the decision and media attacks on the HRA.

the Act – at least, insofar as asylum was concerned.[20] There were also accusations that confidential information about Justice Collins had been 'leaked' to the media by officials in Whitehall.[21] How far this set back the attempts to develop a culture of rights is difficult to assess but an indirect measure is provided by the reluctance of many NGOs, during that time, to give prominence to the HRA (or to the language of rights) because of its unpopularity and the vehemence it attracted from the tabloids.[22] A more direct measure is provided by the findings of this study that shows the development of a culture of rights, in the asylum sector, has stagnated as a result of the government's 'get tough' approach.[23]

5.2.3   The Crisis of Section 55

Soon after the coming-into-effect of Section 55 the NGOs reported an almost immediate increase in their casework of homeless and destitute asylum-seekers:

> We're already seeing hundreds of people denied shelter and
> food, and facing a desperate situation in the middle of winter . . .
> this is an appalling way to treat people – and it's a shameful way
> for the Government to act. It's creating a terrible injustice for the
> sake of looking tough . . . [24]

Irrespective of the reasonableness of its announced objectives Section 55, for most intents and purposes, constituted an attack on asylum rights and asylum-seekers. And the worst fears and predictions of the NGOs were realised. In the hands of the Home Office Section 55 became a tool which targeted almost all in-country asylum-seekers. This was done by an unyieldingly strict interpretation of the legislation, in particular what constituted 'as soon as reasonably practicable', the period within which asylum-seekers are required to file asylum claims. Rather than

---

[20]   S Chakrabarti (2005) 'Rights and Rhetoric: The Politics of Asylum and Human Rights Culture in the UK' 32 Journal of Law and Society 131; A Lester, 'My Misery as a Tethered Goat in Gordon Brown's Big Tent' *Guardian* (27 July 2009) www.guardian.co.uk/ commentisfree/2009/jul/27/constitutional-reform-illiberal-reactionary-labour

[21]   A Bradley, 'Judicial Independence Under Attack' (2003) Public Law 397

[22]   See Chapter 6

[23]   See Chapters 1 and 9

[24]   Liberty, 'Asylum Benefits: Liberty wins emergency injunction' (2003) 17 Jan <www.liberty-human-rights.org.uk/news-and-events/1-press-releases/2003/asylum-benefits-liberty-wins-emergency-injun.shtml>

focus on obvious abusers and long-stay (illegal) residents, as had been the intent of the legislation and as the Home Secretary had repeatedly assured the public and MPs, officers at NASS began systematically rejecting almost all in-country applications:

> They (NASS) were rejecting those who had made claims within 24 hours; we even had cases where applications were refused for a delay of a few hours . . . the NASS told us that there were signs at airports telling asylum-seekers how to claim asylum; some of our staff went to the airports and looked and saw very few such signs. And ones we did see were difficult to find – and we were looking for them. Can you imagine how difficult it is for new asylum-seekers?[25]

The Home Office, prior to implementation of Section 55, had estimated that on average at least 100 asylum-seekers per week would be refused. But the rate of refusal in the first few months was higher than had been predicted;[26] the Home Office put the figure at 200 per week.[27] According to the Refugee Council the refusal rate was between 70-80%, with Refugee Action suggesting in excess of 90% rejection.[28] An average of over 200 asylum-seekers per week was being added to the ranks of the destitute and homeless.[29] Research conducted later by the Inter-Agency Partnership, a consortium of NGOs, estimated the refusal rate at 70% for all of 2003.[30] That the rate should have been so high for the entire duration of 2003 in spite of the various court decisions against Section 55, the efforts of the NGOs, and the Home Secretary's directive to NASS that applications made within 24 hours was to be considered to have been made 'as soon as reasonably practicable', suggests obstinacy on part of the Home Office. The NGOs considered this to be a direct result of a 'culture of disbelief' and

---

[25]   Interview with Uma Joshi, Legal Officer, Shelter (London 25 May 2005); as part of my field work I also visited Heathrow, Stansted, and Gatwick, all major port-of-entry airports, but could find no such signs in the arrivals area; even after searching the likely places where such signs would be posted, I saw none.

[26]   National Coalition of Anti-Deportation Campaigns, 'Beware the 8th January 2003' (2003) <http://www.ncadc.org.uk/archives/filed%20newszines/oldnewszines/news28/8thjan.html>

[27]   Inter-Agency Partnership *The impact of section 55 on the Inter-Agency Partnership of leading UK refugee agencies and the asylum seekers it supports* (2004)

[28]   Shelter, *Briefing: Section 55 of the Nationality, Immigration and Asylum Act 2002. Independent Review* (2004)

[29]   Refugee Council, *Hungry and Homeless: The Impact of the Withdrawal of State Support on Asylum Seekers, Refugee Communities and the Voluntary Sector* (2004) 1-381

[30]   Inter-Agency Partnership *The impact of section 55 on the Inter-Agency Partnership of leading UK refugee agencies and the asylum seekers it supports* (2004) 7

the dehumanisation of asylum-seekers who continued to suffer destitution. One of the key problems, according to the NGOs, was that many officers ignored the Home Office directive; NASS officers continued to maintain that most of the claims had not been made within 24 hours, hence rejection of 70% of Section 55 applications:[31]

> Yes . . . we knew what the courts said (how to assess Section 55 applications). But it doesn't really make much difference. It doesn't change the fact that the application is fraudulent. A lie is a lie no matter what test a Court sets out . . .[32]

The true humanitarian cost and actual numbers of destitute asylum-seekers is difficult, if not impossible, to measure:

> Many (asylum-seekers) sleep outside our offices, in doorways, in the gardens of local churches and sometimes in telephone boxes (the only place where they are able to keep dry). They do not have enough blankets and clothing to keep them warm. They are often lonely, frightened and feel humiliated and distressed . . . staff have seen the condition of asylum-seekers visibly deteriorating after periods of rough sleeping . . . (some) have become depressed and threatened suicide – we see people in this situation on a daily basis.[33]

To the NGOs the approach by NASS almost defied belief. So convinced was the NASS in the rightness of its approach and decision-making that caseworkers simply gave up trying to negotiate with them (providing that they were able contact them in the first place). Some of the NGO caseworkers assisting claimants with their applications quickly realised the futility of their task.[34] It seemed that whatever explanations were offered for late claims many continued to be rejected. Many of the decisions were of the cut-and-paste variety; decisions also seemed overly concerned

---

[31]   ibid

[32]   Interview with anonymous immigration officer at Heathrow Airport (London, December 2005; on file with author); the officer had worked at NASS in 2004.

[33]   H Tristram, Team Leader, Refugee Council (cited in: *R (on application of Adam, Tesema, and Limbuela) v Secretary of State for the Home Department* [2004] EWCA Civ 540, para 92

[34]   Interview with Jonathan Knight, Caseworker, Joint Council for the Welfare of Immigrants (London March 2005)

with assessing the credibility of claimants and focused on substantive issues (pertaining to the merits of the asylum-claim) rather than whether the application had been made 'as soon as reasonably practicable'. Applications for NASS are supposed to be approved if claimants can provide a credible explanation for the delay in filing asylum claims, but even standard reasons (well established in case law and listed in the UN Handbook) such as 'fear of authorities' did not sway NASS officials from rejecting hundreds of applications.[35] Not that it would have likely made much difference because credibility was being assessed by staff far-removed from the process (based on an assessment of written notes by the interviewing officer). Exacerbating the situation was that applicants, facing potentially life-threatening decisions, were not given an opportunity to provide explanations (for the late applications).[36] Many other examples, of what the NGOs termed obstinacy, ineptness, and mismanagement at the Home Office, were documented including sending asylum-seekers to various offices and then re-directing them to another office and then using such delays as reasons for rejecting applications, and then refusing to admit or rectify such errors.[37]

The NGOs were hit hard by Section 55 and its impact was almost immediate. What began as a trickle of homeless and destitute asylum-seekers soon became a flood.[38] The under-resourced and financially strapped NGOs were quickly overwhelmed, unable to cope with such demands on their services:

> They (asylum-seekers) had nowhere to go. They were actually sleeping in our office; on the floor, outside the doors. It was a desperate situation. A lot of our staff would give them money from their own pockets. . .[39]

> There were people sleeping on the pavement outside our offices in Brixton in the middle of winter.[40]

Even though the NGOs had predicted the fallout from Section 55 there was little they could have done to prepare for its impact. There were two primary reasons for

---

[35]   Refugee Council, *Hungry and Homeless* (2004)

[36]   These factors were commented upon by Justice Andrew Collins when he ruled in favour of the applicants in the first test-case challenge in *Q and Others*.

[37]   M Pickett, 'On the asylum frontline ' *Guardian* (02 Feb 2003); Parliamentary and Health Service Ombudsman, *Incorrect Refusal of Application for Asylum: 6th Report of Session 2001-2002* (2002)

[38]   Interview notes (on file with author); also: *The impact of section 55 on the Inter-Agency Partnership of leading UK refugee agencies and the asylum seekers it supports*

[39]   Interview with Claire Sephton, Solicitor, Shelter (London 13 June 2005) (on file with author)

[40]   M Sherlock, 'Asylum seeker destitution' (Church Action on Poverty 2005)

this: insufficient time (the legislation was introduced as a last-minute amendment to a Bill already before the House) and a marked lack of resources. Nonetheless they made concerted efforts to meet the needs of their clients, while at the same time campaigning for a repeal of the legislation. During the early days of Section 55 the various NGOs sought to get in touch with their contacts at the Home Office but most of the calls went unanswered, messages unreturned. The telephone calls were followed by a flurry of letters, pleading and urging a response. But their pleas fell on deaf ears. No one at the Home Office responded:

> We tried everything; we called; we wrote; tried to negotiate. Nothing happened. It soon became very clear that the Home Office wasn't paying any heed to us, didn't care, and was waiting us out.[41]

> It became quite clear that the Home Office had instructions (from higher up) not to provide support; clearly it was a major operation because the amount of money it must have cost (legal costs, court costs, etc.) them to hold firm . . . it got to the stage that they actually said to us 'don't even bother' (contacting us).[42]

Amid the crisis there was nothing but indifference from the Home Office even as stories began to circulate of homeless and hungry asylum-seekers sleeping rough, camping at various churches, huddled in the doorways of various NGO offices – all this in the middle of an unseasonably cold winter.[43] When the unambiguous question of 'sleeping rough' was raised in the House of Commons the government refused to acknowledge that such was the case notwithstanding the evidence presented by the NGOs. The government's response was seen by many as evasive as evidenced, for example, by the following exchange in Parliament (question by Lord Hyton and response by the Parliamentary Under-Secretary of State, Lord Filkin):

> Whether they have received evidence that the new Rules under the Nationality, Immigration and Asylum Act 2002 are leading some new arrivals into rough sleeping and destitution, although they had claimed asylum as quickly as practically possible; and what remedial measures they have in mind.

---

41   Interview with Uma Joshi, Solicitor, Shelter (London 25 May 2005)
42   Interview with Claire Sephton, Solicitor, Shelter (London 13 June 2005)
43   Mayor of London, 'Destitution by Design' (2004)

> We have not received any such evidence in respect of asylum
> seekers who have been judged by the Home Office to have
> made their asylum claim as soon as reasonably practicable. The
> operation of Section 55 is being kept under review.[44]

Notwithstanding the absence of official acknowledgement the impact on the asylum-seekers was severe. Asylum-seekers left without shelter and food spoke of humiliation, of begging in the streets, sleeping in bus shelters and alleyways, and being physically and racially abused:

> I feel really depressed, unhappy and hopeless. I smell filthy and
> cannot walk amongst other people. I feel less than human – like an
> animal. I hate myself. I left my country to escape imprisonment,
> suffering and death. Here I fear hunger and homelessness.[45]

5.2.4   Conclusion

It is difficult to conceive of the Home Office being unaware that such was the impact of its policies. The fact it did not respond cannot but be viewed as demonstrative of a disregard for a vulnerable minority and a focus on policy objectives irrespective of the human cost. No doubt, differences of opinion will often exist as to whether government policies are compatible with the HRA. And the Home Office is entitled to take the view that legitimate policies are exactly that and that differences of opinion should be adjudicated by the courts. But this is also a disingenuous approach because it sidesteps the vexed matter of a gulf which often exists between questions of law and questions of fact, and of inherent delays in the court system, which all acts to exacerbate matters on the ground. While the Home Office was fighting in the courts about whether its policies constituted 'treatment' within the ambit of Article 3, hundreds of asylum-seekers were suffering destitution.

The NGOs were not blind to the contradictions they were witnessing. A culture of rights was not supposed to be just about legal rights. Labour's White Paper had

---

[44]   Hansard HC vol 643 (28 January 2003) www.parliament.the-stationery-office.com/pa/ld200203/ldhansrd/vo030128/text/30128w01.htm#30128w01_sbhd9 accessed 31 August 2006

[45]   M Sherlock, 'Asylum seeker destitution' (2005) (citing an anonymous asylum-seeker from the Sudan)

promised it would be much more.[46] To the NGOs the Home Office approach and what they viewed as hypocrisies raised deeper questions about the government's commitment to the HRA and to bringing about a cultural change. One interviewee commented: 'they (Home Office) are going about the same as before; they don't care about the rights of asylum-seekers'.[47] A similar view was taken by Shami Chakrabharti, Director of Liberty, who criticised the government for 'disowning' the very Act that it passed into law.[48] It is arguable that such an approach also demarcates an apparent point of departure of the government view of what constitutes a 'culture of rights' from that of NGOs, particularly NGOs such as the British Institute of Human Rights working to promote a broader vision of rights. The message which emerged during the campaign suggested a vision of a 'culture of rights' which the NGOs found troubling – where rights exist for some but not for others, as if rights are earned (for example, by virtue of citizenship) rather than something inherent to all humans.[49] The message to asylum-seekers could not have been clearer: do not come to the UK.[50] The message to the NGOs was even clearer: nothing you do is going to stop us (Home Office) from implementing our policy:

> In terms of immigration control and policy, the government
> have been very very clear: 'we are not going to let human rights
> interfere with our objectives'.[51]

5.3   Part II: The Campaign

5.3.1   Challenges, Media Coverage, and Activities

It would be inaccurate to describe the fight against Section 55 as a well-coordinated and orchestrated campaign. It was not. Much of what happened did so by chance. Much was organisationally chaotic, but much happened owing to the determination

---

[46]   Home Office, *Rights Brought Home: the Human Rights Bill* (1997)

[47]   Interview with Marilyn, volunteer, Asylum Welcome (Oxford June 2005)

[48]   S Chakrabarti (2005) 'Rights and Rhetoric: The Politics of Asylum and Human Rights Culture in the UK'

[49]   This view of rights granted by nationality, considered by many to be outdated, has been rejected by courts in Canada and the US; see also: N Blake, 'Why is there no song and dance about this Act?' *Times* (25 Apr 2006) about future legislative plans for citizenship and revocation of status if granted citizenship.

[50]   Interview with Don Flynn, Policy Director, Joint Council for the Welfare of Immigrants (London 14 March 2005)

[51]   Interview with Tauhid Pasha, Legal Director, JCWI (London 16 March 2005)

of a group NGOs who united to fight against what they called 'forced destitution'.[52] Even though they had predicted the impact – to be sure, worst-case scenarios – which would follow upon implementation of Section 55, they were nonetheless surprised at how quickly the impact was felt and the ensuing pressure brought to bear upon their services:

> We were surprised by the influx; the cases came about so
> quickly. It wasn't until much later that we got our act together.[53]

> What we were seeing (destitute asylum-seekers) was just a drop
> in the ocean.[54]

As the humanitarian crisis unfolded, the NGOs were inundated with additional demands by a rapidly increasing work-load. In addition to serving regular clients and performing daily tasks, such as counselling individual asylum-seekers or operating help-lines, the NGOs had to contend with increasing numbers of destitute and homeless asylum-seekers. This stretched, almost to the breaking point, the capability of the NGOs unaccustomed to providing social services. The situation was not helped by a March 2003 Court of Appeal decision (in the first test-case challenge) which accepted the Home Office argument that provision of support by 'charitable bodies or individuals' must be factored when deciding on the likelihood of a breach of convention rights brought about by a lack of support.[55] The NGOs protested that, first, they had no resources to provide the extent of services required; and second, they should not be asked to shoulder responsibilities normally undertaken by government departments or third-party contractors.[56] The government's argument in court, and efforts to offload its responsibilities on organisations unable to afford it, was an irony not lost on the campaigning NGOs who had argued that they had little or no resources to support destitute asylum-seekers. Thus the first test-case challenge, while a victory in some respects for the NGOs, was not the unequivocal victory the campaigners had hoped for.[57]

---

52   Refugee Action, *The Destitution Trap* (2006)
53   Interview with Uma Joshi, Solicitor, Shelter (London May 2005)
54   Interview with Tauhid Pasha, Solicitor, JCWI (London May 2005)
55   *R (on the application of Q and Others) v Secretary of State for the Home Department* [2003] EWCA Civ 364, (CA), para 63
56   F Webber (2004) 'Asylum: From Deterrence to Destitution' 45 Race and Class 77, 82
57   Interview with Tauhid Pasha, Solicitor, JCWI (London May 2005)

5.3.2 Challenges Faced by NGOs

During the crisis brought about by Section 55 some of the NGOs also had to contend with the morale of its under-pressure workforce. While morale issues are not an unusual problem in organisations they presented additional difficulties in a sector constantly struggling with resources. There are no formal records but anecdotal evidence suggested increased attrition in the staff ranks of some NGOs. Several interviewees spoke of the apparent increase in the use of 'sick leave' provisions and of colleagues resigning out of frustration or inability to manage stresses of the work environment.[58] It is worth noting that NGOs, in general, are not known for generous remuneration benefits; many of the NGO offices visited during fieldwork were threadbare and under-resourced operations. The distinguishing feature being that of a workforce generally committed to serving their constituency.[59] Another key feature – and this explains, to some extent, the degree of disorganisation and initial lack of coordination which characterised the campaign – was an absence of professional management in ranks of the NGOs. During the fieldwork, and in interviews with experienced campaigners, it also became apparent that there too many NGOs, mostly small operations, competing for an increasingly smaller funding pie. And while they may share objectives it cannot be said that there is consensus on how best to address issues of mutual interest.

The challenges faced by the NGOs during the early months of Section 55 were many. A key challenge was presented by the inefficiency at the Home Office, the department responsible for asylum, and considered 'the worst performing department in government' failing in almost all key assessment areas in a recent internal review.[60] The Home Office, a massive bureaucracy described as 'not fit for the purpose' by the Minister-in-charge, is a department rife with turmoil owing to unreasonable demands by its political masters, demoralised, poorly-trained and incompetent staff, and rudderless management.[61] It is also a department under

---

[58]   Interview notes (on file with author)
[59]   While this specific area – of employee commitment – was beyond the scope of the research, it is worth noting that there is an element of mythologizing in this respect. Many of the support staff I encountered did not seem particularly motivated and expressed dissatisfaction with their work. The caseworkers and frontline staff, however, in general seemed genuinely interested in the welfare of their clients and committed to their work seeing it as 'making a difference'.
[60]   Civil Service, *Capability Review of the Home Office* (2006); 'Home Office chiefs lose their jobs' *Daily Mail* (19 July 2006)
[61]   P Johnston, 'Reid Blasts Failures at Home Office' *Daily Telegraph* (24 May 2006) 2

investigation for allegations of racism, corruption, and sex-for-visas scandals.[62] An NGO campaigner, with considerable experience in dealing with the Home Office, blames successive governments for failing to 'tackle the rot' claiming the department has grown too large and unwieldy to be effective.[63]

Another challenge was presented by a shortage of resources. Nonetheless the NGOs worked hard to help hundreds of destitute asylum-seekers while at the same time campaigning against the policy. Prior to the formation of the Coalition Against the Destitution of Asylum-Seekers (CADAS) in December 2003, with its specific mandate to fight Section 55, the various NGOs, more or less, battled on their own or in informal 'partnership' with others in attending to the immediate needs of their clients. This is not to say that there was no coordination of activities but, at this early stage, there was an urgent need to look after asylum-seekers left without shelter and food in the middle of winter. It should be noted that prior to the creation of CADAS there were already in place long-standing relationships between various NGOs, formal and informal networks, and existing coalitions such as the Asylum Rights Campaign (ARC), Inter-Agency Partnership (IAP), and the Immigration Law Practitioners Association (ILPA). These coalitions, however, were not oriented towards campaigning and were mainly for sharing of information amongst other like-minded NGOs; further they were not geared towards providing essential services, which is what was needed most at that time by asylum-seekers refused support under Section 55. The use of the term 'coalition' is somewhat misleading in that it is suggestive of structure and organisation, something not readily apparent in this instance. The coalitions, such as they were, usually comprised of a single, and not always the same, representative from member NGOs whose task is to return to their home organisation and communicate the details of the meetings to other staff. At some of the meetings, the feeling of frustration was notable. There was a great deal of discussion but it was also apparent that there was very little follow-up. At best, there was vague talk about follow-up on matters under discussion. One clearly frustrated member voiced her feelings: 'we speak, but action is less; we have to move on this'.[64]

---

62   M Townsend and J Doward, 'Cash for asylum scandal hits Reid' *Guardian* (04 June 2006); B Leapman and M Kite, 'Hundreds of corruption inquiries at Immigration' *Daily Telegraph* (27 July 2006); R Verkaik, 'Investigation into claims of abuse on asylum-seekers' *The Independent* (30 Sept 2008)

63   Interview notes with anonymous source (on file with author)

64   On file with author (observation notes)

From the time that Section 55 came into effect in January 2003 to when CADAS was formed, the various NGOs had their hands full in trying to meet the needs of their clients, a rapidly increasing number of destitute asylum-seekers. This was no easy undertaking as the NGOs were in no position to fill the immense need for services such as housing, food, and funds that the arriving asylum-seekers required. And these needs arose suddenly and seemingly at once. There was no gradual build-up such as would generally occur in a normal course of identifying social services need. But what is remarkable is the degree to which the NGOs were able to manage, particularly, with the help of faith groups and refugee community organizations (RCOs), in meeting such needs. While generally adept and experienced in campaigning and lobbying the NGOs had few staff, little experience, and few resources to provide housing and food. Such services were beyond their capacity and if not for the various faith groups, community organizations, and benevolent individuals the impact upon asylum-seekers would have been potentially worse. But the true extent of the impact on asylum-seekers may never be known. The NGOs are first to admit that, in spite of their best efforts, many asylum-seekers (rejected under Section 55) could not be helped and disappeared from official records or became part of the black-market economy.[65]

5.3.3 Campaign Activities

At the commencement of the campaign against Section 55 the NGOs directed their initial efforts at stopping the clause from becoming law. When that failed they campaigned for its outright repeal. And when that failed, the NGOs sought to have it amended and suggested various alternatives which retained the core of the legislation but sought to ensure protection for asylum-seekers.[66] The suggested amendments were minor and did not substantially change the original draft. Shelter, for example, suggested a right of appeal (to an immigration tribunal) for refused applications. The NGOs also used whatever leverage they had, mainly via sympathetic MPs or MPs in seats considered vulnerable to 'swing' votes, to raise questions in Parliament. At that time the Asylum Rights Campaign, for

---

[65]   Mayor of London, 'Destitution by Design' (2004)

[66]   The efforts to repeal/amend continued even after Section 55 became law. Coming less than a year after Section 55, the Home Office announced yet another legislative change, which became the Asylum and Immigration (Treatment of Claimants, etc) Act 2004. It was during the passage of this most recent legislative reform that the NGOs sought to repeal Section 55.

example, had a list of 'sympathetic' MPs numbering about 60, with an additional 20 considered amenable to lobbying – this out of over 600 MPs in the House of Commons.[67] With such few apparent supporters amongst MPs in the House the NGOs knew that lobbying would not be effective. The House of Lords, on the other hand, has generally been more accessible and accommodating to NGOs: 'the Lords is where our big chance is'.[68] While this may seem a politically astute move by the NGOs, it is one necessitated by pragmatism and not because the Lords are a particularly effective option or sympathetic to their concerns. While the Lords may delay passage of Bills, its powers are severely curtailed by various Acts of Parliament and the inevitable generally does come to pass. Nonetheless, political gamesmanship publicises the issue and raises its profile and increases media coverage, which considerably aids the work of NGOs.[69]

As part of their campaign the NGOs also issued press releases and joint statements urging the government to reconsider its plans. For the NGOs, access to media, or least getting press releases into print, is not an easy task although certain NGOs (such as Liberty or the Refugee Council) are expected to comment on asylum and/or their comments are sought by the media.[70] During the campaign, several press releases, in truncated form or certain quotes (no more than a few lines), did appear in newspapers but, in general, coverage of the NGO campaign was sparse.[71] The broadsheets, particularly those on the left of the political spectrum such as the *Guardian* and *Independent*, devoted considerable space to covering not just the issue of destitution, but of asylum in general. These sources continue to offer extensive coverage of the issue, both in print and their respective websites. The *Guardian/Observer* and BBC have specific pages/links devoted entirely to the subject, and include commentary from established NGOs.[72] But such media coverage was the exception. An extensive review of press coverage during the campaign shows little sustained or regular media attention.

---

[67] On file with author (in 2006, there were 646 seats in the House of Commons)

[68] Interview with Imran Hussain, Parliamentary Officer, Refugee Council (London 12 May 2005)

[69] Ibid; (The House of Lords comprises 741 seats, of which 210 are Labour (the current government); see: www.parliament.uk/directories/house_of_lords_information_office/ analysis_by_composition.cfm accessed 25 September 2006).

[70] Interview with R Benyon, Communications Officer, JCWI (London 15 May 2005); interview with H Rahman, Chairperson, JCWI (London 13 August 2005)

[71] The press releases also featured prominently on various asylum and race-related websites.

[72] See, for example, the Guardian/Observer and BBC webpage: <observer.guardian.co.uk/ asylum/0,,536799,00.html> accessed 25 September 2006 <news.bbc.co.uk/1/hi/in_depth/ uk/2001/destination_uk/default.stm> accessed 25 September 2006

From experience the NGOs are aware that complaining 'something is wrong or unjust' is often ineffective. To support the campaign they conducted or commissioned independent research and published the results.[73] Reports by the Refugee Council (in partnership with Oxfam), the Inter-Agency Partnership, and the Mayor of London were all widely disseminated and quoted in the broadsheets. The NGOs also lobbied individual MPs, MPs serving the 'black minority ethnic' (BME) constituencies, BME MPs, organised rallies, staged a 'soup kitchen' outside the Home Office, and 'sleep-in' protests in various locations across the UK focusing on areas with large asylum-seeker populations. But with a government determined to 'get tough' the NGO campaign, at this stage (prior to Section 55 coming into effect), was not successful insofar as repeal/amendment of the legislation was concerned. Nor could it be considered a success in terms of sustained media coverage and publicity. However the objective behind the campaign was never so single-minded because many in the NGO community knew that the fight would be long and drawn-out.[74]

The combined efforts of the NGOs kept the issue of Section 55 and destitution 'live' and at the forefront of the political agenda. While all these activities may not have succeeded in achieving their central objective, they did have the important effect of galvanising and uniting the NGO community, faith groups, and other like-minded organisations. Several interviewees recalled the campaign and how 'fired-up' they were in their determination to fight Section 55.[75] The various activities, some well attended and some not, were not only aimed at the NGO community but also were meant to create awareness amongst the general public in the hopes of eliciting sympathy/support for the situation of destitute asylum-seekers. In this latter objective, not many were hopeful given the overwhelming opposition and apathy of the general public towards asylum-seekers.[76] Asylum is a highly contested arena where the NGOs have to battle an almost constant barrage of negative tabloid coverage. In this respect, the NGOS employed a 'targeted' approach and turned to their long-time allies, the various churches and faith groups, which in turn addressed their respective congregations on the moral question of the suffering brought about by Section 55. By appealing to the 'immorality' and

---

73   Interview with Habib Rahman, Chairperson, JCWI (London June 2005)
74   Interview notes (on file with author)
75   Interview notes (on file with author)
76   See Chapter 3 for a discussion on public attitudes towards asylum-seekers.

'suffering' (and putting aside any talk of rights) the NGOs succeeded in bringing an important and powerful organisation, the Church of England, on side. For some campaigners the support of the Church of England was crucial, more so than other faith groups, because its constituency represents mainstream England; that is white and Christian and a powerful voting sector.[77] It is the only faith group with seats in the House of Lords; the Lords Spiritual (Bishops and Archbishops) hold 26 seats.[78] The support of the Church of England was crucial to showing the government, and the public at large, that the issue crossed 'colour' and cultural boundaries and that something 'greater' was at stake – about how fellow humans should be treated irrespective of rights, immigration status, or nationality.[79] This is not to say that support of other faith groups were not valued; temples and mosques are important allies which have traditionally supported the marginalised and were involved in providing assistance and food and shelter to destitute asylum-seekers; its members also marched in support of asylum-seekers. But the so-called 'ethnic' faith groups are generally presumed to have other pressing issues unique to their constituency, such as racism and immigration reform, and are not as powerful or influential as the Church of England.[80] The Church's communiqués on asylum – and its abhorrence at Section 55 – made the front pages or were given prominent coverage in many of the major newspapers and websites.[81]

During the campaign senior NGO policy and legal staff criss-crossed the country, travelling to areas with large asylum-seeker populations; they attended meetings, held information sessions, and organised rallies and other protest activities. According to Pasha, one of the major galvanising factors was the impact of Section 55 as experienced by volunteers and NGO staff who were 'appalled and flabbergasted at what they were seeing' and dealing with on a first-hand basis.[82] And based primarily on such feedback the campaign strategy focused on the impact (as measured by the increasing number of destitute asylum-seekers and their plight) of Section 55. Many felt that there was ample evidence with which to highlight the 'inhumane' treatment and suffering and much support would be gained. In this

---

[77] Interview notes (on file with author)

[78] http://news.bbc.co.uk/2/hi/uk_news/politics/82539.stm

[79] Interview notes (on file with author)

[80] Interview with Tauhid Pasha, Solicitor, JCWI (London March 2005)

[81] A Delmar-Morgan, 'Church of England damns Labour on asylum and poverty' *The Times* (14 May 2006)

[82] Interview notes (on file with author)

respect the strategy did succeed in garnering the support of various churches and faith groups.

But during the campaign (from Oct 2002 to November 2005) there also were divisions within the NGO community with some, such as Legal Action for Women, taking a more radicalised stance. Legal Action accused other NGOs, in particular the Refugee Council, of 'being part of the problem'. But so polemic was the position of Legal Action that not many accorded it much credit. It is likely that such a stance (for example, comparing Home Office actions to that of Nazism) served more to alienate than to unite.[83] Legal Action also mounted a protest rally outside the Refugee Council office in Brixton accusing the Council of a 'lack of independence' and colluding with the government.[84] However this is a minority view and not one held by many in the NGO community. There is little evidence to suggest that the Refugee Council is anything but a credible voice for refugees and asylum-seekers.[85]

5.3.4   The *Human Rights Act* and the Campaign Against Section 55

> The *Human Rights Act* was really really useful (against Section 55).[86]

Initially the HRA did not feature in any prominent way in NGO campaigning and lobbying efforts against Section 55. At best it featured peripherally, cementing the findings of this study, and of a previous survey, of the Act perceived as something solely for lawyers and courtrooms and not as a (potential) resource in the wider campaign for social justice and change.[87] In this respect, rights continue to be seen

---

[83]   For example, the following is an excerpt from the Legal Action for Women website: An angry and determined group of 40 women – destitute asylum seekers and anti-racist supporters – who gathered outside the court immediately denounced the verdict as opening the way to mass pauperism in Britain. All were shocked but not surprised that the Home Office should insist on its right to make people destitute in a way that is reminiscent of Nazism, and outraged by the judges who colluded with it. www.allwomencount.net/EWC%20LAW/protests_against_section_55_cont.htm accessed 11 August 2006

[84]   The Refugee Council does provide third-party services (contracted by the Home Office) but there is no evidence to suggest that it colludes with the government or that its campaigning is affected (by fear of losing government contracts).

[85]   Interview notes (on file with author)

[86]   Interview with Claire Sephton, Solicitor, Shelter (London May 2005)

[87]   British Institute of Human Rights, *Something for Everyone: The Impact of the Human Rights Act on Disadvantaged Groups* (2002)

mostly as a matter befitting a legal approach, a reflection of a persistently narrow view of rights held by many in the NGO community.

As the campaign against Section 55 progressed it became quickly apparent that the government would not change its position. This was no surprise to experienced NGO staff; while still campaigning and hoping for repeal, they knew that legal action presented one of the few viable options with which to challenge the policy. And that proved to be the case. It was when Section 55 was challenged in the courts that the HRA achieved prominence and was pivotal in the eventual defeat of the policy. It was also the deciding factor that helped overturn many Section 55 refusals under the NASS reconsideration option.[88] This was of crucial importance on the ground because hundreds, if not thousands, of asylum-seekers were provided with shelter and benefits.

The campaign also brought scrutiny to the government's wider policy objectives on asylum, highlighting its inequities and the human cost. But none of this was achieved without cost, particularly to the HRA itself, as successful test-cases unleashed a spate of vitriolic media coverage. So aggressive and vitriolic was the coverage that both the UN and European Commission against Racism and Intolerance (ECRI) felt compelled to comment, criticising the media for xenophobic and racist reporting.[89] The attack on the HRA and the judiciary (mostly by the tabloid media) was unrelenting and most certainly not the kind of publicity the NGOs had hoped for or wanted.[90] The HRA was portrayed as damaging democracy and subverting the will of the people by stopping the government in the exercise of a legitimate public policy. There were sustained calls for the repeal of the HRA and the government promised legislation to rein in judges, to limit their role in interpreting the Act, in order to re-assert parliamentary democracy.[91] More damaging was the tabloid portrayal of the HRA as working against the interest of Britain and helping 'the other' or 'outsiders' to take advantage of 'Britain's

---

[88]   Mayor of London, 'Destitution by Design' (2004) 20

[89]   UNHCR, 'UN Refugee agency has grave concerns over tabloid reporting of asylum' (2003) <http://www.unhcr.org.uk/press/press_releases2003/pr23Oct03.htm> ; Council of Europe: European Commission Against Racism and Intolerance (ECRI), *Third Report on the United Kingdom* (CRI 27 2005)

[90]   BBC, 'Media linked to asylum violence ' (2004) BBC News <http://news.bbc.co.uk/1/hi/uk/3890963.stm> (09 October 2006)

[91]   P Johnston and G Jones, 'Blair to take on judges over asylum' *Daily Telegraph* (20 Feb 2003) 1

generosity'.[92] The concern that the HRA should be seen or portrayed as something for the other, for 'brown' or 'black' people and not the greater good, continues to be of significant concern, something which the NGOs are working hard to guard against:

> It (HRA) has widened our scope, certainly given us more options
> . . . but, and I think this is crucial; we are losing the argument
> if the general public perceive the Act to be something just for
> unpopular minorities.[93]

5.3.5   The Campaign: October 2002 to January 2003

From October 07, 2002 to early January 2003 (the time of the amendment introducing Section 55 to its coming into effect) the NGOs were primarily focused on repealing the clause. At this early stage, there was some hope that the government would listen to reasoned arguments (against the clause) and repeal it. That hope, however, was not shared by the more experienced campaigners who had noted the machinations at how Section 55 had become law. The campaign, such as it was at this time, focused largely on the 'unworkability' of the clause and its likely impact on asylum-seekers. The NGOs reminded the government of the crisis and collapse of a similar regime which had been introduced by the then Conservative government in 1996 and urged them not to repeat past mistakes. The NGOs also campaigned on compassionate and humanitarian issues, predicting that there would be homelessness and destitution on a grand scale and that it would be morally wrong for an affluent society to treat the less fortunate in such a manner. They also focused their attention on sympathetic Labour MPs and targeted seats with large black and ethnic minority (BEM) constituencies. Labour MP Neil Gerrard, a strong supporter of asylum rights, introduced an Early Day Motion (EDM) in Parliament calling for a repeal of Section 55, but was defeated.

As the campaign progressed it became increasingly clear that the government remained determined to push ahead. At this still early stage not many of the campaigners were thinking of the HRA – insofar as the Act did not feature prominently or at all in campaign literature, press releases, or in lobbying Parliament.

---

92   A Kundnani (2007) 'Britain gripped by populist campaigns against immigrants'
93   Interview with Tauhid Pasha, Solicitor, JCWI

Many of the campaigners viewed the Act as 'something for lawyers'. This view should not be seen as necessarily negative but more a reflection of the campaigners' lack of knowledge about the Act and a preference to let perceived experts (i.e. lawyers) deal with apparent legal matters. The language of rights or an expansive approach to rights as a resource is not yet the currency amongst NGOs advocating and campaigning on asylum issues. An exception is the Refugee Council, one of the primary campaigners for the HRA, which used the Act by specifically targeting the newly established Joint Committee on Human Rights (established by Parliament in January 2001). The Council has worked hard to develop a relationship with the JCHR and the Committee, in turn, has been most receptive to input from the Council and has been highly critical of the government's asylum bills.

> When a Bill is going through Parliament, it (HRA) is an extremely useful tool, for example, in our lobbying work, to say that the Bill, as it stands, is a clear breach of the HRA; remember that the Minister has to clear (declare) its human rights compatibility beforehand . . . it is a very powerful thing for us to be able to say there is a breach. But the government's response is also powerful. They say 'we don't think it is because the Secretary of State has certified that the Bill is compatible'.[94]

According to Imran Hussain, Parliamentary Officer with the Refugee Council, the Council is well aware of the inherent tensions in human rights arguments; of differing views of when, or if at all, any particular legislation is potentially in breach of Convention rights and of the need to tread carefully the minefield that rights arguments potentially present:

> The HRA is a tool which helps us in terms of putting pressure on the government. But the government doesn't turn to us (when we raise concerns) and say: 'oh, we are really sorry, what can we do to make amends' . . . the government knows what it wants to do, and usually the response is 'what we are doing is human rights compliant' . . . the government is not overly impressed with pure human rights arguments. If they want to do certain things, they will do those things.[95]

---

[94] Interview with Imran Hussain, Parliamentary Officer, Refugee Council (London 12 May 2005)

[95] Ibid.

Many Refugee Council staff are well-versed on the HRA (many trained by the BIHR), which is what one would expect in view of the Council's history and involvement with the Act. But what is surprising is a lack of innovation in the deployment of the Act or rights – and the Council acknowledges it:

> It (HRA) is nowhere near the forefront of our work . . . we do
> not use the Act to any great extent in our arguments (with the
> exception of legal strategy, which is left to our lawyers) . . . we
> are guided by what our lawyers tell us.[96]

Nonetheless, on an individual level, particularly in seeking reconsideration from NASS on Article 3 grounds, some of the Council caseworkers claim to have been achieved considerable successes.[97] To what extent this is due to the experience of the Council or its various contacts in the Home Office is difficult to ascertain. What is clear though is the impact of the various test-case challenges. As the various cases progressed through the High Court (and appellate courts), the Home Office was forced to modify its procedures. The NGO caseworkers became more emboldened in using the HRA (in particular Article 3) and the NASS officers became more aware of the need to be HRA compliant. This may explain, to some extent, the subsequent successes in view of the initial obstinacy of NASS:

> We were very aware that the duty of the (NASS) officer was
> not to violate Article 3; and they were also aware. There was
> nothing else in our armoury. We were well aware that the duty
> on the officer was to reinstate support if verging on Article 3
> breach. And that's the point we honed-in on. Article 3 was the
> only thing we could use that would work and the only thing the
> Home Office would consider – albeit quite reluctantly . . .[98]

But, and this is significant, the change of approach by NASS (and the subsequent successes enjoyed by the Refugee Council and other NGOs) had to do with 'reconsideration' applications only. The initial applications for support were still being refused at consistently high rates irrespective of court decisions by officers apparently unaware of requirement to be HRA compliant. The 'verging on Article

---

[96] Ibid.
[97] Interview notes (on file with author)
[98] Anonymous (caseworker at the Refugee Council) (London 13 June 2005)

3 breach' requirement had to do with the Court of Appeal ruling in *Q and Others* – in other words, unless an asylum-seeker (who had already been refused Section 55 support) was fortunate enough to get NGO representation – and only if s/he was verging on Article 3 breach would he succeed in having the initial refusal overturned. How real or substantive a change this represented is difficult to quantify because of an appearance of rights been grudgingly considered and only under certain conditions rather than as a matter of course. And even then, the NGOs had to show real suffering in order to satisfy NASS. Many of those involved in assisting asylum-seekers with reconsideration applications found the process 'perverse' and were left with the task of advising their clients that the more extreme the suffering the better the chances of winning:

> We would tell our clients that if you have been on the streets for
> a day or two, without food or shelter, Home Office isn't going
> to be sympathetic. For a bit longer, then maybe; if sick, even
> better (providing they could get a doctor's letter). The more the
> suffering the easier for us to get a result; don't have any figures
> but we did manage to get quite a few success.[99]

To reconsider an application on Article 3 grounds, the NASS made what NGOS viewed as extraordinary demands – such as evidence that an applicant was 'sleeping rough' or 'having to beg or steal' and how that impacted upon or diminished his/ her 'human dignity'. These requirements, leaving aside the subjectivity of the criteria, were such that it would be unlikely for individual asylum-seekers, without proper representation or NGO assistance, to gather such evidence and present a persuasive argument for support.[100] It became apparent that unless an argument was made on behalf of an applicant on the basis of Article 3 rights, NASS, on its own, was unlikely to reverse its decision leave alone consider the possibility that rights could be breached. It was clear to the NGOs that NASS was 'still not getting the message' and did not appear overly concerned with the statutory obligation to be HRA compliant.[101] That serious flaws and inconsistencies continued to characterise NASS decision-making, particularly a lack of regard for Convention rights, is demonstrated by the fact that two out of three refusals were reversed upon further

[99]   Interview with Imran Hussain, Refugee Council
[100]   Mayor of London, 'Destitution by Design' 21
[101]   Interview with Elisabeth, volunteer, Refugee Council (London, August 2006)

representation by NGOs.[102] These figures raise even more questions about Home Office conduct and its continued insistence that there was no evidence that Section 55 had lead to an increase in asylum-seekers 'sleeping rough' – this in the face of NGO findings showing six out of ten 'sleeping-rough.'[103]

5.3.6   The Legal Strategy Against Section 55

> It had been decided at the campaigning level that the best thing
> was to challenge it (Section 55) by legal action.[104]

Concurrent to lobbying – putting pressure on MPs, conducting research, organising protest rallies, providing support for destitute asylum-seekers – the NGOs also pursued a legal strategy with the HRA key to their efforts. But such was the apparent separation of a 'rights-focused' or legal strategy from other aspects of the 'humanitarian' or 'impact-based' campaign that many, except for the senior campaigners and legal staff, seemed unaware of existence of the HRA and its crucial role in the campaign.

Some of the NGOs, particularly those experienced in ECHR litigation such as Liberty, which had lobbied long and hard for the HRA, had been preparing for a legal battle long before the Section 55 came into effect:

> [The amendments] came into force on the 8th of January, and
> we geared up for that even before the 8th of January, because
> we campaigned against the policy when it was first introduced
> as an amendment to the Act. We campaigned against it, we did
> media work, we said this is appalling . . . And that built up a
> head of steam when the Act was passed. And we coordinated
> meetings with all the major refugee and asylum organisations
> so that essentially people were out looking for just case victims
> from the second the policy came into force.[105]

---

[102]   BBC, 'Asylum seekers 'sleeping rough'' (2004) BBC News <http://news.bbc.co.uk/1/hi/uk_politics/3501779.stm> (10 June 2006)

[103]   ibid

[104]   Interview with Claire Sephton, Solicitor, Shelter (London May 2005)

[105]   R Maiman, 'We've had to raise our game: Liberty's litigation strategy under the Human Rights Act 1998' in S Halliday and PD Schmidt (eds) *Human Rights Brought Home: Socio-Legal Perspectives on Human Rights in the National Context* (2004) (citing Shami Chakrabarti, Director of Liberty)

Notwithstanding such after-the-fact statements there was, nonetheless, an element of 'crap shoot' associated with cases selected for test-case litigation. There was little coordination as to what types of cases were being filed; some of the caseworkers interviewed suggested that the NGOs were competing to get to court first. A veteran caseworker complained that Shelter, an NGO not normally involved in asylum-seeker advocacy, 'went barging in' (for its intervention in *Limbuela*) thereby stealing 'our thunder' and publicity which would have been gained given the high-profile success of *Limbuela*.[106] This view, however, was not widely shared as other staff (in the same NGO) applauded Shelter's efforts viewing it as achieving a shared objective. Nonetheless there was competition to be first. Whether this is healthy in an environment of limited resources and mutual objectives is another matter; it also raises questions about strategy, efficiency, and test-case selection:

> Everybody rushed to court, and we got to the court in the evening, and somebody else got to court in the morning, and they got the case. So we then intervened with all these other organisations . . . we were irritatingly close![107]

For the Joint Council for the Welfare of Immigrants (JCWI) litigation has always been an important component of its overall strategy. It was the JCWI that had successfully challenged similar provisions pre-HRA in 1996; and, although not much experienced with ECHR work, its legal staff was eager to put the HRA to the test and was also in search of test-cases. At this early stage of the campaign many NGOs were aggressively seeking test-cases but without much coordination with other like-minded NGOs. In respect of first major test-case challenge, *Q and Others,* it is unclear whether there had been any communication between JCWI and Liberty. There was much informal discussion but several of the campaigners interviewed do not recall any direct communications specifically related to *Q and Others*.[108] As it turned out both the JCWI and Liberty intervened in the case which was initially proclaimed a success; that is until a later detailed reading of the decision and the Home Office response made apparent that it was not the unequivocal victory the NGOs had hoped for.

---

[106]   Interview notes with anonymous caseworker (14 April 2005) (on file with author)
[107]   R Maiman, 'We've had to raise our game: Liberty's litigation strategy under the Human Rights Act 1998' in Halliday and Schmidt (2004) citing John Wadham, Liberty 108
[108]   Interview notes (on file with author)

In their litigation tactics the NGOs, with the HRA as their 'arrow to the bow', deliberately flooded the courts with judicial review (injunction) applications. The applications argued that leaving asylum-seekers without support risked breaching Convention rights. Within a short time, the first three months of the campaign, almost 900 applications had been filed. The NGOs hoped that pressure on the courts would in turn pressure the government into an about-face. While the injunctions, almost 90% of which were granted, mitigated the impact of Section 55 it had no apparent effect on the government, which publicly vowed to continue the course.[109] Test-case challenges alleging breach of Articles 3, 6, and 8 were initiated, with mixed results, leading to greater confusion in the lower courts as to the application of Section 55 and the vexed question of precisely what constitutes an Article 3 breach for asylum-seekers left without support.[110] Throughout all this, the Home Office remained unmoved and held firm, appealing to higher courts whenever the NGOs were victorious in the courts. The tactic adopted by the Home Office also served to undercut NGO efforts as they conceded on 'strong' cases while appealing *prima facie* weak cases.[111] And this continued for all of 2003, 2004, and up to mid-2005; the key test-cases were *Q and Others,* and *R v S, D, T* until finally the House of Lords (in *Limbuela*) sounded the death knell for Section 55.

5.3.7   Conclusion

> It is time to scrap this unjust and inhumane law once and for all.[112]

While a cursory examination may lead to a conclusion that NGO campaign efforts, such as lobbying MPs and protest rallies, were ineffective, Tauhid Pasha, Legal and Policy Director at JCWI, takes a reflective and pragmatic view of the campaign, viewing their efforts as having a cumulative effect and ultimately leading to the House of Lords decision. According to Pasha, it is a powerful tool to be able to publicly point out the inherent contradictions in government policy which extols

---

[109]   Inter-Agency Partnership (2004) 'The Impact of Section 55 on Inter-Agency Partnership of leading UK Refugee Agencies and the asylum-seekers it supports'.

[110]   See Chapters 6, 7, and 8 for a detailed analysis of the key test-cases.

[111]   Legal Action for Women, 'Press Release' (2003) <http://www.allwomencount.net/EWC%20 LAW/protests_against_section_55_cont.htm>

[112]   BBC, 'Asylum seekers 'sleeping rough'' (2006) (citing Sandy Buchan, Refugee Action)

human rights on one hand while denying, without any apparent sense of injustice, the most fundamental of rights to vulnerable minorities. Courts do not operate in a vacuum and the judges were aware of the consternation that Section 55 had caused and was causing (irrespective of any Convention arguments). The judges were also aware of government indifference and appeared quite fed-up that the courts were being burdened with injunction applications owing to an absence of appeal provisions in the enabling statute.[113] The judges even convened a special meeting to discuss how to approach Section 55 judicial review applications.[114] While the content of the meeting may never be public knowledge it is quite possible that a consensus may have emerged given some of their later critical language on Section 55 in direct reference to government indifference to the scale of suffering.[115] And when the High Court ruled in favour of the NGOs in *Q and Others*, the media maelstrom and government outrage which followed was of a nature not seen in recent years. If press reports are to be believed, the decision ignited 'a (Home Office) battle with the judiciary', 'judicial independence was threatened', and the main villain, the *Human Rights Act*, threatened the very existence of the British way of life.[116] *Q and Others* was followed by Mr Justice Kay's decision in *S, D, T*. And by the end of the year the Home Office had had enough of the HRA and court decisions against its policies. Its response – and it came as no surprise to the embattled NGOs – was to announce new legislation, the centrepiece of which would eliminate the right to judicial review in asylum claims.[117]

---

[113]   C Dyer, 'Judges 'saving asylum seekers from starvation' ' *Guardian* (04 Nov 2003)

[114]   C Dyer, 'Asylum cases 'clogging the courts'' *Guardian* (16 Oct 2003)

[115]   See Chapter 6

[116]   Comment, 'Bogus Asylum and the Judges who have it in for Britain' *Daily Mail* (20 Feb 2003) 12; A Bradley (2003) 'Judicial Independence Under Attack' Public Law Aut 397-405

[117]   F Gibb and P Webster, 'Ministers are breaking the law, say judges' *The Times* (04 March 2004); C Dyer, 'Outrage at plan to end judicial review in asylum cases ' *Guardian* (11 Dec 2003)

6   THE *HUMAN RIGHTS ACT* AND THE FIRST TEST-CASE CHALLENGE TO SECTION 55

6.1   Introduction

When the campaign against Section 55 commenced in October 2002 few in the NGO community would have predicted the 'war' that it became. In many respects the campaign marked by vitriolic and ugly scenes was like no other in recent memory.[1] The campaign, which ended in November 2005, was hard-fought against a government unwilling to concede on its 'get-tough' policy seen as essential to 'halving' asylum-seeker arrivals.[2] During this time countless asylum-seekers suffered deprivation and destitution as the NGOs struggled to keep up with the demands on their services. Migration Watch, a conservative think-tank, acknowledged the suffering but urged the government to remain committed saying that 'tough decisions' have to be made.[3] And the government did stay the course notwithstanding the estimated 10,000 destitute asylum-seekers and concerted campaigning by NGOs and faith groups, including the Church of England.[4] It took three major court challenges, *Q and Others, SDT*, and *Limbuela*, before Section 55 was defeated.

This chapter opens with a brief background to the campaign and sets it against the current events of that time. The focus then shifts to an analysis of how Section 55 became law and examines how the first test-case challenge, *Q and Others,* came about. It concludes with an analysis of the decision and examines the government, NGO, and media response to it.

6.1.1   Background to the Campaign

During the initial stages of the NGO campaign – to 'drive a truck through the legislation'[5] – the HRA played a mostly peripheral role. In other words, it was not initially a rights-based campaign. In general, the campaigners viewed the Act

1   Interview notes (on file with author)

2   P Johnston, 'Court Threat to Blair's Asylum Vow' *Daily Telegraph* (10 Feb 2003)

3   P Johnston and G Jones, 'Blair to take on judges over asylum' *Daily Telegraph* (20 Feb 2003) 1

4   Mayor of London, 'Destitution by Design' (2004)

5   Interview with Tauhid Pasha, Director of Legal Policy, Joint Council for the Welfare of Immigrants (JCWI) (London 29 March 2005)

as something best left to lawyers and courtrooms and not something that could be potentially useful in the wider campaign. The NGOs were also wary of focusing too much on the Act, something that many had long campaigned for, fearing the possibility that it could become devalued and come to be seen as something used by unpopular minorities to extract concessions rather than something for the greater good of society.[6] Such caution was not surprising because the Fall of 2002 was still early days for the untested HRA and, outside and even within legal circles, the Act was a largely unknown factor.[7] The campaigners decided to focus instead on the ground-level impact that Section 55 was having on asylum-seekers. This was a strategic decision based on feedback from front-line caseworkers and grass-roots volunteers who were 'appalled by what they were seeing'.[8] Many campaigners hoped and believed that by highlighting the humanitarian crisis, of asylum-seekers sleeping rough and going hungry, the campaign would send a powerful message and bring about a general repulsion and repeal of Section 55. At least such was the assumption.

The NGOs also expended considerable efforts to keep the issue 'live' but it was not to be as media coverage, while relatively sustained in left-leaning newspapers, petered out as the subject of destitute asylum-seekers failed to excite much interest.[9] This absence of media interest, notwithstanding concerted efforts by NGOs which issued press releases and invited media representatives to various events, must be evaluated in the wider context of an established pattern of apathy towards and dehumanisation of asylum-seekers, something against which NGOs also continue to battle.[10] It therefore came as little surprise that the campaign, on behalf of the 'lowest of the low', created barely a ripple in the halls of power or public opinion.[11]

---

[6] See Chapter 5 for a fuller discussion

[7] British Institute of Human Rights, *Something for Everyone: The Impact of the Human Rights Act on Disadvantaged Groups* (2002)

[8] Interview notes (on file with author)

[9] An analysis of media reporting during this period shows very little continuing coverage of the unfolding events related to Section 55. There were generally supportive articles in all the newspapers (Daily Telegraph, Times, Guardian, Independent, and Daily Mirror) about the wrongness of asylum-seekers suffering from lack of benefits support, but this coverage was not sustained and simply petered out while the crisis continued for most of 2003, 2004, and 2005.

[10] Article 19, What's the Story: Results from Research into Media Coverage of Refugees and Asylum-Seekers in the UK (2003); Oxfam, Asylum: The Truth Behind the Headlines (2001); P Waugh, 'Think-Tank Distorts Asylum Facts, says Former Minister' *The Independent* (19 Nov 2003) 9; A Asthana, 'Asylum policy is 'grotesque' ' *The Observer* (27 Feb 2005)

[11] M McFadyean, 'Centres of barbarism' *Guardian* (02 Dec 2006); it is generally agreed by many observers that asylum-seekers are seen as the 'lowest of the low' in UK society. See, for example, Ipsos MORI *British Views On Immigration* (2003)

The NGOs, however, long-hardened by their battles with the government were under no illusions. Concurrent to the general campaign staff at Liberty, Joint Council for the Welfare of Immigrants (JCWI), Refugee Council, and other NGOs had already been on the lookout for suitable test-cases with which to challenge the policy. And so it was in the courts that the Act achieved prominence. It was the deciding factor in a series of cases resulting in the eventual defeat of a major government policy. Not only that, the Act was also crucial in ensuring that hundreds of newly-arrived asylum-seekers, either via grant of an injunction by the courts or reconsideration by the National Asylum Support Service (NASS), were provided with basic welfare benefits without which countless more would have joined the ranks of the destitute. But for this – which the *Guardian* called 'a victory for humanity' – the Act was not celebrated.[12] Instead the HRA, and the judiciary, came under sustained and unseemly criticism by senior government ministers and vitriolic attack by segments of the media, which condemned the decision and judges and demanded the immediate repeal of the Act. *The Sun,* the largest-selling newspaper in the UK, demanded the Act be revoked and started an online petition which almost immediately garnered 300,000 signatures.[13]

6.1.2 The First Test-Case Challenge in Context

If there was ever a time for the abstract promises and theoretical protection of a 'culture of rights' to ascend upon a powerless and unpopular minority it was during the months of 2002. During that time several factors converged, much of it inflammatory, when an oft-used metaphor of asylum as a battleground morphed into something tangible. In that year alone there were over 100,000 asylum claims in the UK, the highest to date. Of those, about 10,000 were granted asylum, 8,000 returned to their countries or were deported, and 82,000, the number refused, simply vanished from official records and are presumed to be living (and working illegally) somewhere in the UK.[14]

---

12 Leader, 'A victory for humanity ' *Guardian* (20 Feb 2003) referring to the first successful challenge in *Q and Others.*

13 Mr Dolittle, 'The Sun Says' *The Sun* (27 Jan 2003)

14 D Bamber and C Brown, 'Blunkett says Blair's pledge on asylum-seekers 'undeliverable'' *Sunday Telegraph* (09 Feb 2003) 1; P Johnston, 'Asylum seekers reach record 100,000 a year' *Daily Telegraph* (30 Nov 2002)

In June at a European Union summit in Spain, illegal immigration, with dead bodies washing up on the shores no longer an uncommon sight, came to dominate the agenda with the UK seeking Europe-wide cooperation on stricter asylum policies.[15] For most of 2002 the focus on asylum in the UK (by politicians and the media) was at fever pitch with the Prime Minister going as far as suggesting use of the military to intercept asylum-seekers and stop them from setting foot in the UK.[16] In December 2002, a month before Section 55 was to take effect, months of negotiations concerning the closure of Sangatte, an asylum-holding centre near the Eurotunnel terminal in France and a 'festering sore' in Anglo-French relations, came to an end.[17] The tabloids were outraged and headlines proclaimed that Britain was being 'swamped by scroungers' and 'welfare cheats' and speculation was rife that trainloads of asylum-seekers were amassing at UK borders.[18] The then-leader of the opposition wrote an incendiary piece demanding that 'not one of the Sangatte inmates be allowed in' claiming that Britain was being 'taken for a ride' and 'we are at the end of our tether'.[19] And, again, as in recent years, the very concept of asylum was under siege with both the government and opposition openly questioning the merits of the *1951 UN Convention Relating to the Status of Refugees*, the clear inference being those seeking its protection were without merit, economic migrants seeking to take advantage of welfare benefits. The uphill battle that asylum represents in the UK had never been as steep as it was in 2002. Such was the furore that international organisations, Oxfam and Human Rights Watch, were compelled to step in publishing reports highly critical of Labour policies on asylum.[20] It was against this tempestuous

---

[15] CNN, 'Immigration tops EU summit agenda' (2002) CNN World News <http://archives. cnn.com/2002/WORLD/europe/06/20/spain.summit/> (10 Oct 2006); L Fekete, 'The Human Trade: More Dead at Sea' (2002) Institute of Race Relations <https://www.irr.org. uk/cgi-bin/news/open.pl?id=5285> (20 Oct 2006)

[16] M Tempest, 'Duncan Smith: keep Sangatte refugees out ' *Guardian* (24 May 2002). This is not an untried policy; the US, for example, uses its navy to intercept and return asylum-seekers in violation of international law; Canada, in the past, has also used its navy for this purpose (see Chapter 2).

[17] BBC, 'Sangatte closure deal agreed' (2002) BBC News <http://news.bbc.co.uk/2/hi/uk_ news/politics/2533415.stm> (10 Oct 2006)

[18] Article 19, *What's the Story: Results from Research into Media Coverage of Refugees and Asylum-Seekers in the UK* (2003)

[19] ID Smith, 'Why the French are laughing at us this morning' *Daily Mail* (24 May 2002) 4

[20] UN, *Sofia Judicial Round Table on Refugee Protection* (2003); see also: Human Rights Watch, 'UK Asylum Proposal Denounced' (2001) HRW (20 Oct 2006); Human Rights Watch, *Commentary on the United Kingdom Home Office White Paper: Secure Borders, Safe Haven: Integration with Diversity in Modern Europe* (2002)

backdrop, of an image of Britain under siege, that the first test-case challenge to Labour's legislated promise to be tough on asylum-seekers and to end the perception of Britain as a 'soft-touch' was fought.[21]

The fight over Section 55 had the makings of a classic battle, a collision of two opposing forces, the under-resourced and relatively powerless NGOs against a government determined to be tough and be seen as tough on asylum-seekers. And caught in the middle – huddled in doorsteps, sleeping rough – thousands of asylum-seekers from all corners of the globe unaware of the converging forces and the maelstrom to come. *Q and Others* came about during the first month of Section 55 and, on the face of it, presented fairly compelling fact situations albeit not yet tested at this stage of the process.[22] Nonetheless, in determining whether the claimants had made their claims 'as soon as reasonably practicable', the Home Office decided that the respective narratives (to do with the substance of their asylum claims rather than if the claims had been made as 'soon as reasonably practicable') were not credible and refused them welfare and shelter (generally referred to as Section 55 support). Of the six asylum-seekers, which comprised *Q and Others,* 'M' was a Rwandan Hutu who claimed to have been raped and beaten in a refugee camp; 'D' was an Angolan male who claimed to have witnessed the shooting death of his father, the rape and murder of his mother and sister before he himself was beaten and interrogated; 'Q' was an Iraqi Kurd who had entered the UK in a lorry, was dropped off at some unknown locale, and walked three hours before he got to the Home Office where he filed his claim. The applications were assessed by officials removed from the interview process and based entirely on notes by the interviewing officer; exactly how an assessment of credibility was made is unclear but it seems apparent that an ethos of 'disbelief' prefigured much of the decision-making.[23] All were disbelieved, their applications rejected, and left without shelter or benefits in the middle of winter.

Q and Others was the first challenge to Section 55, a much decried legislation which the NGOs had fought hard to repeal, and came about during the infancy

---

21 For a review of Labour's 'get tough' policy on asylum see: Oxfam, *Response to UK Government's White Paper on immigration, citizenship and asylum: Secure Borders, Safe Haven* (2002); and also: Human Rights Watch, *Commentary on the United Kingdom Home Office White Paper: Secure Borders, Safe Haven: Integration with Diversity in Modern Europe* (2002)

22 *R (on the application of Q and Others) v Secretary of State for the Home Department* [2003] 2 All ER 905 (Admin)

23 For a review on NASS procedures see: Mayor of London, 'Destitution by Design' (2004)

of the new policy directed at denying welfare benefits to asylum-seekers who did not make a claim 'as soon as reasonably practicable'. Section 55 represented the latest in a long line of increasingly strict legislation explicitly linking the reduction of benefits (as pull-factors) to deterring asylum-seekers.[24] But the legislation also signalled a marked shift in policy – from that of faster processing of applications, which had been the main objective for years, to stopping asylum-seekers from setting foot in the UK.[25] In other words, the government could not back down without compromising or undercutting its central strategy for dealing with this most intractable of global issues. The case was heard by Justice Andrew Collins in the High Court in February 2003 and his decision on the 19th of that month set off a media maelstrom of a like not seen in recent years.[26] The government response to the defeat of a policy promoted as central to its objective: an openly outraged and clearly frustrated then-Home Secretary, David Blunkett, unmindful of the government's promise of a 'culture of rights', declared he was 'fed-up' with the judiciary. An equally frustrated Prime Minister, Tony Blair, promised legislation to limit the scope of the HRA and rein in judges, widely labelled as defying democracy and the will of Parliament. When told that such a move would ignite a legal battle, the Prime Minister reiterated his determination and said if needed, he would fight a test-case all the way to the European Court of Human Rights.[27] That the judiciary was doing exactly what it is supposed to do (interpreting and applying an Act of Parliament and acting as a check on executive misuse/abuse of power) was lost on the government, particularly a Home Secretary obsessed with and guided by tabloid ranting on major public issues.[28] And a favourite target for both, possibly the most powerless constituency in UK, asylum-seekers:

> Since becoming Home Secretary, David Blunkett, has sought to
> appease and reassure right-wing newspapers in his never-ending

---

[24]   L Pirouet, *Whatever Happened to Asylum in Britain* (2001); H O'Nions (2006) 'The Erosion Of The Right To Seek Asylum' 2 Web Journal of Current Legal Issues ; Leader, 'Asylum rights evaporate ' *Guardian* (10 Feb 2003)

[25]   P Johnston, 'Pledge to Halve Asylum Seekers Derided' *Daily Telegraph* (08 Feb 2003)

[26]   For a summary of the media response see: A Bradley (2003) 'Judicial Independence Under Attack' Public Law Aut 397-405

[27]   P Johnston and G Jones, 'Blair to take on judges over asylum' (20 Feb 2003)

[28]   See, for example, a review of David Blunkett's memoirs: R Hattersley, 'A bit of a wet Blunkett ' *Guardian* (London 15 Oct 2006); also of note: in its criticisms of Labour policy on asylum (and immigration), the *Daily Mail* is careful to exclude David Blunkett from blame; see: Comment, 'Bogus Asylum and the Judges who have it in for Britain' *Daily Mail* (20 Feb 2003) 12

initiates against asylum-seekers. Whenever the *Daily Mail* runs a story aiming to shock, Mr Blunkett surfaces with another headline-grabbing idea for tackling 'the problem'.[29]

6.1.3 Background to *Q and Others* and Section 55

While Section 55 appears on the face of it to be a curious piece of legislation it was, in fact, a masterstroke insofar as the objectives of Labour were concerned and not inconsistent, according to some observers, with the policies of a government that has steadily eroded civil liberties.[30] Section 55 was designed with two objectives in mind: to deter asylum-seekers and to blunt potential court challenges. Leaving aside the question of whether it would have succeeded in its primary objective of deterring asylum-seekers, why it failed in the latter and what possibly led to its downfall was an apparent lack of communication between the policy-makers at the Home Office and those who implement such polices, in this instance, the front-line bureaucrats at the much-ridiculed NASS.[31] If NASS had not been so apparently single-minded in its refusal of over 90% of the applications, the crisis of destitute asylum-seekers most probably would have been averted and court challenges muted. But, if anything, rather than blunting court challenges, the actions of the NASS invited exactly what the drafters had hoped to avoid.[32]

When Section 55 was drafted it specifically excluded appeal rights against a decision not to grant support. A reflection not only of Home Office concern with what it views as 'abuse of the system' via endless appeals, but also of an ethos

---

[29]   Comment, 'A Shameful Asylum Policy' *The Independent* (30 Nov 2003)

[30]   H Porter, 'Blair gets away with his assault on liberty, because we let him' *The Observer* (16 Apr 2006); H Porter, 'How we move ever closer to becoming a totalitarian state ' *The Observer* (05 Mar 2006)

[31]   See Chapter 5 for a fuller discussion; it is also worth noting that front-line staff often see themselves as gate-keepers and that they know best how to enforce or implement policies and view with disdain what they consider 'out of touch' head-office policy-makers. This view is anecdotal and is based on a ten-year career as a front-line immigration officer/investigator and later as policy advisor (in Canada) and interviews with an unrepresentative sample of Home Office officers. See, in general, J Bhabha (2002) 'International Gatekeepers: The Tension between Asylum Advocacy and Human Rights' 15 Harvard Human Rights Journal 155-81

[32]   For a review of NASS decision-making and rejection rates see: Inter-Agency Partnership, *The impact of section 55 on the Inter-Agency Partnership of leading UK refugee agencies and the asylum seekers it supports* (2004); Mayor of London, 'Destitution by Design' (2004); M Taylor, 'Asylum policies 'make 10,000 people destitute a year' ' *Guardian* (09 Feb 2004)

which regards most claims for asylum to be economically motivated and not for reasons of persecution.[33] The only recourse for those refused was to seek judicial review, a fairly narrow basis for redress, which, along with other asylum rights, has been systematically eroded by cuts to legal aid and other obstacles.[34] However the Section did have one saving grace – a requirement for the Secretary of State to act in order to avoid a breach of Convention rights as mandated by Section 55(5):

> This section shall not prevent (a) the exercise of a power by the Secretary of State to the extent necessary for the purpose of avoiding a breach of a person's Convention rights (within the meaning of the Human Rights Act 1998)

Why this should be so legislated is unclear because the HRA would apply irrespective of any such provision. Perhaps it was an acknowledgement of a check on the Home Secretary's powers. But whatever the reasoning, the NGOs knew from experience that it would be unlikely for the Secretary of State (or officials acting on his behalf) to act on his own initiative. This proved to be the case with upwards of 93% applications rejected, the NASS paying scant attention to its statutory obligations under the HRA.[35] But such a hard-nosed approach by NASS unwittingly undercut the saving provision of Section 55(5), which was for all intents and purposes designed to blunt Court challenges.[36] The possibility that the judiciary, which had overruled previous such legislative attempts to restrict welfare benefits, would again do so was something that the Home Office clearly wanted to avoid. In this respect, Section 55(5) mandated officials to act so as not to breach Convention rights, thereby avoiding potential judicial intervention. In other words, officials applying Section 55 should have, as mandated and a matter of course, evaluated human rights implications. The problem, however, was that the NASS

---

[33] For recent comments by the Minister of Immigration on asylum-seekers as economic migrants see: P Barkham, 'Asylum-seeker charities are just playing the system, says Woolas' *Guardian* (18 Nov 2008)

[34] C Dyer, 'MPs attack legal aid cuts ' *Guardian* (23 Oct 2003); D Stevens (2004) 'The Nationality, Immigration and Asylum Act 2002: Secure Borders, Safe Haven?' 67 (4) Modern Law Review 616

[35] Inter-Agency Partnership *The impact of section 55 on the Inter-Agency Partnership of leading UK refugee agencies and the asylum seekers it supports* (2004) 2

[36] A Travis, 'Judge orders urgent asylum case hearings ' *Guardian* (17 Jan 2003); see also Leader, 'A victory for humanity ' (20 Feb 2003) for a similar analysis of legislation designed to 'handicap court challenges'.

seemed oblivious of the HRA in its assessment of the applications. An examination of the standardised screening/interview forms used by NASS officers, at that time, clearly shows that HRA issues were not addressed or solicited, an approach inconsistent with the mandated requirements of the Act.[37] The NASS disbelieved a majority of applicants and refused them irrespective of whether they had food or shelter in the midst of winter, thereby triggering a humanitarian crisis.

For this, however, the NASS is not entirely to blame. There was also confusion as to exactly when or how Convention rights, in this instance Articles 3 and 8, would be breached. Article 3, for example, entails meeting a high threshold and up until Section 55 challenges had never been applied to domestic asylum policies of democratically-elected liberal governments.[38] The article, after all, refers to torture and degrading punishment and generally understood to be something authoritarian governments inflict upon its citizens, neither of which seemed to apply in the UK. And could implementation of public policy be considered 'treatment'. All such issues served to hamper the application of the legislation's saving provision. What the drafters had apparently assumed to be straightforward turned out be anything but. This in itself is not surprising for exactly the same question also vexed the courts as the judges grappled with the issue through several test-cases. If such confusion reigned in the courts, it is not surprising then that the issue on the ground continued to confound many. For example, was it even possible for Article 3 to be engaged: the state was not ill-treating anyone; and, even if it did apply, precisely how much suffering would be enough suffering for Article 3 to be engaged?

According to Don Flynn, then policy analyst at JCWI and now director at Migrant Rights Network (MRN), Home Office solicitors generally concede on cases that they are likely to lose in the courts in order to save major policies.[39] But somewhere along the line communication, between policy-makers at the Home Office and front-line staff at NASS, went awry with the department rejecting applications en masse notwithstanding the HRA. This, in turn, raised the ire of the courts as they found themselves inundated with judicial review applications.[40]Even this seemingly unprecedented numbers of judicial review applications was the tip

---

[37] On file with author; this fact was also commented upon and criticised by Justice Collins in *Q and Others*

[38] The high-threshold 'test' is outlined in *Pretty v United Kingdom* [2002] 35 EHRR 1

[39] Interview notes (on file with author).

[40] C Dyer, 'Judges 'saving asylum seekers from starvation' ' *Guardian* (04 Nov 2003)

of an iceberg because many unrepresented asylum-seekers simply vanished from official records.[41]

Section 55, while seen as 'utterly reasonable' by the *Daily Mail*, was of great concern to the NGOs who campaigned to repeal it before it came into effect.[42] When that failed, they sought the inclusion of appeal rights. That, too, failed. And so it was with a great deal of concern that the NGOs looked ahead to the day labelled 'beware the 8th of January'.[43] When Section 55 came into effect the NGO plan – at least it was for Liberty, JCWI, Refugee Council, and a few others – to challenge the section in the courts did not quite unfold as planned. There were many more players than had been anticipated by the major asylum-seeker serving NGOs; in part, owing to the design of Section 55 itself, an eagerness on part of some to test the nascent HRA, and the politics and competition (amongst NGOs) to be first in what was expected to be a major publicity coup should there be a favourable decision. All of these factors contributed to a chaotic rush for the courts which were flooded with injunction and judicial review applications: [44]

> There were politics about it. A rush to get to court first . . . it's
> good for an organisation's profile, to strike the first blow, to be
> there at the start.[45]

At this stage of the campaign CADAS (Coalition against Destitution of Asylum-Seekers) had not yet come into existence and would not for another twelve months. In short, there was very little oversight or coordination of the cases filling the already overcrowded dockets.[46] The various NGOs, on their own and in competition among themselves, were filing injunction and judicial review applications as were many individual solicitors.[47] For these reasons it is problematic to presume that

---

41   See statement by Justice Collins, in *Q and Others*, acknowledging this.

42   Comment, 'Bogus Asylum and the Judges who have it in for Britain' *Daily Mail* (20 Feb 2003)

43   NCADC, 'Newszine 28' (2002) October - November - 2002 National Coalition of Anti-Deportation Campaigns <http://www.ncadc.org.uk/archives/filed%20newszines/oldnewszines/news28/28index.html> (20 Oct 2006)

44   See R Maiman, 'We've had to raise our game: Liberty's litigation strategy under the Human Rights Act 1998' in S Halliday and PD Schmidt (eds) *Human Rights Brought Home: Socio-Legal Perspectives on Human Rights in the National Context* (2004); also interview notes (on file with author)

45   Interview with Alex Gask, Solicitor, Liberty (London 01 Nov 2006)

46   Interview notes (on file with author)

47   Statement by Alex Gask, Solicitor, Liberty (Personal email correspondence 16 Oct 2006)

a majority of NGOs were united in pursuing a wider policy objective (defeat of legislation). To be sure, that was the announced objective of Liberty, Refugee Council, and JCWI but the field was a crowded one with many other NGOs filing applications. But as stated elsewhere, this was more by accident than design – the key being a marked lack of resources and professional management hindered planning and coordination among the NGOs. This approach was also necessitated by Section 55 itself because the courts were the only option for redress for those refused support. There was no other alternative. Many NGOs and solicitors were seeking immediate redress for their clients, their needs being more pressing than wider policy objectives. But, notwithstanding an absence of coordination amongst those filing judicial review applications, there was an apparent tacit understanding that only those cases where the asylum-seeker was a recent-arrival (as opposed to those who had been in the country for an extended period and were only filing a claim to avoid/delay enforcement action) would be put forward. Not only because such cases were more likely to succeed at judicial review but they would also serve to undermine the Home Office's stated objective behind Section 55 (to address abuse of the system by 'overstayers') and bring to the fore the inhumanity of its application.[48]

6.2   Litigation as a Strategy

> We saw the legislation as dangerous and, even before it came
> into force, we were discussing with other NGOs and concerned
> groups the best way of tackling it . . . once it (Section 55) came
> into force, we were ready to change from policy campaigning to
> litigation campaigning.[49]

At the beginning of the campaign the NGOs did not have in place procedures on how to select or identify Section 55 test-cases, a curious bit of under-planning given their avowed determination to challenge it in the courts.[50] While this may be partially explicable because of the lateness and manner of Section 55's introduction, which took the NGOs by surprise, it is nonetheless surprising because test-case litigation plays an important role in their campaigning efforts in general.

---

[48]   Interview notes (on file with author)
[49]   Interview with Alex Gask, Solicitor, Liberty (London 01 Nov 2006)
[50]   Anonymous sources (on file with author)

According to Tauhid Pasha, Legal Director of Policy at JCWI, an intervenor in *Q and Others,* certain elements must be present for a case to be a 'runner' or test-case.[51] But even before such a consideration, the case must fall within an already identified and defined policy area. From a wide array of issues that are important to the organisation's mandate and objectives test-case areas are prioritised because 'we have to pick our fights'. Various factors, such as the views of its membership, in-house expertise, determine what those priorities will be or are but out of necessity are driven largely by government agenda.[52] Planning is about being able to respond to the shifting tides of political priorities. In this instance, the government's last-minute introduction of Section 55 left the NGOs scrambling but also set the agenda for them.

The JCWI, having previously battled the then-Conservative government over the same issue in 1996, approached the campaign with litigation as a key part of its strategy.[53] There was no question of avoiding litigation. The option of using the HRA as leverage or negotiating a settlement, an approach not uncommon in jurisdictions where a culture of rights or long established history of rights litigation is part of the political and social movement landscape, was considered not viable. In order for leverage to be effective or for negotiations to occur there must be some common ground, where a culture of rights – or at least respect for rights (combined with a healthy wariness for court battles) – is fundamental to the political process and not seen as an impediment.[54] According to the findings of this research, such is not yet the case in the UK insofar as asylum-seekers are concerned.[55] The Home Office showed no interest in negotiating. It was an option not open to the NGOs, particularly with a government determined to be tough on asylum, seemingly indifferent to its own HRA, and wanting to demonstrate its toughness to a highly-sceptical public opposed to asylum. If anything, the Home Office invited court challenges.[56]

---

[51]   Interview with Tauhid Pasha, Solicitor, JCWI (London March 2005)

[52]   Interview with Habib Rahman, Chairperson, JCWI (London March 2005)

[53]   R v Secretary of State for Social Security ex parte Joint Council for the Welfare of Immigrants [1997] 1 WLR 275 (CA)

[54]   See for example: M McCann, 'How Does Law Matter for Social Movements? ' in B Garth and A Sarat (eds) *How Does Law Matter* (1998); M McCann, *Rights at Work: Pay Equity Reform and the Politics of Legal Mobilization* (1994); DA Schultz, *Leveraging the law: using the courts to achieve social change* (1998); GN Rosenberg, *The Hollow Hope: Can Courts Bring About Social Change?* (1991)

[55]   For a fuller discussion see Chapters 1 and 9

[56]   Anonymous legal officer (interview notes on file with author); interview with Clare Shepton, Counsel, Shelter (London 12 April 2005)

Such an uncompromising stance must be evaluated within the context of how Section 55 became law – the policy was implemented by a government well aware that it raised serious human rights issues. This is after all a government which, according to some critics, has steadily eroded civil liberties since coming to power.[57] Not that the NGOs did not make the effort. Caseworkers tried contacting the Home Office only to be met with indifference; telephone calls were not returned and some told 'not to bother'.[58] And in a position borne of experience, and the recent history of repeated government attempts to reduce welfare benefits for asylum-seekers and toughening of laws, the campaigners knew they were in for a long battle and were determined to challenge the matter in the courts:[59]

> 'Not all our policy initiatives have a litigation strategy. Where
> there is one, we will pursue it. It is not a last-resort measure; it's
> a very important part of our overall strategy'.[60]

The JCWI, like Liberty, relied on long established channels (membership, notices in its publications, website, and informal networking) to inform others they were seeking test-cases to challenge Section 55. Notwithstanding the mixed success JCWI has had in the courts litigation remains central to its strategy where changes in law or policy are sought. But there is also a great deal of wariness because the outcome is never certain and a negative decision is sometimes 'worse than no decision at all'.[61] But not always because so wearied are the NGOs in having to continually challenge the Home Office and so restrictive are the policies that, according to Don Flynn, rarely do negative results translate into a situation being 'worse off' than what it was at the outset:

> The negative effect is that the case simply confirms what the
> authorities want to do as being legal. The point of about legal
> casework is that it shouldn't be seen as one-off work, but building
> up a series of arguments which help you to make the case over
> time and tease the decision you want from the courts. From

---

[57]   H Porter, 'Blair gets away with his assault on liberty, because we let him' (16 Apr 2006)

[58]   Interview with Clare Shepton, Counsel, Shelter (London 12 April 2005)

[59]   See Chapter 4 for a review of previous legislative attempts to reduce welfare for asylum-seekers.

[60]   Interview with Tauhid Pasha, Solicitor, JCWI (London May 2005)

[61]   Ibid.

this perspective even losing a case can help, because a good judgment will help mark out the area you need to concentrate on with future cases.[62]

Irrespective of the views on the merits of test-case challenges or the vagaries of judicial decision-making litigation makes for a slow process. The slowness is more pronounced in asylum because faster results are usually crucial. The fight over Section 55, for example, took over three years during which there was immense suffering. However, compared to litigation, worse has been JCWI's success rate at having policy changed or modified via other means, such as lobbying Parliament or petitioning MPs. No one at JCWI was able to provide data in support of this anecdotally-held view because there has been no in-house analysis on the efficacy of its non-litigation campaign work.[63] What there is in abundance is a conviction of belief amongst many NGO staff that the work they do is important and much needed. This belief permeates the ranks of most front-line caseworkers and volunteers interviewed where results are often seen at a micro-level: when a hungry asylum-seeker is fed or given shelter; when a sick asylum-seeker is provided with medical care. All such efforts are seen as part of the bigger battle against an unfeeling bureaucracy and a 'get tough' government.[64]

In any event, it can be problematic to evaluate the successes of such work and not always satisfactory to compare activities, including litigation, in isolation given the close relationships and the complex interplay between them in the campaign. In an arena where scarcity of resources is a constant concern the options available to the JCWI, and other campaigning NGOs, are not limitless. Litigation, on the other hand, is more direct and the NGOs via their networks often secure pro-bono representation by lawyers driven by principles and idealism.[65] Litigation, according to Pasha, gets the attention of policy-makers which is not always the case via other means:

---

[62]   Statement by Don Flynn, Policy Analyst, JCWI (Personal email correspondence 26 Oct 2006)

[63]   Interview notes (on file with author).

[64]   Interview notes (on file with author)

[65]   Several of the lawyers interviewed had left high-paying city jobs for work viewed as more rewarding and interesting; many did not initially describe themselves as cause-lawyers, a terminology in vogue in the US, but agreed that it was an appropriate description. For example, Rabinder Singh, QC, a solicitor of some renown often does pro-bono work for Liberty.

> We try to engage with them directly but it is difficult. We do talk,
> sometimes they consult, sometimes seek our input. But often
> they don't listen. The Minister came to meet us a few weeks ago.
> We had a pleasant discussion but made no inroads. He didn't
> agree with us.[66]

Notwithstanding NGO efforts asylum remains a tough sell with the public and politicians alike. Asylum-seekers remain overwhelmingly unpopular and are almost universally seen and portrayed as cheats and undeserving of protection – and policy-makers know this. It is this very antipathy towards asylum-seekers that makes draconian policies possible and for rights and rights arguments to be little regarded and a measure of how difficult it is for rights or a culture of rights to penetrate the discourse of the day. And, as evidenced by the reaction to *Q and Others*, rights are seen as an obstacle and infringement on the government's ability to deal with the problem of asylum:

> The Home Office is quite sceptical about human rights arguments.
> The feeling is that they (arguments) have gone far enough . . . or
> too far. Their view is that human rights are being tried in cases
> where it doesn't even apply. They don't seem to have much time
> for novel arguments.[67]

While the preceding seems contradictory in view of the government's public claims about 'building a culture of rights', it is nonetheless another indicator of official frustration with the HRA, particularly where court decisions have required a re-design of major policies or have brought about an end to policies central to government objectives (as did eventually happen in the case of Section 55). It also marks a clash between the pragmatic and the rhetorical. The former where the HRA has effectively halted the government's rush to implement policies and the latter being spin-doctoring about building a culture of rights. And no amount of spin-doctoring could hide what bubbled to the surface in the aftermath of the Justice Collin's decision in *Q and Others* – of a government seeking an exit strategy from the HRA to the point of voicing serious consideration to legislating judicial

---

[66]   Interview with Tauhid Pasha, Solicitor, JCWI (London 22 March 2005)
[67]   Interview with Don Flynn, Policy, JCWI (London 22 March 2005)

interpretation of the Act.[68] Such a belligerent stance served to confirm what some have long believed about Labour and the HRA: that had it not been for a major campaign promise, which only a party confined to the wilderness of opposition for eighteen long-years could suggest (the HRA was part of a package concerning radical constitutional reform), the HRA would never have become a reality:[69]

> There has been about one chance in the past 80 years when such a law (HRA) could have been brought in – and it was in the early years of this government. They would never dream of doing it now.[70]

The Home Office nonetheless takes the view, as it must, that its actions in the pursuit of legitimate policy objectives are exactly that and do not violate the HRA. And, notwithstanding persuasive evidence to the contrary, nor do they set out to deliberately breach it.[71] In many ways this is the only position that the Home Office can take notwithstanding inferences which convincingly suggest that they should have known (or reasonably been expected to know), particularly after being repeatedly warned by the Joint Committee on Human Rights that Section 55 posed exactly such a risk.[72]

6.3   The Selection of Test-Cases and *Q and Others*

For the campaigners at JCWI, Liberty, and other NGOs, litigation is central to their efforts for bringing about meaningful changes to policy and advancing social justice issues. That is until their small victories are legislated out of existence and the battle begins anew. Both the JCWI and Liberty take the view that test-cases must ultimately address the wider policy issue(s), even if the intervention may not be in the best interests of an individual litigant though ideally it would serve all interests.[73] In this instance, the crisis and the large number of claims brought about by Section 55 made it difficult for the NGOs to manage the influx of cases

---

[68]   A Lester, 'Don't blame the judges' *Guardian* (25 Feb 2003)
[69]   Prior to its electoral victory in 1997, Labour had spent 18 years in opposition.
[70]   F Gibb, 'Blunkett v the Bench: the battle has begun' *The Times* (04 Mar 2003) 3 citing Lord Lester.
[71]   See Chapters 1 and 9
[72]   See Chapter 5 for a review of how Section 55 came into existence.
[73]   Interview notes (on file with author)

going before the courts. But given that test-case litigation was central to their strategy, it is not readily apparent why there was almost no control mechanism to ensure only those cases which met stated test-case criteria would be filed in the courts, particularly where the issues raised were of such immense importance that losing was not to be thought of. This may be attributable to competition amongst NGOs with everyone in a rush to get to court first and 'strike the first blow'.[74] This haphazard approach could also be attributed, in part, to the various NGOs eagerness to test the promises of the Act.[75] It is a truism that no matter how noble an objective it is not necessarily absent of egos. However, as it turned out, the NGOs did not have much say over which cases were ultimately selected as test-cases before the High Court. Their approach to flooding the courts resulted in the courts, rather than themselves, selecting the test-cases. Such an approach, clearly, takes away a crucial element of control whereby the best cases, ideally those which meet all the NGO criteria, are prosecuted. But, in this instance, the NGOs got lucky.

First, the six test-cases were selected by Justice Sir Andrew Collins, from over 150 applications pending before the courts at that time, as being broadly representative and presenting similar fact situations. Mr Justice Collins, former head of the Immigration Tribunal and well versed in the complex and highly-charged environment of asylum law, selected cases which were quite possibly amongst the strongest. The cases also had the additional bonus of satisfying key NGO criteria for test-cases – that the litigant arouse sympathy and their case expose the excesses of power used against them (in this instance, the enforcement of Section 55 against vulnerable persons caught in a plight not of their making).[76] All six were from known refugee-producing countries, all had claimed to be victims of horrendous suffering, and none had any welfare support (from friends or charity) in the UK.[77] It was hoped by Collins, that providing general guidance on the application of Section 55, would rein in the increasing number of applications before the courts.

Second, Mr Justice Collins has an established pattern of ruling against the government on numerous policy issues much to the ire of various Home Secretaries, and has a history of striking down key policies on asylum. A cursory review of a

---

[74]   Interview with Alex Gask, Solicitor, Liberty (London November 2005)
[75]   R Maiman (2004)
[76]   Interview notes (on file with author)
[77]   For details of the individual cases see *R (on the application of Q and Others) v Secretary of State for the Home Department* [2003] 2 All ER 905 (Admin)

selected sample of his decisions is demonstrative of principled views on social justice and empathy towards the disadvantaged. An indirect measure of that is provided by the fervently right-wing tabloid press, which view him as a 'serial offender', a 'dictator in wigs' and someone who 'constantly sets his will against the government and democracy'. In attacks the *Daily Mail*, for example, listed several cases where the judge had 'defied and set his will above Parliament'.[78]

Third, Collins had previously tackled the same issue (introduced in 1996 by the then Conservative government) and ruled in favour of the NGOs. In a then landmark decision he wrote:

> The regulations (denial of welfare benefits) necessarily contemplate
> for some a life so destitute that to my mind no civilised society can
> tolerate it.[79]

The statement was a precursor for things to come because, if anything, Section 55 was even more restrictive and 'draconian and appalling' than the previous legislation that had been struck down.[80] When Mr Justice Collins selected the six test-cases as representative of pending Section 55 judicial review applications, there was at the time almost 200 other such cases before the courts, with more being filed daily, taxing the court's resources and patience of the judges. But the judges were also aware of the mounting crisis outside their courtrooms and, at the urging of Shelter and Refugee Council, ordered urgent hearings:

> It is apparent from this group of cases and conversations with other
> judges who have received out-of-hours applications that this might
> be the beginnings of a flood.[81]

In other words, the NGOs, without much planning or coordination, had much in their favour before the hearings began. And, true to form, Collins, after a two-day hearing on the test-cases and a week before release of the decision, publicly asked the government to adopt a more 'liberal approach' and restore benefits to asylum-seekers.[82]

---

[78]   Comment, 'Bogus Asylum and the Judges who have it in for Britain' (20 Feb 2003)

[79]   *R v Secretary of State for Social Security ex parte Joint Council for the Welfare of Immigrants* [1997] 1 WLR 275 (CA)

[80]   Press Release, 'New Labour: Government policy to leave thousands homeless and hungry' (2002) AsylumSupport.info <http://www.asylumsupport.info/thousandstobeleftdestitute.htm> (30 Oct 2006)

[81]   Travis, 'Judge orders urgent asylum case hearings ' citing Justice Maurice Kay

[82]   BBC, 'Judge urges asylum rule suspension' (2003) BBC News <http://news.bbc.co.uk/1/hi/uk_politics/2751161.stm> (27 May 2007)

6.4   The Decision in *Q and Others*

During the trial the Home Secretary argued the European Court had set a very high threshold for breaches of Articles 3 and 8 – that destitution and homelessness did not 'inevitably and necessarily' lead to a breach of Convention rights. The Home Secretary maintained that even if the claimants suffered, the suffering would be insufficient to engage Convention rights; or if a claimant's health begins to suffer, he or she would have access to medical treatment and not suffer sufficiently – at least not enough in the Convention sense. And, without any sense of irony, he also argued that claimants were unlikely to starve because the NGOs would step in and look after them. Mr. Justice Collins found the arguments 'unattractive' but not necessarily wrong, but he dismissed the view that NGOs should be expected to shoulder what is a state responsibility.[83] Apparent in the Home Secretary's arguments was the acknowledgement of suffering – but that the suffering would have to be extreme before the protection afforded by Section 55(5) could be effected. In other words a wait-and-see approach to see how much suffering could be endured by asylum-seekers and then an assessment of whether the suffering was sufficient to require government intervention to avoid a Convention breach. The Home Secretary submitted that if the Court was to accept the arguments advanced on behalf of asylums-seekers – that, first, the effect of Section 55 constituted 'treatment' and, secondly, such treatment breached Convention rights – it would render the legislation (and policy objectives) of no effect. The argument was dismissed by Collins:

> If it means that the regime lacks teeth and will not achieve what was hoped, so be it. I must construe the legislation as I find it, since it was clearly Parliament's intention that the defendant (Home Secretary) should not act in a way which meant that any Claimant's human rights were breached.[84]

And there were no mistaking his views on the impact of Section 55:

> There can be no question but that the effect of s 55 as presently being applied by NASS has been and will be that a considerable

---

[83]   *Q and Others* para 64 and 65
[84]   ibid para 58

number of asylum seekers will be left destitute with no means of
support. It is obvious that they will be likely to resort to begging
or other more serious criminal activities in order to survive.[85]

In further examining how Section 55 applications were being processed Collins
reviewed Home Office guidelines issued to NASS officers. How is it possible, he
asked, for the NASS to make an informed and fair decision when its procedures
provided no means by which to assess human rights implications?

It is noted that there is no guidance provided as to how human
rights issues should be investigated and no questions in the form
give much, if any, assistance in that respect.[86]

Quite apart from its legal implications such an omission raised further questions:
was it oversight on part of the Home Office or was it deliberate? Did the Home
Office, criticised as a 'dysfunctional' organisation 'not fit for the purpose' and
widely derided as a bureaucratic mess, simply bungle?[87] But, given how Section
55 was introduced and implemented – for example, as a last-minute amendment,
the use of guillotine motion to limit debate, and its rush through both Houses
of Parliament – there are reasons to infer that it was deliberate.[88] And later, in
implementation, the apparent cavalier attitude towards HRA obligations continued.
For example, guidelines issued to field officers contained no instructions on how to
assess HRA issues. Some observers have argued that to accept the neglect of such
basic obligations as an oversight stretches credulity.[89] But whatever the real reason
the lack of attention to the HRA was a key factor in the case:

The standard form rejection of any application of s 55(5) in all
the refusal letters demonstrates that insufficient consideration

---

[85]   ibid para 11

[86]   ibid para 19

[87]   P Johnston, 'Reid Blasts Failures at Home Office' *Daily Telegraph* (24 May 2006) 2; BBC,
'Immigration System Unfit – Reid' (2006) BBC News <news.bbc.co.uk/2/hi/uk_news/
politics/5007148.stm> ; B Leapman and M Kite, 'Hundreds of corruption inquiries at
Immigration' *Daily Telegraph* (27 Jul 2006)

[88]   See Chapter 5 on the background to Section 55

[89]   Interview notes (on file with author); see also F Webber 'NASS: Chronicle of Failure' (2003)
Institute of Race Relations http://www.irr.org.uk/2003/july/ak000010.html; C Brown,
"Kirk attacks 'forced poverty' policy of discouraging asylum seekers." *The Scotsman* (09
May 2006); BBC, 'Asylum hardships 'are deliberate' (2007) BBC News <news.bbc.co.uk/1/
hi/uk_politics/6507961.stm>

has been given to the issue (human rights)[90] . . . I am conscious that this will weaken the anticipated effect of s 55(1). But Parliament itself recognised that possibility by enacting s 55(5). Furthermore, Parliament can surely not have intended that genuine refugees should be faced with the bleak alternatives of returning to persecution (itself a breach of the Refugee Convention) or of destitution.[91]

In finding that Section 55 breached Article 3 and Article 6 Mr Justice Collins concluded:

> Asylum has created and is continuing to create was seems an intractable problem . . . attempts have been made by various means to stem the flow. Section 55 represents one such attempt. I am conscious that this decision will mean it is unlikely to work, at least to the extent which was hoped . . . but (whatever) is to be done must accord with those fundamental rights which are to be found enshrined not only in the European Convention of Human Rights but in the . . . constitutions of many civilised countries.[92]

6.4.1   Response to *Q and Others*

Just as the months of 2002 had been dominated by negative coverage on asylum, the first few months of 2003 were no different. Across Britain, in various communities, protestors amassed in angry and sometimes violent denunciation of Home Office plans to house asylum-seekers in their communities in so-called 'accommodation centres'.[93] There were also various reports, including some from the official opposition, blaming asylum-seekers for NHS failures and accusing them of 'health

---

90   *Q and Others* para 73

91   ibid para 74

92   ibid para 87

93   BBC, 'The trouble with asylum centres' (2004) BBC News <http://news.bbc.co.uk/1/hi/uk/3604553.stm> (27 May). Accommodation centres were supposed to alleviate housing and other pressures by dispersing asylum-seekers from major centres (i.e. London) to smaller towns and villages to be housed in accommodation centres. The centres were planned to be self-supporting (complete with schooling services, etc.). The resistance and opposition, particularly in the towns selected, was fierce and widespread. After spending millions the plans were quietly shelved. To date not a single centre has been built.

tourism' by taking up hospital beds intended for native Britons. Meanwhile *The Sun* and the *Mail on Sunday* published stories about 'imported plagues' that asylum-seekers were bringing into the country. By the end of January of 2003, *The Sun* had gathered 300,000 signatures, the largest such poll on record, in an on-line petition to 'stop Britain becoming a soft touch for illegal asylum seekers' and in inflammatory language implored a stop to 'this sea of humanity polluted with terrorism and disease and threatens our way of life'.[94] In a survey conducted by Ipsos/MORI, a week before the decision, 85% of the respondents disagreed that the government had immigration under control; and, almost 70% said laws on asylum should be much tougher.[95] It was into this fray that Mr Justice Collins released his decision on 19 February. The effect was such that many observers were left shocked and alarmed; and, an 'all out war' erupted.[96] Voices of reason, voices extolling the humanity of the decision, voices praising the principled decision and the HRA, and voices of moderation were drowned out by voices of anger and vitriolic attacks on the judiciary and HRA. The tabloid media, some of the broadsheets, and high-profile members of government reportedly 'spitting blood' exploded in frenzied outrage.[97]

6.4.2   The NGO Response

For the right-wing tabloids, which view refugee NGOs with disdain and suspicion, there was little doubt as to how the campaigners would view the High Court decision:

> Not surprisingly, refugee organisations reacted ecstatically to his
> judgement, which will surely – as they well know – encourage
> others to come here . . .[98]

---

[94]   R Winnett and D Leppard, 'Shires buckle under migrant tension' *Sunday Times* (29 Aug 2004); D Leppard and R Winnett, 'Memo leak exposes asylum meltdown in middle England' *Sunday Times* (29 Aug 2004); A Kundnani, 'Britain gripped by populist campaigns against immigrants' (2003) Institute of Race Relations <http://www.irr.org.uk/2003/january/ak000017.html> (May 27); Mr Dolittle, 'The Sun Says' (27 Jan 2003)

[95]   Ipsos MORI *British Views On Immigration* (2003)

[96]   M Phillips, 'Judicial Hubris and Asylum Policy' *Daily Mail* (21 Feb 2003); R Tyler, 'Britain: Government and media conspire to whip-up anti-immigrant hysteria' (2003) World Socialist Web Site <http://www.wsws.org/articles/2003/feb2003/brit-f10.shtml> (04 Dec 2006)

[97]   Comment, 'Rethink Asylum Policy' *Daily Telegraph* (20 Feb 2003) 23; Comment, 'Ministers Must Learn to Respect Their Own Human Rights Laws' *Independent* (20 Feb 2003); T Kavanagh, 'Blunkett Fury as Judge Boots Out New Asylum Law' *The Sun* (20 Feb 2003); Leader, 'Asylum rights evaporate' *Guardian* (10 Feb 2003)

[98]   Comment, 'Bogus Asylum and the Judges who have it in for Britain' (20 Feb 2003)

But the NGOs were far from ecstatic. What they had sought – 'to drive a truck through the legislation' – was not the outcome. For example, breach of Article 6 (a central NGO contention) was held not to be fatal provided that the state changed its procedures. The decision, while positive in some ways and highly critical of the policy, left enough openings via which the government could more or less continue as before. And the NGOs knew it and knew well just how the government would respond to the ruling. High Court criticisms, while encouraging in some respects, do not provide an effective bulwark against an impervious Home Office, particularly in an area where the general public feel the government is failing and is not tough enough.[99]

Notwithstanding deep disappointment that the decision did not go far enough in repudiating a despised policy, the NGOs were nonetheless quietly elated with the decision confirming, as it did, the rightness of their convictions and reward for a hard-fought campaign. But they knew that the fight was far from over. The central players in the test-case (JCWI, Refugee Council, Refugee Action, and Liberty) simply issued press releases saying that they 'welcomed the ruling'. The Refugee Council added that the decision 'confirms our view that the implementation of section 55 has been unreasonable and unjustifiable'. The Refugee Legal Centre said they were 'pleased that the High Court has granted the applications for judicial review'.[100] The NGOs were all too aware of the raging animosity and choose to take the route of moderation in their celebrations while already anticipating the government's next move at the Court of Appeal.

For the purposes of their campaign, the NGOs hailed the decision as a victory for humanity but not much mention was made of the role of the HRA. The language of rights or rights discourse did not dominate campaigning literature and nor did it figure much in the celebrations. This was not by design as a large part of the grassroots campaign had been focused on what was seen by them as 'appalling' conditions to which asylum-seekers were subjected. Many of NGO caseworkers interviewed did not ascribe the victory to the HRA or were unaware of the role of the HRA in the decision. Many saw the court victory as 'just and correct' in dealing with the crisis. In any event, those leading the campaign downplayed the role of the

---

[99]   YOUGOV/Mail on Sunday, *Survey* (2004)

[100]   Refugee Council, 'High Court ruling restores food and shelter to destitute asylum seekers' (2003) <http://www.refugeecouncil.org.uk/news/press/2003/february/20030219high.htm> (25 May)

HRA because of fears, later to be justified, of the Act coming to be seen as somehow opposed to the interests of the majority of Britons. Their celebrations were mostly characterised by feelings of relief but tempered with pragmatism in anticipation of appellate court hearings already scheduled for early March.[101] Not that much of this mattered because not many were paying much attention to what the NGOs had to say. Their voices were drowned out by the furore which followed. Much of the focus was on senior government ministers and the news media, particularly the tabloids, which launched tirade after tirade at Mr Justice Collins and the HRA.

6.4.3   An Attack on the HRA

Almost immediately following Justice Collins's decision, David Blunkett, the Home Secretary, was seemingly everywhere – on talk-shows, television, and giving interviews – condemning the decision. He made no secret of his outrage and railed against the decision and judiciary in emotive and intemperate language, playing to a constituency as 'fed-up' as he over asylum and the judiciary's apparent refusal to countenance his 'draconian' policies.[102] The Home Secretary made it clear that notwithstanding the decision – and the HRA or no HRA – he was not about to change his policies directed at dealing with a major public policy issue and dispelling a view, a self-created one at that, of a Britain 'soft' on asylum:

> This measure is an important part of our asylum reform .
> . . dealing with widespread abuse of the system . . . we must
> continue to be able to operate a robust policy and people who
> try to abuse our asylum system will not find us a soft touch . . .
> I'm personally fed up with having to deal with a situation where
> Parliament debates issues and the judges then overturn them . . .
> Parliament did debate this, we were aware of the circumstance,
> we did mean what we said and, on behalf of the British people,
> we are going to implement it.[103]

---

[101]   Interview notes (on file with author)
[102]   According to a MORI survey 80% of respondents supported much tougher immigration laws
[103]   R Verkaik, 'Asylum system flawed, rules High Court' *The Independent* (20 Feb 2003) quoting David Blunkett, Home Secretary.

> We don't accept what Justice Collins said and will seek to overturn
> his judgment. We don't want any confusion and mixed messages.[104]

The level of the Home Secretary's heated criticisms of the judiciary and, by implication, the HRA cannot be understated and it reached the level of incitement as the media picked up the thread – and many in the media cheered him on.[105] The *Daily Mail*, for example, was careful to exempt Blunkett from its strident criticism of Labour's approach to asylum and the decision. All the major newspapers, particularly the tabloids, quoted Blunkett at length describing him as 'spitting blood', 'furious',[106] 'declaring war on meddling judges', 'ripping into the judiciary', and having 'blown a fuse'[107] and that a 'battle has begun'.[108] Both Prime Minister Tony Blair and Blunkett were reported to have 'reacted furiously' at the defeat and that the Prime Minister was 'prepared for a showdown with the judiciary' and was considering legislation to limit the role of judges and their interpretation of the HRA.[109]

But the invective heaped upon the judiciary by politicians paled in comparison to attacks by large sections of the media. Voices of moderation, and there were a few, were drowned out by the many who had never supported the HRA to begin with. They found in the decision vindication of their long-held views that the HRA, often derided as a foreign imposition or 'European law', should never have become part of British law in the first place.[110] Steve Pound, a Labour MP, wrote a piece in the *Sunday Express* blaming the courts, not the fundamentally flawed piece of legislation or its harsh regime, for making it tougher for the government to address the problem(s) of asylum:

> Collins has driven a horse and carriage through a key piece of
> legislation and dodgy asylum lawyers will be rubbing their hands
> in glee . . .[111]

---

[104]   T Kavanagh, 'Blunkett Fury as Judge Boots Out New Asylum Law' (20 Feb 2003)

[105]   According to many observers David Blunkett, particularly in his attitude towards the judiciary, was an unusually vocal and strident critic and many in the legal profession were pleased when he was forced to resign over an unrelated scandal – see, for example: BBC, 'QC calls for political politeness ' (2005) BBC News <http://news.bbc.co.uk/1/hi/uk_politics/4285339.stm> (25 May 2007)

[106]   T Kavanagh, 'Blunkett Fury as Judge Boots Out New Asylum Law' (20 Feb 2003)

[107]   Comment, 'Bogus Asylum and the Judges who have it in for Britain' (20 Feb 2003)

[108]   F Gibb, 'Blunkett v the Bench: the battle has begun' (04 Mar 2003)

[109]   M Clarke and S Greenhill, 'So what have our judges got against Britain?' *Daily Mail* (20 Feb 2003) 1

[110]   J Young, 'The Politics of the Human Rights Act ' 26 Journal of Law and Society 1 27-37

[111]   S Pound, 'Judge Makes Tackling Asylum Even Tougher' *Sunday Express* (23 Feb 2003)

Melanie Phillips, former writer for the leftist *Guardian* and now columnist for the right-wing *Daily Mail* and author of the provocatively titled 'Londonistan', was at the forefront in attacking the decision. For her the culprit was clear – the HRA, and human rights lawyers. The HRA, she argues, is a 'bad mistake' and another measure in a long line of measures symptomatic of a Britain which has lost its way:

> We should withdraw from the human rights convention . . . and tear up our Human Rights Act altogether. For this culture of rights . . . has given power to unelected judges to make questionable decisions . . . only things that have expanded exponentially are judicial hubris and the parasitical industry of human rights lawyers.[112]

For the tabloids, particularly *The Sun* and *Daily Mail,* the culprits were equally clear: undemocratic judges or 'dictators in wigs' and the 'foolish' HRA. With an estimated readership in excess of 20 million, the tabloids, with their own brand of misleading and inflammatory reporting, called for an immediate repeal of the HRA.[113] The tabloids went even further linking and conflating the decision (and the HRA) to a wide array of major public policy issues such as terrorism, benefits fraud, and the so-called porous borders of Britain. And how did the *Daily Mail,* which called the situation 'dangerous', substantiate such linkage – on nothing more than 'attitude' that 'drips, at least implicitly, from every phrase of the decision'.[114] An extensive review of the online blogs of several major newspapers, including tabloids and broadsheets, leaves little doubt as to the reader's viewpoints. Almost all (in the hundreds) lambasted the government, the courts, and the HRA letting vent to their feelings about a Britain no longer the mythologized Britain of old. And many readers urged a repeal of the HRA – an Act now increasingly seen as an affront to the sensibilities *and* rights of ordinary Britons.

The voices of moderation, or least newspapers which generally would be expected to be more reasoned in their approach, also had difficulty in expressing support for the HRA or the decision, a measure of an ingrained opposition to asylum and the HRA. What the decision did was to bring to the fore the combined

---

[112]   M Phillips, 'Judicial Hubris and Asylum Policy' (21 Feb 2003)
[113]   Institute for Public Policy Research, *Seeking Scapegoats: The Coverage of Asylum in the UK Press* (2005)
[114]   Comment, 'Bogus Asylum and the Judges who have it in for Britain' (20 Feb 2003)

forces of resentment – that which had always been evident and that which had been long simmering, since at least the 1990s (as indicated by numerous legislative attempts to shut the gates to asylum-seekers).[115] In a nation traditionally opposed to immigration (for a wide variety of reasons), and by extension, asylum, the courts again telling Parliament that it could not do as it wished in trying to control its borders (insofar as the UN Convention and HRA were concerned) was too much. The conservative *Daily Telegraph* headlines on the day following the decision proclaimed:

> Damning verdict on judge: One man's rulings have thwarted all
> moves meant to stem the tide of refugees.[116]

In the same article the newspaper left no doubt as to how it viewed asylum-seekers referring to them as 'economic migrants', a pejorative the paper knows to be misleading.[117] While such deliberate misuse is expected of tabloids it is not usually the case with broadsheets. In an editorial, in the same issue, the paper wrote:

> It is quite understandable that Mr. Blunkett is upset that his plan
> to remove benefits has been shot down. The benefit system is
> undeniably attractive . . . and is one of the principal reasons that
> so many asylum-seekers make a beeline for Britain.[118]

Again the newspaper repeats what it ought to know is unsupported by evidence but which is persistently cited by many, including government ministers, as to why asylum-seekers enter Britain: not for reasons of persecution but to take advantage of its supposed generous benefits system. The editorial board did admonish the Home Secretary for attacking the judiciary but suggested that he design better legislation in order to withstand HRA challenges. Failing that the paper suggested that legislation reining in the judiciary was a 'step in the right direction and certainly worth trying'. The editorial board, silent on asylum rights, concluded that if all else failed then withdrawing from the 1951 UN Convention, or amending its domestic application, should be considered.[119]

---

[115]   See Chapter 3 for a review of the recent history of asylum in the UK
[116]   P Johnston, 'Damning Verdict on Judge' *Daily Telegraph* (20 Feb 2003) 2
[117]   R Greensdale *Seeking Scapegoats: The Coverage of Asylum in the UK Press* (2005)
[118]   Comment, 'Rethink Asylum Policy' (20 Feb 2003)
[119]   ibid

Migration Watch, a conservative think-tank opposed to almost all immigration and which views the HRA as an infringement to parliamentary supremacy and obstacle to immigration controls, was equally dismayed at the decision calling it 'good news for asylum-seekers but bad news for Britain' and concluded:[120]

> Increasingly it appears that if the government wants to effectively deal with the growing problem of asylum-seekers it will have to make more derogations from the Human Rights Convention . . .[121]

A week later as the fallout from the decision continued the Chairman of Migration Watch, Sir Andrew Green, felt compelled to issue another press release:

> One day the government will have to face up to the fact that very substantial changes to international Conventions, if not actual withdrawal, are the only answer. We hope that this is sooner rather than later.[122]

The centre-right *Times* was much more restrained and balanced – neither praising nor criticising the decision, HRA, or the judiciary – focusing instead on what options a 'justifiably incensed' Home Secretary should consider in responding to 'this cleverly constructed challenge to the law'. It is noteworthy, however, that the paper felt no need to come to the defence of the HRA in the face of unseemly conduct by senior government ministers and the vitriolic attack of the tabloids. The paper commented that a 'narrow interpretation of Section 55 had led to miscarriages of justice' and made some rather pragmatic and fair recommendations, not much different from what the NGOs had suggested months ago and almost exactly how the-then Immigration Minister had said the law would operate once in effect: that asylum-seekers be given a reasonable period of time in which to file a claim.[123] The irony, of course, is that had this pragmatic and not unreasonable approach being followed Section 55 most likely would have withstood legal challenges leaving alone the central platform of the legislation to work as intended – as a means of cracking down on the obvious abusers, those who had been in the country for long

---

[120]   Migration Watch, 'Response to High Court ruling' (2003) <http://www.migrationwatchuk. org/pressreleases/>

[121]   Migration Watch, 'Implications of the Government's Appeal on Asylum Benefits' (2003)

[122]   Migration Watch, 'Appeal outcome could be 'tip of iceberg'' (2003) <http://www. migrationwatchuk.org/pressreleases>

[123]   Comment, 'Asylum Angst' *The Times* (20 Feb 2003) 21

periods and only filed claims to avoid enforcement action. But this premise does not consider what some viewed as a sinister element of the plan – it was never intended solely for that purpose – it was meant as another signal that Britain's gates are shut to all asylum-seekers, not just to those who abuse the system. The objective: to deter asylum-seeker arrivals and to make life so difficult for those in the UK that returning to the home country becomes the better option.[124]

The *Times* concluded its commentary on the decision by expressing support to the Home Secretary for his work on 'shaping asylum reform . . . (because) skyrocketing numbers have strained the tolerance of a tolerant country'.[125] There is much agreement on this sentiment. The NGOs do not deny the asylum system is chaotic and agree there is an urgent need for reform. The question is whether ill-treating fellow humans to a point beyond endurance is the way to go about it or worthy of a society which espouses human rights values but fails, with some deliberation, to uphold them for the most vulnerable.

6.4.4 Support for the Decision and the HRA

In addition to asylum-seeker and refugee serving NGOs, many social justice and left-leaning organisations, such as Fortress Europe, Operation Black Vote, and Institute of Race Relations, also featured the decision prominently on their websites. However it is difficult to gauge the impact of such sites preaching as they do to the converted. In any event their voices were lost in the tide of invective which swept the nation in the early months of 2003. A major newsmagazine, the *New Statesman* and two major newspapers – the *Guardian* and *Independent* – came down strongly in favour of the decision and the beleaguered HRA. The *Guardian* called the decision a 'victory for humanity' while the *Independent* wrote:

> The European Convention of Human Rights was incorporated
> into British law not for the benefit of government ministers
> but for the sake of those whose fundamental rights are being

---

[124] Interview notes (on file with author). Several NGO interviewees – many of them with years of experience in asylum – expressed this view. See also: F Webber, 'NASS: Chronicle of Failure' (2003) Institute of Race Relations <http://www.irr.org.uk/2003/july/ak000010.html> ; F Webber, 'Asylum: From Deterrence to Destitution' 45 Race and Class 77; see also BBC, 'Asylum hardships 'are deliberate'' (2007) BBC News <//news.bbc.co.uk/1/hi/uk_politics/6507961.stm>

[125] Comment, 'Asylum Angst' (20 Feb 2003)

> threatened . . . it bears repeating that a Human Rights Act is of
> no use at all if every time it runs foul of government policy it is
> ignored or reversed . . . we can be sure that Mr Blunkett will do
> all that he can to overturn a perfectly correct decision . . . [126]

Both newspapers have an established track-record of supporting the HRA and asylum often devoting considerable space demystifying the complexities of the issue. However these papers have a combined daily circulation of about 300,000 compared to about 4 million for the tabloids and 2 million for the broadsheets (*Times* and *Telegraph*).[127] Leaving aside the empirical question of (negative) impact of media coverage on public opinion, events, or any particular issue, it is clear that most of UK was blanketed by negative, and much of it rabid, reporting on the decision and the HRA. What effect this had on the British public already opposed to asylum and the HRA is difficult to gauge? But one thing was certain and it was precisely what the NGOs had feared and that is the HRA would be devalued and come to be seen as something for the 'other' or the outsider and not something for the greater good. At least it was judging by the almost 300,000 Sun readers who signed an online petition to repeal the Act, the very public attacks on the judiciary by the government, the unwillingness of two major broadsheets, the *Times* and the *Telegraph* to support the HRA, and the ranting of the tabloids:

> Yesterday the High Court declared that (Section 55) . . . was a
> breach of – you guessed it – human rights . . . is it any surprise
> that the interpretation of the Human Rights Convention . . . has
> created a hugely lucrative asylum industry[128]

6.5   Conclusion

Several months into life under Section 55, it had become apparent to many observers, including the judiciary which urged the government to take a reasoned approach, that the policy could not continue on its present trajectory of adding to the ranks of destitute asylum-seekers and a durable solution was needed. The

---

[126]   Comment, 'Ministers Must Learn to Respect Their Own Human Rights Laws' (20 Feb 2003)

[127]   R Greensdale (2005)

[128]   Comment, 'Bogus Asylum and the Judges who have it in for Britain' (20 Feb 2003)

court decisions, while promising in some respects, did little to address the wider questions with the Home Office showing little inclination to change its policy. For the NGOs the situation, in many respects, remained dire and they continued to struggle with increasing numbers of destitute asylum-seekers. In some ways the situation, seemed to some NGOs, to be one of brinkmanship. The Home Office continued to resist pressure from some powerful and influential groups such as the Church of England and members of the judiciary who urged a rethink of the policy. The Home Office was also under intense pressure from even more powerful groups – the media, think-tanks, opposition parties, and the electorate – to continue the course. The NGOs, at this stage of the campaign, had very few options. Not much had worked and the crisis of destitute asylum-seekers showed few signs of abating. They were well-aware that much depended on the Court of Appeal and looked ahead to the hearings, with considerable trepidation, but also hope for a more definitive ruling.

7 THE CONTINUING CAMPAIGN AGAINST SECTION 55

7.1 Introduction

By the time the Court of Appeal decided *Q and Others* in March 2003 the furore over the High Court's decision had subsided, at least, as evidenced by the relatively muted media response to the appellate decision.[1] As many expected the tabloids again bashed asylum-seekers, the perceived softness of UK asylum laws, and complained that the *Human Rights Act* (HRA), now increasingly being portrayed as un-British and a European imposition, had again trumped the rights of hard-working, tax-paying native Britons.[2] But there was no vitriolic from elected officials or attacks on the judiciary, which had characterised the High Court decision.[3] And for very good reasons: in several key areas the Court of Appeal, while admonishing the Home Secretary, ruled in his favour. For the NGOs the decision, with some minor exceptions, was a major setback to their objective of 'driving a truck through the legislation'.

This chapter first examines the decision and why it was a defeat for the NGOs. The second part is an overview of the government response and status of Section 55 after the decision. The third part examines the progression of the next set of test-cases from High Court to the Court of Appeal. The chapter concludes with an analysis of how the NGOs regrouped and continued the campaign and how early 2004 marked the beginning of the end of Section 55.

7.2 *Q and Others* at the Court of Appeal

On March 01, 2003, two days before the Court of Appeal commenced hearings on *Q and Others*, David Blunkett, the-then Home Secretary, mounted a public relations offensive and disclosed to the media that costs associated with asylum for the current financial year would be almost £2 billion (the figure for the preceding two years totalled £3.5b).[4] By any accounting such costs are staggering and Blunkett's

---

[1]   *Q and Others v Secretary of State for the Home Department* [2003] EWCA Civ 364

[2]   A Kundnani, 'Britain gripped by populist campaigns against immigrants' (2003) Institute of Race Relations <http://www.irr.org.uk/2003/january/ak000017.html> (May 27)

[3]   See Chapter 6 for a review of media reaction to the decision.

[4]   P Johnston, '£2bn Bill for Flood of Asylum Seekers' *Daily Telegraph* (01 March 2003)

disclosure appeared to be playing to the public's fear and perception of an asylum system out of control, a drain on taxpayers, and in need of severe measures.[5] For the NGOs the timing of the disclosure had the appearance of a Home Secretary, already engaged in a battle with the judiciary, trying to influence an institution which he had earlier criticised for defying democracy.[6] At that time (after the High Court decision in *Q and Others*) Blunkett had argued that Section 55 had been debated and passed by Parliament and it was, therefore, undemocratic for judges to rule against his policy. In the first instance the Home Secretary was not entirely accurate, if not outright disingenuous. The tenuous nature of such an argument and the irony of his claims, while obvious to the NGOs, were not apparent to the Home Secretary who had used a 'guillotine' motion to cut off debate and push through Section 55 into law in late 2002. There had been very little debate on the legislation.[7] While the coincidence and effect of the release of such information on judicial decision-making is unlikely ever to be public knowledge, judges do not exist in a vacuum and this information most probably would have been known to them. In any event the judges were well-aware of the situation on the ground inundated as the courts were with hundreds of judicial review applications.[8] Whatever the case, it was the Home Secretary who prevailed when the Court of Appeal released its decision a few weeks later.

The malleable nature of legal reasoning and judicial decision-making can be such that it often allows both parties to claim victory. And such was case when the Court of Appeal decided *Q and Others*. Both the Home Secretary and NGOs claimed victory, but, in truth, it was the Home Secretary who emerged the victor. To be sure the NGOs won, but mostly on procedural matters. The Home Secretary, on the other hand, won the more important substantive issues which to the dismay of NGOs left Section 55 completely unscathed. This, as the NGOs soon realised and notwithstanding admonishments of the Court, allowed the Home Office to continue as before, as if *Q and Others* and the related activities (protests, sleep-ins, letter writing campaigns, etc.) challenging Section 55 had never happened.[9] But

---

5   See Chapter 3 for a review of how asylum is viewed in the UK.

6   R Sylvester, 'Blunkett accuses judges of damaging democracy' *Daily Telegraph* (21 Feb 21 2003); interview notes (on file with author)

7   See Chapters 4 and 5 for a detailed discussion in how Section 55 was introduced as a last-minute amendment and pushed through both Houses.

8   C Dyer, 'Asylum cases 'clogging the courts'' *Guardian* (16 Oct 2003)

9   See, for example, P Johnston, 'Blunkett defies appeal ruling on asylum benefits' *Daily Telegraph* (19 March 2003)

initially many in the NGO community viewed the appellate decision as the 'nail in the coffin' for Section 55; that the battle had been won and the fight over.[10] Within weeks, however, the NGOs realised that not much had changed; and the front-line caseworkers were the first to notice:

> It wasn't very long after the decision . . . we were seeing the same numbers, even more than before. I thought we had won, all that work . . . but we quickly realised, bloody hell, there's still people out in the streets, homeless, sleeping in the streets, committing crimes, begging.[11]

But the first few weeks following the decision were still heady days and there was much that was misinterpreted about the decision. There was also much that was selectively interpreted by all parties to suit their respective agendas. The NGOs claimed victory owing mostly to the language of the decision or what the Court had to say about rights, in particular, that the regime created by Section 55 constituted 'treatment' within the Article 3 meaning of the word and that that treatment could be 'inhumane and degrading' and therefore 'potentially engage' Convention rights.[12] And this was not an insignificant aspect of the decision. The legal team in *Q and Others*, including the interveners, had fashioned an innovative argument and succeeded in having Section 55 judged from the perspective of an absolute right (Article 3 of the Convention cannot be derogated from and brokers no exception). In this respect many of the caseworkers and volunteers interviewed for this study found in the words of the Court a powerful affirmation of their own convictions:

> For the Court to actually say that the Home Office is treating asylum-seekers inhumanely; well, we knew that, but never before had a court actually said that about the rights of these people. It felt really good to hear that. I was really proud of the court that day, proud of being English . . . it was such a strong thing to say . . .[13]

---

10   Interview notes (on file with author)
11   Interview with Maurice Wren, Asylum Aid (London 27 March 2005); this view was also expressed by several interviewees (on file with author). It is important to note that the supposed link between 'sleeping on the streets', 'begging', and 'crimes' has been cited by many, including politicians, judges, and NGO caseworkers, but there is little evidence to support such claims.
12   *Q and Others* (para 108)
13   Interview notes with Elizabeth, volunteer, Jesuit Refugee Service (London 12 Mar 2005).

But the Court did not actually make such a statement. The justices had been referring generally to Article 3 and the requisite severity of treatment necessary for that treatment to fall within the ambit of 'inhumane and degrading'. Such misunderstanding and misinterpretation of the decision, however, was not uncommon. Many had also assumed, mistakenly, that the courts (both the High Court and Court of Appeal) had struck down the legislation when no such thing had happened.[14] Notwithstanding the misconceptions and inaccuracies such views served to vindicate the work of the NGOs; that after a long and arduous battle they had actually 'won' against a powerful adversary, an inhumane and impersonal Home Office. This was particularly important for the front-line caseworkers and volunteers who wanted to see some tangible proof of their efforts:

> I remember that day quite well because we had been waiting
> for the decision. Some of us went to the Court to wait . . .
> there were protestors there as well because I think they were
> expecting to lose. I felt numb when they told us the Court had
> thrown out Section 55 and we won . . .[15]

> It was anti-climatic. We were exhausted. It was a long campaign
> and I really didn't think we would win. All this talk about rights.
> Even now I am not sure what it all means. We know refugees in
> the UK have no rights. But it was a relief . . .[16]

7.2.1   What Did the Court Decide?

So what did the Court of Appeal actually decide? While the court complimented Mr Justice Collins on the thoroughness of his analysis, the judges disagreed with him in several key areas. First, the Court of Appeal ruled that just because 'there is a real risk that an asylum-seeker will be reduced to degradation' owing to lack of welfare support does not in itself engage Article 3. The threshold, ruled the Court,

---

[14]   See also: R English, 'Failure to support destitute asylum seekers' (2003) Lawtel (10 Oct 2006). Under the HRA courts cannot strike down legislation (but can issue declarations of incompatibility).

[15]   Interview with Catherine, volunteer, Churches Commission for Racial Justice (London 17 April 2005)

[16]   Interview with volunteers/caseworkers at the Refugee Council (Brixton March-April 2005)

because of the seriousness of such a finding is much higher.[17] More importantly, the Court added, it was not unlawful for the Secretary of State to refuse support because that is what Section 55 mandated unless it was clear that charitable or other support was not available and the individual was unable to fend for himself. This test was particularly galling to the NGOs who resented the Home Office (and the courts) placing such a burden on their limited resources and had argued precisely that – that they were unable to provide such support. They argued that their resources were already stretched and they should not be expected to assume duties properly the responsibility of the government.[18] But the Court of Appeal seemed unwilling to accept that the Home Office would use denial of welfare support or forced destitution as a deliberate policy. This would not be an accepted view until about four years later when under the weight of evidence the Joint Committee on Human Rights (JCHR) concluded exactly that, confirming what the NGOs and other observers had warned of before the inception of Section 55 and had seen first-hand since implementation – that forced destitution was deliberate, an enforcement measure designed to deter arrivals and make life so intolerable for those in the UK that returning to the home country, from where asylum-seekers had fled fearing persecution, would present as a more attractive option.[19]

That such a conclusion by a Parliamentary body, by most measures a most serious finding, barely registered outside of a few editorials itself is another indication of the powerlessness of asylum-seekers in the UK and the immense challenges faced by NGOs advocating on their behalf. A content analysis of media coverage during the period of the publication of the Committee's report yielded just two critical editorials in *The Guardian* and *The Independent*; coverage in other major publications was confined to a few paragraphs. There were no apparent repercussions as a result of the report. Such a blithe attitude raises several questions: could it be that a seemingly constant stream of negative news about asylum has inured the public, policy-makers, and media? Or could it be a reflection of public resentment or apathy giving license to increasingly tougher policies? Whatever the case, there is every indication that

---

[17]   *Pretty v United Kingdom* [2002] 35 EHRR 1

[18]   Liberty, *Submission to the Court of Appeal in Q and Others* (2003); interview notes (on file with author)

[19]   Joint Committee On Human Rights, *The Treatment of Asylum-Seekers* (HL 81-1 2007); BBC, 'Asylum hardships 'are deliberate'' (2007) BBC News <http://news.bbc.co.uk/1/hi/uk_politics/6507961.stm> (29 Jun)

get-tough policies will continue to dominate the government's approach to asylum in the foreseeable future.[20]

7.2.2   Article 6 of the ECHR

The Court did rule that Article 6 of the Convention (right to fair trial) had been infringed because of the unfairness of the decision-making process. The Court, however, held that the Home Secretary's assurance the procedures would be changed to remedy Article 6 deficiency and the common law right to judicial review was sufficient to satisfy Convention requirements. In this respect the Court prescribed procedural changes; mainly, that the decision-maker (for the Section 55 application) be the same person as one conducting the initial interview (based on the presumption that this would allow the decision-maker to better assess credibility, the key to determining Section 55 applications). The Court also ruled the applicant must be provided with an opportunity to respond to issues of credibility and that 'as soon as reasonably practicable' must be evaluated from the perspective of the asylum-seeker rather than some assumed objective test (generally deemed by the Home Office to be at time of arrival at a port of entry). These were sensible suggestions which, in theory, should have ensured a more flexible and pragmatic approach to Section 55. However what was not in evidence before the Court was what many in the NGO community regard as possibly the biggest obstacle to a humane and fair process and that is the dominance of 'a culture of disbelief' at the Home Office. It was this culture that virtually ensured procedural changes prescribed by the Court would have little noticeable impact at the ground level.[21] And it was precisely such attitudes and behaviour that the HRA was supposed to change, by bringing about a new respect for human rights in agencies serving the public.[22]

---

[20]   B White, 'New Labour's bare-knuckle fight against asylum seekers' *Guardian* (25 July 2008)

[21]   Interview notes (on file with author): almost every NGO interviewee (supported by various reports) view the Home Office decision-making process as permeated by a 'culture of disbelief'. In my interviews with a non-representative sample of IND immigration officers, it became apparent that a majority view asylum-seekers as economic migrants and cheats. The officers, having witnessed 'fraud on a massive scale', disbelief most claimants as a matter of course and expressed particular antipathy towards human rights lawyers and the *Human Rights Act*; that antipathy extends to their work as public servants, with the Act seen as an impediment to their duties.

[22]   Home Office, *Rights Brought Home: the Human Rights Bill* (1997)

According to the findings of this study, the HRA has had little impact insofar as the lot of asylum-seekers are concerned and on the Home Office, which has been repeatedly criticised and has repeatedly failed to take into account its mandated obligations under the Act. These findings are consistent with an established pattern of Home Office treatment of asylum-seekers, some egregious, focused more on enforcement than a regard for rights.[23]

7.3   Section 55 after the Court of Appeal Decision

What effect did the Court of Appeal ruling have on NASS? Almost none, for all intents and purposes, the decision allowed the Home Office to continue as before, with the NGOs noticing little discernible change. The Home Secretary, in newspaper interviews, made clear that the get-tough policy was necessary and would continue because, as he put it, 'we won'.[24] And he was right. NASS resumed assessing Section 55 applications, and refusing them at roughly the same rate as before the decision.[25] Applications which had been filed or held in abeyance during the court challenge, and which had been given Section 55 support pending outcome of the test-case, were re-assessed and a majority of them rejected:[26]

> Yes . . . we know what the courts said (how to assess Section 55
> applications) but it doesn't change the fact that the application is
> fraudulent, the story full of holes. A lie is a lie no matter what test
> a Court sets out. The judges don't have a clue what's happening
> in the real world.[27]

---

23   V Dodd, 'Home Office ignored law, says judge' *Guardian* (08 April 2006); BBC, 'Asylum
      seekers policy 'unlawful'' (2007) <http://news.bbc.co.uk/1/hi/uk_politics/6302919.stm>
      (04 Feb 2007); R Verkaik, 'Investigation into claims of abuse on asylum-seekers' *The
      Independent* (30 Sept 2008); J Burns, 'Abuse of detainees puts asylum policy in the spotlight'
      Financial Times (03 March 2005); M Townsend and J Doward, 'Cash for asylum scandal
      hits Reid' *Guardian* (04 June 2006); B Leapman and M Kite, 'Hundreds of corruption
      inquiries at Immigration' *Daily Telegraph* (27 July 2006)

24   P Johnston, 'Blunkett defies appeal ruling on asylum benefits' (19 March 2003)

25   Minutes of Meeting - British Institute of Human Rights and Joint Council for the Welfare of
      Immigrants, 'Workshop - Section 55 and Human Rights' (BIHR/JCWI Conference 2003)

26   Mayor of London, 'Destitution by Design' (2004) ; Inter-Agency Partnership, *The impact of
      section 55 on the Inter-Agency Partnership of leading UK refugee agencies and the asylum
      seekers it supports* (2004)

27   Interview with anonymous immigration officer at Heathrow Airport (December 2005; on
      file with author); the officer had worked at NASS in 2004.

Some in the NGO community had hoped that the Court's admonishments and clarification on 'reasonably practicable' and guidance on Article 6 defects would be sufficient to end or at least mitigate the apparent policy of playing 'hard ball' in rejecting applications. Amongst the battle-hardened campaigners, accustomed to lip-service by senior officials, the apparent non-compliance with the Court's ruling came as little surprise. Few were surprised that assurances by senior officials, including the then-Home Secretary, that procedures would be changed to reflect the Court's decision, failed to translate into real change (measured by the continuing negative NASS decisions and increasing numbers of destitute asylum-seekers). And the impact upon asylum-seekers: once again they crowded into already overcrowded shelters and camped outside NGO offices (for the hot breakfasts, showers, and temporary respite from the elements provided by some of the NGOs, especially the Refugee Council location in Brixton).[28] To a person almost all those interviewed, front-line caseworkers, volunteers, campaign organisers, and lawyers, echoed the comments of Jonathan, a caseworker at the Joint Council for the Welfare of Immigrants (JCWI):

> It doesn't matter what the courts say. The government will do as it wishes. How many times have we seen it before? Anytime they lose, they change the law or make new laws and continue as before. We have been fighting this same battle over and over again. It just doesn't change. I don't know much about the *Human Rights Act* but I thought it was supposed to change all this . . . I don't see it.[29]

The action or inaction on part of the Home Office in response to the Court's decision, and what the NGOs were seeing on the ground, confirmed what many front-line workers had long-believed – that the HRA or no HRA, and no matter how many asylum-seekers were left destitute, nothing was going to stop the government from continuing its get-tough policy. The degree of resistance experienced by the NGOs

---

[28] I made several visits to the Brixton location and at all times found it chaotic; the waiting room was always full and the staff clearly overworked (but remarkably patient). My visits took place over several months in 2005 and 2006; often I would sit in the waiting area and observe just to get some sense of what it must have been like during most of 2003 when destitute asylum-seekers would 'camp' outside the doors waiting for the office to open.

[29] Interview with Jonathan, caseworker, JCWI (London March 2005); also, see Chapter 4 for a history, from 1993 to present, of government use of refusal/reduction of welfare as a means of deterrence.

and veteran campaigners convinced them that the orders were coming from senior officials. According to a senior solicitor at Shelter 'it was clearly a message from the top; to hold tough'.[30] Another campaigner added:

> These court challenges, the workload on the courts, cost them (the government) a lot of money. And they were clearly determined to hold tough . . . and to push back. Clearly they were in for the long haul.[31]

The non-compliance with the Court's decision caused a great deal of frustration amongst the campaigners. The leading human rights and refugee advocacy NGOs, including the Refugee Council, Liberty, Shelter, and JCWI, asked the government some pointed questions:

> We ask the government to explain how it is honouring the recent Court of Appeal's judgement, which ruled that the government's previous implementation of section 55 was unlawful . . . we have serious concerns. . . and no evidence that decisions are being made in a fair and consistent manner? We again ask the Government to explain how a policy, which could leave many people impoverished and homeless, can be justified. There is no excuse for employing such a tactic against people whose asylum claims have yet to be decided. [32]

There was no reply because the government took the view that the Court had upheld its policy and that its approach was lawful. For the government, particularly in view of the position very publicly staked by the then-Home Secretary, David Blunkett, that defeat of its asylum-policy to which Section 55 was central was not an option, the decision was proclaimed a vindication. It had to be seen as such and actually be that in fact.

The government had no interest in changing a policy that it viewed as crucial to dealing with the crisis of asylum. And, notwithstanding differences of

---

[30]   Interview with Clare Shepton, Solicitor, Shelter (London April 2005)
[31]   Interview with Uma Joshi, Solicitor, Shelter (London May 2005)
[32]   Joint Council for the Welfare of Immigrants, 'A Joint Statement on the withdrawal of asylum support for in-country applicants' (2003) <http://www.jcwi.org.uk/archives/ukpollcy/statementsec55.html> (Apr 25)

opinion, there is a crisis in asylum. The increasing number of arrivals continues to pose significant policy challenges and have, as the editorial in the *Times* said 'strained the tolerance of a tolerant country'.[33] The key setback, however, was that a policy the NGOs had worked so hard to defeat now had the stamp of an appellate court approval. More importantly the Court had found it not wanting on the more serious of allegations – that Section 55 infringed Article 3 of the Convention.

7.4   The NGO Reaction

Many in the NGO community, notwithstanding public statements to the contrary, were experienced enough to know that the campaign against Section 55 was far from over. *Q and Others* was just the first step in what was expected to be long drawn-out fight. But notwithstanding what was a significant setback the decision was trumpeted as a victory. It had to be seen as such because it was crucial to maintaining the momentum of their campaign and the spirits of the volunteers who had mobilised in large numbers. Many of the veteran campaigners had not seen such a groundswell of support from such a wide variety of groups in recent times and they wanted to maintain it. In this respect, it was important that the decision was seen as a defeat for the government and a victory for the hard work of a disparate group of campaigners (grass-roots volunteers, church groups, front-line case-workers, and lawyers working pro-bono) who had mobilised over what was seen as an 'absolutely appalling' treatment of a particularly vulnerable minority.[34]

> *Q and Others* was trumpeted as a victory because it was useful for us to do so at the juncture of the campaign. The Court was critical of the government in the way they were using Section 55. We used that to focus the media – and we got lots of media attention . . . because, look, the Court said that this practice by the government can lead to serious violations of human rights.[35]

It is important to note that all this time (up to, during, and after the Court of Appeal decision) the NGOs had been campaigning with relatively little coordination. To be sure there was ad-hoc organising and sharing of information via established networks and there was wide-spread support for fighting the policy, but there was no agreed upon tactic or focused strategy:

---

[33]   Comment, 'Asylum Angst' *The Times* (20 Feb 2003) 21
[34]   Interview with Alex Gask, Solicitor, Liberty (London 01 Nov 2006)
[35]   Ibid.

> Maybe strategy's too grand a word for it . . . in practice, how the litigation strategy works is that people work here for awhile and they work on subjects and they begin to pick up stuff from other lawyers or from the calls we get, and they have a kind of strategy in their head. . . . So it's not as much of a strategy as perhaps it should be, but that's because we are a small organisation and we do the best we can.[36]

And this was the case when the NGOs met after the Court's decision to discuss options on what to do next. Attendees and volunteers at the various meetings reported that there was a great deal of talk but no one seemed to be in charge:

> There were lots of great ideas but no implementation or action plan or anything. I didn't see any . . .[37]

The one issue on which there was near unanimity was the conviction that more test-case challenges were needed. There was still no refined or focused strategy except what had been the strategy from the day Section 55 came into effect: keep going to court and filing as many judicial review applications as possible. The NGOs wanted to maintain and increase the pressure on the courts (and, by extension, the Home Office). The intent was to obtain immediate relief for failed Section 55 applicants, while at the same time demonstrating the 'un-workability' of Section 55. But there was also an element of simply 'hoping for the best' – either the courts would decide in their favour or the government, faced with hundreds of applications, would concede because of pressure from the courts.[38]

7.5   *Q and Others*, the HRA, and Publicity

The publicity generated by *Q and Others,* particularly following the High Court decision, kept the issue live for weeks. While most of the coverage was negative,

---

[36]   R Maiman, 'We've had to raise our game: Liberty's litigation strategy under the Human Rights Act 1998' in S Halliday and PD Schmidt (eds) *Human Rights Brought Home: Socio-Legal Perspectives on Human Rights in the National Context* (2004) citing John Waldham, the then-Director of Liberty. This view was also confirmed by Alex Gask, Solicitor, Liberty, when I interviewed him in 2006.

[37]   Interview with anonymous caseworker, Asylum Welcome (Oxford 12 June 2005)

[38]   Interview notes (on file with author)

much rabidly so, there were some heavy-hitters on the NGO side. The Church of England and at least two major newspapers, *The Guardian* and *The Independent,* were firmly on their side and highly critical of the government's policy. While publicity is an important factor given the 'indirect effects' of test-cases litigation, the adverse publicity in the aftermath of *Q and Others* was of considerable concern to the NGOs and the subject of heated debate as to the strategic direction of the campaign.[39] The options, however, were limited. Notwithstanding the apparent 'rightness' of the cause, there were not many lining up to defend this most unpopular of minorities. The NGOs were well aware that they were battling against a tide of public opinion opposed to asylum-seekers (and the HRA) and firmly in support of the government's get-tough approach, an approach which a majority of the public, and tabloids serving a readership of over 20 million, considered 'not tough enough'.[40] And scattered throughout dozens of articles and commentary on *Q and Others* were derisive comments on rights, asylum-seekers, and 'refugee organisations rubbing their hands in glee' – the implication was clear: the HRA was being used to deny Britons their rights and everything was being given away to foreigners who were abusing and cheating the system.[41]

While publicity and media attention are important to the work of NGOs this was not the type of publicity they desired. The NGOs did make attempts to counter the tide of negative reporting and publicity, but it was difficult to be heard under the barrage of such sustained vitriolic. An added concern was that somehow, in the process, rights had become an apparent pejorative. While 'asylum' and 'refugee' have long since been imbued with a particularly venomous connotation, the tabloid and right-wing attacks on the HRA had given 'rights' an almost sinister meaning: that officials and authorities charged with protecting the public had suddenly become weakened because of the HRA.[42] Some of the solicitors working for the NGOs reported facing derision from colleagues and others for their work in human rights and refugee-serving NGOs.[43] According to Shami Chakrabarti, Director of

---

[39]   See, for example, T Prosser, *Test Cases for the Poor: Legal Techniques in the Politics of Social Welfare* (1983).

[40]   Article 19, *What's the Story: Results from Research into Media Coverage of Refugees and Asylum-Seekers in the UK* (2003)

[41]   A Green, 'What About Our Human Rights?' *Daily Mail* (27 July 2005)

[42]   BBC, 'Human rights 'blaming' under fire' (2006) 14 Nov <//news.bbc.co.uk/1/hi/uk_politics/6144804.stm> ; Article 19 *What's the Story: Results from Research into Media Coverage of Refugees and Asylum-Seekers in the UK* (2003)

[43]   Interview with Sameena Ahmed, Solicitor, JCWI (London 08 June 2005)

Liberty, the fight over Section 55 had, in some ways, become a battle over 'making human rights not a dirty term'.[44]

7.6   Conclusion

It remains curious but not surprising that many commentators, particularly the tabloids, viewed the appellate decision as a victory for the NGOs and asylum-seekers when it was in fact a major defeat. The defeat had significant ramifications for the NGOs: in the immediate sense it meant that asylum-seekers would be again left without welfare benefits and shelter and dependent on resource-starved NGOs for support. And, in the longer term, prospects for bringing about wider changes in policy or repealing the law seemed a lot bleaker. By happenstance, a day after the Court released its decision, the Joint Committee on Human Rights issued a report on the culture of rights which the HRA was supposed to develop.[45] And what it had to say, though hardly news to the NGOs, was not promising:

> We have not found evidence of the rapid development of awareness of a culture of respect for human rights and its implications throughout society, and what awareness there is often appears partial or ill-informed. We fear that the high-water mark has been passed, and that awareness of human rights is ebbing, both within public authorities and within the public at large.[46]

And nowhere is the ambivalence towards and, in many cases, an outright rejection of a 'culture of rights' more evident than in the arena of asylum rights. The fight over Section 55, pitting the NGOs against the Home Office, is the most recent manifestation of a seemingly unending contest. As the finding of this research (and other commentators) suggest, asylum is a no-holds barred 'bare-knuckle' fight which the Labour government is determined to win irrespective of what the courts decide.[47]

---

[44]   Cited in R Maiman (2004).

[45]   See Home Office, *Rights Brought Home: the Human Rights Bill* (1997)

[46]   Joint Committee On Human Rights, *The Case for a Human Rights Commission (Sixth Report of Session 2002-03)* (HC 489-1 2003) 9

[47]   The Labour government has come under criticisms for ignoring the law and riding 'rough-shod' over civil liberties; see, for example: Dodd, 'Home Office ignored law, says judge' (18 April 2006); C Dyer, 'Outrage at plan to end judicial review in asylum cases ' *Guardian* (11 Dec 2003); H Porter, 'Blair gets away with his assault on liberty, because we let him' *The Observer* (16 Apr 2006); B White, 'New Labour's bare-knuckle fight against asylum seekers' *Guardian* (25 July 2008)

And during that period Labour stood firm on its 'get tough' policy irrespective of increasing numbers of destitute asylum-seekers.

7.7   The Next Test-Cases: *R on the Application of S, D, T:* July 2003[48]

Following the setback in *Q and Others* it was back to the drawing board in search of a strategy. The NGOs asked: 'what is the best way of fighting this?' The answer was unanimous: 'keep going to the courts.'[49] For the NGOs the choice of tactic was mainly determined by resources and the awareness that not much else had worked or was working. Recourse to the courts, with the HRA serving as a 'bow to the arrow', was seen as the most effective means, and the only means as protests, sleep-ins, letter-writing, lobbying MPs had not produced any apparent results.[50] If anything the situation seemed to be getting worse, the get-tough approach even more entrenched.

That NGOs, fighting for unpopular causes or politically weak and disadvantaged groups, should consistently and persistently turn to the courts is consistent with research in rights and social change.[51] For the NGOs in the asylum sector, litigation has been and continues to be central to their objective of bringing about wider changes in policy, improving the treatment of asylum-seekers and immigrants, and promoting social justice.[52] But this is not to say that courts are particularly receptive to the marginalised or powerless.[53] There is significant evidence to suggest that they are not but it is where the NGOs have had some successes in having their voices heard, with Justice Maurice Kay, in *SDT* for example, calling their arguments 'formidable'.[54] But success is relative, and if it does happen, it is often in small incremental steps. And such was the case with the next series of test cases in *SDT.*

---

[48]   *R (on the application of S, D, T) v Secretary of State for the Home Department* [2003] EWCH 1941 (Admin)

[49]   Interview with Alex Gask, Solicitor, Liberty

[50]   Interview with Don Flynn, JCWI (London March 2005)

[51]   A Hunt, *Explorations in Law and Society: Towards a Constitutive Theory of Law* (1993); GN Rosenberg, *The Hollow Hope: Can Courts Bring About Social Change?* (1991); M Mandel, *The Charter of Rights and the Legalization of Politics in Canada* (1994)

[52]   Interview with Tauhid Pasha, JCWI (London April 2005)

[53]   KD Ewing (2004) 'The Futility of the Human Rights Act' Winter Public Law 829; see also Chapter 2 for a review of the literature on 'Rights and Social Change'.

[54]   See Chapter 2 for a review of theory and literature and case studies on rights and social change.

However before *SDT,* there was *R (on the application of D)* challenging the fairness of the procedures adopted as a result of the Court of Appeal decision in *Q and Others*.[55] In June 2003, the Court of Appeal refused leave because it found the procedures to be fair. In other words, the only way forward for the NGOs' objective of dismantling the Section 55 regime was for a court finding an Article 3 breach.

The lead-up to the High Court's decision in *SDT* in July 2003 was not dissimilar to that of *Q and Others* just four months earlier. There was little coordination and not much strategising. The approach was the same as it had been since the campaign began: file as many judicial review applications as possible. Four months into the Section 55 regime and the situation for asylum-seekers continued to deteriorate; solicitors and NGOs faced with destitute asylum-seekers (refused under Section 55) continued to seek immediate relief for their clients. And, as before, there was also competition amongst the NGOs to be first. This unsaid objective was important to some NGOs eager to enhance their reputations and gain much-needed publicity for their organisation. As stated elsewhere, the human rights field since the advent of the HRA had become increasingly crowded with many making the argument that Article 3 of the Convention had been breached in respect of their clients. However the tactic of crowding the court's dockets (coupled with almost no coordination and screening of cases that were being filed) took away a crucial element in test-case litigation: control over cases selected for test-case litigation. Many cases were poorly prepared or had been rushed to the courts and few addressed wider policy issues. Much was due to the fact that many of those filing court applications had little experience in public interest litigation.[56] The major players in asylum – Liberty, JCWI, the Refugee Council, and since early 2003, Shelter – recognised that many cases were ill-prepared and intervened making submissions to inform the Court of broader issues; attached to the legal arguments was recent research on the impact of Section 55.[57]

The cases of asylum-seekers identified only as S, D, and T, were selected by Justice Kay, as representative of the hundreds on the court's docket. But, as it turned out, the selection of the test-cases, particularly *T* was indeed poor. While *S* and *D* appeared to have relatively strong facts, *T* did not. T had delayed ten days before

---

[55]   *R (on the application of D) v Secretary of State for the Home Department*
[56]   Interview with Tauhid Pasha, Senior Solicitor, JCWI (London 13 March 2005); interview with Uma Joshi, Solicitor, Shelter (London March 2005)
[57]   Copies of the respective submissions on file with author.

making an asylum claim, clearly the 'unreasonable delay' that Section 55 was designed to tackle. Furthermore T was manifestly suffering from a mental malady in that his claim was premised on alleged persecution owing to his preference for European women rather than Chinese (his nationality). T also claimed that his thoughts and actions were being controlled by unknown others, a most unusual set of 'facts' for an asylum claim. At the time of the High Court decision T had shelter and food albeit his circumstances were less than ideal as he sheltered at Heathrow airport. Nonetheless T, along with S and D, was found to have had his Article 3 rights violated.

7.7.1   *SDT*: A Victory for Rights?

The decision was a victory for the NGOs when the High Court ruled that Article 3 rights of each of the applicants had been violated. This was a first for a UK court in finding that the treatment imposed by Section 55 (refusal by the Home Secretary to provide welfare support) was 'degrading and inhumane'. The NGOs had learned from the defeat in *Q and Others* and had fashioned an innovative argument exclusively on Article 3 rights. The test suggested by the NGOs, from a 1997 Court of Appeal victory for the NGOs during an earlier battle over benefits, that Section 55 resulted in a 'life so destitute that no civilised nation can tolerate it' was adopted by Justice Kay in his ruling.[58] But given that this was a High Court ruling, the campaigners knew that the fight was far from over. While their joint press release concluded with a hopeful message to the government (to repeal Section 55), they knew the message would be disregarded no matter how principled the position:

> We hope that this judgement will convince the Government that it is unacceptable for vulnerable people to have to sink to desperate levels of destitution before they can have their human rights upheld.[59]

While, in some respects, historic, *SDT* was also a decision unlikely to stand. Arguably it was a decision that only a court with no precedent setting authority

---

[58]   *R v Secretary of State for Social Security ex parte Joint Council for the Welfare of Immigrants* [1997] 1 WLR 275 (CA)

[59]   Joint Council for the Welfare of Immigrants, 'Section 55 Asylum Support Law Denounced' (2003) JCWI <www.jcwi.org.uk/archives/ukpolicy/sec55_4aug03.html> (Mar 10)

could make. In any event, the High Court hedged its bets by making it clear that its ruling on the test-cases only applied to the three applicants and that it was not 'inevitable' that all those refused Section 55 support would suffer Article 3 infringement. Mr Justice Kay made clear that the cases had been heard on an expedited basis to resolve 'recurring issues in this difficult area'. But his decision clarified little and left the subject as muddled as it had been before his ruling. In any event the categorical nature of the decision meant that the Home Office could continue its policy as before. But in many ways the decision of the High Court was almost predictable. Justice Maurice Kay, like Justice Collins preceding his decision in *Q and Others*, had made his views apparent on the issue of destitute or near-destitute asylum-seekers and expressed displeasure at the increased workload brought about by Section 55.[60]

It is arguable that *SDT* was a direct message to the Home Secretary – perhaps a reflection of a meeting the High Court justices had held to on the very issue of workloads owing to increasing numbers of judicial review applications.[61] In any event there was no mistaking Mr Justice Kay's indignation at both the suffering brought about by Section 55 and the obstinacy of the Home Office in failing to respect the human rights of asylum-seekers. His ruling set out a test (when denial of support would breach of Article 3) and included an explicit barb directed at public officials and the-then Home Secretary, whose submissions he found 'bizarre and distasteful':

> When a person . . . is refused asylum support and must wait for a protracted time for the determination of his asylum claim . . . (and is) denied access to employment and other benefits . . . *our public authorities are required to respect (his) human rights. . . no one should be surprised if, within a short period of time, the demands of Article 3 require the relief of damage to human dignity caused by . . . a life so destitute that . . . no civilised nation can tolerate it. I do not suppose that any reasonable person, including the Secretary of State, views the alternative with equanimity.*[62] (emphasis added)

---

[60] A Travis, 'Asylum Policy Degrading, High Court Rules' *Guardian* (01 Aug 2003)

[61] P Johnston, 'Judges denounce Blunkett's policy on asylum claims' *Daily Telegraph* (31 July 2003)

[62] *SDT* (at para. 27 and 33)

The Home Secretary, however, remained unmoved and immediately announced his intention to appeal the decision. His office issued a statement claiming that its tough measures (Section 55) were a success having reduced asylum applicants by a third. Again that persistent and unfounded claim that the Section 55 was working as intended and weeding out 'bogus' asylum claims when, in practice, it was mostly increasing hardships on NGOs and asylum-seekers.[63] The NGOs again pointed out that senior Ministers had repeatedly assured Parliament that Section 55 was intended to deal with applicants who had been sustaining themselves for long periods in the UK (not recent arrivals), and was not being applied as Parliament had been told it would be but to little avail.[64]

Notwithstanding the preceding factors, the NGOs were elated with the decision and its condemnation of Section 55. Such strong words coming from the High Court made it an important (incremental) victory and maintained the momentum of the campaign. Shelter, Liberty, and the JCWI issued press releases praising the decision and the HRA; various NGOs were quoted in the press claiming that the victory meant an end to the policy of 'forced destitution' and Section 55.[65] This view, however, was not one that pragmatic and experienced campaigners believed and nor was it the case. But it was important for the campaign to project an image of momentum – of continued human rights victories, proclaimed as major victories, for the NGOs and defeats for the Home Office. For the NGOs to state that the Courts had again found in their favour was a powerful message, confirming and legitimising the rightness of their position, while at the same time conveying to the public the inhumanity of the Home Office. The NGOs, supported by the Church of England and other faith groups, continued to repeat the message that the inhumanity and suffering brought about by Section 55 was unworthy of a society where respect for human rights are held as fundamental values. Again the NGOs focused on the contradictions of a government extolling the virtues and importance of the principle of human rights while, at the same time, ignoring the rights of a vulnerable minority and causing undue suffering.[66]Whether this found an audience beyond the converted is another matter, but the messages continued to emphasise

---

[63]   See Chapter 5 for a review of various reports/findings on the impact of Section 55

[64]   Home Office, *Building Trust and Confidence - Home Secretary Tackles Asylum Abuse* (2002)

[65]   A Travis, 'Asylum Policy Degrading, High Court Rules' (01 Aug 2003)

[66]   Refugee Council, 'High Court rules Home Office in breach of Human Rights Convention' (2003) <http://www.refugeecouncil.org.uk/news/press/2003/august/20030801high.htm>

the importance of continuing the fight to the hundreds of exhausted volunteers and front-line caseworkers. To what extent this was a concerted effort in using rights as a catalyst to motivate and organise opposition to Section 55 is difficult to assess, particularly given that the NGOs had focused on the impact of the policy as the driving force in mobilising opposition. The stark picture of human indignities and suffering that the NGOs portrayed caused anger and consternation amongst the supporters, including major newspapers, but the Home Office remained unmoved and continued to maintain a hard-line.[67]

While the use of rights as catalyst is commonplace in other jurisdictions (for example the US and Canada) with established traditions of using rights in social justice campaigns it has not yet found currency in the UK. This research has found little to suggest that such was the case in the fight against Section 55; outside of courtrooms and lawyers the use of rights, language of rights, did not play a major role in the campaign.[68] However, over the course of the campaign, a subtle change seemed to emerge when some of the major media outlets, the BBC, and *The Guardian* and *The Independent* in particular, began to refer to refugee-serving NGOs as human rights organisations rather than refugee organisations.[69]

SDT and the test suggested by Justice Kay, admittedly imprecise, had little noticeable effect and did little to stop the flow of cases to the courts as NASS continued to reject a majority of Section 55 applications. Rather than accepting the letter if not the spirit of the *SDT* test – that a person without access to shelter and support benefits would soon be reduced to a level of suffering consistent with Article 3 – the Home Office instead imposed additional evidentiary requirements asking applicants to provide supporting medical and physical evidence of suffering. No mention was made how such evidence would be assessed or what would be deemed Article 3 treatment by low-level bureaucrats unversed and untrained in assessing such evidence. Logistically and financially this also presented further challenges to the NGOs, amongst them, how to obtain medical certification for a largely transient and homeless population? And even if medical certification was obtained how would it be paid for, and how would such evidence be assessed given the culture of disbelief at the Home Office?

---

[67] A Travis, 'Asylum Policy Degrading, High Court Rules' (01 Aug 2003) ; see also Chapter 5 for a review of various reports on the impact of Section 55
[68] See Chapters 1 and 9 for a detailed analysis.
[69] Based on a cursory review of the respective websites and publications

The answer again, and the only apparent effective option, was to keep going to the courts. In some respects the NGOs were assisted by the chaos at NASS, an organisation in 'continuous crisis management' and 'error-prone' in delivery of services, with the courts displaying little confidence in the ability of NASS to discharge its mandate.[70] The NGOs, using the HRA, continued with judicial review applications (challenging the initial decision by NASS) combined with seeking injunctive relief, which the courts invariably granted ordering emergency aid/support in over 90% of the cases:[71]

> To rescue them (asylum-seekers), judges of the administrative court have made over 800 emergency orders . . . every week about 60 (are made). It is thanks to the safety of the Human Rights Act . . . and perhaps also to the judiciary's unwillingness to pass by on the other side, that these people are not starving in the streets.[72]

While the courts had yet to make a definitive ruling on Section 55, they were more than receptive to applications for injunctions. The NGOs regarded this as their 'one real success' in that the relief ordered by the courts kept hundreds of asylum-seekers housed and provided welfare benefits.[73] The state of affairs, however, remained unsatisfactory. What the NGOs wanted was a durable resolution, a complete dismantling of Section 55 and the apparatus which existed to support it. And *SDT* had failed in that respect. In any event, what little relief had been provided by *SDT* was undone by the Court of Appeal a few months later. The Home Office fell back on its usual (and legitimate) tactic – conceding *S* and *D*, the stronger of the cases – knowing that administrative court decisions do not establish precedence and appealed *T*, the weakest of the three claims. A tactic that the NGOs were too familiar with but still failed to take into consideration in their litigation strategy.[74] Many of the senior policy officers and legal staff, experienced in dealing with the Home Office, acknowledged that such was the case but continued to be hindered by a lack of resources to counter it. But the underlying problem, a lack of planning and coordination, remained constant given that the test-cases were selected by

---

[70]   O Bowcott and D Pallister, 'Rich pickings in the world of asylum seekers' *Guardian* (03 Aug 2005) (referring to the crisis at NASS in 2003)

[71]   C Dyer, 'Asylum cases 'clogging the courts'' (16 Oct 2003)

[72]   C Dyer, 'Judges 'saving asylum seekers from starvation' ' *Guardian* (04 Nov 2003)

[73]   Interview with Don Flynn, Policy Advisor, JCWI (London, April 2005)

[74]   ibid

the High Court rather than the NGOs themselves, which, ideally, is how it should have been done and according to the NGOs own criteria for selecting test-cases.[75] The NGO approach in this instance does not compare well with social movements in jurisdictions where test-case litigation is central to policy objectives; but, as documented in Chapter 2, they too stumble when poor cases are put forward.[76]

This apparent lack of foresight, while primarily a result of an ever-present shortfall in human and financial resources, was compounded by a lack of coordination amongst the sometimes competing NGOs. The Court of Appeal gave short shrift to Justice Kay's ruling and, in overturning it, expressed astonishment that *T* with its bizarre facts had succeeded in the lower court. In what was also a message to the NGOs, other advocates, and the lower courts, the Court made it clear that a case as weak as *T* should never have been prosecuted as a test-case:

> It is also relevant to ask why, instead of becoming involved in the present convoluted dispute over benefits, nobody seems to have confronted the fact . . . that T does not have a viable asylum claim . . . (his) fears seem delusional and not (related) to any form of persecution within the 1951 (Refugee) Convention.[77]

7.8   After SDT: October 2003

Notwithstanding Mr Justice Kay's intention of providing guidance and lessening the workload on the courts, it was back to square one following the Court of Appeal decision. Justice Kay, in charge of the administrative court list, had hoped that his ruling would clarify the law and resolve the problem (of judicial review applications). It is unclear why he should have thought so given the rather convoluted and vague nature of the test he had outlined. Whatever the reason the courts were again inundated with asylum-seekers applying for injunctive relief and seeking judicial review of their rejected Section 55 applications. This again raised the ire of the courts which, in turn, urged the NGOs and Home Office to resolve the

---

[75]   See Chapter 6 for a fuller discussion on the NGO criteria for test-case selection.

[76]   See, for example, FL Morton, *Law, Politics and the Judicial Process in Canada* (2002) for a review of how the women's movement in Canada organised test-case challenges; how they raised funds and created an inventory of issues to challenge several months before the equality provisions of the *Canadian Charter of Rights and Freedoms* came into effect.

[77]   *R ('T') v The Secretary of State for the Home Department* [2003] EWCA Civ 1285

issue without involving the courts. The pleas fell on deaf ears as the Home Office was not about to change its policy nor was it prepared to negotiate with NGOs.

In view of the continuing morass, and given that not much had changed, Mr Justice Kay again decided to select test-cases with the intention of providing guidance. Not all NGOs were pleased given his earlier attempt but they had little choice.[78] This displeasure, however, extended to judicial efforts in general in dealing with Section 55, with some calling the courts' efforts 'unsatisfactory' in reference to what was regarded as an apparent reluctance to make a definitive ruling.[79] At this point many in the NGO community were asking what more it would take for the courts to be persuaded of the merits of their argument; larger questions were also raised about tactics and strategy, and what could be done to be more effective.[80]

Notwithstanding the frustration and on-going debate in the NGO community Justice Kay selected four new cases as possible test-cases, much to the surprise of the respective counsels who then asked for time to consider whether they wanted their clients to be treated as test-cases.[81] The cases were heard in October 2003, but the guidance – a list of four criteria on how Section 55 should be assessed – turned out to be a non-event and quickly faded into obscurity.[82] Like his decision in *SDT, Q* was non-binding, offered recommendations and suggestions leaving it to NASS to decide which, if any, it would follow.[83] And consistent with its approach to Section 55 NASS ignored Justice Kay's ruling; the guidelines had no noticeable effect. The NGOs had not been expecting any substantive changes and were not surprised. What they really wanted was a definitive ruling, a strong test-case that would go to the House of Lords and settle the vexed matter.[84]

7.9   A New Direction?

At this stage of the campaign, the NGOs had come to the realisation that a re-evaluation of their strategy was in order. Many of the senior campaigners and

---

[78]   Interview notes (on file with author)

[79]   Doughty Street Human Rights Unit, 'Comments and Analysis' (2003) Doughty Street (Mar 11)

[80]   Interview with Uma Joshi, Solicitor, Shelter (London 13 March 2005)

[81]   C Dyer, 'Asylum cases 'clogging the courts'' (16 Oct 2003)

[82]   *R (on the application of Q) v Secretary of State for the Home Department* [2003] All ER (D) 409

[83]   Refugee Council, *Update: Withdrawal of in-country asylum support* (2003) Press Release

[84]   Interview notes (on file with author)

organisers, interviewed for this research, had known all along that battle would be long and hard but nonetheless expressed surprise at the degree of government resistance and determination.[85] To be sure the NGOs, in a relatively short period, had accomplished much: they had garnered extensive media coverage and attention on the issue, succeeded in hundreds of injunctions which provided asylum-seekers with benefits and saved them from destitution, amassed a groundswell of support amongst the mainstream media such as the *Guardian, Independent, New Statesman,* and the *Daily Mirror,* major faith organisations, such as the Church of England, were on side; and, they had also won some not insignificant court cases, though mostly on procedural issues. But their persistence, challenges, and court decisions seemingly in their favour had also unleashed a level of vitriolic not recently seen in the UK – commentary bordering on outright racism, a siege mentality exacerbated by tabloids and politicians urging even tougher measures against asylum-seekers – further entrenching government determination.[86]

At this stage of the campaign many NGOs had come to realise that much more was needed to defeat Section 55, but were unsure what to do next. However, there was recognition that careful planning and coordination was needed; there were simply too many organizations, with no clear or apparent strategy, chasing the same goal. At this juncture, however, many were exhausted and tired of the battles and resigned to the apparent futility of their task:

> The Home Office had deliberately done this and wasn't going to budge. It was quite an emotional campaign and there was so much at stake for these people (asylum-seekers), with so little on their side. It was just us (NGOs) against the Home Office, against a huge swathe of public opinion, and so much negativity. *There is a feeling you really need to fight hard or else . . . but there is less fight on our side now, less energy . . . the government has worn down so many people;* each time you have to fight a new piece of legislation, you have to fight a new fight – and you think, wait a minute, we fought that two years ago . . . but always more legislation which goes even further than the one we

---

85   Interview notes (on file with author)
86   Article 19, *What's the Story: Results from Research into Media Coverage of Refugees and Asylum-Seekers in the UK* (2003)

had fought already. And it keeps coming. At the same time there is reduction in legal aid money (and people think the money is going to lawyer's pockets). And people – solicitors – are leaving immigration work. We (Liberty) used to run workshops on immigration and human rights; we were getting over 100 people attending; now, we get barely 30 or so. The whole thing . . . it's exhausting.[87] (emphasis added)

Don Flynn, Policy Director (then at the JCWI), with decades of experience in the field, is even blunter about government motives and intentions:

I honestly think that if they (Labour) had known they'd be in the position (vis-à-vis asylum issues) they are today, they probably would not have passed the HRA.[88]

7.10   The Campaign (November – December 2003)

A review of minutes of a meeting held in late November 2003 show the NGOs poised to 'tug at the heartstrings' by contrasting the season of goodwill with the plight of destitute asylum-seekers.[89] But it was unmistakably a time of hardening and getting even tougher with asylum-seekers. In keeping with the 'crisis in asylum theme' the Home Secretary announced another major legislative overhaul with more promises to yet again tackle abuses in asylum: the *Asylum and Immigration (Treatment of claimants, etc)* Bill, the fifth overhaul in ten years.[90] The Bill contained several provisions which raised concerns in the NGO community, with many dismayed to note an explicit linkage of asylum with crime:[91]

There will be no let up in the Government's drive to tackle abuse of the asylum system and the organised criminals behind it, said the Home Secretary.[92]

87 Interview with Alex Gask, Solicitor, Liberty (London 01 Nov 2006)
88 Interview notes (London 22 March 2005) (on file)
89 On file with author
90 L Smith, 'Britain: Government steps up attacks on asylum seekers' (2004) World Socialist Web Site <http://www.wsws.org/articles/2004/jan2004.bak/asyl-j05.shtml> (16 Oct 2006)
91 Refugee Council, 'UK Asylum: new Bill endangers refugee protection in UK' (2003) <http://www.refugeecouncil.org.uk/news/press/2003/december/20031217ukas.htm>
92 Home Office, No Let Up Combating Abuse Of The Asylum System-Home Secretary (press release) <http://press.homeoffice.gov.uk/press-releases/No_Let_Up_Combatting_Abuse_Of_Th> (2003)

While the criminalisation of asylum remains of significant concern the NGOs were taken aback by an even more troubling provision: an end to judicial review. It was a clear message that the Home Secretary was fed-up with the courts weakening his policies and the NGOs using the courts to challenge those policies. The Home Office also announced a reduction in legal aid for asylum claims, proposals which the *Guardian* called 'almost beyond belief'. The combined effect of both provisions, the NGOs feared, would see checks on executive power via court challenges drastically reduced.[93] In other words the notoriously poor decision-making in asylum would be even less subject to court challenges (owing to lack of legal aid) and scrutiny by higher courts (absence of judicial review).[94] But there was also a token gesture. After months of pressure, an apparent thawing on part of the Home Secretary who announced a modification to Section 55, viz. that applications made within three days of arrival would be deemed to have been made 'as soon as reasonably practicable'. The Refugee Council and the other NGOs received the news cautiously and called it a 'welcome step' but urged the government to go further and repeal the legislation.[95] The NGOs knew from experience that the minor modification in policy would not have much effect on the decision-makers at the Home Office. And it did not.[96] The crux of the problem remained the 'culture of disbelief' and the ingrained belief – shared by politicians, policy-makers, and front-line officers – that most asylum claims were for reasons of economic betterment not persecution.[97]

The effect of the new Bill was to create yet another battleground for the ill-resourced NGOs. On top of battling the policy of forced destitution, the NGOs were now confronted with additional fights over the right to judicial review and cuts to legal aid. It was not a good end to one of the most difficult periods on record.[98]

---

[93] Leader, 'Almost Beyond Belief' *Guardian* (25 Nov 2003); Refugee Council, 'UK Asylum: new Bill endangers refugee protection in UK' (2003)

[94] For a report on the Home Office record on asylum decision-making see: House of Commons, *Asylum Applications* (2004)

[95] Refugee Council, 'Home Secretary announces policy change regarding Section 55' (2003) <http://www.refugeecouncil.org.uk/news/press/2003/december/20031218home.htm>

[96] Inter-Agency Partnership *The impact of section 55 on the Inter-Agency Partnership of leading UK refugee agencies and the asylum seekers it supports* (2004)

[97] H Crawley, 'Tackling the Causes of Asylum' *Guardian* (11 May 2003); A Travis, 'Blunkett aims to axe asylum legal aid ' *Guardian* (25 Nov 2003); C Dyer, 'Top judge condemns asylum proposals ' *Guardian* (11 Feb 2004)

[98] BBC, 'Asylum: Getting tough in 2003 ' (2003) BBC News <http://news.bbc.co.uk/1/hi/uk/3333865.stm> ; interview notes (on file with author)

7.11   Coalition Against the Destitution of Asylum-Seekers (CADAS)

> The principled arguments have failed . . .[99]

For the various NGOs working alone, in ad-hoc partnerships, or loose coalitions not much had worked in their efforts to change the policy or repeal the legislation. Particularly dispiriting had been the Court of Appeal decisions in *Q and Others* and *SDT* – both of which overturned victories achieved at lower courts. The elation, particularly after the two High Court victories, had long faded. Many staffers, echoing Gask's comments (above) had become resigned to what was now regarded as inevitable: that the government would have its way no matter what they did. But to give up and accept defeat would mean that asylum-seekers would have an even lesser voice. Moreover the situation raised some profound questions in the NGO community about the purpose, vision, and mission of fighting for the rights of those least able – the thousands of destitute asylum-seekers. Many volunteers and staff found solace and motivation in their most fundamental objective: what and who are we fighting for? This question was raised repeatedly by organisers as they worked hard to motivate all those involved and reinvigorate the campaign:

> We all need such reminders. It's a simple thing to say but it is what we (NGOs) are all about. What's the alternative – give up – that was unthinkable?[100]

While there had long been recognition that better coordination and management was needed no one had taken the initiative to do much about it. In December 2003, following the appellate setbacks in *Q and Others* and *SDT* and realising the ineffectiveness of their campaigning, a coalition of over twenty refugee-serving and human rights NGOS decided to form a single body, Coalition against the Destitution of Asylum-Seekers (CADAS), dedicated to fighting Section 55. The coalition, comprised of representatives of member NGOs, agreed to work together 'strategically and complementarily rather than duplicating efforts'.[101] The coalition, a diverse range of organisations, included the Salvation Army, Oxfam, the UNHCR, Churches Commission for Racial Equality, law firms, student organisations,

---

[99]   Minutes of Meeting (CADAS 21 Nov 2003) (on file with author)
[100]   Interview notes (on file with author)
[101]   Interview with Habib Rahman, Chairperson, JCWI (London 13 June 2005)

religious orders, and all major refugee-serving NGOs. The first order of business was their mission statement – to fight for the 'rights and dignity of refugees and asylum-seekers and bring about a repeal of legislation' – posted at various meetings as a reminder to all.[102]

7.11.1 CADAS: Reclaiming Rights

The need for a coalition devoted solely to fighting Section 55 had been in gestation for several months but came into fruition at a joint British Institute of Human Rights (BIHR) and JCWI conference in early November of 2003.[103] Observing the furore over the High Court decision in *Q and Others* and continuing attacks on asylum-seekers and the HRA, the BIHR had become concerned at the level and tone of debate, mostly negative and shrill, about the HRA. This was not the vision of a culture of rights which had been promoted by Labour and lobbied for by some the UK's leading advocacy NGOs.[104]

While rights – for example, the interpretation of constitutional rights in Canada or the US[105]– has long been a robustly contested field, in the UK the notion of rights had somehow become symptomatic of all that was (is) wrong in Britain.[106]Not only were the NGOs battling against a swathe of negativity about asylum-seekers, but one of the most important tools at their disposal, the HRA, had now acquired a taint, with many calling for its complete revocation.[107] But such views, particularly so misinformed and misanthropic, did not go unchallenged. The Lord Chief Justice, Lord Woolf, entered the fray and offered a spirited defence of the HRA signalling that rights continue to hold resonance, legitimacy, and power. In direct response

---

[102] Minutes of Meeting (CADAS 21 Nov 2003)
[103] Minutes of Meeting (BIHR/JCWI Conference 11 November 2003)
[104] Home Office, *Rights Brought Home: the Human Rights Bill* (1997)
[105] For example: P Sharma, *Aboriginal Fishing Rights: Laws, Courts, Politics* (1998); M Mandel (1994); J Hucker (1999) 'Theory Meets Practice: Some Current Human Rights Challenges in Canada ' 26 Journal of Law and Society 1 54-71
[106] M Phillips, 'Judicial Hubris and Asylum Policy' *Daily Mail* (21 Feb 2003); M Clarke and S Greenhill, 'So what have our judges got against Britain?' *Daily Mail* (20 Feb 2003) 1; R Tyler, 'Britain: Government and media conspire to whip-up anti-immigrant hysteria' (2003) World Socialist Web Site <http://www.wsws.org/articles/2003/feb2003/brit-f10.shtml> (04 Dec 2006)
[107] Mr Dolittle, 'The Sun Says' *The Sun* (27 Jan 2003); an online review of tabloids blogs in 2003, including those of broadsheets such as the Daily Telegraph and the Times, revealed thousands of negative comments about the HRA and how it had become a 'burglar's charter'.

to the Home Secretary's criticisms he said that judges applying the HRA are not defying Parliament but protecting the public by ensuring compliance with the law.[108] The BIHR also stepped up its programs on educating and training NGOs and others on how to claim and use rights as a means of empowerment. To date the BIHR (and to a lesser extent, JUSTICE) remains one of the few organisations devoted to an expansive exploration of rights other than as an instrument for lawyers and courts:

> We believe that the full value (of human rights) is lost unless we articulate, claim and actively use them in our everyday lives. Our driving ethos is to shift human rights from the realm of abstract, legal documents into living, breathing tools that individuals and organisations can use in all aspects of their lives.[109]

The BIHR, aware of the potential and successes of a rights framework, sought to reframe the debate to that advocated by seasoned campaigners in jurisdictions with established tradition of rights campaigning.[110] And CADAS, at this early stage, while not wholly convinced that a rights-based campaign was the way forward, began speaking more about rights and challenging the government over its contradictions. Many in CADAS (including the wider NGO community) still feared that too much emphasis on the HRA, like the events which followed the High Court decision in *Q and Others*, would create a backlash. Such apprehension was not surprising given the experience of the past several months; and, in the face of Home Office resistance, many in the NGO community felt that the HRA would be of little use outside the courts. The Home Office, during the campaign, had been very clear about its stance and policies – that they were HRA compliant. When challenged the Home Office position was even clearer: take us to court if we are in breach of the HRA.[111] To the frustration of the NGOs, the Home Office's attitude was simply another in a long line of offences; of a department resistant to the objectives and promises of *Rights Brought Home*.[112]

The first meeting of CADAS was held later that month and what the NGOs found, following a 'balance-sheet' analysis of what had worked and what had not, provided

---

[108]   Notes from a lecture by Lord Justice Woolf on the 'Impact of Human Rights' (Oxford Lyceum 06 March 2003); Lord Justice Woolf declined to be interviewed for this research. See also: C Dyer, 'Woolf defends judge over rights ruling' *Guardian* (07 Mar 2003) 11

[109]   www.bihr.org

[110]   For a review of literature on rights and social change see Chapter 2

[111]   Interview with Uma Joshi and Clare Shepton, Solicitors, Shelter (London 2005)

[112]   Home Office, *Rights Brought Home: the Human Rights Bill* (1997)

little encouragement. The balance sheet was clearly tilted towards the government: at this stage of the campaign the media attention had faded and there was little coverage of the NGO efforts or of the plight of destitute asylum-seekers. The cost-benefits arguments (on the economic benefits of immigration and allowing asylum-seekers to work), which did not go unchallenged by conservative organisations, had few takers.[113] Principled arguments (i.e. the inhumanity and cruelty of starving human beings) also had little apparent effect and were considered to have failed. In an era of a supposed new dawn for human rights, arguments based on the HRA, particularly on the apparent contradiction in government policies which the NGOs highlighted in the campaign and for which the government was severely criticised by the courts, major newspapers, and the JCHR, also failed.[114] The government remained steadfast during a year judged by many observers to be the 'toughest' on asylum.[115] Even more importantly during the year it had become apparent that, notwithstanding promises by Labour to usher in a new era of human rights, the HRA was having little effect on a government and bureaucrats determined to be tough on asylum.[116] At about the same time the JCHR took stock of the human rights situation in the UK and concluded:

> It is clear to us that . . . public authorities . . . do not give a high priority to placing respect for human rights at the heart of their policies and practices.[117]

7.12   HRA Successes

While the NGOs had some, albeit modest, successes with the HRA in test-cases before the lower courts, the Act was the key factor in winning over 90% of applications for injunctive relief. When NASS refused welfare benefits the NGOs immediately filed for judicial review of the decision and sought injunctions at the

---

[113]   This particular argument does not appear to be very persuasive insofar as British attitude towards immigration (and asylum) is concerned; in any event, it is a position which has been challenged by conservative organizations such as Migration Watch and Civitas.

[114]   Minutes of Meeting (CADAS 21 November 2003) (on file with author); see Chapter 9 for a fuller discussion

[115]   BBC, 'Asylum: Getting tough in 2003 '

[116]   Interview with Don Flynn, Policy Advisor, JCWI (London 14 March 2005)

[117]   Joint Committee On Human Rights *The Case for a Human Rights Commission (Sixth Report of Session 2002-03)* (2003)

same time. The courts readily intervened and ordered NASS to provide relief (on Article 3 grounds and without determining if the claim had been made 'as soon as reasonably practicable').

In other respects, however, such as using the HRA as leverage or in negotiations with the Home Office, the successes for the NGOs were few. There were anecdotal reports of 'small victories', particularly by caseworkers at the Refugee Council who reported some successes in securing benefits for refused Section 55 applicants without judicial intervention. But whether this was due to the human rights arguments or the clout and size of the Refugee Council, which has offices across the UK, is uncertain; even a senior officer was unable to explain the reason of such apparent success.[118] What is clear, however, is that almost all the caseworkers interviewed for this study (working for organisations other than the Refugee Council) had little success with human rights arguments in convincing the Home Office to reconsider its initial refusal. In fact, many recall the Home Office challenging the merits of human rights arguments – i.e. – NASS officers would counter the arguments by assertions such as: 'we don't think this particular claim raises HRA issues' and/or 'we believe our refusal is HRA compliant'.[119] The NGOs were aware that there was resentment and resistance to HRA arguments in the Home Office, with CADAS reporting that officials felt 'forced'; that 'human rights arguments were being foisted on them'; and this 'is not about how the HRA was supposed to work'.[120] That government officials, duty-bound and mandated to consider the HRA in their day-to-day work, should hold such views or be so resistant is a measure of how little inroad the Act has made in changing the 'culture of disbelief' at the Home Office. This finding is consistent with the findings of the JCHR which, upon review of the state of HRA compliance at that time, expressed concern at the state of affairs and concluded that public officials were paying scant attention to human rights obligations.[121]

7.13   A Campaign Reinvigorated?

Notwithstanding some disagreements at CADAS on how the campaign should be refocused, it remained almost unanimous that litigation was to be central. This

---

remained the view notwithstanding setbacks in *Q and Others* and *SDT.* Some of the campaigners felt that it was a matter of time and all that was needed was a strong test-case.[122] That such a view should persist, in spite of a mixed results in the courts, is consistent with research in rights and social change. Mandel (1994), for example, ascribes this to the power of law to seduce the unwary of what are ultimately empty promises.[123] But, as Epp argued, a persistent push from below is a major factor in bringing about social change.[124] And this approach prevailed. There was a strong feeling amongst some of the legal staff that a strong case would result in a finding of a breach of Article 3. This feeling was based on a reading of various court decisions, including the High Court decision in *SDT* (which had found Article 3 breach) and the comments of the Court of Appeal in *Q and Others*, which had examined at length what would be required for 'treatment' to breach Article 3. At this stage the NGOs were confident that they had amassed sufficient evidence – studies, witness statements, and reports – on the effects of Section 55.[125] And irrespective of the case that would actually go before the courts, the major refugee-serving and human rights NGOs (Refugee Council, JCWI, Liberty, Shelter, and JUSTICE) had already prepared intervener submissions focused on 'treatment' and Article 3 breach. The submissions also contained witness statements about the lack of capacity of NGOs to provide charitable relief (in absence of government welfare benefits) and empirical reports on the impact of Section 55 and suffering it was causing asylum-seekers.[126] In this respect, the NGOs were fully prepared and confident but also wary given the vagaries of judicial decision-making.[127]

There is little doubt that the flurry of activities under CADAS also had the effect of conveying a unity of purpose. The campaign, which had become disorganised and dispirited, appeared reinvigorated: meetings were held across the country, with organisers criss-crossing to 'hot-spots' and rallying the supporters. A review of the

---

[122] CADAS Minutes of Meetings (11 Nov 2003; 21 Nov 2003; 04 Feb 2004; 10 Feb 2004)
[123] M Mandel (1994)
[124] CR Epp, *The Rights Revolution: Lawyers, Activists, and Supreme Courts in Comparative Perspective* (1998)
[125] The reports included: Refugee Council, *Hungry and Homeless: The Impact of the Withdrawal of State Support on Asylum Seekers, Refugee Communities and the Voluntary Sector* (2004); Inter-Agency Partnership, *The impact of section 55 on the Inter-Agency Partnership of leading UK refugee agencies and the asylum seekers it supports* (2004); Oxfam and Refugee Council, *Poverty and asylum in the UK* (2002); Mayor of London, *Destitution by Design* (2004)
[126] Copies of submissions by Liberty, Shelter, JCWI, and Justice (on file with author)
[127] Interview notes (on file with author)

minutes of several meetings held in the early months of 2004 show a coalition deeply angered and concerned at the continued plight of destitute asylum-seekers. There was also some division on how to continue the fight and radical elements were showing some signs of coming to the fore. Some expressed the view that the courts were not the proper venue for the campaign and that more aggressive tactics were needed:

> The only way to deal with Section 55 is not through the courts but to have it repealed . . . lobby MPs and move away from legal challenges; access to lawyers is limited . . . itself a worrying situation if we have to rely on lawyers to do this. It's local action that will count . . .
>
> We need to carry this to the streets . . .
>
> Approach all political parties campaigning to be elected (and put) Section 55 repeal on the agenda . . . [128]

Lobbying of MPs (mostly targeting of known and sympathetic supporters, 'swing' seats, BME (black, minority, and ethnic) MPs, and constituencies with large BME population) was renewed. The NGOs succeeded in having sympathetic MPs table an Early Day Motion (EDM) in the House of Commons to repeal Section 55, but it was received with little enthusiasm.[129] The NGOs then lobbied the House of Lords (during the Committee Stage of hearings into the most recent Bill on asylum) and succeeded in having their motion (an amendment to repeal Section 55) debated at length. While there was sympathy and support the amendment was ultimately withdrawn from further debate. A review of the Hansard record of the debate show a committee deeply divided. It was clear that there was much unease within the House over Section 55, particularly its impact and purported effectiveness in weeding out abusive claims.[130] During this time the office of the Mayor of London became actively involved in working with the NGOs to repeal Section 55. The office, under Ken Livingstone's mayoralty, had always been sympathetic but became active following the publication of its report on the impact that the policy was having in London communities.[131]

---

[128]   Minutes of Meeting of CADAS (04 Feb 2004)
[129]   Minutes of Meeting of CADAS (10 Mar 2004)
[130]   www.publications.parliament.uk/pa/ld200304/ldhansrd/vo040426/text/40426-27. htm#40426-27_head0
131   Mayor of London, *'Destitution by Design'* (2004)

A flurry of emails between the NGOs and the Mayor's office show them working closely on strategy, gathering supporters, and organising opposition.[132]There was also increased media attention on the campaign, but not as much as the NGOs would have preferred – a few of the campaign events, such as sleep-ins, were usurped by other news events. The NGOs also appeared at a Home Affairs Committee examining asylum and gave evidence, much of which was later incorporated in the Committee's critical report urging the government to be more humane in its policies and reconsider some of the provisions of its new immigration Bill.[133]

7.14   The End of Section 55

For many front-line caseworkers, volunteers, and others involved in the campaign the cumulative effect of the various activities undertaken by CADAS conveyed a sense of a gradual building of opposition, of an almost inexorable force compelled forward by the justness of its position. As some of the campaigners later recalled the momentum seemed firmly in their favour.[134] At this time, with the exception of a minor modification in policy which had little discernible effect on decision-making at NASS, the Home Office remained steadfast. But, in many ways, the early months of 2004 marked the beginning of the end of Section 55. To be sure the legislation and policy remained intact but, in practical terms, the regime had been hobbled by the various court actions. By now the courts had been granting injunctive relief in 90% of the applications before them; in effect, nullifying NASS rejections of Section 55 applications. And, in April 2004, the Home Office, facing the inevitable and at the request of the courts fed-up with unnecessary applications, agreed to provide support to applicants until the outcome of another group of test-cases (which were, at that time, making their way through the Court of Appeal).[135]

7.15   Conclusion

At this stage of the campaign, the middle of 2004, much had improved for the NGOs. The number of asylum-seekers suffering destitution had slowed considerably from

---

132   Copies of emails (dated Feb 2004) on file with author

133   House of Commons, *Asylum Applications* (2004) para 191-2, 200

134   Interview notes (on file with author); Minutes of Meeting of CADAS (11 Nov 2003; 21 Nov 2003; 04 Feb 2004; 10 Feb 2004)

135   www.asylumsupport.org.uk/whatsnew.htm

the early days of Section 55. This was due, in part, to court injunctions and the fact that government efforts at strengthening border controls had reduced the number of new arrivals.[136] Nonetheless Section 55 had been more or less reined-in. With the exception of legal tactics, it remains, on the whole, difficult to assess what affect the various NGO activities – such as protests, letter-writing – had on the campaign or even if it is possible or instructive to break them into constituent parts. 'It's the force of the opposition' according to Tauhid Pasha, the then-senior solicitor with JCWI, who described the campaign as having a cumulative effect: the various actions, each incrementally important to the campaign:

> All our activities – litigation, letter-writing, lobbying, etc. – are underpinned by human rights. It goes to the very core of what we are all about. Whether we say human rights or not, that is what it's all about . . . we will continue to challenge the government; point out the contradictions in its policies . . . it's a very powerful thing to say 'hey, your policies are in conflict with your own human rights act'. And we do focus on that – but we also do other things . . . I won't deny that in asylum, it's very very difficult . . . never really sure if they (government) are listening . . . we have seen in this instance that they were single-minded and nothing – not even the HRA – was going to stop them from that policy.[137]

Not surprising, Pasha, a veteran of challenging government policies on immigration and asylum, considers litigation ('because that is the only way we can get the government's attention') to be one of the most effective means of action; of effectively and forcefully conveying the NGO message. But Pasha also views publicity as crucially important 'because judges read newspapers and watch television . . . as do MPs, labour unions and, at some level, there is an effect'.

While the NGOs waited for another test-case, there was consensus to continue filing as many judicial review applications as possible to continue to drive home the un-workability of the current process and increase the pressure on the government to change its policy. The NGOs reasoned that judges expressing concern about destitute asylum-seekers and increasing workloads were more likely

---

136   Home Office, *Government Reply: Asylum Applications* (2004)
137   Interview with Tauhid Pasha (London 13 Apr 2005)

to get the attention of the Home Office and the media than any statements they issued. By this time there was a strong feeling, amongst many campaigners, that judges were sympathetic to the cause; that the judges, too, were troubled by the crisis, to which the Home Office continued to turn a blind eye.[138]And when the judiciary, which had been signalling its displeasure at the policy through a series of decisions (including applications for injunctions against Section 55), finally responded, it was a resounding 5-0 House of Lords decision for the NGOs.[139]

---

[138] Minutes of Meeting (CADAS 10 Mar 2004); interview notes (on file with author)
[139] *Limbuela*

8   THE END OF SECTION 55?

8.1   Introduction

The fight over welfare benefits for asylum-seekers, which began in the early 1990s, shows little sign of abating and continues to pit the Home Office against NGOs which work for and advocate on behalf of asylum-seekers. November 2005 may have marked the end of one such fight when the House of Lords ruled 5-0 that Section 55, a policy that left over 10,000 asylum-seekers destitute and without shelter, was in breach of the *European Convention of Human Rights* (ECHR). But it was a temporary respite. This chapter examines the events leading up to the House of Lords decision in *Limbuela* and what the fight over Section 55 has meant for the NGOs, asylum-seekers, and the development of a culture of rights. The chapter concludes with a review of how the policy of limiting welfare benefits continues as an enforcement measure.

8.2   Overview of *Limbuela*

In early February 2004 three judicial review applications were being heard in the High Court. On the face of it they were fairly routine, indistinguishable from the hundreds of other applications filed by asylum-seekers refused welfare support under Section 55. At that time, and given that they were lower court proceedings, not many were paying much attention. To be sure, there was ad-hoc monitoring, and the NGOs had put out several messages networked via caseworkers to watch for potential test-cases with which to continue challenging the much criticised policy of refusing welfare benefits to asylum-seekers determined not to have applied 'as soon as reasonably practicable'. This particular requirement, a legally mandated criterion, was considered by many observers to be a cover for the real objective, which was to refuse anyone who did not submit an asylum application at a port-of-entry.[1] In other words, the policy was designed to force asylum-seekers into destitution as an enforcement measure – to deter them from entering the UK, and compel those already here to return to their countries of nationality.[2]

---

[1]   See, for example: Inter-Agency Partnership, *The impact of section 55 on the Inter-Agency Partnership of leading UK refugee agencies and the asylum seekers it supports* (2004)

[2]   See Chapters 5 and 6 for a fuller discussion

One of the applications, *Limbuela*, was presided over by Mr Justice Collins;[3] the others, all later co-joined at the appellate level, were *Tesema* (Mr Justice Gibbs) and *Adam* (Mr Justice Charles).[4] As if moved by a singular motivation, all three justices found for the applicants. Mr Justice Gibbs followed what Collins had termed 'common sense' that the applicants would be subjected to degrading treatment, within the ambit of Article 3, if refused permission to work and not provided with welfare support. Mr Justice Charles disagreed with Collins's approach calling it no different from the 'real risk' test (expressly rejected by the Court of Appeal in *Q and Others*) and applied a stricter test, but nonetheless found an Article 3 breach.[5] Later that year in a 2–1 decision the Court of Appeal agreed with Mr Justice Collins's reasoning.[6] And in November 2005 the House of Lords in a 5–0 unanimous decision agreed sounding the death knell for Section 55.[7]

For the NGOs it was victory at last. A fight that had began in October 2002 ended just over three years later with a legal victory against an unyielding Home Office which had fought them every step of the way. It was a significant victory for human rights in general and the HRA in particular. The notion of rights and the Act itself had withstood sustained and vitriolic attacks during the campaign and, in the end, was the deciding factor in the long battle over Section 55. Also subjected to vitriolic attacks were 'anti-democratic' judges ('dictators in wigs'), 'parasitical' human rights lawyers, and refugee-advocacy NGOs 'rubbing their hands in glee' (at the prospect of more asylum-seekers entering the UK).[8] During the campaign the NGOs faced immense challenges – fighting the policy while at the same time struggling to provide support for destitute asylum-seekers in the face of public apathy, political determination, and tabloid anger. But they remained undeterred from what was an 'exhausting' battle and achieved their objective of 'driving a truck through the legislation' and dismantling the much-reviled Section 55 regime.[9] How

---

3   *R (on the application of Limbuela) v Secretary of State for the Home Department* [2004] EWCH 219 (Admin)
4   *R (on the application of Tesema) v Secretary of State for the Home Department* [2004] All ER (D) 247; *Adam v Secretary of State for the Home Department* [2004] All ER (D) 264
5   *Q and Others v Secretary of State for the Home Department* [2003] EWCA Civ 364
6   *Secretary of State for the Home Department v Limbuela, Tesema & Adam* [2004] EWCA Civ 540
7   *R. v. Secretary of State for the Home Department ex parte Limbuela* [2005] UKHL 66
8   See Chapter 6 for a fuller discussion on the reaction to the first test-case challenge of the campaign.
9   Interview with Alex Gask, Solicitor, Liberty (London November 2005)

did the test-case responsible for dismantling Section 55 come about? It happened by chance.[10] And was it the victory that the NGOs had worked for?

8.3 *Limbuela* (High Court)

Wayoka Limbuela, a national of Angola, arrived in the UK on 6 May 2003 and claimed asylum the following day. He was provided with accommodation, but a few weeks later NASS decided that he had not made his claim 'as soon as reasonably practicable' and refused further support. He was evicted from shelter and spent a few nights on the street. Later he was able to obtain charitable shelter but was asked to leave after four nights and advised to contact a solicitor, who then wrote to NASS advising that Limbuela faced violations of Article 3 and 8 (because he was without shelter and welfare support). Limbuela's situation should have qualified him for Section 55 support under guidelines issued by Mr Justice Kay.[11] But, true to form, there was no reply from NASS.[12] Limbuela then sought the intervention of the courts. On 28 July 2003 he was granted an interim injunction enabling him to obtain shelter and welfare support while he awaited the determination of his asylum claim.[13] Limbuela's application for judicial review was heard by Mr Justice Collins, a High Court judge with a record of striking down 'draconian' polices on asylum-seekers and considered a 'serial offender' and 'thorn in the side' by the Home Office.[14] Collins was the same justice who had set off the furore over Section 55 when he had first considered the policy and ruled against it. And, now, he was again asked to consider the very same issue he had first decided in *Q and Others* (which was later overturned by the Court of Appeal).[15]

In what was, for all intents and purposes, a fine tuning of *Q and Others*, Mr Justice Collins dismissed two of the central arguments of the Home Secretary. First, he ruled that the possibility or option of finding charitable support or shelter (to fend of Article 3 breach) was more illusory than real and therefore

---

10   Interview with Claire Sephton, Solicitor, Shelter (London 13 June 2005)

11   See Chapter 7 for a review of various guidelines issued by the courts.

12   See Chapters 5 and 6 for a discussion on the Home Office, an organisation 'not fit for the purpose'.

13   *Limbuela* (para 18-19)

14   Comment, 'Bogus Asylum and the Judges who have it in for Britain' *Daily Mail* (20 Feb 2003) 12; see also Chapter 6 for a brief on Mr Justice Collins's previous decisions on asylum.

15   *Q and Others v Secretary of State for the Home Department* (2003)

not a bar to pursuing action under Articles 3 or 8. And, second, he dismissed the 'wait and see' approach (to see if the actual suffering would be severe enough *before* intervening to avoid Article 3 breach) advocated by the Home Secretary as 'distasteful' and 'impossible to accept' (paragraphs 32-33; Gibbs, in *Tesema*, described it as 'abhorrent' and 'contrary to any reasonable concept of justice').[16] The 'common sense' test was even more expansive and flexible than the 'real risk' test he had advocated earlier in *Q and Others*; that that test was later overturned on appeal did not deter Collins from continuing his opposition to a policy viewed by many as 'abhorrent'. For some of the campaigners, at this stage, it had become apparent that Mr Justice Collins, and other like-minded judges, was determined to hobble the regime. That such a reasoned decision should emanate from Collins did not surprise the campaigners who were well aware of his previous approach to the vexed question of welfare benefits for asylum-seekers and his established record, arguably a sympathetic view of vulnerable groups.[17] It was open to Collins to adopt the position advocated by Mr Justice Newman just a week earlier in *Zardasht* rejecting Article 3 arguments; Newman wrote: 'I am unable to accept the breadth of generality of the (common sense) submission'.[18] This very position was advanced by the Home Secretary rejecting as 'too general' the very proposition accepted as 'common sense' by Collins, mainly that those left without shelter and no benefits would soon suffer the required severity to breach Article 3. Mr Justice Collins wrote:

> I am afraid I cannot go as far as Newman J in rejecting the
> application of common sense . . . if the (applicant) can show .
> . . that no assistance is available except by begging and hoping,
> then the fact he will have to sleep rough, he has no money, he
> has no proper access to food or other facilities, will be likely to
> establish his case.[19]

And in direct reference to the additional and onerous evidentiary burdens placed on the NGOs and asylum-seekers by NASS (later adopted by Newman in *Zardasht* in requiring detailed evidence before determining Article 3 breach), Mr Justice

---

[16] *R (on the application of Tesema) v Secretary of State for the Home Department* (para 59)

[17] Interview notes (on file with author)

[18] *Zardasht v Secretary of State* [2004] EWHC 91 Admin (para 21)

[19] *R (on the application of Limbuela) v Secretary of State for the Home Department* (para 36-7)

Collins explicitly rejected such requirements, adding that no medical or specific evidence was needed to 'establish what, after all, is a matter of common sense.'[20]

It is of significant import that the decisions in *Limbuela, Tesema,* and *Adam* had come after a meeting amongst High Court judges concerned with the crisis of destitute asylum-seekers and the mounting workload on the courts. It was also apparent that the judges were fed-up with the courts being the only option of redress, perturbed at the Home Secretary failing to acknowledge clear signals from the courts to resolve the matter without litigation, and fed-up with the obstinacy of the Home Office in refusing to address what was seen as a humanitarian crisis.[21] While it is apparent that the judges were united in certain aspects there was, however, no unanimity in approach with judges seemingly split into two camps: the tough approach of Newman and the 'common sense' advocated by Collins. During the early days of Section 55 (in February 2003) Mr Justice Collins had pointedly asked the Home Secretary to adopt a more 'liberal approach' towards asylum-seekers; and, in October 2003, Mr Justice Maurice Kay (of *SDT*), in a draft statement supported by other nominated judges, had urged a practical approach because the Secretary of State's 'policies were not working'.[22] Aside from a minor concession that did nothing to stem the flow of cases to the courts, the Home Secretary continued as before.[23] In many ways, this was a court pushed to a corner by the actions of the-then Home Secretary, David Blunkett, determined to ride rough-shod over rights and judges with whom he was 'fed-up' and viewed as 'interfering' and 'anti-democratic'.[24] This, some observers considered, was Blunkett's 'war' against the judiciary.[25] But the judges in the High Court were equally determined and pushed

---

[20]   ibid (para 38); see Chapter 7 for further discussion. The NGOs regarded NASS demands for medical evidence as another example of obstinacy. The requirement, while seemingly reasonable, had the effect of creating further hurdles for asylum-seekers.

[21]   C Dyer, 'Judges 'saving asylum seekers from starvation' ' *Guardian* (04 Nov 2003)

[22]   *Secretary of State for the Home Department v Limbuela, Tesema & Adam* (para 108)

[23]   See Chapter 7 for a discussion on the concession (i.e. an application filed within three days of arrival would be considered 'as soon as reasonably practicable) which had no noticeable impact upon NASS decision-making.

[24]   See Chapter 6; also BBC, 'Judge urges asylum rule suspension' (2003) BBC News <http://news.bbc.co.uk/1/hi/uk_politics/2751161.stm> (27 May 2007); R Hattersley, 'A bit of a wet Blunkett ' *Guardian* (15 Oct 2006)

[25]   See, for example: J Rozenberg, 'Judges prepare for battle with Blunkett' *Daily Telegraph* (26 Feb 2003); F Gibb, 'Blunkett v the Bench: the battle has begun' *The Times* (04 Mar 2003) 3; P Johnston, 'Blunkett defies appeal ruling on asylum benefits' *Daily Telegraph* (19 March 2003); R Sylvester, 'Blunkett accuses judges of damaging democracy' *Daily Telegraph* (21 Feb 2003)

back. And perhaps emboldened by the HRA did not hesitate to step into what Lord Justice Laws (later in dissent at the Court of Appeal) viewed as:

> We are left with a state of affairs in which our public law courts are driven to make decisions whose dependence on legal principle is at best fragile, leaving uncomfortable scope for the social and moral preconceptions of the individual judge . . .[26]

What was it that compelled Justices Collins and Gibbs to move in the direction that they did, while Justices Newman and Charles (notwithstanding his finding in favour of the applicant) moved in the opposite direction? The applications could just as easily have been dismissed as per *Zardasht*. To be sure such a position would have entailed the Court turning a blind eye to the suffering of thousands of destitute humans (which is precisely what *Zardasht* had done). This would not have been inconsistent with other rulings on asylum (or immigration) by courts in the UK which have not always viewed asylum-seekers with much leniency and have a demonstrable history of marked reluctance to step into an arena of apparent policy-making.[27] In *Zardasht* Mr Justice Newman acknowledged that his decision may be viewed as 'harsh' but sought refuge in the words of Section 55 itself which he described as 'not intended to be a benevolent piece of legislation'. It is the law and must therefore be applied as Parliament intended was the approach taken by Newman.[28]

For the NGOs the position taken by Newman seemed too convenient; a refuge for judges disregarding their obligations under the HRA and avoiding controversial issues as best left to policy-makers.[29] The NGOs regarded such reasoning as contradictory to the spirit of human rights outlined in *Rights Brought Home*. They argued that a culture of rights requires a robust application of the HRA, which is also the law and must be applied as Parliament intended.[30] For the NGOs Mr Justice Newman's reasoning signalled a less than robust approach to

---

[26]   *Secretary of State for the Home Department v Limbuela, Tesema & Adam* (para 58)
[27]   See for example: L Pirouet, *Whatever Happened to Asylum in Britain* (2001); C Harlow and R Rawlings, *Pressure through law* (1992); also: Amnesty International, *Seeking asylum is not a crime: Detention of people who have sought asylum* (2005); *Secretary of State for the Home Department ex parte Saadi (FC) and Others (FC)* [2002] UKHL 41
[28]   *Zardasht v Secretary of State* (para 9-10)
[29]   C Harlow and R Rawlings (1992)
[30]   See Home Office (1997)

rights, a primary reason for their frustration with how the courts have applied the HRA.[31] Moreover *Zardasht* also meant turning a blind eye to the evidence which was before the courts of wide-spread suffering. This is something that Collins and others (for example Justices Gibbs and Kay) refused to countenance.[32] They could have taken the *Zardasht* approach or fallen back on the doctrine of deference and leave to the legislature to deal with matters of public policy. But much to the later relief of the NGOs, Collins did not hesitate to deliver a decision reasoned in condemnation of Section 55.

There is much to infer that the decision by Collins was a rebuke to Newman's self-acknowledged 'harsh' ruling, an indicator of apparent tension in the administrative court over the issue.[33] It is also arguable that the decision was Collins's riposte to an obstinate Home Secretary. There is no denying however that the crisis – and that is what it was notwithstanding the views of conservative organisations, the Home Office, and some members of the judiciary that tough measures were necessary[34] – of destitute asylum-seekers cried out for a humane intervention. The case had everything to do with the human rights of a powerless constituency for whom the suffering was extreme; essentially strangers in a strange land, refused welfare and permission to work, left to fend for themselves. Many volunteers and front-line caseworkers described it as 'appalling'; and, during interviews some were moved to tears when recounting the suffering they had witnessed.[35] Mr Justice Collins, and the other judges, were well aware of the situation and refused to turn a blind eye.

The ruling was consistent with how Mr Justice Collins had previously approached the vexed issue of welfare support for asylum-seekers. It was also consistent with his approach to human rights – principled and robust, combined with a strong sense of social justice.[36] Any review of several decisions by Collins during that time, including his ruling against the detention of asylum-seekers

---

[31] Interview notes (on file with author)

[32] In *R (on the application of S, D, T) v Secretary of State for the Home Department* [2003] EWCH 1941 (Admin)

[33] See for example transcript of conversation following Justice Collins's ruling in *R (on the application of Limbuela) v Secretary of State for the Home Department* (para 49-59)

[34] See for example: Migration Watch, 'Appeal outcome could be 'tip of iceberg'' (2003) <http://www.migrationwatchuk.org/pressreleases> and Justice Newman's comments in *Zardasht v Secretary of State*

[35] Interview notes (with caseworkers and volunteers) (on file with author)

[36] This view was expressed by several lawyers and policy advisors (interview notes on file with author).

(later overturned on appeal),[37] is demonstrative of principled compassion for those subjected to the full powers of the government and least able to fight back. And clearly his common-sense 'test' was expansive, perhaps deliberately so, because it captures *all* Section 55 applicants without welfare support even though it is apparent that not everyone denied support will automatically fall within the ambit of Article 3. It is also arguable that it would not have been unreasonable for applicants to provide corroborative evidence before a finding that they had been treated in an 'inhumane or degrading' manner, which as acknowledged by Collins, is one of a high threshold. The explicit rejection of corroborative evidence was possibly a measure of Collins's criticism of and lack of faith in Home Office decision-making, a department considered 'not fit for the purpose' and seemingly oblivious to its mandated obligations under the HRA.[38]

8.3.1   Conclusion

The expansive nature of the Collins test could also be construed as a message to the Home Secretary; and, in the words of the decision itself, a reflection of Mr Justice Collins's abhorrence at the policy, its effect on the vulnerable, and his desire to see it changed. There is no doubt that Collins (along with other judges at the High Court) was convinced of the rightness of his approach, and he said as much. At the end of the hearing, recognising the importance of issues addressed in his decision, Collins granted the Home Secretary leave to appeal. Mr Justice Newman, on the other hand, who had decided *Zardasht* just a week earlier, had pointedly refused leave. In granting leave Collins noted, possibly a commentary on the 'harsh' ruling of his colleague, that he understood why Mr Justice Newman had refused. And, as if in a dare, he said that it was better for the appellate courts to decide which of the two was the correct approach leaving no doubt as to which he felt was correct:

> I will give you leave, *not because I think there is any real*
> *prospect of succeeding on the facts of the case* ... since I adopted

---

37   *Saadi & Ors, R (on the application of) v Secretary Of State For Home Department* [2001] EWHC Admin 670

38   Collins had criticised NASS for its lack of attention to the HRA in his earlier decision: *R (on the application of Q and Others) v Secretary of State for the Home Department* [2003] 2 All ER 905 (Admin); for an independent review – and criticisms – of Home Office decision-making see: National Audit Office, *Improving the Speed and Quality of Asylum Decisions* (2004); R Verkaik, 'UN criticises Home Office over refugees' *Independent* (28 June 2006) 4

an approach which differs from Newman J . . . it is right to enable
the Court of Appeal to say which is correct.[39] (emphasis added)

What the above, the differences in approach to Section 55 and how the HRA
was interpreted by judges at the High Court (i.e. Collins versus Newman), made
apparent was an emerging consensus towards a humane intervention. Of this the
NGOs were certain. They knew that some judges were sympathetic and this was
gleaned from a 'gut instinct', the very words of the judges themselves, including
off-the-cuff comments to solicitors and caseworkers. The campaigners were not
naïve and many had noted the undercurrent and were aware of the 'word on the
street' – of an imperceptible shift in their favour.[40] Even if Newman's views had
prevailed, it would not have stopped the more enlightened approaches eventually
coming to the fore. But all this would have been meaningless if not for an equally
enlightened approach by the Court of Appeal, albeit by a narrow 2-1 margin (and,
finally, the House of Lords).

8.4   *Limbuela* at the Court of Appeal

As the cases made their way to the appellate court not many in the NGO community
had noticed the import of what Mr Justice Collins had decided in *Limbuela*. There
were no press releases by any of the major refugee-serving NGOs, which is
understandable given that *Limbuela* was a lower court decision and not yet law. *Q
and Others* and *T*, at the time, were the leading cases. But if they had been paying
closer attention the NGOs would have noticed that the nature of Collins's ruling
had actually delineated an expansive test for how Section 55 applications should
be assessed by NASS and, if upheld, would have the effect of hobbling the regime.
Nonetheless when the campaigners at Shelter became aware of *Limbuela's* passage
to the Court of Appeal it was by chance. An informal review of cases going before
the appellate court alerted campaigners to the import of what Collins had decided.
Shelter then quickly applied for and received permission as intervenor. The Court
noted the lateness of the application but nonetheless granted permission, later
scolding Shelter for submitting 'substantial written evidence' for which permission

---

[39]   *R (on the application of Limbuela) v Secretary of State for the Home Department* (para 51-
59)
[40]   Minutes of Meeting of CADAS (10 March 2004); interview notes (on file with author)

had not been granted. Nonetheless the court called their submissions 'useful'.[41] The Refugee Council also provided witness statements and other evidence in support of Shelter's intervention. In submissions, Stephen Knafler, the pro-bono counsel, honed in on Mr Justice Collins's rejection of the 'wait and see' approach arguing that human rights are supposed to be 'practical and effective' and 'abhorrent' to wait for an asylum-seeker to 'undergo a period of destitution' to determine level of suffering.[42] And the majority agreed.

It was also clear that the fate of hundreds of asylum-seekers, who were receiving welfare support because of intervention by the courts, was of considerable concern to the Court. Lord Justice Carnwarth, writing for the majority, acknowledged the practical effects and human rights implications if the appeals by the Home Secretary were allowed:

> We cannot ignore the fact that the likely result of allowing these
> appeals is that the safety net of interim relief . . . will be removed
> (for hundreds of applicants).[43]

And this is precisely what Laws LJ (in dissent) had said should not be a consideration; that irrespective of the practical implications judges should confine their remit to the law. But, and not for the first time, the Court reminded the Home Secretary and public servants of their mandated obligations under the HRA and, as Shelter had argued, rights must be given practical effect. The Court noted that the Home Office had provided extensive guidelines, including hypothetical case studies, to frontline officers on how to interpret 'as soon as reasonably practicable' but devoted the briefest of attention to the question of human rights; in particular, how to address potential Article 3 breach. The Court said the guidelines were of 'little practical' use and insufficient to discharge the Home Secretary's responsibilities under the HRA.[44]

The guidelines in question, while consistent with *Q and Others,* were devoid of any consideration for the everyday realities of life under Section 55 and merely a reiteration of the legislation. For all intents and purposes, the guidelines were a charter for refusal. An example:

---

[41]   *Secretary of State for the Home Department v Limbuela, Tesema & Adam* (para 9)
[42]   Shelter, *Submissions (The Queen on Application of Limbuela, Tesema, and Adam)* (2004) p. 8
[43]   *Secretary of State for the Home Department v Limbuela, Tesema & Adam* (para 113)
[44]   ibid (para 125)

It is lawful to for the Secretary of State to refuse to provide support unless and until it is clear that charitable support has not been provided and the individual is incapable of fending for himself such that his condition verges on the degree of severity described in *Pretty*.[45]

It is difficult to envision circumstances, in view of the generality of the preceding and the high threshold of the *Pretty* test, when NASS caseworkers would have felt compelled to act to avoid Article 3 breach, particularly, convinced as they apparently were that (a) most asylum-seekers were not truthful, (b) most were economic migrants, and (c) charitable support was readily available and easily attainable.[46] In the early stages of the Court of Appeal hearings a debate had ensued between counsel for *Adam* and a NASS officer on the latter point, with the officer in vehement disagreement that charitable support and shelter was *not* readily available. This notwithstanding the fact that the officer was relying upon a list (of shelters) published by the very NGOs providing those shelters and who, at that time, had testified that they were over-subscribed and unable to meet the demands.[47]

The blame for the lack of attention to the HRA does not rest entirely with frontline Home Office staff but also on the vagueness of guidance issued presumably from a higher level. That those responsible for defining public policy in such a sensitive, high-profile, and critical area of government responsibility should be so bereft of human rights awareness is another measure of how unlikely Section 55 applicants were to receive benefits or to have found to have met the *Pretty* threshold. Was this mere oversight or deliberate instructions from political masters? In view of the high-profile nature of the issue, and the circumstances surrounding how Section 55 became law, the inference that it was the latter remains the most likely and credible explanation.[48] In any event, it remains the firm opinion of many in the NGO community and other observers that it was deliberate and came from the 'very top'.[49]

---

[45]   ibid (referring to *Home Office Policy Bulletin 75* at para 124)

[46]   *Pretty v United Kingdom* [2002] 35 EHRR 1(HL)

[47]   Inter-Agency Partnership, *The impact of section 55 on the Inter-Agency Partnership of leading UK refugee agencies and the asylum seekers it supports* (2004)

[48]   See Chapter 5 for a discussion on how Section 55 became law.

[49]   Interview with Claire Sephton, Solicitor, Shelter (London 2005) (on file with author); F Webber, 'NASS: Chronicle of Failure' (2003) Institute of Race Relations <http://www.irr.org.uk/2003/july/ak000010.html>

The general view, that the directions must have come from senior levels, was later confirmed some three years later by the JCHR when it reviewed the implementation of Section 55 and treatment of asylum-seekers.[50] The courts (Collins in *Q and Others*) had previously noted and criticised the complete absence of guidance on the HRA for NASS caseworkers. How, the court asked, were front-line officers making decisions which had immense human rights implications with no training or guidance?[51] This in face of the fact that the HRA, passed in into law in 1998, did not come into effect until two years later to allow public service agencies to become HRA ready. During that time the government spent millions in training and other related matters to ensure readiness.[52] The NGOs were incredulous asking why front-line officers were absent such fundamentals.

From February 2003 (when *Q and Others* was decided in the High Court) to the Court of Appeal in *Limbuela* (March 2004), what substantive efforts had NASS made in response to various court decisions on Section 55 and the HRA? What efforts did NASS make to ensure compliance with the HRA? Almost none; for example, knowing that many applicants were potentially without shelter, NASS simply issued leaflets advising asylum-seekers of charities to contact for housing, without making any effort to substantiate whether in fact housing was available or even if the charities were able to provide support.[53] The lists, in fact, were carbon copies of what the NGOs had compiled and had testified in lower courts that the shelters were over-subscribed and unable to accommodate the hundreds needing shelter.[54] And, this, defence for the Home Secretary, argued was sufficient to discharge HRA responsibilities to those left without shelter as a direct result of government policy.

Such deficit in considering rights, given that Article 3 was and had been raised in hundreds of applications, while of concern came as little surprise to the NGOs. It was something they had become accustomed to in dealing with the bureaucrats at the Home Office and knew that HRA obligations played a negligible role in asylum

---

[50] Joint Committee On Human Rights, *The Treatment of Asylum-Seekers* (2007) (para 120)

[51] See Chapter 5

[52] CJ Harvey and British Institute of Human Rights, *Human Rights in the Community: Rights as Agents for Change* (2005); Home Office, *Rights Brought Home: the Human Rights Bill* (1997)

[53] Interview notes (on file with author)

[54] Inter-Agency Partnership, *The impact of section 55 on the Inter-Agency Partnership of leading UK refugee agencies and the asylum seekers it supports* (2004)

policies.[55] But for the Home Secretary to defend the practical workings of his policy when it clearly was not was more than the Court could countenance, particularly in face of evidence submitted by Shelter. It is apparent that intervention by Shelter was crucial to the final decision. While it cannot be stated with certainty that it was the turning point, it is clear that Shelter opened up the wider picture; its evidence, a package of witness statements and empirical studies, presented a stark picture of events on the ground and the un-workability of the policy. Shelter also honed in on its list of shelters, relied upon by the Home Secretary, submitting evidence that the shelters were unable to meet the demands of homeless and destitute asylum-seekers. The Court made several references to Shelter's evidence as they struggled with the ramifications to all asylum-seekers of *not* deciding in favour of Limbuela, Adam, and Tesema. And clearly the Court was divided over the issue. Laws LJ (in dissent) urged his colleagues against exceeding what he considered the Court's proper role:

> Such matters, however pressing, cannot be allowed to divert us into accepting a role which is not our own. We cannot don the mantle of the statue's practical administrators . . . in particular we cannot strain and extend the obligations of the United Kingdom . . . under Article 3 beyond what, judicially, we conceive to be their proper limits.[56]

But the majority, a 2-1 decision, disagreed and dismissed the appeals by the Home Secretary ruling: 'we must also give effect to Parliament's intention to abide by the Convention'.[57] In doing so the Court also made clear that the Home Secretary cannot ask charitable organisations to bear the burden of providing shelter and support (properly the duty of government) to asylum-seekers left destitute by his policies.[58]

8.5   The End of Section 55?

The campaigners were overjoyed. It appeared then to be the victory they had worked so long and hard to achieve. Internal letters paint a picture of ecstatic campaigners

---

55   Interview with Tauhid Pasha, Solicitor, JCWI (London 25 May 2005)
56   *Secretary of State for the Home Department v Limbuela, Tesema & Adam* (para 80)
57   ibid (para 97)
58   ibid (para 91)

celebrating a hard-won victory.[59] And it was a major victory.[60] Shelter, in its press release, called the decision 'ground-breaking' and added: 'This is a vindication for those of us campaigning for the human rights of destitute people'.[61] But, in the euphoria of victory, Shelter also got carried away claiming the ruling could potentially apply to homelessness in general – i.e. a right to shelter for the homeless – when it did no such thing. The Refugee Council, a bit more constrained, added:

> We welcome this decision. We have long argued that Section 55 breaches basic human rights and there is mounting and unavoidable evidence that it is doing so on a large scale. Consistent court cases have shown how inhumane this legislation is. It is surely time now for the Government to repeal Section 55 . . .[62]

The Home Office did not agree. Section 55 was a major policy initiative designed to tackle an issue, which months earlier the Prime Minister had mooted the use of military to combat, and it was not about to admit defeat. The Home Office had ignored earlier calls and court decisions and it remained of the view that the policy should continue. Just a few months earlier, in January 2004, a Home Affairs Select Committee looking into asylum applications became so concerned about Section 55 that it called for an independent review of the policy.[63] In March of the same year, however, the Home Secretary rejected the call claiming a review was neither 'necessary nor desirable' and the problems which had arisen at implementation had now been resolved.[64] In other words, what the NGOs, some members of the judiciary, and the Home Affairs Select Committee viewed as a crisis was not how the Home Office regarded the matter. For it the policy was working exactly as intended. And so it came as no surprise that the Home Office response to the Court of Appeal decision was described as 'defiant'.[65] A press release expressed 'disappointment' with the 2-1 ruling and made clear that leave to appeal would be sought, while at the same time claiming that the 'basic thrust of the policy

---

[59]   On file with author

[60]   Letter from Deborah Garvie, Senior Policy Officer, Shelter (London 21 May 2004) (on file)

[61]   Shelter, *Shelter is a basic human right, says Court of Appeal* (2004) press release

[62]   Refugee Council, *Refugee Council welcomes Court of Appeal decision to uphold asylum seekers' right to shelter* (2004) press release

[63]   House of Commons, *Asylum Applications* (HC 218-1 2004)

[64]   Home Office, *Government Reply: Asylum Applications* (2004)

[65]   D Callaghan, 'Court rejects Blunkett's asylum support appeal' *Guardian* (21 May 2004)

had been vindicated in the courts'.[66] It is unclear how the Home Office concluded such was the case when it is not readily apparent on an objective reading of the decision. The Home Office stated that the policy had already been modified earlier (the concession that applications submitted within three days are deemed timely; this however had little effect on NASS decision-making) then added:

> The essential point of section 55 is that we are not prepared to use taxpayers' money on supporting people who make speculative asylum claims . . . Section 55 is working in tackling this kind of abuse . . . It is a tough measure, but there are safeguards to protect the vulnerable. [67]

The tone of such statements coming from the Home Office (with its emphasis on the minority dissent) bemused and dismayed the campaigners. In face of compelling evidence that the 'safeguards' were not working and, far from tackling abuse, Section 55 was indiscriminately subjecting a vast majority of asylum-seekers to 'inhumane and degrading treatment', the Home Office projecting a tone of an 'injured' party was a 'bit rich'. Many campaigners found it objectionable, inaccurate, and typical Labour spin but not surprising.[68]

The message, however, remained unmistakable (both to the public and public servants) that asylum claims (in general) were not meritorious and the courts (and HRA) were again thwarting public servants from carrying out their duties and the government from legitimate public policy aimed at stopping abuse and economic migrants. What were the effects of such messaging on public servants, the front-line Home Office officers, who are mandated to consider the HRA in their decision-making but generally view it as a hindrance to their duties, when their political masters continued to extol such messages? The effects, a peripheral regard for human rights, was readily apparent to the NGOs. This is supported by various studies and reports – by the National Audit Office, Home Affairs Committee, and Joint Committee on Human Rights – and the day-to-day experiences of NGO caseworkers interviewed for this study.[69] All of these findings paint a picture of rights which is far from positive and discouraging insofar as creating a rights culture

---

66   *Nationality, Immigration & Asylum Act 2002: Court Judgement* (2004)
67   ibid
68   Interview with anonymous representative, Asylum Rights Campaign (London March 2005)
69   National Audit Office, *Improving the Speed and Quality of Asylum Decisions* (2004); Joint Committee On Human Rights, *The Treatment of Asylum-Seekers* (2007); House of Commons, *Asylum Applications* (2004)

is concerned. Making matters even worse are the conclusions of another report asking senior ministers, including the Prime Minister, to stop blaming the HRA for shortcomings in their respective departments.[70] What conclusions can be drawn from this? While many in the NGO community maintain that disregard of the HRA in asylum policy was deliberate, another view would be to accept that mishaps in the implementation of major public policies happen. To assume otherwise – that the misinformation and disparagement of HRA obligations are deliberate – raises some troubling questions. While misinformation and blame are not uncommon in politics, the inference is inescapable – and that is, a government going out of its way to discredit the HRA; or, according to the Director of Liberty, a government seeking to 'disown the Act'.[71] Anthony Lester, a human rights lawyer, is blunt:

> The government damaged (the HRA) by blaming the act for
> its own political mistakes. It never campaigned effectively to
> explain why human rights protection matters . . . the sad reality
> is that the government is illiberal and often deeply reactionary. It
> lacks imagination, ambition and respect for personal liberty . . .[72]

Is a culture of blame to develop instead of the much talked-about culture of rights? At date of writing the Home Office continues to come under severe and sustained criticism by various bodies in how it manages asylum. And credible stories continue to persist of officers displaying unethical, abusive, violent, and racist attitudes and behaviour towards migrants and asylum-seekers in almost complete disregard for the most fundamental of human rights.[73] The Home Office response, in general, has been to ignore or deny allegations of malfeasance. But in a recent instance it could do so no longer. After months of strenuous denials of serious allegations, including hundreds of allegations of corruption, sex-for-visas, and cash for asylum scandals,

---

[70] BBC, 'Human rights 'blaming' under fire' (2006) 14 Nov <http://news.bbc.co.uk/1/hi/uk_politics/6144804.stm>

[71] S Chakrabarti, 'So much freedom lost and on my watch' *Daily Telegraph* (20 May 2007)

[72] A Lester, 'My Misery as a Tethered Goat in Gordon Brown's Big Tent' *Guardian* (27 Jul 2009)

[73] Independent Asylum Commission, *Deserving Dignity - A Nationwide Review of the UK Asylum System* (2008); P Legrain, 'Tear down the walls' *Guardian* (08 Aug 2008); Birnberg Peirce & Partners, Medical Justice, and NCADC, *Outsourcing Abuse: The use and misuse of state-sanctioned force during the detention and removal of asylum seekers* (2008); R Verkaik, 'Asylum-seekers put at risk by law, warns top judge' *The Independent* (02 Jul 2008); M McFadyean, 'Centres of barbarism' *Guardian* (02 Dec 2006)

the Minister responsible for the Home Office was forced into an about-face and ordered an independent investigation.[74]

8.5.1   Conclusion

There is little doubt among many in the NGO community that the Home Office knew full well the human rights implications of Section 55 and deliberately ignored them?[75] Presumably there must have been intense debate and discussion in the halls of government about a legislative regime that the Home Secretary, in a process which can only be described as disingenuous, had forced into law.[76] Starting in October 2002, the Home Office had withstood and ignored pressure and campaigning by the NGOs; ignored the warnings of its own parliamentary committee on the human rights implications of Section 55; ignored various studies on the impact of Section 55, including a report by the Mayor of London; ignored persistent requests from the administrative courts 'to do something'; and, ignored various court decisions which had made apparent a move towards finding a Convention breach. But after the Court of Appeal in *Limbuela* it could do so no longer. Even then it took the Home Secretary a month to respond and it was a grudging concession.[77] On the 25th of June, 2004, the Home Office finally seemed to acknowledge the import of what the Court of Appeal had decided and announced major changes to the policy, which had the effect of bringing to a (temporary) end measures which had caused such widespread suffering.[78] The legislation remained – none of the courts had found it incompatible with the HRA – but the policy was drastically modified and reinstated basic levels of support for all applicants (who were without benefits) even if asylum claims had not been made 'as soon as reasonably practicable'. However at the same time as the Home Secretary announced the change in policy, he also announced his intention to appeal to the House of Lords and, as defiant as ever, added:

---

[74]   M Townsend and J Doward, 'Cash for asylum scandal hits Reid' *Guardian* (04 June 2006); B Leapman and M Kite, 'Hundreds of corruption inquiries at Immigration' *Daily Telegraph* (27 July 2006); R Verkaik, 'Investigation into claims of abuse on asylum-seekers' *The Independent* (30 Sept 2008); R Verkaik, 'How 'Independent' story was denied – then accepted' *The Independent* (30 Sept 2008)

[75]   Interview notes (on file with author)

[76]   See Chapter for an analysis of how Section 55 became law

[77]   BBC, 'Asylum seekers to be housed' (2004) 25 June <http://news.bbc.co.uk/1/hi/uk_politics/3840439.stm>

[78]   See, for example, Refugee Council, *Hungry and Homeless: The Impact of the Withdrawal of State Support on Asylum Seekers, Refugee Communities and the Voluntary Sector* (2004) 1-38

> We are determined to ensure that we are not obliged to provide
> support for those who have deliberately not applied for asylum
> at the earliest opportunity – we are not the welfare system of the
> world.[79]

Some of the campaigners, accustomed to Home Office obstinacy, were nonetheless
privately bitter, frustrated, and angered but restrained in their public criticisms of
a government they viewed as defying its own HRA and common sense.[80] They
applauded the changes in policy, which meant, at least temporarily, fewer destitute
clients and, not desiring another potentially lengthy and costly court battle, urged
the government not to appeal and said:

> We hope now in practice that [the government] will fully comply
> with the judgement.[81]

8.6   *Limbuela* at House of Lords

While changes by the Home Office to its Section 55 policy were significant and
signalled a marked shift the NGOs were under no illusion that the fight was over.
The NGOs had urged the government not to appeal and re-fashion a humane policy
in dealing with asylum-seekers. But the grudging changes in policy and tone of
statements emanating from the Home Office left the NGOs with little doubt as to the
fragile nature of their victory. Something more definitive was needed. And it would
have to be something that would, once and for all, confine Section 55 to the 'trash
heap'.[82] While the NGOs had known that some judges at the administrative court
were sympathetic to their cause, much was unknown about the House of Lords.
The NGOs would have preferred for the Home Office to accept the Court of Appeal
decision and not appeal. In view of the fact that earlier victories (*Q and Others* and
SDT) in the administrative courts had been overturned on appeal, and the narrow
victory in this instance, the NGOs approached the hearings with some trepidation.
And the concerns were not insignificant because a defeat would be 'catastrophic'.[83]

---

[79]   BBC, 'Asylum seekers to be housed' (25 June 2004)

[80]   Interview notes (on file with author)

[81]   BBC, 'Asylum seekers to be housed' (25 June 2004)

[82]   Interview with Imran Hussain, Parliamentary Officer, Refugee Council (London 12 May
       2005)

[83]   Interview with Alex Gask, Solicitor, Liberty (London 01 Nov 2006)

It would mean a return to the status quo of destitute asylum-seekers, more test-case challenges, and possibly continuing the fight to the European Court of Human Rights. While this was an option that Liberty had contingently planned for there was little desire amongst the campaigners to prolong the fight.[84] Moreover, the resource-strapped NGOs knew they would be severely limited in their ability to help destitute and starving humans, particularly with winter approaching. At the House of Lords, Shelter and the Refugee Council were joined by two additional interveners, Liberty and JUSTICE. Rabinder Singh, QC, considered one of the leading human rights lawyers in the UK and who had represented JCWI and Liberty in *Q and Others*, appeared pro-bono for Liberty.[85]

It was the general view of many that the Court of Appeal had a taken a thoughtful view of human rights and the role of the courts in protecting those rights.[86] And the House of Lords in a 5-0 unanimous ruling agreed signalling an end to Section 55. But given its history, particularly the furore over Mr Justice Collins's decision in *Q and Others*, the House of Lords, like the Court of Appeal below, seemed wary of entering into what they viewed as policy-making. That the apex court felt so compelled is suggestive of a less than robust approach to the HRA; and, this is something that dismayed some of the senior campaigners who regarded it as limiting the HRA.[87] The decision also suggested a court lacking the courage of its conviction as some of the Lordships seemed at pains to emphasise that theirs was not a political decision but a legal one. Baroness Hale, perhaps mindful of the Home Secretary's and tabloid media's earlier criticisms of judges defying Parliament added (unnecessarily): 'we are respecting, rather than challenging the will of Parliament'.[88]

The apex Court recognised that homelessness and destitution are 'unfortunate' facts of life for many, not just asylum-seekers. However, Lord Brown wrote: 'it is quite another matter to single out a particular group to be left utterly destitute on

---

84 R Maiman, 'We've had to raise our game: Liberty's litigation strategy under the Human Rights Act 1998' in S Halliday and PD Schmidt (eds) *Human Rights Brought Home: Socio-Legal Perspectives on Human Rights in the National Context* (2004); also, interview notes (on file with author)

85 www.matrixlaw.co.uk/WhoWeAre_Members_RabinderSinghQC_WhatOthersSay. aspx

86 A Hardiman-McCartney (2006) 'Absolutely Right: Providing Asylum Seekers with Food and Shelter Under Article 3' 65 Cambridge Law Journal 01 4-6

87 Interview notes (on file with author)

88 *Limbuela* (para 75)

the streets as a matter of policy'.[89]Lord Bingham, echoing what the NGOs had been saying since day one of the policy coming into effect, was succinct:

> Treatment is inhuman or degrading if, to a seriously detrimental extent, it denies the most basic needs of any human being . . . I would accept that in a context such as this, not involving the deliberate infliction of pain or suffering, the threshold is a high one . . . but I have no doubt that the threshold may be crossed if a late applicant with no means and no alternative sources of support, unable to support himself, is, by the deliberate action of the state, denied shelter, food or the most basic necessities of life.[90]

In his conclusion Lord Bingham, again echoing the NGO argument and fulfilling their major objective, drove a 'horse and carriage' through the 'late applicant' provision and made clear that the duty to provide support arises:

> When an individual faces imminent prospect of serious suffering caused or materially aggravated by denial of shelter, food or the most basic necessities of life.[91]

The House of Lords decision had been eagerly awaited, and on the whole, delivered to the NGOs what they had fought for from day one of the campaign. But there were some significant exceptions. One of the major concerns had to do with Laws LJ's dissent, in the Court of Appeal, whereby he had outlined a 'spectrum' approach to Article 3, turning what was considered an absolute right into a qualified right. In other words harm as a result of government policies, unless severe enough to meet the *Pretty* threshold, would not fall within the ambit of Article 3. The NGOs had argued at length that such an approach was anathema to the concept of human rights and would have the effect of reducing Article 3 protection to 'hierarchies of species of harm' and an obstacle to giving rights practical effect.[92] Worryingly, however, only two of the Lordships saw fit to reject the 'spectrum' analysis outright.

---

[89]   ibid (para 99)
[90]   ibid (para 7)
[91]   ibid (para 8)
[92]   Liberty and JUSTICE, *Written Intervention (Limbuela) before the House of Lords* (2005) (para 21-26)

In other words, a majority of the judges at the Court of Appeal and House of Lords, by their silence on the issue, appeared to approve of an approach which the NGOs had argued should broker no justification for state sponsored violence or harm occurring as a result of government policies.[93] The campaigners were dismayed because they realised that this presented a potential saving grace for future policies similar to Section 55 – particularly since a key objective of the campaign, repeal of Section 55, was not achieved. And, in case there was any doubt about future Home Office intentions, the immigration minister, while conceding that the Section 55 regime would undergo changes to comply with the ruling, made clear that tough policies would continue:

> The judgment leaves intact a fundamental principle within our approach to asylum which is that people should claim as soon as they arrive in the country . . . (the Court) has recognised that there are difficult decisions to be made and each case has to be judged on its individual merits . . . we are adopting tough new means to crack down on opportunistic behaviour. In particular, we are setting up tightly managed new processes for handling late and opportunistic claims.[94]

The NGOs knew well what the Minister meant – yet another legislative reform and/or new policies on immigration and asylum were on the horizon.[95] This, in itself, was not surprising given the Home Office proclivity for legislative changes, averaging one every 18 months since 1999 and each heralded as 'tackling abuse in the asylum system'. The certainty that the NGOs had fought for seemed less attainable.[96]

8.7 Reaction to *Limbuela*

In many ways the House of Lords decision was anticlimactic. The NGOs were pleased. But the celebrations were muted and sense of victory, of an unnecessary

---

[93] ibid (para 21-26)
[94] Tony McNulty cited in: BBC, 'Lords throw out key asylum rule ' (2005) 03 Nov <http://newsvote.bbc.co.uk/1/hi/uk/4402596.stm>
[95] At that time a bill, later to become the Immigration, Asylum and Nationality Act 2006 , was making its way through the various readings; the Asylum and Immigration (Treatment of Claimants, etc.) bill, announced in November 2003, had become law in July 2004.
[96] *Immigration, Asylum and Nationality Bill - Briefing for Commons Second Reading* (2005)

fight hard-won, was tempered by questions of 'what next?' by campaigners all too familiar with the hardening of positions and legislation and continuing erosion of asylum rights in the UK.[97] A sense of exhaustion marked the victory for other battlefronts, new polices and legislation with welfare again as a coercive measure, had already opened.[98] The NGOs press-releases praised the victory of human rights over draconian policies but a sense of resigned pessimism, if not hopelessness, remained:

> We welcome the unanimous decision of the House of Lords. It should not have been necessary to go to our highest court in order to establish that a destitute person forbidden to work is in an intolerable position.[99]

> We are delighted with this unanimous judgement. It was disgraceful that vulnerable refugees were left to starve on the streets. Section 55 brought immeasurable harm to many innocent refugees who were guilty of nothing more than asking for protection here . . . (and refused) by this unjust law.[100]

In comparison to the media attention to earlier test-case challenges the reaction to the House of Lords decision, a ground-breaking one at that, was muted. Unusually, and it is not clear why this was so, the tabloids had little to say about the decision. To be sure negative stories about asylum still featured prominently but there was no mention of the decision. A website search of the *Sun* and *Daily Mail* yielded dozens of 'hits' but nothing specifically on the decision. The *Sun*, for example, had eighteen (negative) stories on asylum in November 2005 (when the House of Lords decided the case) but no mention of *Limbuela*. The broadsheets, too, had limited coverage. The National Coalition of Anti-Deportation Campaigns (NCADC), which maintains an extensive archive of press coverage on asylum, lists only two pieces – both relatively short summaries of the decision in the *Guardian* and *Independent;* the BBC website devoted a page.

---

97 See, for example, K Puttick (2005) 'Strangers at the welfare gate: asylum seekers, welfare and Convention rights after Adam' 19 Immigration, Asylum and Nationality Law 4 214-34; A Porter, 'Labour: Rights Act is mess' *The Sun* (15 May 2006); D Stevens (1998) 'The Asylum and Immigration Act 1996: Erosion of the Right to Seek Asylum' 61 Modern Law Review 2 207-222; H O'Nions (2006) 'The Erosion Of The Right To Seek Asylum' 2 Web Journal of Current Legal Issues

98 T Shifrin, 'Lords threaten to vote against asylum benefits ban ' *Guardian* (20 May 2004)

99 Refugee Council, *Law Lords unanimously condemn withdrawal of support for asylum seekers* (2005) press release

100 Refugee Council, *House of Lords backs judgement restoring support to destitute asylum seekers* (2005) press release

There are various possible explanations but crucially a landmark decision – with the highest court in the land ruling that the government had breached the human rights of an entire class of persons, a serious finding by most measures – failed to generate much attention or even elicit outrage. As the Chairperson of JCWI explained: 'asylum just isn't sexy'; Jonathan, a caseworker at JCWI, is blunter: 'no one gives a shit about asylum-seekers'.[101] In other words, one of the key objectives of test-case litigation by NGOs, to garner media coverage and publicity for the cause, failed to materialise. Undoubtedly the victory was over-shadowed by continuing developments in asylum, but the decision, which came about as a result of almost unprecedented mobilisation efforts by NGOs and was a major victory for human rights, vulnerable asylum-seekers, and the HRA itself, had faded in importance. The ruling may remain a legal landmark but in many other respects – such as its effect on asylum policy, asylum-seekers, and NGOs – it can no longer be considered as such. In part this is because of the very nature of asylum. It is a fluid and dynamic arena, subject to frequent legislative and policy changes. Be that as it may, it remains unequivocal that during a period of over three years, from October 2002 to November 2005, a group of determined campaigners using the *Human Rights Act* obtained emergency injunctions which saved hundreds of asylum-seekers from being homeless and without welfare; and, won significant concessions to the government's 'get tough' policy.

8.8   Conclusion

The fight over asylum has been a losing fight since it began in earnest in the late 1990s. And, in many ways, it has been a fight long lost. Various deterrent and enforcement measures have allowed many receiving states to circumvent their obligations under international treaties and conventions, and this has been done with planning and deliberation.[102] The numbers of asylum-seekers entering the West

---

[101]   Interview notes (on file with author)

[102]   C Dyer, 'Top judge condemns asylum proposals ' *Guardian* (11 Feb 2004); BBC, 'Asylum laws under fresh attack' (2004) BBC News <http://news.bbc.co.uk/1/hi/uk_politics/3501702.stm> (10 June 2006); A Delmar-Morgan, 'Church of England damns Labour on asylum and poverty' *The Times* (14 May 2006); R Verkaik, 'UN criticises Home Office over refugees' (04 June 2006); G Tremlett, 'Under fire at Europe's border ' *The Observer* (02 Oct 2005); L Smith, 'Britain: Government steps up attacks on asylum seekers' (2004) World Socialist Web Site <http://www.wsws.org/articles/2004/jan2004.bak/asyl-j05.shtml> (16 Oct 2006); BBC, 'Asylum hardships 'are deliberate'' (2007) BBC News <http://news.bbc.co.uk/1/hi/uk_politics/6507961.stm> (29 Jun); J Huysmans, *The Politics of Insecurity: Fear, Migration, and Asylum in the EU* (2006); G Loescher A Betts and J Milner, *The United Nations High Commissioner for Refugees (UNHCR): The Politics and Practice of Refugee Protection into the Twenty-first Century* (2008)

have been reduced dramatically. And it is not because the world is suddenly a safer place; flashpoints, strife, and war-zones remain but the gates to safety have been effectively shut. But the problem of what to do with asylum-seekers once they are within the borders of receiving states continues to confound governments.[103] In this respect, forced destitution has become a policy of choice. The use of destitution, along with a host of other enforcement and deterrent measure, continues unabated in Europe and the UK.[104] While the courts brought an end to Section 55 welfare as a coercive measure remains a key component of 'get tough' policies. The defeat of Section 55 has meant the policy of destitution has legislatively 'migrated' to other categories of asylum-seekers. Section 4, for example, another point of contention for NGOs, pertains to the provision of hardship funds as inducements to leave the UK notwithstanding significant obstacles (i.e. return to unstable or unsafe countries such as Zimbabwe or Iraq).[105] Section 9, another inducement to leave introduced in 2004, targets destitute asylum-seeker families with the threat of having children taken into care by social services (on the grounds that the family is financially unable to care for the needs of their children).[106] The Home Office, however, was forced into an about-face on Section 9 after pilot projects backfired and social workers refused to participate in a program seen as unethical and mean-spirited.[107] Without debating but accepting that the government may have legitimate policy objectives the NGOs argue whether 'starving humans to the point of submission' is consistent with human rights or the behaviour of 'civilised' countries.[108]

Notwithstanding the assumptions about why asylum-seekers come to the UK and irrespective of its effectiveness as an enforcement measure, forced destitution remains central to policy-making.[109] It is worth noting, however, that the House

---

[103]   See Chapter 3 for a fuller discussion on 'Asylum in the Wider Context' and the gradual erosion in asylum rights.

[104]   SD Lomba (2006) 'The threat of destitution as a deterrent against asylum seeking in the European Union' 23 Refuge 1 78-93

[105]   *Asylum and Immigration Act 1999*

[106]   *Asylum and Immigration Act 2004*

[107]   G Hinsliff and J Doward, 'U-turn on plan to take babies from refugees' *Guardian* (29 Jan 2006); S Cunningham and J Tomlinson (2005) "Starve them out': does every child really matter? A commentary on Section 9 of the Asylum and Immigration (Treatment of Claimants, etc.) Act, 2004 ' 25 Critical Social Policy 2 253-275

[108]   Refugee Council, 'Section 9 is a question of morality, not law, says the Refugee Council' (2005)   <http://www.refugeecouncil.org.uk/news/press/2006/january/20060131secti.htm> press release

[109]   See Chapters 3-5 for a fuller discussion

of Lords (in *Limbuela*) established a general proposition: that asylum-seekers unable to support themselves, denied basic necessities by the deliberate action of the state, and where suffering is imminent, fall within Article 3. Arguably this is an unambiguous proposition. But it seems to have bedevilled the Home Office because there is much upon which to conclude that it has failed, with apparent deliberation, to give practical effect to the House of Lords decision. For example, almost three years after *Limbuela*, various reports and studies have concluded that destitution amongst asylum-seekers remains a crisis and, in some cases, has increased.[110] In an open letter to the *Times* the Church of England (signed by over 40 bishops and church leaders) expressed its concern about destitution and urged a change in policy:

> As a society we have international moral and legal responsibilities
> to welcome those fleeing adversity from other parts of the world
> and provide social security.[111]

In March 2007 the Joint Committee on Human Rights published its report after an extensive review on the treatment of asylum-seekers and Section 55 and concluded:

> The continued use of Section 55 provision to deny support in
> subsistence-only cases leaves many asylum-seekers . . . with no
> regular means of providing for their basic daily necessities. We
> believe that this treatment does not comply with the House of
> Lords Limbuela judgement, and is in clear breach of Article 3
> ECHR. We recommend that section 55 be repealed.[112]

The Committee also added:

> We have been persuaded by the evidence that the Government
> has indeed been practising a deliberate policy of destitution
> of this highly vulnerable group. We believe that the deliberate
> use of inhumane treatment is unacceptable . . . Government's

---

[110]   Amnesty International UK, *Down and Out in London: The Road to Destitution for Rejected Asylum-Seekers* (2006); BBC, 'Asylum hardships 'are deliberate''; Refugee Action, *The Destitution Trap* (2006); A Delmar-Morgan, 'Church of England damns Labour on asylum and poverty' (14 May 2006); The Joseph Rowntree Charitable Trust, *More Destitution in Leeds* (2008); *Shaming Destitution - Briefing* (2006)

[111]   www.timesonline.co.uk/tol/comment/letters/article745101.ece

[112]   Joint Committee on Human Rights *The Treatment of Asylum-Seekers* (2007) para 92

treatment of asylum seekers and refused asylum seekers falls below the requirements of the common law of inhumanity and of international human rights law . . . the policy of enforced destitution must cease.[113]

And, in March 2007, Amnesty International, in coalition with over twenty other NGOs, commenced a new campaign 'Still Human Still Here' to fight against the continuing destitution of asylum-seekers.[114] For the NGOs, it is yet another fight over an issue just hard-fought over. According to Alex Gask, Solicitor at Liberty, the continual battles with the government has 'worn the NGOs down and there is less fight. We keep having to fight the same issues over and over again.'[115] A few months later the government responded to the JCHR's report and recommendations and made clear the foreseeable future for asylum-seekers and NGOs: 'There are no plans at present for section 55 to be repealed.'[116]

---

[113]   ibid (para 120-121)
[114]   www.stillhuman.org.uk/
[115]   Interview notes (on file with author).
[116]   Joint Committee on Human Rights, *Government Response to the Committee's Tenth Report of this Session: The Treatment of Asylum Seekers* (2007) para 5

9 CONCLUSION: ASYLUM AND A CULTURE OF RIGHTS?

9.1 Introduction

> Our *Human Rights Act* is pretty tame protection . . . [1]

That the *Human Rights Act* should be introduced at about the same time as Labour intensified its offensive against asylum implementing such measures as pre-clearance (at embarkation points abroad), vouchers instead of cash payments for welfare support, increased use of detention, including detention of children, dispersal of asylum-seekers away from urban centres and support networks to council estates characterised by urban decay and racist violence, and other punitive and coercive measures, was for the NGOs an irony too far.[2] The NGOs, which work with and advocate on behalf of asylum-seekers and long accustomed to increasingly stricter controls on asylum and welfare, were caught by surprise in late 2002 by the introduction of Section 55, a legislation designed to limit welfare support for asylum-seekers. The policy, 'a cruel piece of law', became a major battleground and represented the very antithesis of what the HRA promised.[3] It was never supposed to be this way when the HRA was first introduced with its promise of a culture of rights. How is it that the early days of the Act have come to be associated with continuing attacks on the concept of affording protection to humans seeking sanctuary? Of deliberately forcing asylum-seekers into destitution as a means of deterring them from entering the UK; and, if already in the country, making life so intolerable as to make returning back to a country from which they fled a better option. What does this say about a culture of rights? What does the battle over Section 55 say about the role of rights in the fight for social justice or to change policies? What does it say about the health of rights? What are the prospects for using rights in bringing about social change in the UK?

The findings of this research – a case study of rights at work between the period October 2002 to November 2005 – which examined the NGO campaign against Section 55, the role of the HRA in the campaign, and the treatment of

---

[1] Shami Chakrabarti, Director of Liberty, cited in: BBC, 'Viewpoints: The Human Rights Act' (2006) BBC News <http://news.bbc.co.uk/1/hi/uk/4990414.stm> (26 June 2006)

[2] See Chapter 3 for an overview on the treatment of asylum-seekers and a review of legislation on asylum and previous conflicts over welfare benefits.

[3] Interview with Alex Gask, Solicitor, Liberty (London Nov 2005)

asylum-seekers are that there are very few signs of a culture of rights taking hold or developing insofar as asylum is concerned. And that powerful forces opposed to asylum have trumped the process of building a culture of rights, often at the expense of fundamental rights.[4] The findings of my research are consistent with other contemporaneous (between 2002 and 2008) reviews of asylum and rights in the UK by the Council of Europe,[5] Independent Asylum Commission,[6] Joint Committee on Human Rights,[7] Ministry of Justice,[8] various NGOs,[9] and other seasoned observers.[10] These reports and my findings also echo those of earlier reports by the British Institute of Human Rights and the Audit Commission.[11]

This concluding chapter frames the analysis against why asylum has become such a challenging policy issue, and examines what the NGO campaign against

[4]   BBC, 'Watchdog criticises asylum decisions' (2004) 23 June <http://news.bbc.co.uk/1/hi/uk_politics/3831163.stm>; BBC, 'Asylum seekers 'denied justice'' (2005) BBC News <http://news.bbc.co.uk/1/hi/uk/4552523.stm> (10 Oct 2006); BBC, 'Asylum detentions 'breaking law'' (2005) BBC News <http://news.bbc.co.uk/1/hi/uk/4109406.stm> (10 Oct 2006); BBC, 'Asylum seekers policy 'unlawful'' (2007) <http://news.bbc.co.uk/1/hi/uk_politics/6302919.stm> (04 Feb 2007); N Blake, 'Why is there no song and dance about this Act?' *Times* (25 Apr 2006); LM Clements (2007) 'Asylum in Crisis, An assessment of UK Asylum law and policy since 2002: Fear of Terrorism or Economic Efficiency?' 3 Web Journal of Current Legal Issues; Comment, 'A Shameful Asylum Policy' *The Independent* (30 Nov 2003); Comment, 'Ministers Must Learn to Respect Their Own Human Rights Laws' *Independent* (20 Feb 2003); S Daghlian, 'Asylum seekers are the victims, not the problem' *The Scotsman* (26 March 2005); A Delmar-Morgan, 'Church of England damns Labour on asylum and poverty' *The Times* (14 May 2006); V Dodd, 'Home Office ignored law, says judge' *Guardian* (08 April 2006); R Dunston, 'Blunkett's uncivilised act' *New Statesman* (11 Aug 2003); Ekklesia, 'World churches criticise UK policies on asylum and immigration' (2005) Ekklesia <http://www.ekklesia.co.uk/content/news_syndication/article_050222asylum.shtml> (10 Oct 2006)

[5]   Commissioner for Human Rights of the Council of Europe, *Memorandum   by Thomas Hammarberg* (2008)

[6]   Independent Asylum Commission, *Deserving Dignity - A Nationwide Review of the UK Asylum System* (2008)

[7]   Joint Committee On Human Rights, *The Treatment of Asylum-Seekers* (2007)

[8]   Ministry of Justice, *Human Rights Insight Project* (2008)

[9]   Amnesty International UK, *Down and Out in London: The Road to Destitution for Rejected Asylum-Seekers* (2006); Asylum Rights Campaign, 'Providing Protection in the 21st Century' (2004); Oxfam and Refugee Council, *Poverty and Asylum in the UK* (2002); Amnesty International UK, *Seeking Asylum is not a Crime: Detention of People who have sought Asylum* (2005); Amnesty International, *Human Rights: A Broken Promise* (2006)

[10]   Liberty, *Evidence to the Joint Committee on Human Rights: Treatment of Asylum Seekers* (2006); BBC, 'Asylum hardships 'are deliberate'' (2007) BBC News <http://news.bbc.co.uk/1/hi/uk_politics/6507961.stm> (29 Jun)

[11]   British Institute of Human Rights, *Something for Everyone: The Impact of the Human Rights Act on Disadvantaged Groups* (2002); Audit Commission, *Human rights: Improving Public Service Delivery* (2003); British Institute of Human Rights and Joint Council for the Welfare of Immigrants, 'Workshop - Section 55 and Human Rights' (BIHR/JCWI Conference 2003)

Section 55 means for asylum rights and development of a rights culture in the UK. The chapter also examines government failings on human rights measured against its own definition of a culture of rights. It incorporates the concept of the 'outsider' and rights and compares it with similar events in Canada to further the analysis. The final section draws in the earlier theoretical discussion about rights and social change for an assessment on the future of human rights in the UK.

9.2   The Question of Asylum

'Liberty is ill in Britain' wrote Professor Dworkin reflecting on the years preceding 1988.[12] Ewing (2004) in a lecture examining the impact of the HRA concluded that the Act has done little to change Dworkin's views and that it is too weak to be an effective bulwark against increasingly illiberal policies.[13] Lord Steyn, a former law lord, commenting generally on Labour policies was even less encouraging: 'Absolute power encourages authoritarianism which is a creeping phenomenon. Our government has been prone to it'.[14] In various columns in *The Observer* Henry Porter documents the attacks on civil liberties in Britain and the guile of ministers in obfuscating the real intentions of laws being legislated.[15] Shami Chakrabarti, former Home Office solicitor and now director of Liberty, laments the many authoritarian laws passed by Labour since coming into power in 1997.[16] And Liberal-Democrat peer Anthony Lester, a human rights activist and long-time campaigner for the HRA, is also critical claiming that Labour has both ignored and damaged the HRA.[17]

While none of the preceding commentators were referring specifically to asylum, their views, in general, speak to the malaise in UK society concerning

---

[12]   Cited in: KD Ewing (2004) 'The Futility of the Human Rights Act' Winter Public Law 829

[13]   ibid

[14]   Cited in: H Porter, 'Blair gets away with his assault on liberty, because we let him' *The Observer* (16 Apr 2006); D Galligan (2001) 'Authoritarianism in Government and Administration: The Promise of Administrative Justice' 54 Current Legal Problems 79-102

[15]   H Porter, 'Only a constitution can save us from this abuse of power' *The Observer* (02 Apr 2006); H Porter, 'How we move ever closer to becoming a totalitarian state ' *The Observer* (05 Mar 2006)

[16]   S Chakrabarti, 'So much freedom lost and on my watch' *Daily Telegraph* (20 May 2007)

[17]   A Lester, 'My misery as a tethered goat in Gordon Brown's big tent' *Guardian* (27 Jul 2009); A Lester, 'Ignorant Opposition: The prime minister is undermining public confidence in the rule of law and the judiciary' *Guardian* (16 May 2006)

rights and liberties.[18] Such comments are a measure of the dominance of an ethos, at least for the marginalised and powerless, which bears little resemblance to the 'culture of rights' promoted in *Rights Brought Home*. And it has been primarily in two major policy areas, asylum and terrorism, where the passage of illiberal and draconian laws have been most in evidence.[19] Since winning a majority in 1997 Labour has passed several major pieces of legislation on asylum – at the rate of one almost every two years, each successively regressive and tougher.[20] The measures have included increased use of administrative detention (including detention of children),[21] criminalisation and prosecution of those seeking asylum in contravention of international law,[22] cuts to legal aid,[23] and the use of welfare (forced destitution) as a coercive measure.[24] These policies have also drawn international criticism but with little apparent effect on policy-makers.[25]

Asylum, as an arena in which to examine rights at work or look for signs of an emerging culture of rights, presents a volatile mix. It is where politics, public opposition, NGO advocacy, and the HRA have collided over the rights of a powerless constituency. Politics in the form of *both* the government and official opposition competing to be tougher over an issue consistently rated among the top three of public policy concerns in the UK; public opposition in the form of a public

---

18   Some of the same authors have been critical of government policies on asylum, particularly Chakrabarti, but not in the articles cited in this instance.

19   S Chakrabarti (2005) 'Rights and Rhetoric: The Politics of Asylum and Human Rights Culture in the UK' 32 Journal of Law and Society 131; C Gearty (2005) '11 September 2001, Counter-terrorism, and the Human Rights Act' 32 Law and Society 1 18-33; C Harlow, 'Can Human Rights Survive the War on Terror and the War on Crime' (2006) <http://arts.anu.edu.au/democraticaudit/papers/20060809_harlow_hr_wars.pdf.>

20   This is the case, at least, until late 2009 (the date when this thesis was finalised).

21   A Aynsley-Green, 'No place for children' *New Statesman* (04 Sept 2008)

22   See for example *R v Asfaw* [2008] UKHK 31in which the House of Lords expressed astonishment with such prosecutions and considered it an 'abuse of process' (para 31)

23   Refugee Council, *The Refugee Council's submission to the Campaign Against Legal Aid Cuts (CALAC) about the impact of changes to legal aid* (2005); C Dyer, 'MPs attack legal aid cuts' *Guardian* (23 Oct 2003)

24   See Chapters 1, 4 - 8

25   Amnesty International, *Human Rights: A Broken Promise* (2006); R Verkaik, 'UN criticises Home Office over refugees' *Independent* (28 June 2006) 4; Oxfam and Refugee Council, *Poverty and asylum in the UK* (2002); Human Rights Watch, *Human Rights Overview: European Union* (2004); Human Rights Watch, 'UK Asylum Proposal Denounced' (2001) HRW (20 Oct 2006); A Majid (2005) 'Do We Care About the Rule of Law' *New Law Journal* ; Leader, 'A Political Debate that Shames Us' *The Observer* (06 Feb 2005); G Hinsliff and M Bright, 'Labour Fuels War on Asylum' *The Observer* (06 Feb 2005); F Gibb and P Webster, 'Ministers are breaking the law, say judges' *The Times* (04 Mar 2004); C Dyer, 'Top judge condemns asylum proposals' *Guardian* (11 Feb 2004)

ostensibly supportive of the concept, but overwhelmingly dissatisfied with the government's approach and demanding tougher action; NGO advocacy in the form of dedicated organisations with limited resources fighting a determined but losing battle; and, in the middle, the *Human Rights Act* providing sporadic protection but blamed for various ills and battered by concerted opposition, including by the very government which brought it into existence.[26] Asylum is also a toxic mix when the issues of race, racism, and xenophobia, never far from the surface, enter the equation. No matter the perspective the subject of asylum arouses intense emotion and public concern about undeserving foreigners, 'outsiders', using the HRA to exploit the (supposed) generosity of Britain's welfare benefits, the fiction of multiculturalism, and of a Britain no longer the mythic Britain of old.[27] There exists a real fear that Britain is changing or has changed for the worst because of an assumed 'soft-touch' towards asylum-seekers and liberal immigration policies. Charles Moore, former editor of the *Daily Telegraph*, is succinct:

> Britain is basically English speaking, Christian and white, and if
> one starts to think it might become basically Urdu speaking and
> Muslim and brown one gets frightened.[28]

It is in the arena of asylum that the HRA, still in its early days, has most entered the public consciousness. It has been, on the whole, a mostly negative introduction; of a perception of rights of 'outsiders' trumping the rights of native-born Britons. When needed the most – to protect a vulnerable minority from the excesses of a government comfortable that its 'get tough' policies have public support – the HRA has failed to deliver. Or, more accurately, it is where administrative convenience and political imperative, in the form of highly restrictive and punitive laws and policies, have trumped rights.[29]

---

[26] See Chapters 1 and 5

[27] S Heffer, 'Labour is malignant, not incompetent' *Daily Telegraph* (02 April 2008); in various columns Mr. Heffer continues to express such fears with a 'savage gusto'; F Bodi, 'Fear and loathing ' *Guardian* (21 Jan 2003); Commission for Racial Equality, *Attitudes Towards Asylum-Seekers, Refugees and Other Immigrants* (2004); Ministry of Justice *Human Rights Insight Project* (2008)

[28] cited in R Greensdale, 'Seeking Scapegoats: The Coverage of Asylum in the UK Press' (2005) 6

[29] See also: J Huysmans, *The Politics of Insecurity: Fear, Migration, and Asylum in the EU* (2006); H O'Nions (2006) 'The Erosion Of The Right To Seek Asylum' 2 Web Journal of Current Legal Issues

9.3   Asylum and Rights

The current state of affairs does not bode well for a culture of rights in asylum. And there is little sign that it is about to change anytime soon. The findings of this study are that the hope with which some of the NGOs had greeted the arrival of the *Human Rights Act* has waned considerably since the Act came into effect.[30] True, the HRA was used creatively and effectively by NGOs in court battles over asylum rights and was instrumental in defeating Section 55, a major government policy aimed at deterring and reducing asylum-seeker arrivals. But the hope that rights would expand outside its legal boundaries, away from the courtrooms and lawyers, and take root in everyday practice has not been the general experience of NGOs working on behalf of asylum-seekers or of asylum-seekers themselves. And, equally importantly, there are few indications that a culture of rights is emerging in the public agencies and authorities which deal with asylum-seekers, mainly the Home Office which, by its actions such as the manner of its approach to Section 55, has demonstrated a resistance to the principles of the Act and the spirit and objectives behind *Rights Brought Home*. According to Pasha:

> The government has an objective, which I feel conflicts with the objectives of the *Human Rights Act*. Their objective is to limit the numbers (of asylum-seekers) who enter; limit the numbers who are actually granted asylum . . . they pay lip-service to the Geneva Convention . . . they do not want asylum-seekers; they want to keep them out. And they are not going to let the HRA stop them in any of these processes.[31]

For the NGOs a sense of pessimism, disappointment, and frustration have come to replace the initial optimism when the HRA was first introduced. This is the very Act which some NGOs, in particular, Liberty, had lobbied for when Labour was then in opposition and still developing its manifesto of what it later termed 'radical' reforms.[32] For the Home Office the HRA comes into play almost as an

---

[30]   Home Office, *Rights Brought Home: the Human Rights Bill* (1997); see Chapters 1, 6 – 8.

[31]   Interview with Tauhid Pasha, Solicitor, Joint Council for the Welfare of Immigrants (London April 2005)

[32]   R Maiman, 'We've had to raise our game: Liberty's litigation strategy under the Human Rights Act 1998' in S Halliday and PD Schmidt (eds) *Human Rights Brought Home: Socio-Legal Perspectives on Human Rights in the National Context* (2004)

afterthought; and, for the front-line officers who see themselves as 'gate-keepers', it is considered a hindrance, an obstacle to dealing with what they regard as the crisis of asylum.[33]

On the whole, and this became apparent during the course of the study, what best describes the NGO experience in the asylum sector is a sense not of defeat but rather resignation, of continually asking 'what next?' Increasingly there is 'less fight'. The NGOs have been 'worn down' by repeated battles, often over the same issues such as welfare benefits, and constant legislative changes. They are acutely aware of public opposition to asylum and general apathy to their work and that they are up against a formidable opponent, the Home Office, unwilling to bend in pursuit of policy objectives.[34] And those objectives are clear and have been since the early 1990s when the number of asylum-seeker arrivals skyrocketed – from about 1500 annually (in the late 1970s) to a peak of almost 9000 per month in 2002 to about 2000 per month in 2007.[35] Asylum-seekers are not wanted and must be stopped them from entering the UK.[36] The findings of this study, and several others, supports the comments of Pasha (above) that the government is paying lip-service to its obligations under both the *1951 UN Convention* and the HRA because its policies persistently undermine them.[37]

Asylum-seekers are quite possibly the most vulnerable peoples in UK society. More than any other group they are most dependent upon the government for welfare and other support, including seeking from the state the right to residency.[38] It is in the fight for the rights of these 'outsiders' that the HRA has met its match in the form of policies which presume that many asylum-seekers enter the UK, not for sanctuary, but for its generous welfare provisions. It is this

---

[33]   Interview notes (on file with author); see also comments by Mr Justice Collins in *Q and Others* (Chapter 6); see, in general, J Bhabha (2002) 'Internationalist Gatekeepers?: The Tension Between Asylum Advocacy and Human Rights' *Harvard Human Rights Journal*

[34]   Interview with Alex Gask, Solicitor, Liberty (London November 2005); see Chapter 8 for a fuller discussion.

[35]   Euromove, 'Asylum, Illegal Immigration & the European Union' (2007) <http://www.euromove.org.uk/index.php?id=6511>

[36]   For a review of immigration and asylum controls see: L Pirouet, *Whatever Happened to Asylum in Britain* (2001); for an overview see Chapter 3

[37]   See Chapter 3 for an overview of various policies and legislation which have reduced rights to asylum; see Chapters 1, 6, 7 and 8 on how Home Office actions have undermined the HRA.

[38]   R Sales (2002) 'The deserving and the undeserving? Refugees, asylum seekers and welfare in Britain' 22 Critical Social Policy 3 456-478

assumption, a belief widely shared by politicians, the public, and media, which makes draconian and regressive policies not only possible but standard practice.[39] And the policies keep getting progressively tougher. When the might of a powerful state is matched against that of a powerless, demonised, and disliked minority there can be little doubt of the outcome.[40]

9.4   A Culture of Rights?

When the HRA was first introduced as a key component of constitutional reforms by then-newly elected Labour government, a widely-promoted objective of the Act was to bring about a cultural change. While cultural change was not clearly defined it was inferred to mean the promotion of progressive social goals directed at empowering citizens and providing a real measure of protection for the powerless of society. The Act was introduced during a period of much soul searching about the nature of British society and a perception of a society rife with racism, social exclusion, and a deepening divide between the haves and have-nots.[41] These very issues were being laid bare in the late 1990s, particularly by the events leading up to the-then ongoing public inquiry into the race-motivated murder of Stephen Lawrence and its scandal of indifferent, racist, and uncaring authorities and bungled investigations.[42] The HRA was borne of an ambitious hope that enhancing awareness of human rights would in turn result in a culture of rights, in a more inclusive, more caring Britain.[43]

In a 2003 report the JCHR said that such a culture was a goal worth striving for; and, fundamental to its development was to create a culture in public life where human rights are central to policy, legislation, and public services (see section 1.3).[44] The definition of a culture of rights was reinforced by Labour in its third term of office when Harriet Harman, the Minister of State at the Department for Constitutional Affairs, appeared before the JCHR in January 2006 and added:

---

[39]   See Chapters 3 and 5 for a discussion on public attitudes and media reporting on asylum.

[40]   See: Joint Committee on Human Rights *The Treatment of Asylum-Seekers* (2007)

[41]   R Norton-Taylor, *The Colour of Justice* (1999)

[42]   William MacPherson and Home Office, *The Stephen Lawrence Inquiry: Report of an Inquiry* (1999)

[43]   Home Office, *Rights Brought Home* (1997)

[44]   Joint Committee on Human Rights, *The Case for a Human Rights Commission*, Sixth Report of Session 2002-03 (2003) HL Paper 67-I p. 5

'human rights protection is important for all who are vulnerable'.[45] This was later expanded in the Department's guide to the Act clarifying what it meant by a culture of rights:

1.   Convention rights and responsibilities form a common set of binding values for public authorities right across the UK;

2.   Public authorities must have human rights principles in mind when they make decisions about people's rights;

3.   Human rights must be part of all policy making.[46]

It is recognised that creating a culture of rights is not an overnight project; it is an ambitious and arguably laudable undertaking to bring about societal-wide changes. But now, almost ten years into the Act, it is time to ask about the status of those objectives. The findings of this study and other reviews while suggesting some positives are, on the whole, far from encouraging. In 2003 the JCHR expressed concerns that they had 'not found evidence of the rapid development of a culture of rights' and identified asylum as an area of particular concern.[47] In the same year the Audit Commission took stock of the situation and concluded: 'three years on, the impact of the Act is in danger of stalling and the initial flurry of activity surrounding its introduction has waned'.[48] Again, in 2006, the JCHR noted 'there remain unresolved questions about how far a culture of human rights is developing'.[49] And on various occasions the Committee, noting the apathy, ambivalence and resistance to the HRA, has seen fit to remind the government of its stated objective to 'bring about a fundamental transformation of the relationship between individuals and the state, a shift towards a culture of human rights'.[50] But how far the government

45   Joint Committee On Human Rights, *The Human Rights Act: the DCA and Home Office Reviews* (HL Paper 278 2006) (para 143)

46   Department of Constitutional Affairs, *A Guide to the Human Rights Act, 1998: Third Edition* (2006) (para. 1.14)

47   Joint Committee On Human Rights, *The Case for a Human Rights Commission (Sixth Report of Session 2002-03)* (2003) (para. 9)

48   Audit Commission, *Human rights: Improving Public Service Delivery* (2003) p.8

49   Joint Committee On Human Rights, *The Human Rights Act: the DCA and Home Office Reviews* (2006) (para. 138-46)

50   Joint Committee on Human Rights *The Case for a Human Rights Commission (Sixth Report of Session 2002-03)*; *The Human Rights Act: the DCA and Home Office Reviews* (at para. 139)

is willing to move or moves on such concerns remains to be seen. In asylum, for example, it has demonstrated a marked reluctance. And the public appears to be in step with its views on the HRA and the culture of rights:

> I am really disappointed in this culture of rights. Everyone wants something for nothing. What has this culture done but create entitlement. I am not sure I like it. I don't like what it has done to this country. What about my rights, all we hear of are rights of criminals, people who don't want to work, people who come to this country and make no effort to fit in expecting everything to be given to them.[51]

In many respects, notwithstanding its arguably broad and ambitious nature, the preceding definition of a culture of rights, as articulated by the JCHR and Department of Constitutional Affairs, is fairly straightforward. And when applied to asylum, particularly the events before and after the introduction of Section 55, the failings of the government become apparent. For example the HRA mandates that public authorities must not act in a manner contrary to the Act; and that Parliament must declare the laws it enacts are HRA compatible. The absence, and arguably deliberate circumvention or putting aside that which inconvenienced government policies in asylum, of almost all that had been outlined as essential for creating a culture of rights provides a measure of government failings. The campaign against Section 55 reinforced what many in the NGO community have been saying about Labour policies – that the HRA or no HRA, nothing is going to stop 'get tough' policies and the shutting of gates to asylum-seekers.[52] This includes implementing laws the government knew, or ought to have known after being warned by a parliamentary committee, raised serious human rights concerns. And those warnings were stark and prescient. Even as the impact of Section 55, of destitute and homeless asylum-seekers, was becoming known the government refused to act arguing that it was not obligated to act until the suffering had reached a sufficiently serious level, a threshold high enough to meet Article 3 requirements.[53] How that would have been

---

[51]   Anonymous source (interview notes on file with author); for similar comments see: Telegraph Speaker's Corner, 'Time for a rethink on human rights?' *Daily Telegraph* (11 May 2006)

[52]   For a review of toughening of policies see: BBC, 'Asylum: Getting tough in 2003 ' (2003) BBC News <http://news.bbc.co.uk/1/hi/uk/3333865.stm>

[53]   For a discussion on 'threshold levels' of suffering see: *Pretty v United Kingdom* [2002] 35 EHRR 1

measured was not clear as witnesses described 'extreme suffering' to which the Home Office remained blind.[54] The government actions and Section 55, criticised as 'draconian', 'distasteful', 'abhorrent' by High Court judges, 'inhuman and grotesque' by church leaders, 'almost beyond belief' by the *Guardian*, and 'cruel' and 'nasty' by NGOs, was defended all the way to the House of Lords as necessary to dealing with the crisis in asylum.[55] And even after a 5-0 defeat at the apex court the government, while changing the way Section 55 was applied, remained defiant promising to maintain its tough course on asylum.[56] If there was ever any doubt of government intention it became clear when the Home Office refused to repeal Section 55 when asked to do so by the JCHR.[57]

When all the above criteria, particularly criteria 1 and 2, are applied to the campaign against Section 55, it makes clear government abdication of its own publicly stated objectives.[58] That such a finding should be of some concern is not an impression a reader of most major newspapers, during the period of 2002 to 2005, would have had. Similarly, the House of Lords decision in *Limbuela* which found the government in breach of Article 3 rights, a serious finding by any measure, barely created a ripple. Later when the JCHR reviewed Section 55 and issued its report confirming what the NGOs had been saying all along – that the policy of forced destitution was a deliberate measure – not many, as measured by media coverage and Hansard record of debates in both Houses, paid attention.[59]

9.5   Outsiders and Rights

The process of dehumanisation of asylum-seekers has also included a systematic socio-legal construction and division of asylum-seekers into various categories (via frequent legislative changes), each entitled to varying levels of support (generally

---

54   Interview notes (on file with author)
55   Leader, 'Almost Beyond Belief' *Guardian* (25 Nov 2003); A Asthana, 'Asylum policy is 'grotesque' *The Observer* (27 Feb 2005); interview notes (on file with author); see Chapters 6 – 8 for an overview of various court challenges.
56   Tony McNulty, Immigration minister, cited in: BBC, 'Lords throw out key asylum rule ' (2005) 03 Nov <http://newsvote.bbc.co.uk/1/hi/uk/4402596.stm>
57   Joint Committee on Human Rights, *Government Response to the Committee's Tenth Report of this Session: The Treatment of Asylum Seekers* (2007) para 5
58   See: Department of Constitutional Affairs, *A Guide to the Human Rights Act, 1998: Third Edition* (2006) for the criteria (quoted earlier in this text)
59   Joint Committee on Human Rights *The Treatment of Asylum-Seekers* (2007)

at or below subsistence levels) and rights.[60] However, notwithstanding such categories, most asylum-seekers have been effectively constructed as undeserving 'outsiders' cheating a 'soft-touch' system (including a welfare system to which they have not contributed) and taking advantage of rights to which they ought not be entitled.[61] While this is a recurring and powerful theme in anti-asylum rhetoric and fodder for tabloids it also facilitates the process of exclusion. It is no accident that asylum-seekers do not factor in the mandate of the Social Exclusion Task Force (formerly Social Exclusion Unit) established to support evidence-based policy-making. Its mandate is to suggest ways to address ills that foster exclusion and marginalisation.[62] At that time, in support of the Unit's mandate, Prime Minister Tony Blair (1999) had said:

> On the eve of the 21st century it's a scandal that there are still people sleeping rough on our streets. This is not a situation we can tolerate in a modern and civilised society.[63]

The Prime Minister, however, was not referring to asylum-seekers. That the situation of asylum-seekers should be absent from a committee with a mandate to reduce social exclusion amongst vulnerable populations is another measure of their status as outsiders who have not earned rights or benefits which accrue to citizens. The House of Lords (in *Limbuela*) acknowledged that the policy (of reducing social exclusion) was never intended to apply to asylum-seekers, but Lord Brown had difficulty reconciling the Prime Minister's words with the suffering brought about by Section 55.[64] That the House of Lords, in this instance, was

---

[60] R Sales (2002) 'The deserving and the undeserving? Refugees, asylum seekers and welfare in Britain' ; S Chakrabarti (2005) 'Rights and Rhetoric: The Politics of Asylum and Human Rights Culture in the UK'

[61] See, for example: J Hampshire, *Citizenship and Belonging: Immigration and the Politics of Demographic Governance in post-war Britain* (2005); S Spencer, *The Politics of Migration: Managing Opportunity, Conflict and Change* (2003); P Dwyer (2005) 'Governance, forced migration and welfare' 39 Social Policy & Administration 6 622-639; A Green, 'What About Our Human Rights?' *Daily Mail* (27 July 2005)

[62] www.cabinetoffice.gov.uk/social_exclusion.aspx. The Unit was first established in 1997 and restructured in 2006; initially established when Prime Minister Tony Blair declared homelessness to be a scandal: BBC, 'Blair pledge to reduce rough sleeping ' (1999) 14 Dec <http://news.bbc.co.uk/1/hi/uk_politics/565001.stm>

[63] BBC, 'Blair pledge to reduce rough sleeping' (1999) 14 Dec <http://news.bbc.co.uk/1/hi/uk_politics/565001.stm>

[64] *R. v. Secretary of State for the Home Department ex parte Limbuela* [2005] UKHL 66 (para. 99)

unable to countenance the exclusion of asylum-seekers provides a measure of the government's determination and harsh nature of its policies.

If anything government policies – such as dispersal of asylum-seekers to various areas of the country (including placing them in condemned housing, toxic council estates, and remote regions away from community and other support infrastructure), the now-defunct voucher system, separate welfare system, increasing use of detention, varying socio-legal categorisation, etc. – have served to exacerbate exclusion, which some argue is the real objective behind the policies.[65] There is much to infer the drafters never envisioned the HRA applying to outsiders. What this study has shown is a government backtracking on a central platform of its manifesto, to foster a culture of rights, quite possibly because it never expected that non-citizens or 'outsiders' would seek the protection of the HRA and want to be a part of the proposed culture of rights. If not part of it then at least ask that their rights are protected under a convention which speaks of 'human' not 'British' rights. While it may be suggested that this view veers towards the speculative a closer review of *Rights Brought Home* offers some insight. That document extols the virtues of rights and speaks of benefits to 'British people' and home-grown judges putting a uniquely 'British' interpretation to Convention rights:

> Bringing these rights home will mean that the British people
> will be able to argue for their rights in the British courts . . .
> Our aim is a straightforward one. It is to make more directly
> accessible the rights which the British people already enjoy
> under the Convention.[66]

To be sure promotional material – which is what the manifesto, in part, was – should be viewed with scepticism and not as direct evidence of an intention to stop 'outsiders' from accessing the HRA. Nonetheless it should not be wholly disregarded when seeking to understand how the Act came about or the intention of drafters. There are good reasons to suggest that barring outsiders was precisely the intent in this instance. An example from Canada and its experience with constitutional reform and rights, which was studied extensively by the drafters of the HRA, illustrates.[67]

---

[65] See: R Sales (2002)

[66] Home Office, *Rights Brought Home: the Human Rights Bill* (para 1.14 and 1.19)

[67] R Penner (1996) 'The Canadian Experience with the Charter of Rights: Are there Lessons for the UK' Spring Public Law, 104-25

9.6 Rights, Outsiders, and the Canadian Experience

Much like the events preceding the HRA and constitutional reform in the UK, constitutional reform in Canada also was, in part, premised on an imperative to address tensions in Canadian federalism and a perception of society characterised by fissures and social exclusion. A key part of the reform was to include the *Canadian Charter of Rights and Freedoms,* to build a stronger, more inclusive and united Canada.[68]

But much to the later and continuing consternation of many outsiders did crash the party. More than twenty-five years since coming into effect arguments still continue whether *Charter* protection should ever have been extended to non-citizens. According to *The Globe and Mail* political columnist Jeffrey Simpson, who has written dozens of pieces about the *Charter* and interviewed the drafters (both elected officials and civil servants), 'none thought in using the word "persons" that they were extending *Charter* protection to non-citizens'.[69] But, just like the fight over Section 55, NGOs in Canada fought to have *Charter* protection extended to asylum-seekers. At that time, in 1985, a siege mentality (not unlike the events of 2003 in the UK) prevailed in Canada as boatloads of Sri Lankan and Indian asylum-seekers fleeing separatist violence in their respective homelands entered the country and sought refuge. A central argument and debate of the day focused on whether *Charter* rights applied to non-citizens – the Canadian government argued that it did not; that non-citizens had not earned the right to its protection. The Supreme Court of Canada disagreed. One of the justices dismissed the government position as mere 'administrative inconvenience';[70] that inconvenience, however, resulted in an almost immediate backlog of claims exceeding 100,000 and annual costs since then in excess of hundreds of millions of dollars.[71] It changed fundamentally the refugee determination process in Canada – from one of bureaucratic administration to judicial determination. In other words, the government effectively lost control over decision-making in asylum. To this day, many continue to rue the decision; 84% of the cases before the Federal Court (seeking judicial review) concern asylum.

---

[68] M Mandel, *The Charter of Rights and the Legalization of Politics in Canada* (1994); FL Morton, *Law, Politics and the Judicial Process in Canada* (2002)
[69] Personal communication (Jeffrey Simpson, Globe and Mail, Toronto, Canada 08 Sept 2008)
[70] Justice Bertha Wilson in *Singh v. Minister of Employment and Immigration* [1985] 1 S.C.R. 177
[71] M Mandel (1994)

And this granting of *Charter* protection to non-citizens and outsiders, according to Simpson and other observers, is the key reason behind the 'shambles' that is the Canadian refugee determination system. A view shared by many, including senior politicians, is that the Canadian system is 'badly broken'. A former Deputy Prime Minister has suggested that the government consider legislation restricting access to the *Charter* for non-citizens.[72] But the Canadian system, reviled in many quarters and subject of severe criticisms at home with regular calls for its reform and/or abolition, also has many supporters and is often held up as an example for the UK to emulate.[73] Not surprising it is mostly the NGOs in the UK who are saying so, the government, on the other hand, has shown no interest.[74] It comes as little surprise that the very criticisms voiced in Canada have a familiar ring in the UK dealing with its own 'not fit for the purpose' and 'chaotic' system and the rights of outsiders and of legislating limitations to the HRA.[75] In view of the UK's long and continuing battle over asylum, and the annual costs in excess of a billion (and increasing), it is more probable than not that the drafters of the HRA were keen to avoid the Canadian experience. How else to reconcile the comments of the Minister for the Department of Constitutional Affairs (above) extolling human rights 'for all who are vulnerable' while being apparently oblivious to the vulnerability of asylum-seekers or the irony of her government's policies in asylum and social exclusion.[76]

The drafters of the HRA also included other safeguards against what were considered negative aspects of the Canadian experience; for example, supremacy of Parliament was retained (in Canada judges can declare laws unconstitutional, of no force or effect; in the UK there is no such power). In Canada a special fund was created to encourage groups (other than the victim) wishing to commence Charter

---

[72]   John Manley, former Deputy Prime Minister cited in: M Jimenez, 'Broken Gates: Canada's welcome mat frayed and unravelling' *Globe and Mail* (16 Apr 2005)

[73]   During its tenure as the official opposition the Conservative Party's (formerly Reform Party of Canada) mantra was the abolition of the IRB; the Conservatives, now in government, have not made the IRB an issue given that it holds the slimmest of margins in Parliament. However, according to anonymous sources within the IRB, the process of 'hollowing-out' seem to be in the works; there are currently over 40 vacant judicial or board member positions, generally filled by patronage appointments, which the government has made very little effort to staff (interview notes on file with author).

[74]   Interview notes (on file with author)

[75]   Joint Committee on Human Rights *The Treatment of Asylum-Seekers* (2007)

[76]   Joint Committee On Human Rights, *The Human Rights Act: the DCA and Home Office Reviews* (2006) 98

challenges;[77] the HRA, on the other hand, contains a specific provision stipulating that only victims can commence action for breaches of Convention rights.[78] This would appear to exclude actions by third-parties seeking broader policy changes rather than redress for a specific victim. It is common knowledge that few asylum-seekers have the wherewithal to initiate legal battles; few are aware of their rights and are generally reluctant to challenge the very government before whom they are seeking asylum. Moreover most are primarily concerned with seemingly mundane but fundamental matters such as 'making it through the day' and 'having shelter and food to eat'.[79] Without third-party interveners it is unlikely that *Singh* in Canada would have happened; and, the fight over Section 55 and other court battles over asylum rights would have been just as unlikely in the UK. While the drafters of the HRA were careful to avoid provisions for third-party intervention – a subject of much debate during the Bill stages of the Act – the judiciary, to the probable dismay of the drafters, has been fairly open to such applications.[80] In any event, it is not unusual for judges to disregard procedural rules which have the effect or appearance of fettering decision-making.[81] Liberty, for example, is often welcomed as *amicus curiae* by courts seeking its expertise.[82]

While it was the announced intention of policy-makers to avoid creating a culture of litigation – in fact, the HRA was promoted on the basis that as a culture of rights developed it would somehow lessen the need to litigate – it remains the case that third-party intervention in the public interest has an important role to play in the interpretation of rights; of giving meaning to rights and pushing the

---

[77] For a discussion of the political machinations behind the Court Challenges Program see: I Brodie (2001) 'Interest group litigation and the embedded state: Canada's court challenges program' 34 Canadian Journal of Political Science 2 357-376. The program later became a contentious issue for successive governments fed-up with legal challenges; it was ended by the Conservative government in 2006: H Henderson 'Government expects no outcry over axing of court challenges program' *Toronto Star* (28 Sep 2006)

[78] Section 7(1): A person who claims that a public authority has acted (or proposes to act) in a way which is made unlawful . . . may (a) bring proceedings against the authority under this Act in the appropriate court or tribunal, or (b) rely on the Convention right or rights concerned in any legal proceedings, but only if he is (or would be) a victim of the unlawful act.

[79] Interview with Maurice Wren, Asylum Aid (London March 2005)

[80] C Harlow (2002) 'Public Law and Popular Justice' 65 Modern Law Review 1 1-18

[81] AC McHugh, 'Tensions Between the Executive and the Judiciary' (2002) Australian Bar Association Conference <http://www.hcourt.gov.au/speeches/mchughj/mchughj_paris.htm>

[82] R Maiman (2004)

boundaries in a continually-evolving rights landscape. And this is as true for the UK – for example, as seen in this study of the fight over Section 55 and creative use of rights or what *The Times* called a 'cleverly constructed challenge to the law' – as it has been for the US and Canada.[83] As documented in this study, the efforts directed at defeating Section 55 required a great deal of resources, persistence, creativity, and determination. Without third-party interveners, who organised and fought lengthy and expensive court battles over the course of three years, it is unlikely that Section 55 would have been defeated. Those efforts included fighting against public opinion and dealing with significant setbacks in the courts.

The defeat of Section 55 did not happen overnight. It required a massive effort. From front-line caseworkers and volunteers assisting asylum-seekers navigate the bureaucracy, helping with their day-to-day needs and, at the same time, working to identify possible cases for test-case challenges; to NGO staff raising funds and awareness; to campaigners organising protests, writing letters, educating the public, and seeking publicity for the efforts; to legal staff, some working pro-bono, developing strategy and filing applications for prerogative writs seeking shelter and benefits for destitute asylum-seekers. All this had to be sustained over a period of over three years before the policy was defeated. It is difficult to envision how the policy would have been defeated had it not been for the combined efforts of a disparate group – NGOs, faith groups, and volunteers – of organisations who came together and intervened on behalf of a vulnerable and powerless constituency.

9.7   The Human Rights Act

In a relatively short period of time (since coming into force in 2000) the *Human Rights Act* has come to be seen by many as un-British; for creating a culture of entitlement, not of rights; of protecting the rights of outsiders at the expense of citizens.[84] How has this come about? Why and what is it that so many find so objectionable about the HRA?

---

[83]   Comment, 'Asylum Angst' *The Times* (20 Feb 2003) 21; FL Morton (2002); C Harlow and R Rawlings, *Pressure through law* (1992); T Prosser, *Test Cases for the Poor: Legal Techniques in the Politics of Social Welfare* (1983)

[84]   BBC, 'Human rights 'blaming' under fire' (2006) 14 Nov <http://news.bbc.co.uk/1/hi/uk_politics/6144804.stm>; Ministry of Justice *Human Rights Insight Project* (2008); also see Chapter 6. Many examples of 'human rights blaming' are found in print media (both tabloids and broadsheets) – see C Moore, 'Our human rights culture has now become a tyranny' *Daily Telegraph* (18 Dec 2009)

In examining such questions it is instructive to first examine the Act itself. Not unusually in an Act for the protection of human rights it contains lofty and noble ideals which are perhaps more inspirational than achievable. But there are also provisions – for example, the right to liberty, freedom from cruel and unusual punishment, freedom of conscience – found in the Bills of rights in many liberal-democratic nations, for example, Canada and the US. These are fairly standard and uncontroversial provisions, which, not many would dispute are worthy of protection. Yet the Act, in its short existence, continues to attract controversy and has generated legions of detractors united in vehement opposition. Many, it seems, want the Act to be limited in application if not outright repealed in law.[85] This process of denigration, according to the JCHR, has been aided and abetted at the highest levels of government for whom the Act has become a convenient scapegoat for administrative shortcomings.[86] This includes the party which first promoted the concept of an HRA when in opposition and brought it into existence when in government. Tony Blair, during his term as Prime Minister, made several public comments of his determination to limit the reach and applicability of the Act. And his senior ministers have railed against it (and the courts) in intemperate language.[87] The public servants, who are mandated to apply the Act in their work, view it as a hindrance.[88] The opposition Conservatives, under various leaders, including the present continue to make the Act a key political issue with promises, depending on the perceived electoral mood, to review, amend and/or repeal it.[89] Major newspapers, such as the *Daily Telegraph* have called for its repeal claiming that the Act has not stopped the government from passing illiberal laws and that the only beneficiaries have been 'criminals' and 'terrorists'.[90] *The Times* has also questioned its merits and has supported legislation which would limit its application.[91] Conservative think-tanks such as Civitas blame the Act for

---

[85] British Institute of Human Rights, *The Human Rights Act - Changing Lives* (2008)
[86] BBC, 'Human rights 'blaming' under fire' (citing Andrew Dismore, Chair, JCHR) (14 Nov 2006); S Chakrabarti, 'So much freedom lost and on my watch' *Daily Telegraph* (20 May 2007)
[87] BBC, 'Blair 'to amend human rights law'' (2006) 14 May <http://news.bbc.co.uk/1/hi/uk/4770231.stm>
[88] Joint Committee On Human Rights, *Human Rights Policy: Oral and Written Evidence* (2007)
[89] BBC, 'Cameron 'could scrap' rights act ' (2006) 25 June <news.bbc.co.uk/1/hi/uk_politics/5114102.stm> ; at time of writing (2009) David Cameron was leader
[90] Leader, 'It is time to protect the public's human rights' *Daily Telegraph* (11 May 2006)
[91] Comment, 'Asylum Angst' (20 Feb 2003)

various policy failures and have called for an outright repeal because 'no good has come of it at all, only harm'.[92] Migration Watch, an organisation opposed to most immigration, continues to urge the government to derogate from the Act in favour of a robust enforcement of immigration control measures, including restricting the entry of asylum-seekers and carrying out deportations to countries where their lives may be at risk because 'tough decisions have to be made'.[93] And, last but not least, the Act provides fodder for tabloids which rail against its existence and have persistently called for its repeal. The tabloids, with its unique blending of fact and fiction and large readership, continue to portray the Act in negative terms with stories of its purported harm to UK society dominating headlines.[94]

There are several explanations for such strident opposition to the HRA and nowhere is that opposition amplified as it is in asylum. As wryly noted by some observers the HRA is unlikely to be called into service by the 'haves' of society. It is generally those on the margins – on the outside – subjected to excesses or abuses of government power who have occasion to call upon its protection.[95] High profile cases of serious criminals and prosecutions under terrorism laws in which the HRA supposedly weakened the government's case, coming at the heels of intense spotlight on asylum (particularly during 2003), have served to cement an overwhelmingly negative view of the Act.[96] But it has been mostly in asylum that the Act has met with outrage, and calls for its repeal.[97] Asylum, in the UK, is seen almost exclusively as being about undeserving outsiders, a perception that the UK has lost control of its borders and is being 'swamped' by 'diseased

---

[92] BBC, 'Viewpoints: The Human Rights Act' (2006)

[93] Migration Watch, 'Response to High Court ruling' (2003) <http://www.migrationwatchuk. org/pressreleases/> ; also cited in: P Johnston and G Jones, 'Blair to take on judges over asylum' *Daily Telegraph* (20 Feb 2003) 1

[94] Greensdale (2005)

[95] Interview notes; see also: T Campbell KD Ewing and A Tomkins, *Sceptical Essays on Human Rights* (2001); L Clements (1999) 'The Human Rights Act – A New Equity or a New Opiate: Reinventing Justice or Repackaging State Control?' 26 Journal of Law and Society 1 72-85; R Cotterrell, Law *and Society* (1994) citing Marc Galanter (Why the "Haves' Come Out Ahead). Also see Chapter 2.

[96] The high-profile examples included the case of a convicted murderer, Andrew Rice, who murdered again while on release; prison officials claimed that their concern for Rice's human rights had resulted in his release. The matter was reviewed by the JCHR which found government officials using the Act as a scapegoat for their department's shortcomings and errors. See: BBC, 'Human rights 'blaming' under fire' (2006)

[97] See Chapter 6 for an overview of media and official reaction to the first Section 55 test-case challenge.

hordes'[98] – a view which the government has indirectly and directly created and has done little to counter.[99] For this apparent calamitous turn of events, the media, politicians, including senior government ministers and commentators have blamed the HRA and decisions by 'dictators in wigs defying democracy'.[100] The NGOs and international organisations, on the other hand, have put the blame squarely on politicians and the media for scapegoating the HRA and for targeting vulnerable peoples.[101] Quite possibly no other public policy issue generates as much negativity and opposition, particularly because those seen as 'winning' human rights claims are almost universally considered 'cheats' and worse.[102] As a former leader of the Conservatives wrote: Britain is being 'taken for a ride' (by asylum-seekers) and 'we are at the end of our tether'.[103]

In some respects the Act has come to be seen as something which acts against the interest of society and feeds into fears of a Britain no longer the Britain of old. Such fears are exploited and give credence by relentless tabloid attacks blaming the HRA, for example, for hindering public officials in protecting Britain from 'invading hordes' of asylum-seekers.[104]An extensive and detailed review of a cross-section of newspaper blogs, letters to the editor, complaints to MPs, creation of ad-hoc organisations (i.e. Bicester Action Group), and interviews conducted for this study are reflective of those fears and paint a picture of a society deeply concerned about and opposed to asylum.[105] Moreover, the findings of this and other studies also point to fears – exaggerated and unfounded but nonetheless real to those holding such fears – about the impact of asylum in communities across the UK: of asylum-seekers

---

[98]   D Leppard, 'Focus: Ministers lose control of Britain's borders' *The Times* (04 April 2004)

[99]   R Sales (2002); Comment, 'Leading article: Damned lies and targets' *The Times* (04 April 2004). See also Chapters 6-9 for examples of comments by government officials and senior ministers blaming various social challenges on asylum; also see: BBC, 'Human rights 'blaming' under fire' (14 Nov 2006) //news.bbc.co.uk/1/hi/uk_politics/6144804.stm

[100]   See Chapter 6 for media coverage following Justice Collins's decision in *Q and Others*.

[101]   R Tyler, 'Britain: Government and media conspire to whip-up anti-immigrant hysteria' (2003) World Socialist Web Site <http://www.wsws.org/articles/2003/feb2003/brit-f10.shtml> (04 Dec 2006)

[102]   N Cohen, 'How we scape-goated asylum-seekers' *New Statesman* (17 Apr 2000); also Chapters 3, 4 and 6 for a fuller discussion on why asylum remains such a 'hot' issue

[103]   ID Smith, 'Why the French are laughing at us this morning' *Daily Mail* (24 May 2002) 4

[104]   Institute for Public Policy Research, *Seeking Scapegoats: The Coverage of Asylum in the UK Press* (2005); A Green, 'What About Our Human Rights?' (27 July 2005); BBC, 'Human rights 'as British as beer' ' (2006) BBC News <http://news.bbc.co.uk/1/hi/uk_politics/6097634.stm> (30 Oct 2006); BBC, 'Human rights 'blaming' under fire' (2006); also Greensdale (2005)

[105]   See, for example, Telegraph Speaker's Corner, 'Time for a rethink on human rights?'

'stealing' jobs, swamping schools, committing crimes, terrorism.[106] While such fears are largely without substance they are nevertheless an indication of societal attitudes making asylum and the HRA a controversial mix, and the HRA, in particular, a difficult sell.

Such negative views of the HRA and asylum are not limited to 'tabloid readers' or middle-England but are more generalised.[107] In interviews and discussions with a cross-section of students in Oxford, including several faculty members, such views cropped up with regularity. Even some human rights advocates expressed little sympathy feeling that the system was being abused.[108] In interviews with residents of Bicester, a village in Oxfordshire, the resentment was palpable; a sense of victimhood and being taken advantage of by asylum-seekers.[109] This was during the period when the Home Office was planning to build an accommodation centre to house asylum-seekers in Bicester.[110] The Bicester Action Group organised opposition to the plan arguing that the human rights of asylum-seekers would be violated if housed in the project. The concern here was not with the rights of the asylum-seekers but an overwhelming objection to having asylum-seekers in their community; fear of collapse in property values; fear of asylum-seekers 'roaming the streets' and committing crimes.[111] The rights argument, in this instance, had nothing to do with the rights of asylum-seekers but it served as a convenient gloss over the real reasons for community opposition.[112] And this turning of rights on its head, by a group opposed to asylum, is a reminder that social justice groups are not alone in deploying rights for the furtherance of

---

[106] R Winnett and D Leppard, 'Shires buckle under migrant tension' *Sunday Times* (29 Aug 2004)

[107] Commission for Racial Equality, *Attitudes Towards Asylum-Seekers, Refugees and Other Immigrants* (2004); Information Centre about Asylum and Refugees, *Key issues: Public opinion on asylum and refugee issues* (2005)

[108] Interview notes (on file with author). It should be noted that such views are consistent with other such surveys on human rights, in particular with the findings of the Ministry of Justice's *Human Rights Insight Project* (2008)

[109] See also: P Johnston, 'Uproar over asylum centre plan' *Daily Telegraph* (12 Feb 2003)

[110] BBC, 'The trouble with asylum centres' (2004) BBC News <http://news.bbc.co.uk/1/hi/uk/3604553.stm> (27 May)

[111] The group, Bicester Action Group, no longer exists; bowing to intense public pressure the Home Office abandoned its plans to build accommodation centres after spending millions on feasibility studies; not a single accommodation centre was built anywhere in the UK; see: BBC, 'Scrapped asylum centre cost £28m' (2007) Nov 8 <http://news.bbc.co.uk/1/hi/uk_politics/7084200.stm>

[112] Interview notes (with respondents in Bicester and Oxford 2003-2005;on file with author)

political agendas.[113] The findings of this study are also a reminder that rights often and with predictable regularity serve the interests of the powerful at the expense of the powerless, favouring the haves over the have-nots.[114]

That the early days of the HRA should be associated with battles over asylum with outsiders seen as winning at the expense of the rights of citizens, has not been a positive factor in the development of a culture of rights. As this research, and a recent survey conducted for the Department of Constitutional Affairs, has found public opinion, while generally favourable to the concept of human rights, changes sharply when it comes to outsiders and human rights, with a majority of respondents holding the view that 'asylum-seekers and foreigners take advantage of the Act'.[115] There is little evidence to support such views but the government has done little to counter them. If anything its undeclared war on asylum and get-tough policies makes a bad situation worse.[116] In 2003, at the height of the crisis brought about by Section 55, the Prime Minister suggested using the military to stop asylum-seekers from entering the UK serving to drive home the war metaphor.[117] When considered in conjunction with the government's undeclared war on asylum, backtracking, and talk of limiting the applicability of the HRA, it is not surprising that the public would make the assumption that the HRA serves as a conduit by which asylum-seekers take advantage of 'soft-touch' Britain. And that is precisely what the headlines in 2003, following Mr Justice Collins's decision in *Q and Others,*[118]conveyed to an outraged public.[119]

---

[113] See, for example, JP Heinz A Southworth and A Paik (2003) 'Lawyers for Conservative Causes: Clients, Ideology, and Social Distance' 37 Law and Society Review 1 5-50; I Brodie and FL Morton, 'Do the 'Haves' Still Come Out Ahead in Canada' (1998) University of Calgary <http://publish.uwo.ca/~irbrodie/newman.pdf>

[114] See, for example, K Hull (2001) 'The Political Limits of the Rights Frame: The Case of Same-Sex Marriage in Hawaii' 44 Sociological Perspectives 2 207-32; M Malik, 'Minority Protection and Human Rights' in T CampbellKD Ewing and A Tomkins (eds) *Sceptical Essays on Human Rights* (2001)

[115] *Human Rights Insight Project*

[116] B White, 'New Labour's bare-knuckle fight against asylum seekers' *Guardian* (25 July 2008)

[117] G Hinsliff and M Bright, 'Labour fuels war on asylum' *The Observer* (06 Feb 2005); L Smith, 'Britain: Government steps up attacks on asylum seekers' (2004) World Socialist Web Site <http://www.wsws.org/articles/2004/jan2004.bak/asyl-j05.shtml> (16 Oct 2006)

[118] *R (on the application of Q and Others) v Secretary of State for the Home Department* [2003] 2 All ER 905 (Admin)

[119] See, for example, Article 19, *What's the Story: Results from Research into Media Coverage of Refugees and Asylum-Seekers in the UK* (2003); as part of data-gathering, I also reviewed hundreds of blogs (from a cross-section of newspapers) linked to the coverage of the decision and close to 90% of the commentary expressed hostility towards asylum-seekers and the courts, including the HRA.

The events of 2003 – the battle over Section 55 and subsequent backlash against the HRA and asylum – brought about a major re-think with Labour backtracking and 'disowning' the HRA.[120] If anything the battle between the NGOs and Home Office highlighted the shortcomings of rights as a means of advancing social justice issues. True, there were some important short-term wins – such as 'winning' injunctions and forcing the Home Office to provide support to asylum-seekers refused welfare under Section 55. And the importance of this should not be understated – for destitute asylum-seekers, hungry and without shelter, to have been provided with welfare benefits were of immeasurable importance. It was the difference between extreme suffering and respite. However, in the long-term, the results have been less positive as seen in the continuing get-tough measures and increasing destitution and ill-treatment of asylum-seekers.[121] And it is the latter, long-term results, by which the effectiveness of a rights strategy should be assessed. As one NGO caseworker lamented: 'it doesn't matter what we do, the government simply changes the law and continues as before'.[122] Alex Gask, solicitor at Liberty, offers an equally resigned view: 'it's the same battles; we keep fighting them over and over again. It has worn us down. There is less fight left in us'.[123]

9.8   The Fight Over Section 55

The fight over Section 55 was the first major test for the HRA. At least it was in November 2005 when the House of Lords decided *Limbuela*. At that time Section 55 represented a litmus test for the nascent Act. There is no question that the campaign was a major victory for the NGOs and *Limbuela*, remains to date, a landmark legal victory in which the HRA was the deciding factor in a decision which the *Guardian* called 'a victory for humanity'.[124] Beginning in early 2003, a group of disparate organisations with limited financial resources came together, initially in an ad-hoc fashion, but later better coordinated, and fought a long and bruising battle against

---

[120]   See Chapter 6
[121]   The Joseph Rowntree Charitable Trust, *More Destitution in Leeds* (2008); Amnesty International, *Down and Out in London* (2006); Refugee Action, *The Destitution Trap* (2006)
[122]   Interview with Jonathan Knight, caseworker, Joint Council for the Welfare of Immigrants (London, March 2005)
[123]   Interview notes (on file with author)
[124]   Leader, 'A victory for humanity ' *Guardian* (20 Feb 2003)

a 'tough as old boots' Home Office – and won.[125] But the victory came at a cost: the immeasurable cost in human suffering; increased division and mistrust between NGOs and the Home Office and retrenching of positions; further marginalisation of a vulnerable constituency; and, further polarisation on a major public policy issue which was then and continues to be marked by an absence of informed debate and discussion. The three-year battle fought out in courtrooms and the campaign trail was a major financial drain on organisations ill-able to afford it. Monies which could have been better utilised were, according to the campaigners, instead devoted to fighting a wholly unnecessary battle. During the crisis, funds were also used to provide support to destitute asylum-seekers and there was suffering on a large scale, with some estimates putting the number of destitute at over ten thousand.

At the height of the crisis homeless asylum-seekers crowded the offices of the NGOs, sleeping on floors until closing time forced them onto the streets; NGO caseworkers spoke of using their own monies to buy them food; the Refugee Council strained under the pressure of helping large numbers, with many sleeping outside their office (in Brixton) waiting for it to open (for food and showers); and, pregnant women sleeping in bus shelters during some of the coldest months of the year.[126] These stories were not uncommon during the three-year long campaign. For asylum-seekers the NGO efforts and eventual victory was the difference between extreme hardship and survival and hundreds were helped. But what has the legal victory meant for the NGOs? And what has it meant for asylum-seekers, the thousands fleeing misfortune, who enter the UK seeking sanctuary?

9.9   A Deliberate Attack on Asylum

When the fight over Section 55 is examined in its entirety – beginning when it was first introduced as a late amendment to a Bill already before the House – there is every suggestion of a government being deliberate, underhanded, and determined to implement a policy it knew or ought to have known had serious human rights implications. And Labour, which long-ago abandoned its traditional ideology of social inclusion and social justice, has not been averse to engaging in

---

[125]   Don Flynn, formerly policy director, JCWI, uses this term to describe the government's approach to asylum and immigration.

[126]   See Chapter 5

sleights of hand to expedite (illiberal) legislation.[127] Law-making, including policy development, generally follows a well-established and deliberative process making it more probable than not that Section 55 was a planned and deliberate attack on human rights. That such a major policy should not have been in the planning stages for considerable time stretches credulity, particularly in view of previous and persistent attempts at legislating against welfare support for asylum-seekers.[128] That previous such legislative attempts had been defeated in the courts was most probably the reason for introducing the amendment at such a late hour. This was clearly a government trying to hide something. For the NGOs, particularly those who had reviewed and commented on the White Paper introducing the Bill and in which there was no mention of what later became Section 55, the manoeuvrings set off alarm bells? And these concerns became even more pronounced when after its introduction, and immediate questions about human rights issues, the government used a guillotine motion to limit debate to less than 15 minutes and forced the legislation through both Houses. And, then, thereafter the government's approach – its behaviour, attitude, and responses – added to those concerns.[129] Later, in response to the first test-case challenge, *Q and Others*, decided in favour of the NGOs, the-then Home Secretary attacked the High Court for defying democracy arguing that the legislation had been properly vetted in Parliament when nothing of the sort had been permitted by his own underhanded actions. In brief, the government:

- failed to heed the warnings of the JCHR on the human rights implications of the amendment;
- failed to respond to a direct and repeated requests from the JCHR to provide timely information;
- failed to implement Section 55 according to what Parliament had been told;
- failed to provide human rights training to officials responsible for Section 55;
- refused to acknowledge that Section 55 was causing widespread suffering;

---

127 R Sales (2002) 459; H Porter, 'Blair gets away with his assault on liberty, because we let him' (16 April 2006)

128 See Chapter 4 for a review of policies on welfare for asylum-seekers. For general information on law-making see the UK Parliament website: www.parliament.uk/about/how/laws/new_laws.cfm

129 See Chapters 5, 6 and 7 for a fuller discussion on how the Home Office responded to NGO lobbying and court decisions.

- failed to censure senior ministers for attacks on the HRA and judiciary;

- failed to heed repeated warnings from members of the judiciary;

- failed to acknowledge various independent reports and studies on the impact of Section 55;

- in response to questions raised in the House of Commons denied that Section 55 was causing suffering (contrary to various reports then-already in the public domain).

These and other actions all point to deliberation and directly to a demonstrable failure of a government uncommitted to a culture of rights, at least, insofar as asylum is concerned. Such actions are also an unequivocal measure of a government prepared to ride roughshod over rights in pursuit of policy objectives, which according to some observers seem to be dictated in part by the tabloid media and its all important constituency of over 20 million readers.[130]

These are not actions conducive to building a culture of rights described in *Rights Brought Home;* and, rather than lessen litigation, Home Office actions during the height of the campaign against Section 55, instead, actively invited litigation. The Home Office, which ought to have known that its actions were causing hardship and potentially contrary to Convention rights, nevertheless maintained a hard-line throughout the campaign and made clear to the NGOs that it believed its actions to be HRA compliant; its challenge to the NGOs: if you disagree, take us to court.[131]

9.10   The Future of Human Rights in the UK

In a recent report the JCHR, comprised of cross-party senior MPs and peers, criticised senior members of the government, including the Prime Minister, for fuelling misunderstandings about the HRA particularly in the area of major public policy issues.[132] And in the face of persistent attacks voices of moderation and in

---

[130]   For some insight into the workings of the then-Home Secretary, David Blunkett, see a review of his autobiography in R Hattersley, 'A bit of a wet Blunkett ' *Guardian* (15 Oct 2006); also, Comment, 'Ministers Must Learn to Respect Their Own Human Rights Laws' (20 Feb 2003)

[131]   Interview notes (on file with author); see also Chapter 5.

[132]   A Travis, 'Ministers accused of fuelling myths on human rights' *Guardian* (14 Nov 2006); Joint Committee on Human Rights, *The Human Rights Act: the DCA and Home Office Reviews* (2006)

support of rights and the HRA have struggled to be heard. But the voices continue to persist that rights have an important role to play in social justice and can be a force for social change. Liberty, the Refugee Council, JUSTICE, British Institute of Human Rights, Public Law Project, and others remain steadfast in their believe and hope in the power of the Act to make real on its promises of a culture of rights; for those rights to be used in innovative ways to bring about changes in policy, promote issues of social justice, and improve the treatment of vulnerable groups.[133]

Notwithstanding what some have called the 'futility of rights' and the findings of various studies, including this study, which have not found much evidence that a culture of rights is developing, some NGOs remain committed to 'bringing rights to life'; by promoting its use in everyday interaction, for improving the quality of life for individuals and, more broadly, bringing about wider social change.[134] The BIHR has recognised that the development of a culture of rights has stalled or is not developing as many had hoped when the HRA came into existence and has embarked on an ambitious series of education programs and initiatives designed to promote the use of rights in everyday life.

Another potentially promising initiative was the establishment, in October 2007, of the *Equality and Human Rights Commission* with a mandate for 'championing equality and human rights for all'.[135] The body, the establishment of which had been long promoted by activists and resisted by Labour, has a wide-ranging and ambitious mandate to make Britain 'a fairer, more equal Britain'.[136] Whether this is a step in the right direction or if the initiatives by the BIHR are successes are, however, empirical questions for future researchers.

On the whole, however, it cannot be unequivocally said that the HRA has been without successes. There are many anecdotes and examples of the HRA affecting the lives of individuals in bringing about the changes they sought. There are examples, in the field of mental health, where the language of rights and the Act itself has brought about marked improvement in how patients are treated; of people

---

[133] See, for example: www.publiclawproject.org.uk/whatisPLP.html; www.justice.org.uk; www.bihr.co.uk

[134] British Institute of Human Rights, *The Human Rights Act - Changing Lives* (2008); KD Ewing (2004)

[135] www.equalityhumanrights.com/en/aboutus/pages/aboutus.aspx

[136] S Spencer (2008) 'Equality and Human Rights Commission: A Decade in the Making' 79 Political Quarterly 1 6-16

using rights in creative ways to improve lives and communities.[137] Such examples can also be found in asylum; as already noted in these pages, the HRA played a crucial role in defeating Section 55 and ensured that asylum-seekers were provided with welfare support.

However, notwithstanding the importance of individual experiences and apparent signs of a culture of rights, questions remain. It is about the extent and true nature of such changes. At an individual or micro level the HRA has made important contributions to the protection of human rights. But the examples in the field of mental health or other areas need to be subjected to an empirical inquiry before one can conclude that a culture of rights is in fact taking root in those areas. To be sure there are some positive signs. But this study is concerned with the 'lowest of the low', an idiom common amongst NGO caseworkers in referring to asylum-seekers.[138] An idiom not intended as a pejorative but as an indicator of how thoroughly marginalised asylum-seekers have become in the UK. It is in the battle over the rights of those who need its protection the most that arguably the true nature of rights emerges. Many interviewees echoed the sentiment: what good are rights if it doesn't protect those who need it the most; what good are rights if the government continues to ignore them; or, what's the point if the government changes the law in response to defeats in the courts and continues as before?[139] A culture of selective rights (i.e. for mental patients) is very different from a culture of rights. The former, arguably, exacerbates inequalities and increases divides while the latter promotes them. Rights for some and not for others – particularly the outsider in society serves to further marginalise the vulnerable. To assume that somehow a culture of rights will eventually trickle down to the most vulnerable as it expands for others is to ignore the very notion of human rights. The so-called 'trickle-down' effect (in other areas such as economics) has not withstood scientific scrutiny and there is little to suggest that such views have merit in other arenas.

A Bill of rights is not just for the protection of vulnerable health patients or those in care-homes but for everyone – most especially the 'lowest of the low'. And, in this respect, the Act has not lived up to expectations. It has failed to deliver.

---

[137] British Institute of Human Rights, *The Human Rights Act - Changing Lives* (2008); Joint Committee on Human Rights, *Monitoring the Government's Response to Court Judgments Finding Breaches of Human Rights* (2007)

[138] Interview notes (on file with author)

[139] Interview notes (on file with author)

But, in many ways, that is not where the problem lies. True, the Act, in the form of incremental court victories against Section 55, eventually did deliver but there are few signs that it has taken hold outside the world of courtrooms and lawyers. And even in the court decisions, following successive challenges to the policy, gaps were evident from what the courts decided to how the Home Office responded. The Home Office responses were viewed as 'grudging' by some observers. Mostly the Home Office was defiant in attitude and response. Many also found that test-case challenges, ostensibly victories for the NGOs, had little apparent effect on bureaucratic decision-making.[140] The changes in policy did come about eventually, but over a long-period of time, grudgingly, and not until after the House of Lords decision.[141]

In many respects the findings of this study are not inconsistent with what critical scholars have concluded about the ability of law or rights to bring about social change. The findings are also consistent with research in the area – changes occur over time, are incremental, and often begrudging.[142] As demonstrated by this study the arena where the NGOs engage with rights is one that is fiercely contested. The arena is also dynamic and constantly changing where the 'contestants' challenge, resist, and adapt. The fight over Section 55 underscores the ambivalent nature of rights – they can be 'paradoxical and perverse'[143] – holding potential and pitfalls; incremental victories, set-backs, and government resistance and counter-attacks characterised much of the campaign. This study, while suggesting hope and potential for social reformers, also offer much for critical scholars such as Mandel (1994) and Rosenberg (1991) who argue that rights offer 'hollow' victories. The findings demonstrates that the powerful do win most of the time; the have-nots do not come out ahead; gaps – sometimes glaring – continue between law on the books and law in action; and, as Sir Stephen Sedley had warned, society's existing 'winners and losers' are turning out to be the same winners and losers under the HRA.[144] Possibly too much was expected of the HRA – commentators, politicians,

---

[140] See, generally, also: S Halliday (2000) 'The Influence of Judicial Review on Bureaucratic Decision-Making' *Public Law* Spring: 110-22

[141] See Chapters 6 and 7 for a fuller discussion on the Home Office reaction and response to court decisions and its effect on Section 55 applications which continued to be rejected notwithstanding Home Office directives to front-line officers.

[142] See Chapter 2 for an overview on theory and case studies on rights and social change.

[143] See N Milner and J Goldberg-Hiller (2002) 'Reimagining Rights.' *Law and Social Inquiry* 1-18, p.1

[144] L Clements (2005) 'Winners and Losers' 32 Journal of Law and Society 1 34-50

academics, and advocates were carried away by the rhetoric and promises of a new dawn for human rights in the UK – because, to date, there has been little evidence of a rights revolution that some had predicted.[145]

But, at the outset, the point of departure for this study was that rights have power and represent potential to bring about change; that if harnessed in creative and innovative ways by advocacy groups rights can be a powerful tool – as demonstrated, to some extent, during the campaign against Section 55.[146] According to Hershkoff (2009) the fact that rights, specifically rights litigation, 'neither promises nor delivers utopian transformation is beside the point'.[147] What it does provide is a forum – a very public forum – where governments can be challenged and, on occasion, defeated. This is of particular import to powerless groups for whom other arenas, such as the political process, may be closed or inaccessible. Rights offer resonance and power allowing groups to challenge the status quo, to push for reform, acquire legitimacy and publicity for a cause, gain alliances, to rebuke the government from exalted chambers such as the courts. All this was on display during the campaign against Section 55. To be sure much of the victory was effectively nullified by the Home Office, but few other options could have accomplished for the NGOs what they managed to achieve during a long and arduous campaign. As detailed in the preceding sections, the NGOs had limited resources and few options; the HRA offered a viable and, as it turned out, effective short-term option for challenging the Home Office.

In some ways, however, the failings in asylum have also come about from a want of action by advocacy groups – in failing to use the Act creatively, failing to engage with rights in a sustained manner, and a short-sighted approach to challenging policy. To be fair, the NGOs are not entirely at fault. They simply do not have the resources to engage with rights in a sustained long-term manner. For example, during the campaign against Section 55 much of their resources had to be diverted to helping the thousands left destitute by the policy. And this is something that the Home Office, oblivious to the irony, relied upon to bolster its argument in the courts: that the asylum-seekers were not suffering (in the Convention sense) because their needs were being met by the NGOs.

---

[145] BBC, 'Human Rights Act: A social revolution' (01 Oct 2000) //news.bbc.co.uk/2/hi/uk_news/949078.stm; T Kirby, 'The Human Rights Act: 800 years in the making' *Guardian* (undated), available at: //www.guardian.co.uk/humanrightsandwrongs/800-years-making; P Wintour et al., 'Brown adviser: Labour's rights record dismal' *Guardian* (11 Dec 2008)

[146] ibid.

[147] p. 160

In the no-holds barred fight which characterises the conflict over asylum rights in general, and welfare for asylum-seekers in particular, the Home Office is well aware that such tactics, such as forcing the NGOs to court, weakens the resource-starved NGOs. What became apparent during the course of the study, particularly in view of the strength of the entrenched opposition to asylum, is that there is 'less fight' in the NGOs 'worn-down' by repeated battles with the government.[148]

Notwithstanding the experiences in asylum, or backtracking by the government on its promise of building a culture of rights, it is not inconceivable that such a culture will develop eventually – signs are slowly emerging in some policy areas. Whether it achieves all that was promised in Labour's manifesto is another matter – the benchmarks, ambitious and laudable, remain vague. How is one to measure, for example, the increase in respect for human dignity? One also has to be clear and recognize that for the foreseeable future a culture of rights will remain a work in progress. Even more importantly the arena of rights will remain highly contested; hard-won victories, rights, or policy changes will remain under attack and are not irreversible. Examples can be readily found in other social justice battles such as affirmative action programs, gay rights and gay marriage in the US, and aboriginal rights in Canada.[149] For example, a common complaint of aboriginal leaders is the constant fight required to assert constitutionally protected rights: 'we are supposed to have all these rights. But yet we must keep fighting for them. It shouldn't be like that'.[150]

Cultural changes also require ideological shifts – from viewing rights as unnecessary in common law UK (i.e. that common law offers sufficient protection) or viewing rights as a charter for criminals and outsiders (at the expense of the rights of Britons) to viewing rights as important for the individual and greater good in a rapidly changing world. And changes of such a profound nature, whether ideological or societal-wide, occur gradually and over extended periods of time. For such changes, or as Epp (1998) argued, a 'rights revolution' to occur a persistent push from below is also necessary. And it must be of a sustained nature.[151] For

---

[148]   Interview with Alex Gask, Solicitor, Liberty (London November 2006)

[149]   See, in general, Editorial, 'A Setback for Equality' *The New York Times* (29 May 2009)

[150]   Personal observation (Fort Saint John, British Columbia, Canada 12 Dec 2008). This view was expressed to me at a recent meeting of aboriginal elders (respected statesmen in the community).

[151]   CR Epp, *The Rights Revolution: Lawyers, Activists, and Supreme Courts in Comparative Perspective* (1998).

the NGOs Section 55 was a start but much remains to be done. While the NGOs advocating for asylum-seekers continue to be committed to their cause they are hampered by a persistent lack of resources. And by powerful forces opposed to asylum and determined to keep out asylum-seekers irrespective of international obligations and the HRA.

9.11   Asylum and a Culture of Rights

One of the key reasons why a culture of rights has yet to take hold in asylum has been mostly because of government actions and policies, much of which has had the effect of undermining rights and the HRA. And those actions, in many ways, have been deliberate.[152] The politics of asylum has turned out to be a much more powerful force than rights.[153] Human rights in the UK face many challenges and these challenges will persist in the near future. This is not only the case in asylum but also in other major public policy areas. The so-called 'war on terror ',' war on crime', and 'war on asylum' have all proven resistant to rights. The politics of fear which has come to dominate public policy (in most of the western world) since late 2001, in the so-called post 9/11 world, has shown little respect for rights.[154] And that is not about to change anytime soon. It is no accident that asylum continues to be conflated with terrorism and other security concerns. Further exacerbating matters is the perception of asylum-seekers as undeserving cheats which makes advocacy more difficult, public opinion more compliant, and draconian measures more expedient.[155]

On the whole, the victory over Section 55 has had little effect on those who flee war, persecution, and other injustices and arrive on the shores of the UK seeking protection only to be subjected to further indignities and injustice. A right enshrined in international law but increasingly a right almost impossible to exercise. The uphill

---

[152]   BBC, 'Asylum hardships 'are deliberate" (2007)

[153]   S Chakrabarti (2005); G Loescher A Betts and J Milner, *The United Nations High Commissioner for Refugees (UNHCR): The Politics and Practice of Refugee Protection into the Twenty-first Century* (2008)

[154]   See also: C Harlow (2006) 'Can Human Rights Survive the War on Terror and the War on Crime'; C Gearty (2005) ; since 9/11 most Western liberal-democracies have enacted ill-liberal laws – some draconian – to combat perceived threats of terrorism. Some, the US and UK in particular, have done so with almost complete disregard for fundamental rights.

[155]   Amnesty International, *Human Rights: A Broken Promise* (2006); A Bloch and L Schuster (2002) 'Asylum and welfare: contemporary debates ' 22 Critical Social Policy 3 393-414

fight over asylum rights that NGOs have battled since the early 1990s continues to present significant challenges. The 'get-tough' policies continue getting tougher. It is a fight which shows no sign of abating. It still remains the Home Office against an outmatched group of under-resourced and ill-equipped organisations driven by a commitment to human rights and the still noble but under attack concept of asylum. For asylum-seekers not much has changed. To be sure the number of applications has been reduced significantly, not because there are fewer asylum-seekers in the world, but owing to enforcement and other measures.[156] As a group they are viewed with resentment and continue to be regarded as 'bogus scroungers' 'polluted with disease and terrorism' taking advantage of 'soft-touch' Britain.[157] In late 2008 the Council of Europe took stock of the situation in the UK and commented:

> Improvements must be introduced to strengthen effective respect
> for the rights of asylum-seekers and immigrants in the United
> Kingdom . . .[158]

A 2008 report by the Independent Asylum Commission recommended, as if something so obvious needed reiteration, that all those who seek sanctuary should be treated with dignity.[159] By most measures, and a parliamentary committee agrees, a government seeking to build a culture of rights must do much more than give lip-service to the concept.[160]

In some respects a search for explanations holds the potential for introducing complexity where simplicity would suffice. And it this: asylum-seekers are not wanted in the UK and, irrespective of the HRA, policies directed at deterring and reducing the number of arrivals will continue. Asylum consistently ranks among the very top of public policy concerns. There is overwhelming public opposition and that it should continue as such suggests the NGO efforts aimed at educating and informing the public about asylum, its benefits and the UK's international

---

[156]   BBC, 'Asylum applications continue fall ' (2006) 28 Feb <http://news.bbc.co.uk/1/hi/uk/4758144.stm> ; Joint Committee on Human Rights, *The Treatment of Asylum-Seekers* (2007)

[157]   See Article 19, *What's the Story* (2003); R Greensdale (2005)

[158]   Commissioner for Human Rights for the Council of Europe *Memorandum by Thomas Hammarberg* (2008)

[159]   Independent Asylum Commission, *Deserving Dignity - A Nationwide Review of the UK Asylum System* (2008)

[160]   See Joint Committee on Human Rights *The Case for a Human Rights Commission (Sixth Report of Session 2002-03)* (2003)

obligations, has had little apparent effect. Further a majority of the public continue to feel that the government is not tough enough and has lost control over its borders; a majority of the media (from almost all political spectrums except the Left) support tough measures; the major political parties, including the government, favour stringent controls and are determined to reduce the number of arrivals and its related costs to the public purse – exceeding billions, a staggering sum by any measure. Into the mix are the added strains of providing housing, medical, and other services, services which are already under significant domestic pressures. And adding volatility to an already combustible mix are the issues of race and racism; of outsiders taking advantage of 'soft touch' Britain. In the face of such overpowering forces rights and the HRA have not fared well.

9.12   Conclusion

The fight over welfare benefits for asylum-seekers is a battle the NGOs are unlikely to win. The fight over Section 55 adds to the picture of how asylum-seekers are treated in the UK. But it is not the whole picture. It provides a prism through which to understand the entrenched nature of opposition to asylum and the challenges faced by NGOs fighting for the right to asylum and rights of asylum-seekers. The fight is more than just about benefits and goes to the very heart of a major policy issue for the government. And the government has clearly demonstrated that it is not about to compromise.

The history of increasingly stricter and punitive controls in asylum precedes that of the coming into effect of the *Human Rights Act.* In this one of the most volatile and contentious of public policy issues the HRA has been primarily a mitigating force, helping to limit some of the excesses of government policies. But, on the whole, its impact has been negligible so extreme have the policies been and so determined has the government remained. The HRA has so far failed to effectively rein in government excesses directed against asylum-seekers. While it is arguable that the battle over Section 55 represents a major victory for the HRA and for the NGOs who battled long and hard against the policy, it also remains the case that one would be hard-pressed to find many NGOs who continue to regard it as a victory. Even before the House of Lords had sounded the death knell for Section 55, the government introduced Section 9 in yet another major legislative overhaul, the fifth since 1993, with benefits again as a coercive tool. Section 4, another destitution inducing provision commonly known as 'hard-case' support for failed asylum-seekers, also remains in effect. If there was any doubt on future policies on asylum, the Home Office made clear its intentions when it pointedly refused to repeal Section 55 when asked to do so by the Joint Committee on Human Rights.[161] It is also the case that gains or victories are reversible, as demonstrated by the continuing legislative actions on asylum. Often hard won victories must be defended against attacks and erosion via legislative action. In this instance – a long, expensive, and bitter campaign against a 'cruel nasty piece of law' which forced destitution upon thousands of vulnerable people – a fight may have been won but the battle has been long lost.

---

[161]   Joint Committee on Human Rights, *Government Response to the Committee's Tenth Report of this Session: The Treatment of Asylum Seekers* (2007)

APPENDIX

SURVEY QUESTIONNAIRE

Thank you for agreeing to participate in this research. The purpose of this questionnaire is to gauge the impact of the Human Rights Act (HRA), *if any*, on your work. You may use point-form in answering any of the questions. Confidentiality and Privacy assured.

Section A (basic information):

* Name of your organization?

* What is your position and the general nature of your duties?

Section B (before the HRA came into effect in the UK):

* Were you aware of the HRA's impending passage into UK Law?

* If yes, did your organization support its implementation?

* How did your organization support it (i.e. lobbying, campaigning, and participation in consultation process)?

* Prior to the coming in effect of the HRA, were you offered any training on the Act?

Section C (after the passage of the HRA into UK law):

* Did you receive any training after the Act came into effect?

- Do you receive training to update your knowledge of the Act as a result of litigation or policy changes or case law?

- Is the training done on a regular basis or is it ad-hoc (i.e. in response to any changes in law or policy)?

- How would you rate your general awareness of the HRA?

  Poor   Good   Very Good

- Do you use the HRA in your work; if yes, can you briefly describe how? (i.e. campaigns, lobbying MPs, media releases, fundraising, on behalf of individual clients)?

- In what area of your work do you use the HRA the most?

- In what area of your work do you use the HRA the least?

- Do you use the HRA in the daily routine of your work (for example, contacting Home Office/IND officers if you feel that a particular case merits a 'second-look' or re-review because of a potential/actual violation of the HRA?

- If yes to above, how responsive is the Home Office to HRA arguments in individual cases such as described above (please circle):

  Hostile   not-responsive   somewhat responsive   very responsive

- Can you think of examples (of which you are personally aware) where the Home Office has taken account of the HRA in their decision-making?

- Can you think of cases where the Home Office has NOT taken account of the HRA in their decision (after a HRA argument had been raised)?

- Does your organization seek examples (real-life cases) where the HRA has been infringed in order to do all or any of the following?

    - Highlight the example to put pressure on the government to change its policy or law?

    - Use that example as a test-case challenge before the courts?

    - Use that example to lobby for change in law or policy?

    - Use that example to in order to get media publicity?

- Is there any particular Article of the HRA which your organization has focused as part of an overall strategy?

- Has the HRA helped you in your work; if yes, how would you rate its effectiveness:

    No change   poor   good   very good

- Your general thoughts on the usefulness of the HRA:

BIBLIOGRAPHY

Allison, Eric. 2004. "Asylum seekers still held in jail." *Guardian*, 01 September.

Amnesty International. 2005. "Spain/Morocco: Migrant rights between two fires." London: Amnesty International.
———. 2005. "Ten years of EUROMED: Time to end the human rights deficit." London: Amnesty International.
———. 2006. "Human Rights: A Broken Promise." London: Amnesty International.

Amnesty International UK. 2005. "Seeking asylum is not a crime: Detention of people who have sought asylum." London: Amnesty International UK.
_____. 2006. "Down and Out in London: The Road to Destitution for Rejected Asylum-Seekers." London: Amnesty International UK.

Anleu, Sharyn L Roach. 2010. *Law and Social Change*. London: Sage

Anonymous. 2005. "Driven underground." *Guardian*, 06 April.

Archibold, Randal, and Abby Goodnough. 2008. "California Voters Ban Gay Marriage." *The New York Times*, Nov 05.

Article19. 2003. "What's the Story: Results from Research into Media Coverage of Refugees and Asylum-Seekers in the UK." London: Article 19.

Asthana, Anushka. 2005. "Asylum policy is 'grotesque' " *The Observer*, 27 Feb.

Asylum Rights Campaign. 2004. "Providing Protection in the 21st Century." London: Asylum Rights Campaign.

Asylum Support Appeals Project. 2008. "Unreasonably Destitute?" London.

Athwal, Harmit. 2006. *Two asylum seekers took their own lives within 24 hours*. Institute of Race Relations 2005 [cited 10 Oct 2006]. Available from http://www.irr.org.uk/2005/september/ha000021.html.

Audit Commission. 2003. "Human rights: Improving Public Service Delivery." London: Audit Commission.

Aynsley-Green, Al. 2008. "No place for children." *New Statesman*, 04 Sept.

Baggini, Julian. 2008. "Consensus of hard and soft." *Guardian*, 24 July.

Bail for Immigration Detainees. 2005. "Justice Denied." London: Bail for Immigration Detainees (BID) and Asylum Aid.

Bamber, D, and C Brown. 2003. "Blunkett says Blair's pledge on asylum-seekers 'undeliverable'." *Sunday Telegraph*, 09 February, 1.

Barek-Erez, Daphne. 2002. "Judicial Review of Politics: The Israeli Case." *Journal of Law and Society* 29 (4):611-31.

Barkham, Patrick. 2008. "Asylum-seeker charities are just playing the system, says Woolas." *Guardian*, 18 Nov.

Barrett, David. 2009. "How migrant crackdown opened the floodgates." *Daily Telegraph*, Dec 06

Barnett, Antony. 2006. "MoD targets Libya and Iraq as 'priority' arms sales targets" *Guardian*, 24 Sep.

Bates, Stephen. 2000. "Catholic bishops attack 'emotive' asylum language." *Guardian*, 05 May.
———. 2005. "Help refugees, churchgoers told" *Guardian*, 22 March.
———. 2008. "Profile: Keir Starmer." *Guardian*, 01 Aug.

Batty, David. 2005. "Family face benefit cut despite court victory" *Guardian*, 11 Aug.

BBC. *Blair pledge to reduce rough sleeping* (14 Dec) 1999 [cited. Available from http://news.bbc.co.uk/1/hi/uk_politics/565001.stm.
_____. *Human Rights Act: A social revolution* (Oct 01) 2000 http://news.bbc.co.uk/2/hi/uk_news/politics/5007148.stm
———. *Landmark human rights law enforced* (Oct 02) 2000 [cited. Available from http://news.bbc.co.uk/2/hi/uk_news/951753.stm.
_____. *A Short History of Immigration* (2002)[cited. Available from http://news.bbc.co.uk/hi/english/static/in_depth/uk/2002/race/short_history_of_immigration.stm.

————. *Asylum system 'failing' refugees* (20 Feb) 2002 [cited. Available from http://news.bbc.co.uk/1/hi/uk/1830886.stm.

————. *Blair sold jets at Kashmir talks.* 21 Oct 2002 [cited. Available from http://news.bbc.co.uk/2/hi/uk_news/politics/2345127.stm.

————. *Extremists 'must not drive out' refugees* (Sep 27) 2002 [cited. Available from http://news.bbc.co.uk/1/hi/england/2284800.stm.

————. 2006. *Sangatte closure deal agreed.* BBC News 2002 [cited 10 Oct 2006]. Available from http://news.bbc.co.uk/2/hi/uk_news/politics/2533415.stm.

————. 2006. *Analysis: Battle over Asylum Bill* (26 Nov). BBC News 2003 [cited 26 May 2006]. Available from http://news.bbc.co.uk/1/hi/uk_politics/3240956.stm.

————. 2009. *Asylum: Attacks and deaths 2001 - 2003* (22 July). BBC News 2003 [cited 2009]. Available from http://news.bbc.co.uk/2/hi/uk_news/3087569.stm.

————. 2003. *Asylum: Getting tough in 2003* BBC News 2003 [cited 2003]. Available from http://news.bbc.co.uk/1/hi/uk/3333865.stm.

————. 2007. *Judge urges asylum rule suspension.* BBC News 2003 [cited 27 May 2007]. Available from http://news.bbc.co.uk/1/hi/uk_politics/2751161.stm.

————. 2006. *Asylum laws under fresh attack.* BBC News 2004 [cited 10 June 2006]. Available from http://news.bbc.co.uk/1/hi/uk_politics/3501702.stm.

————. 2006. *Asylum seekers 'sleeping rough'* [Website]. BBC News 2004 [cited 10 June 2006]. Available from http://news.bbc.co.uk/1/hi/uk_politics/3501779.stm.

————. *Asylum seekers to be housed* (25 June) 2004 [cited. Available from http://news.bbc.co.uk/1/hi/uk_politics/3840439.stm.

————. 2006. *Jailing asylum seekers 'must end'.* BBC News 2004 [cited 10 June 2006]. Available from http://news.bbc.co.uk/1/hi/uk/3564968.stm.

————. 2006. *Media linked to asylum violence* BBC News 2004 [cited 09 October 2006]. Available from http://news.bbc.co.uk/1/hi/uk/3890963.stm.

————. 2006. *Peers urged to wreck Asylum Bill.* BBC News 2004 [cited 20 June 2006]. Available from http://news.bbc.co.uk/1/hi/uk_politics/3722163.stm.

————. 2006. *Q and A: Immigration detention.* BBC News 2004 [cited 10 October 2005 2006]. Available from http://news.bbc.co.uk/2/hi/uk_news/3910193.stm.

————. 2007. *The trouble with asylum centres.* BBC News 2004 [cited 27 May 2007]. Available from http://news.bbc.co.uk/1/hi/uk/3604553.stm.

————. *Watchdog criticises asylum decisions* (23 June) 2004 [cited. Available from http://news.bbc.co.uk/1/hi/uk_politics/3831163.stm.

————. 2006. *Asylum detentions 'breaking law'.* BBC News 2005 [cited 10 Oct 2006]. Available from http://news.bbc.co.uk/1/hi/uk/4109406.stm.

————. 2006. *Asylum seekers 'denied justice'.* BBC News 2005 [cited 10 Oct 2006]. Available from http://news.bbc.co.uk/1/hi/uk/4552523.stm.

————. *Election issues: Immigration* (April 05) 2005 [cited. Available from http://news.bbc.co.uk/1/hi/uk_politics/vote_2005/issues/4352373.stm.

————. *How many have died in Darfur?* (16 Feb). BBC 2005 [cited. Available from http://news.bbc.co.uk/1/hi/world/africa/4268733.stm.

————. *Lords throw out key asylum rule* (03 Nov) 2005 [cited. Available from http://newsvote.bbc.co.uk/1/hi/uk/4402596.stm.

————. 2007. *QC calls for political politeness* BBC News 2005 [cited 25 May 2007]. Available from http://news.bbc.co.uk/1/hi/uk_politics/4285339.stm.

————. *Asylum applications continue fall* (28 Feb) 2006 [cited. Available from http://news.bbc.co.uk/1/hi/uk/4758144.stm.

————. *Blair 'rattled' over immigration* (17 May) 2006 [cited. Available from http://news.bbc.co.uk/1/hi/uk_politics/4988816.stm.

————.*Immigration system 'unfit' – Reid* (23 May) 2006 http://news.bbc.co.uk/2/hi/uk_news/politics/5007148.stm

————. 2006. *Human rights 'as British as beer'* BBC News 2006 [cited 30 Oct 2006]. Available from http://news.bbc.co.uk/1/hi/uk_politics/6097634.stm.

————. *Human rights 'blaming' under fire* (14 Nov) 2006 [cited. Available from http://news.bbc.co.uk/1/hi/uk_politics/6144804.stm.

————. 2006. *Viewpoints: The Human Rights Act* [Website]. BBC News 2006 [cited 26 June 2006]. Available from http://news.bbc.co.uk/1/hi/uk/4990414.stm.

————. 2007. *Asylum hardships 'are deliberate'.* BBC News 2007 [cited 29 Jun 2007]. Available from http://news.bbc.co.uk/1/hi/uk_politics/6507961.stm.

————. *Asylum seekers policy 'unlawful' 2007* [cited 04 Feb 2007. Available from http://news.bbc.co.uk/1/hi/uk_politics/6302919.stm.

————. *Scrapped asylum centre cost £28m* (Nov 8) 2007 [cited. Available from http://news.bbc.co.uk/1/hi/uk_politics/7084200.stm.

Benjamin, Alison. 2005. "Charities fear drop in lottery grants to 'unpopular' causes" *Guardian*, 11 Jan

————. 2006. "No going back." *Guardian*, 09 Aug.

Bennett, Rosemary. 2004. "Asylum cases take a chunk of legal aid bill." *The Times*, 30 April.

Bhabha, Jacqueline. 2002. "International Gatekeepers: The tension between asylum advocacy and human rights" *Harvard Human Rights Journal* 15: 155-81

Birnberg Peirce & Partners, Medical Justice, and NCADC. 2008. "Outsourcing Abuse: The use and misuse of state-sanctioned force during the detention and removal of asylum seekers." London: Medical Justice.

Blair, Tony. 2006. "I don't destroy liberties, I protect them." *The Observer*, 26 Feb.

Blake, Nicholas. 2006. "Why is there no song and dance about this Act?" *Times*, 25 Apr.

Bloch, Alice, and Liza Schuster. 2002. "Asylum and welfare: contemporary debates " *Critical Social Policy* 22 (3):393-414.

Bodi, Faisal. 2003. "Fear and loathing" *Guardian*, 21 Jan.

Bowcott, Owen, and David Pallister. 2005. "Rich pickings in the world of asylum seekers." *Guardian*, 03 Aug.

Bradley, A. 2003. "Judicial Independence Under Attack." *Public Law* (Aut):397-405.

Brides without Borders. 2006. *National Campaign*. Brides without Borders 2005 [cited 10 Oct 2006]. Available from http://www.ncadc.org.uk/archives/filed%20 newszines/oldnewszines/Newszine62/brides.htm.

British Institute of Human Rights. 2002. "Something for Everyone: The Impact of the Human Rights Act on Disadvantaged Groups." London: British Institute of Human Rights.
_____. 2008. "The Human Rights Act – Changing Lives." London: British Institute of Human Rights.

British Institute of Human Rights and Joint Council for the Welfare of Immigrants. 2003. Workshop - Section 55 and Human Rights. Paper read at BIHR/JCWI Conference, 11 Nov 2003.

Brodie, Ian. 2001. "Interest group litigation and the embedded state: Canada's court challenges program." *Canadian Journal of Political Science* 34 (2):357-76.

Brodie, Ian and F. L. Morton. *Do the 'Haves' Still Come Out Ahead in Canada.* University of Calgary 1998 [cited. Available from http://publish.uwo.ca/~irbrodie/newman.pdf.

Brooks, Libby. 2003. "5 tough questions about asylum" *Guardian,* 01 May.

Brown, Colin. 2004. "Blunkett exposes feared invasion of foreign benefit scroungers as myth." *The Independent,* 08 July, 12.

Brown, Craig. 2006. "Kirk attacks 'forced poverty' policy of discouraging asylum seekers." *The Scotsman,* 09 May.

Burns, Jimmy. 2005. "Abuse of detainees puts asylum policy in the spotlight." *Financial Times,* 03 March.

Burstein, Paul. 1991. "Legal Mobilization as a Social Movement Tactic: The Struggle for Equal Employment Opportunity." *American Journal of Sociology* 96 (5):1201-25.

Callaghan, David. 2004. "Court rejects Blunkett's asylum support appeal." *Guardian,* 21 May.

Campaign Against Arms Trade. 2006. *Fanning the Flames: How UK Arms Sales Fuel Conflict.* CAAT.ORG 2003 [cited 10 Nov 2006].

Campbell, Tom. 1999. "Human Rights: A Culture of Controversy " *Journal of Law and Society* 26 (1):6-26.

Campbell, Tom, K. D. Ewing, and Adam Tomkins. 2001. *Sceptical Essays on Human Rights.* Oxford: Oxford University Press.

Canadian Press. 2003. "Ontario Appeal Court rules in favour of same-sex marriage." *The Globe and Mail,* June 10.

Cannon, Bradley C. 1998. "The Supreme Court and Policy Reform: The Hollow Hope Revisited " In *Leveraging the Law,* ed. D. A. Schultz. New York: P. Lang.

Casciani, Dominic. *Secret Life of the Office Cleaner* (19 Sep). BBC 2005 [cited.

Castles, Stephen and Mark J. Miller. 2009. *The Age of Migration: International Population Movements in the Modern World.* 4th ed. New York: Palgrave Macmillan.

Chakrabarti, Shami. 2005. "Rights and Rhetoric: The Politics of Asylum and Human Rights Culture in the UK." *Journal of Law and Society* 32:131.
———. 2007. "So much freedom lost and on my watch." *Daily Telegraph*, 20 May

Child Poverty Action Group. 2003. "Parallel Lives: Poverty Among Ethnic Minority Groups in Britain." London: Child Poverty Action Group.

Citizens Advice Bureau. 2006. "Shaming Destitution - Briefing." London.

Civil Service. 2006. "Capability Review of the Home Office." In *Capability Reviews.* London: Civil Service.

Clark, Campbell. 2003. "Government steers vote on accepting same-sex ruling." *The Globe and Mail*, June 13.

Clarke, Michael and Sam Greenhill. 2003. "So what have our judges got against Britain?" *Daily Mail*, 20 Feb, 1.

Clayton, Gina. 2004. *Textbook on Immigration and Asylum Law.* 1st ed. Oxford: Oxford University Press.

Clements, Luke. 1999. "The Human Rights Act – A New Equity or a New Opiate: Reinventing Justice or Repackaging State Control?" *Journal of Law and Society* 26 (1):72-85.
———. 2005. "Winners and Losers." *Journal of Law and Society* 32 (1):34-50.
———. 2007. "Asylum in Crisis, An assessment of UK Asylum law and policy since 2002: Fear of Terrorism or Economic Efficiency?" *Web Journal of Current Legal Issues* 3.

Clements, Luke and Philip A. Thomas. 2005. "The Human Rights Act: A Success Story? Introduction." *Journal of Law and Society* 32 (1):1-2.

Clements, Luke and James Young. 1999. "Human Rights: Changing the Culture "*Journal of Law and Society* 26 (1):1-5.

CNN. 2006. *Immigration tops EU summit agenda.* CNN World News 2002 [cited 10 Oct 2006]. Available from http://archives.cnn.com/2002/WORLD/europe/06/20/spain.summit/.

Coglianese, Gary. 2001. "Social Movements, Law, and Society: The Institutionalization of the Environmental Movement." *University of Pennsylvania Law Review* 150:85-118.

Cohen, Nick. 1999. "Asylum Bill - Anne Frank would be turned away." *New Statesman* 03 May.

———. 2000. "How we scape-goated asylum-seekers." *New Statesman*, 17 Apr.

Cohen, Steve. 2002. "The local state of immigration controls." *Critical Social Policy* 22 (3):518-43.

Cohen, Steve, Beth Humphries, and Ed Mynott. 2002. *From immigration controls to welfare controls.* London: Routledge.

Colorful. 2008. *Life of an asylum seeker in Britain* (26 Feb) 2006 [cited 2008]. Available from www.iamcolourful.com/news/details/2031/politics/.

Comment. 2003. "Asylum Angst." *The Times*, 20 February

———. 2003. "Bogus Asylum and the Judges who have it in for Britain." *Daily Mail*, 20 Feb.

———. 2003. "Ministers Must Learn to Respect Their Own Human Rights Laws." *Independent*, 20 Feb.

———. 2003. "Rethink Asylum Policy." *Daily Telegraph*, 20 Feb.

———. 2003. "A Shameful Asylum Policy." *The Independent*, 30 Nov.

———. 2004. "Leading article: Damned lies and targets." *The Times*, 04 April.

———. 2005. "Common Sense and Human Rights." *Daily Mail*, March 05.

Commission for Racial Equality. 2004. "Attitudes Towards Asylum-Seekers, Refugees and Other Immigrants." London: Commission for Racial Equality.

Commissioner for Human Rights. 2005. "Report by the Commissioner of Human Rights on his visit to the United Kingdom 2004." Strasbourg: Council of Europe.

Commissioner for Human Rights of the Council of Europe. 2008. "Memorandum by Thomas Hammarberg." Commissioner for Human Rights of the Council of Europe.

Costigan, Ruth, and Philip A. Thomas. 2005. "The Human Rights Act: A View from Below." *Journal of Law and Society* 32 (1):51-67.

Cotterrell, Roger. 1992. *The Sociology of Law: An Introduction.* 2nd ed. London: Butterworths.
_____. 1994. *Law and Society.* (ed) New York: New York University Press

Cowan, Dave. 2004. "Legal Consciousness: Some Observations." *Modern Law Review* 67 (6):928.

Crawley, Heaven. 2003. "Tackling the Causes of Asylum." *Guardian*, May 11.

Cunningham, Steve, and Jo Tomlinson. 2005. "'Starve them out': does every child really matter? A commentary on Section 9 of the Asylum and Immigration (Treatment of Claimants, etc.) Act, 2004 " *Critical Social Policy* 25 (2):253-75.

Daghlian, Sally. 2005. "Asylum seekers are the victims, not the problem." *The Scotsman*, 26 March.

Dallaire, Româeo and Brent Beardsley. 2005. *Shake Hands with the Devil: The Failure of Humanity in Rwanda.* New York: Carroll & Graf.

Dauvergne, Catherine. 2004. "Sovereignty, Migration and the Rule of Law in Global Times." *Modern Law Review* 67 (4):588.

Delmar-Morgan, Alex. 2006. "Church of England damns Labour on asylum and poverty." *The Times*, 14 May.

Dickson, Brice. 2006. "Safe in their hands? Britain's Law Lords and human rights." *Legal Studies* 26 (3):329-46.

Dodd, Vikram. 2006. "Home Office ignored law, says judge." *Guardian*, 08 April.

Doughty Street Human Rights Unit. 2006. *Comments and Analysis.* Doughty Street 2003 [cited Mar 11 2006].

Doward, Jamie. 2004. "Abuse is 'systematic' at asylum detention centres" *Guardian*, 23 May.

Dunston, Richard. 2003. "Blunkett's uncivilised act." *New Statesman*, 11 Aug.

Dupuy, Pierre-Marie, and Luisa Vierucci. 2008. *NGOs in International Law: Efficiency in Flexibility?* Cheltenham: Edward Elgar.

Dwyer, P. 2005. "Governance, forced migration and welfare." *Social Policy & Administration* 39 (6):622-39.

Dyer, Clare. 2003. "Asylum cases 'clogging the courts'." *Guardian*, 16 October.
———. 2003. "Asylum Error to Cost Millions." *Guardian*, 02 October.
———. 2003. "Judges 'saving asylum seekers from starvation' " *Guardian*, 04 November.
———. 2003. "MPs attack legal aid cuts" *Guardian*, 23 Oct.
———. 2003. "Outrage at plan to end judicial review in asylum cases" *Guardian*, 11 December.
———. 2003. "Woolf defends judge over rights ruling." *Guardian*, 07 Mar, 11.
———. 2004. "Top judge condemns asylum proposals" *Guardian*, 11 February.

Edelman, Laura and Mia Cahill. 1998. "How Does Law Matter in Disputing and Dispute Processing." In *How Does Law Matter*, ed. B. G. Garth and A. Sarat: Northwestern University Press.

Editorial. 2006. *The coal miner's canary.* Legal Action Group 2004 [cited 10 Oct 2006].
———. 2006. *A look on the bright side.* Legal Action Group 2004 [cited 10 Oct 2006].
———. 2006. *Chickens home to roost.* Legal Action Group, June 2005 [cited 10 Oct 2006].

Editorial. 2008. "Another Invitation to Abuse." *The New York Times*, Oct 18.
———. 2009. "A Setback for Equality." *The New York Times*, 29 May.

Edwards, Alice. 2005. "Human Rights, Refugees, and The Right 'To Enjoy' Asylum " *International Journal of Refugee Law* 17 (2):293-330.

Edwards, Richard A. 2002. "Judicial Deference under the Human Rights Act." *Modern Law Review* 65 (6):859-82.

Eizenstat, Stuart E. 2004. "Nongovernmental Organizations as the Fifth Estate." *Seton Hall Journal of Diplomacy and International Relations* (Summer/Fall):15-27.

Ekklesia. 2006. *World churches criticise UK policies on asylum and immigration* [Website]. Ekklesia 2005 [cited 10 Oct 2006]. Available from http://www.ekklesia.co.uk/content/news_syndication/article_050222asylum.shtml.

Elliott, John and Zoe Brennan. 2006. "The ultimate sacrifice." *Sunday Times*, 24 Sept.

Ellis, Kathryn. 2004. "Promoting rights or avoiding litigation? The introduction of the human rights act 1998 into adult social care in England." *European Journal of Social Work* 7 (3):321-40.

Engel, David. 1988. "How Does Law Matter in the Constitution of Legal Consciousness " In *How Does Law Matter*, ed. B. G. Garth and A. Sarat: Northwestern University Press.

English, Rosalind. 2006. *Failure to support destitute asylum seekers* [Lawtel Database]. Lawtel 2003 [cited 10 Oct 2006].

Epp, Charles R. 1998. *The Rights Revolution: Lawyers, Activists, and Supreme Courts in Comparative Perspective*. Chicago: University of Chicago Press.

European Commission against Racism and Intolerance. 2005. "Third Report on the United Kingdom." Strasbourg: Council of Europe: European Commission Against Racism and Intolerance (ECRI).

Ewick, Patricia, and Susan S. Silbey. 1998. *The Common Place of Law: Stories from Everyday Life*. Chicago: University of Chicago Press.

Ewing, Keith D. 2004. "The Futility of the Human Rights Act." *Public Law* Winter: 829.

Feeley, Malcolm, and Edward L. Rubin. 1998. *Judicial Policy Making and the Modern State: How the Courts Reformed America's Prisons*. Cambridge: Cambridge University Press.

Fekete, Liz. 2006. *The Human Trade: More Dead at Sea*. Institute of Race Relations 2002 [cited 20 Oct 2006]. Available from https://www.irr.org.uk/cgi-bin/news/open.pl?id=5285.

————. 2005. "The Deportation Machine: Europe, Asylum and Human Rights." *Race & Class* 47 (1):64-91.

Feldman, Eric A. 2000. *The Ritual of Rights in Japan: Law, Society, and Health Policy.* Cambridge: Cambridge University Press.

Fesshaye, Semret. 2003. "Rape, hunger and homelessness" *Guardian*, 01 November.

Ford, Richard. 1998. "Asylum-seekers to lose benefits." *The Times*, 25 Nov.
————. 2006. "Britain accused of refusing visas to prevent entry of world's poor." *The Times*, 08 Aug.

Friedman, W. 1951. *Law and Social Change in Contemporary Britain*. London: Stevens & Sons.

Fudge, Judy. 2001. "The Canadian Charter of Rights: Recognition, Redistribution, and the Imperialism of the Courts." In *Sceptical Essays on Human Rights*, ed. T. Campbell, K. D. Ewing and A. Tomkins. Oxford: Oxford University Press).

Galligan, Denis. 2001. "Authoritarianism in Government and Administration: The Promise of Administrative Justice." *Current Legal Problems* 54:79-102.
————. 2006. *Law in Modern Society*. Oxford: Oxford University Press.

Garth, Bryant G. and Austin Sarat. 1998a. *How Does Law Matter?* Chicago: Northeastern University Press.
————. 1998. *Justice and Power in Sociolegal Studies*. Chicago: Northwestern University Press.

Gearty, Conor. 2005. "11 September 2001, Counter-terrorism, and the Human Rights Act." *Law and Society* 32 (1):18-33.

Gibb, Frances. 2003. "Blunkett v the Bench: the battle has begun." *The Times*, 04 Mar
————. 2006. "Law chief defiant on human rights." *The Times*, 29 Sept.

Gibb, Frances and Philip Webster. 2004. "Ministers are breaking the law, say judges." *The Times*, 04 March

Goodwin-Gill, Guy S. 1985. The Determination of Refugee Status: Problems of Access to Procedures and the Standard of Proof. *Yearbook of the International Institute of Humanitarian Law,* 56-75.

Goodwin-Gill, Guy S., and Jane McAdam. 2007. *The Refugee in International Law*. 3rd ed. Oxford: Oxford University Press.

Green, Andrew. *Opinion: This influx 'must stop'* (07 Sep). BBC 2005 [cited. Available from http://news.bbc.co.uk/1/hi/uk/4222362.stm.
———. 2005. "What About Our Human Rights?" *Daily Mail*, 27 July.

Greensdale, Roy. 2005. "Seeking Scapegoats: The Coverage of Asylum in the UK Press." London: Institute for Public Policy Research.

Hall, Sarah. 2004. "Lords reject new rules for asylum appeals" *Guardian*, 08 June.
———. 2004. "Newspapers flout ruling on asylum seekers" *Guardian*, 31 Dec.

Halliday, Simon. 2000. "The Influence of Judicial Review on Bureaucratic Decision-Making." *Public Law* Spring: 110-22.

Halliday, Simon and Patrick D. Schmidt. 2004. *Human rights brought home: socio-legal perspectives on human rights in the national context*. Oxford: Hart.

Haltom, William and Michael McCann. 2004. *Distorting the law: politics, media, and the litigation crisis*. Chicago, Ill.; London: University of Chicago Press.

Hammond, John. 1999. "Law and Disorder: The Brazilian Landless Farmworkers' Movement." *Bulletin of Latin American Research* 18 (4):469-89.

Hampshire, James. 2005. *Citizenship and Belonging: Immigration and the Politics of Demographic Governance in post-war Britain*. Basingstoke: Palgrave Macmillan.

Hardiman-McCartney, Anna. 2006. "Absolutely Right: Providing Asylum Seekers with Food and Shelter Under Article 3." *Cambridge Law Journal* 65 (01):4-6.

Harlow, Carol. 2002. "Public Law and Popular Justice." *Modern Law Review* 65 (1):1-18.
———. *Can Human Rights Survive the War on Terror and the War on Crime* 2006 [cited. Available from http://arts.anu.edu.au/democraticaudit/papers/20060809_harlow_hr_wars.pdf.

Harlow, Carol and Richard Rawlings. 1992. *Pressure through law*. London: Routledge.

Harvey, Colin J. and British Institute of Human Rights. 2005. *Human Rights in the Community: Rights as Agents for Change*. Oxford: Hart.

Hathaway, James C. 1991. *The Law of Refugee Status*. Toronto: Butterworths.

Hattersley, Roy. 2006. "A bit of a wet Blunkett" *Guardian*, 15 Oct

Hawkins, Keith. 2002. *Law as Last Resort: Prosecution Decision-making in a Regulatory Agency*. Oxford: Oxford University Press.

Heffer, Simon. 2008. "Labour is malignant, not incompetent." *Daily Telegraph*, April 02.

Heinz, John P, A Southworth, and Anthony Paik. 2003. "Lawyers for Conservative Causes: Clients, Ideology, and Social Distance." *Law and Society Review* 37 (1):5-50.

Helton, Arthur C. 2002. *The Price of Indifference: Refugees and Humanitarian Action in the New Century*. Oxford: Oxford University Press.

Henderson, Helen. 2006. "Government expects no outcry over axing of court challenges program." *Toronto Star*, Sept 28

Herbert, Ian. 2005. "Asylum seeker kills himself so child can stay in Britain." *The Independent*, 17 Sept

Hershkoff, Helen. 2009. Public Law Litigation: Lessons and Questions. *Human Rights Review* 10 (2) 157-81

Hertogh, Marc. 2004. "A 'European' Conception of Legal Consciousness: Rediscovering Eugen Ehrlich." *Journal of Law and Society* 31 (4):457.

Hertogh, Marc and Simon Halliday. 2004. *Judicial review and bureaucratic impact: international and interdisciplinary perspectives*. Cambridge: Cambridge University Press.

Hiebert, Janet L. 2006. "Parliament and the Human Rights Act: Can the JCHR help to facilitate a culture of rights." *International Journal of Constitutional Law* 4 (1):1-38.

Hillyard, Paddy. 2002. "Invoking Indignation: Reflections on Future Directions of Socio-Legal Studies." *Journal of Law and Society* 29 (2):654-56.

Hinsliff, Gaby. 2004. "Big fall in numbers seeking asylum" *Guardian*, 22 August.
———. 2006. "Blair savages critics over threat to civil liberties." *The Observer*, 23 Apr.

Hinsliff, Gaby and Martin Bright. 2005. "Labour fuels war on asylum." *The Observer*, 06 Feb.

Hinsliff, Gaby and Jamie Doward. 2006. "U-turn on plan to take babies from refugees." *Guardian*, Jan 29.

Hirsch, Afua. 2008. "Asylum tribunal apologises for questioning academic's evidence." *Guardian*, Oct 27.

Home Affairs Committee. 2004. "Asylum Applications." In *Second Report of Session 2003-04*: (HC 218) House of Commons.

Home Office. 1997. *Rights Brought Home: the Human Rights Bill*. London: Stationery Office.
———. 1998. "Fairer, Faster and Firmer - A Modern Approach to Immigration and Asylum." Home Office.
———. 2001. "Bridging the Information Gaps: A Conference of Research on Asylum and Immigration in the UK." London: Home Office.
———. 2002. "Building Trust and Confidence - Home Secretary Tackles Asylum Abuse." Home Office.
———. 2002. "Secure Borders, Safe Haven: Integration with Diversity in Modern Britain." Home Office.
———. *No Let Up Combating Abuse Of The Asylum System-Home Secretary* 2003 [cited. Available from press.homeoffice.gov.uk/press-releases/No_Let_Up_Combatting_Abuse_Of_Th
———. 2003. "Policy Bulletin 75 (on withholding and withdrawing support)." Home Office.
———. 2004. "Government Reply: Asylum Applications." Home Office.
———. 2004. "Nationality, Immigration & Asylum Act 2002: Court Judgment." In *Press Release*.

Horowitz, Donald L. 1977. *The Courts and Social policy*. Washington: Brookings Institution.

House of Commons. 2004. "Asylum Applications." (HC 218-1). House of Commons.
————. 2006. "Returning Failed Asylum Applicants." In *Thirty-fourth Report of Session 2005-06*, ed. Committee of Public Accounts: House of Commons.

Hucker, John. 1999. "Theory Meets Practice: Some Current Human Rights Challenges in Canada " *Journal of Law and Society* 26 (1):54-71.

Hull, Kathleen. 2001. "The Political Limits of the Rights Frame: The Case of Same-Sex Marriage in Hawaii." *Sociological Perspectives* 44 (2):207-32.

Human Rights Watch. 2001. *UK Asylum Proposal Denounced*. HRW 2001 [cited 20 Oct 2006].
————. 2002. "Commentary on the United Kingdom Home Office White Paper: Secure Borders, Safe Haven: Integration with Diversity in Modern Europe." New York: Human Rights Watch.
————. 2002. "E.U.: Protect the Rights of Migrants and Asylum Seekers in Seville Policy Proposals - Letter to E.U. Heads of State ". New York: Human Rights Watch.
————. 2002. "Sri Lanka: Human Rights and the Peace Process." Human Rights Watch.
————. 2004. "Human Rights Overview: European Union." Human Rights Watch.
————. 2005. "Targeting the Fur: Mass Killings in Darfur." New York: Human Rights Watch
————. 2006. "Defending the Human Rights of Migrants and Asylum Seekers in Western Europe." Human Rights Watch.

Hunt, Alan. 1993. *Explorations in Law and Society: Towards a Constitutive Theory of Law*. New York: Routledge.

Hunt, Murray. 1999. "The Human Rights Act and Legal Culture: The Judiciary and the Legal Profession " *Journal of Law and Society* 26 (1):86-102.

Huysmans, Jef. 2006. *The Politics of Insecurity: Fear, Migration, and Asylum in the EU*. London: Routledge.

Hyland, Julie. 2006. *58 Chinese migrants found dead in lorry at Dover, Britain*. World Socialist Web Site 2000 [cited 20 Oct 2006]. Available from http://www.wsws.org/articles/2000/jun2000/immi-j21.shtml.

Independent Asylum Commission. 2008. "Deserving Dignity - A Nationwide Review of the UK Asylum System." London: Independent Asylum Commission.

Information Centre about Asylum and Refugees. *Dead migrant photo: truth worse than fiction?* (Nov 9) 2006 [cited. Available from www.icar.org.uk/?lid=7773.
———. 2006. "Key Issues: UK Asylum Law and Process." ed. K. Ward. London: Information Centre about Asylum and Refugees.

Institute of Development Studies. 2006. *The Rise of Rights*. IDS 2003 [cited 10 Oct 2006]. Available from http://www.ids.ac.uk/ids/bookshop/briefs/index.html.

Inter-Agency Partnership. 2004. "The impact of section 55 on the Inter-Agency Partnership of leading UK refugee agencies and the asylum seekers it supports." London: Inter-Agency Partnership.

International Organization for Migration. 2005. "World Migration: Costs and Benefits of International Migration ". Geneva: International Organization for Migration.

Ipsos/MORI. 2003. British Views on Immigration. www.ipsos-mori.com/researchpublications/researcharchive/poll.aspx?oItemId=847 <accessed 18 Jan 2009>

Jenkins, Simon. 2006. "Not too round, not too precise: that's why 11,000 is a magic number." *Guardian*, 19 May.

Jimenez, Marina. 2005. "Broken Gates: Canada's welcome mat frayed and unravelling." *Globe and Mail*, Apr 16.

Johnston, Ian. 2004. "Worked to death." *The Scotsman*, 08 Feb.

Johnston, Jenifer. 2004. "Most asylum seekers 'come to UK because lives are in danger'." *Sunday Herald*, 13 June.

Johnston, Philip. 2002. "Asylum group to keep £340,000 lottery cash." *Daily Telegraph*, 23 Oct.

————. 2002. "Asylum seekers reach record 100,000 a year." *Daily Telegraph*, 30 Nov.

————. 2002. "Turning the tide of asylum seekers is an impossible task." *Daily Telegraph*, 30 Nov.

————. 2003. "£2bn Bill for Flood of Asylum Seekers." *Daily Telegraph*, March 01.

————. 2003. "Blunkett defies appeal ruling on asylum benefits." *Daily Telegraph*, March 19.

————. 2003. "Court Threat to Blair's Asylum Vow." *Daily Telegraph*, 10 Feb.

————. 2003. "Damning Verdict on Judge." *Daily Telegraph*, 20 Feb, 2.

————. 2003. "Judges denounce Blunkett's policy on asylum claims." *Daily Telegraph*, July 31.

————. 2003. "Pledge to Halve Asylum Seekers Derided." *Daily Telegraph*, 08 February.

————. 2003. "Tough New Asylum Laws 'Too Draconian'." *Daily Telegraph*, 09 Jan.

————. 2003. "Uproar over asylum centre plan." *Daily Telegraph*, 12 Feb.

————. 2003. "Wanted: country houses for asylum seekers." *Daily Telegraph*, 20 Jan.

————. 2006. "Reid Blasts Failures at Home Office." *Daily Telegraph*, 24 May, 2.

Johnston, Philip and G. Jones. 2003. "Blair to take on judges over asylum." *Daily Telegraph*, 20 February, 1.

Joint Committee On Human Rights. 2001. "Nationality, Immigration and Asylum Bill: Further Report on the Twenty-third Report of Session 2001-02." London: Joint Committee On Human Rights. HL 176.

——————. 2002. "Nationality, Immigration and Asylum Bill: *Seventeenth Report of Session 2001-02.*" London: Joint Committee on Human Rights. HL 132.

——————. 2003. "The Case for a Human Rights Commission *(Sixth Report of Session 2002-03).*" London: Joint Committee On Human Rights. HL 67.

————. 2004. "Asylum and Immigration (Treatment of Claimants, etc.) Bill. ." In *Fifth Report of Session 2003-04*. London: Joint Committee On Human Rights. HL 35.

————. 2004. "Asylum and Immigration (Treatment of Claimants, etc.) Bill: New Clauses - *Fourteenth Report of Session 2003-04.*" London: Joint Committee On Human Rights. HL 130.

————. 2006. "The Human Rights Act: the DCA and Home Office Reviews." London: Joint Committee On Human Rights. *32nd Report of Session 2005-06*. HL 278.

_____. 2007. "Government Response to the Committee's Tenth Report of this Session: The Treatment of Asylum Seekers." London: Joint Committee on Human Rights. HL 134.

_____. 2007. "Human Rights Policy: Oral and Written Evidence." London: Joint Committee On Human Rights. HL 174.

_____. 2007. "Monitoring the Government's Response to Court Judgments Finding Breaches of Human Rights." In *Sixteenth Report of Session 2006–07*. London: Joint Committee on Human Rights. HL 128.

_____. 2007. "The Treatment of Asylum-Seekers." In *Tenth Report of Session 2006-07*. London: Joint Committee On Human Rights. HL 81-1.

_____. 2008. "A Bill of Rights for the UK? *Twenty–ninth Report of Session 2007–08*." London: Joint Committee on Human Rights. HL 165-1.

Joint Council for the Welfare of Immigrants. 2007. *A Joint Statement on the withdrawal of asylum support for in-country applicants* 2003 [cited Apr 25 2007]. Available from http://www.jcwi.org.uk/archives/ukpollcy/statementsec55.html.

———. 2007. *Section 55 Asylum Support Law Denounced*. JCWI 2003 [cited Mar 10 2007]. Available from www.jcwi.org.uk/archives/ukpollcy/sec55_4aug03.html.

Joppke, Christian. 1999. *Immigration and the Nation-State*. Oxford: Oxford University Press.

JUSTICE. 2007. *Refugees: Renewing the Vision* 2004 [cited 2007]. Available from http://www.justice.org.uk/ourwork/asylum/index.html.

_____. 2005. "Immigration, Asylum and Nationality Bill - Briefing for Commons Second Reading."

———. 2005. "Law Lords unanimously condemn withdrawal of support for asylum seekers." In *Press Release*. London.

Kantor, Jodi. 2008. "As a Professor, a Pragmatist About the Supreme Court." *The New York Times*, 02 May

———. 2008. "Teaching Law, Testing Ideas, Obama Stood Apart" *The New York Times*, 30 Jul.

Kavanagh, Trevor. 2003. "Blunkett Fury as Judge Boots Out New Asylum Law." *The Sun*, 20 Feb.

Kettle, Martin. 2005. "We hate our politicians, but we've never had it so good: Fear of immigration and crime is driving the parties to outbid each other." *Guardian*, Feb 08.

Kirby, Terry (undated). "The Human Rights Act: 800 years in the making." *Guardian* www.guardian.co.uk/humanrightsandwrongs/800-years-making

Kirchner, Stefan. 2007. "Hell on Earth - Systematic Rape in Eastern Congo." *Journal of Humanitarian Assistance*.

Kundnani, Arun. 2007. *Britain gripped by populist campaigns against immigrants*. Institute of Race Relations 2003 [cited May 27 2007]. Available from http://www.irr.org.uk/2003/january/ak000017.html.

Lazarus-Black, Mindie and Susan F. Hirsch. 1994. *Contested States: Law, Hegemony, and Resistance*. London: Routledge.

Leader. 2003. "Almost Beyond Belief." *Guardian*, 25 November.
———. 2003. "Asylum rights evaporate" *Guardian*, 10 Feb.
———. 2003. "Judges v ministers: Courts step in where MPs fear to tread." *Guardian*, 24 Feb.
———. 2003. "Swamped by pledges." *Daily Telegraph*, 10 Feb.
———. 2003. "A victory for humanity" *Guardian*, 20 Feb.
———. 2005. "A political debate that shames us" *The Observer*, 06 Feb.
———. 2006. "It is time to protect the public's human rights." *Daily Telegraph*, 11 May.
———. 2006. "Strangers at our gates." *Guardian*, 20 April.

Leapman, Ben, and Melissa Kite. 2006. "Hundreds of corruption inquiries at Immigration." *Daily Telegraph*, 27 July.

Legal Action for Women. *Press Release* 2003 [cited. Available from http://www.allwomencount.net/EWC%20LAW/protests_against_section_55_cont.htm.

Legrain, Philippe. 2008. "Tear down the walls." *Guardian*, 08 Aug.

Leppard, David. 2004. "Focus: Ministers lose control of Britain's borders." *The Times*, 04 April.
———. 2004. "Shambles of the asylum cheats' charter." *The Times*, 14 Nov.

Leppard, David, and Robert Winnett. 2004. "Memo leak exposes asylum meltdown in middle England." *Sunday Times*, 29 August.

Lester, Anthony. 2003. "Don't blame the judges." *Guardian*, 25 February.
———. 2003. "The Human Rights Act - Five Years On." In *Third Annual Lecture Law Reform Committee of the Bar Council*.
_____. 2006. "Ignorant Opposition" *Guardian*, 16 May
———. 2009. "My Misery as a Tethered Goat in Gordon Brown's Big Tent." *Guardian*, 27 July.

Liberty. *Asylum Benefits: Liberty wins emergency injunction* (17 Jan) 2003 [cited. Available from www.liberty-human-rights.org.uk/news-and-events/1-press-releases/2003/asylum-benefits-liberty-wins-emergency-injun.shtml.
———. 2007. *Liberty Reaction to High Court Ruling on Asylum* (19 Feb) 2003 [cited 20 June 2007]. Available from http://www.liberty-human-rights.org.uk/news-and-events/1-press-releases/2003/reaction-to-high-court-ruling-on-asylum.shtml.
———. 2003. "Submission to the Court of Appeal in Q and Others." London: Liberty.
———. 2006. "Evidence to the Joint Committee on Human Rights: Treatment of Asylum Seekers." London: Liberty.

Liberty and JUSTICE. 2005. "Written Intervention (Limbuela) before the House of Lords." (Confidential – on file with author).

Lido, Catherine. 2006. "Negative Press Gives Asylum-seekers a Bad Name." London: Economic and Social Research Council.

Lipman, Maureen. 2006. "In the hysteria over illegal asylum seekers, refugees like my Nepalese friend Tham are being let down by the system." *Guardian*, 24 March.

Llewellyn, Jennifer J. 2002. "Dealing with the Legacy of Native Residential School Abuse in Canada: Litigation, ADR, and Restorative Justice." *The University of Toronto Law Journal* 52 (3):253-300.

Loescher, Gil, Alexander Betts, and James Milner. 2008. *The United Nations High Commissioner for Refugees (UNHCR): The Politics and Practice of Refugee Protection into the Twenty-first Century*. London: Routledge.

Lomba, Sylvie Da. 2006. "The threat of destitution as a deterrent against asylum seeking in the European Union." *Refuge* 23 (1):78-93.

MacKinnon, Catharine A. 1993. "Crimes of War, Crimes of Peace." In *On Human Rights: the Oxford Amnesty lectures 1993*, ed. S. Shute and S. L. Hurley. New York: Basic Books.

_____. 1989. *Towards a Feminist Theory of the State*. Cambridge: Harvard University Press.

MacKinnon, Ian. 2009. "Thailand accused of setting migrants adrift at sea." *Guardian*, 19 January.

Maiman, Richard. 2004. "We've had to raise our game: Liberty's litigation strategy under the Human Rights Act 1998." In *Human Rights Brought Home: Socio-Legal Perspectives on Human Rights in the National Context*, ed. S. Halliday and P. D. Schmidt. Oxford: Hart Publishing.

Majid, Amir A. 2005. "Do we care about the rule of law?" *New Law Journal* 155 (7197):1561.

Makin, Kirk. 2002. "Indigent Optimistic Despite Loss at Top Court." *Globe and Mail*, 20 Dec

Malik, Maleiha. 2001. "Minority Protection and Human Rights." In *Sceptical Essays on Human Rights*, ed. T. Campbell, K. D. Ewing and A. Tomkins. Oxford: Oxford University Press.

Mandel, Michael. 1994. *The Charter of Rights and the Legalization of Politics in Canada*. Toronto: Thompson

Marais, E. 2005. "Wives Unite to Fight Against 'Inhumane' System'." *Hounslow Guardian*, 29 Sep.

Marsden, Chris. 2006. *Britain: Labour government steps up persecution of asylum seekers*. World Socialist Web Site 2001 [cited 20 Oct 2006]. Available from http://www.wsws.org/articles/2001/apr2001/asyl-a28.shtml.

Martin, Lorna. 2004. "Asylum losers spark city crisis." *Observer*, 13 June, 13.

Mayor of London. 2004. *Destitution by Design*. London: Greater London Authority.

McCann, M. 1994. *Rights at Work: Pay Equity Reform and the Politics of Legal Mobilization*. Chicago: University of Chicago Press.

———. 1998. "How Does Law Matter for Social Movements?" In *How Does Law Matter*, ed. B. Garth and A. Sarat. Illinois: Northwestern University Press.

———. 1999. "The common place of law: Stories from everyday life." *American Journal of Sociology* 105 (1):238-40.

McCann, M. and W. Haltom. 2006. "On analyzing legal culture: A reply to Kagan." *Law and Social Inquiry-Journal of the American Bar Foundation* 31 (3):739-55.

McCormick, P. 1993. "Party Capability Theory and Appellate Successes in the Supreme Court of Canada, 1949-1992. . ." *Canadian Journal of Political Science* 26 (3):523-40.

McFadyean, Melanie. 2006. "Centres of barbarism." *Guardian*, 02 Dec.

———. 2006. "A lapse of humanity." *Guardian*, 16 Nov

McHugh, A C. 2002. *Tensions Between the Executive and the Judiciary*. Australian Bar Association Conference 2002 [cited. Available from http://www.hcourt.gov.au/speeches/mchughj/mchughj_paris.htm.

McIlroy, Anne. 2006. "Severance payments." *The Guardian*, Jan 03.

McIntyre, Lisa J. 1994. *Law in the Sociological Enterprise: A Reconstruction*. Boulder: Westview Press.

McMahon, Barbara. 2005. "Asylum seekers' voyages of hell." *The Observer*, 17 July.

McMahon, Kevin J. and Michael Paris. 1998. "The Politics of Rights Revisited: Rosenberg, McCann, and the New Institutionalism." In *Leveraging the Law*, ed. D. A. Schultz. New York: Peter Lang.

Migration Watch. 2006. *Appeal outcome could be 'tip of iceberg' 2003* [cited 2006]. Available from http://www.migrationwatchuk.org/pressreleases.

———. 2006. *Implications of the Government's Appeal on Asylum Benefits*. Migration Watch 2003 [cited 2006].

————. 2006. *Response to High Court ruling* 2003 [cited 2006]. Available from http://www.migrationwatchuk.org/pressreleases/.

Milner, Neal and Jonathan Goldberg-Hiller. 2002. "Reimagining Rights." *Law and Social Inquiry* Spring: 1-18.

Ministry of Justice. 2008. "Human Rights Insight Project." In *Ministry of Justice Research Series*. London: Ministry of Justice.

Moore, Charles. 2009. "Our Human Rights Culture Has Now Become a Tyranny." *Daily Telegraph,* 18 Dec

Morris, Lydia. 2007. "New Labour's Community of Rights: Welfare, Immigration and Asylum." *Journal of Social Policy* (36):39-57.

Morton, F. L. 2002. *Law, Politics and the Judicial Process in Canada.* Calgary: University of Calgary Press.

Moxon, S. 2006. "Ineptitude and Political Correctness Gone Mad" *Daily Mail*, 28 April.

Mr Dolittle. 2003. "The Sun Says." *The Sun*, 27 Jan.

Mulholland, Helene. 2003. "Lottery lost £1m a week after asylum row" *Guardian*, 09 October.

Murdoch, Dan. 2002. "Welfare Rights in a Modern State: A Theoretical Approach to Gosselin v. Quebec." *Journal of Law and Equality* 1 (1):25-53.

National Audit Office. 2004. "Improving the Speed and Quality of Asylum Decisions." National Audit Office.

National Coalition of Anti-Deportation Campaigns. 2006. *Newszine 28* (October - November - 2002) 2002 [cited 20 Oct 2006]. Available from http://www.ncadc.org.uk/archives/filed%20newszines/oldnewszines/news28/28index.html.
————. *Beware the 8th January 2003* [cited. Available from http://www.ncadc.org.uk/archives/filed%20newszines/oldnewszines/news28/8thjan.html.

Nicol, Danny. 2004. "The Human Rights Act and the Politicians." *Legal Studies* 24 (3):451-79.

Norton-Taylor, Richard. 1999. *The Colour of Justice*. London: Oberon Books.

———. 2006. "Arms sales record as firms duck controls with 'flat-pack' weapons." *Guardian*, 03 Oct.

———. 2006. "Huge jump in arms sales to Israel." *Guardian*, 06 April.

Nye, Joseph. *The Rising Power of NGOs*. Daily Times 2004 [cited. Available from http://www.dailytimes.com.pk/default.asp?page=story_27-6-2004_pg3_7.

Oakeshott, Isabel. 2006. "Blears warns over 'explosive' immigration." *Sunday Times*, 10 Dec.

Oxfam. 2001. "Asylum: The Truth Behind the Headlines." London: Oxfam.

———. 2002. "Response to UK Government's White Paper on immigration, citizenship and asylum: Secure Borders, Safe Haven ". London: Oxfam.

Oxfam and Refugee Council. 2002. "Poverty and asylum in the UK." London: Oxfam and Refugee Council.

O'Nions, Helen. 2006. "The Erosion Of The Right To Seek Asylum." *Web Journal of Current Legal Issues* 2.

Parliamentary and Health Service Ombudsman. 2002. "Incorrect Refusal of Application for Asylum: 6th Report of Session 2001-2002." In *6th Report of Session 2001-2002*. London: Parliamentary and Health Service Ombudsman.

Pedriana, N. 2006. "From protective to equal treatment: Legal framing processes and transformation of the women's movement in the 1960s." *American Journal of Sociology* 111 (6):1718-61.

Penner, Roland. 1996. "The Canadian Experience with the Charter of Rights: Are there Lessons for the UK." *Public Law,* Spring: 104-25.

Petr van Tuijl. 1999. "NGOs and Human Rights: Sources of Justice and Democracy." *Journal of International Affairs* 52.

Phillips, Melanie. 2003. "Judicial Hubris and Asylum Policy." *Daily Mail*, 21 Feb.

Phuong, Catherine. 2005. "The removal of failed asylum seekers." *Legal Studies* 25 (1):117-41.

Pickett, Mel. 2003. "On the asylum frontline" *Guardian*, 02 February.

Pilger, John. 2008. "Under cover of racist myth, a new land grab in Australia." *The Guardian*, Oct 24.

Pirouet, Louise. 2001. *Whatever Happened to Asylum in Britain?* Oxford: Berghahn.

Pollock, Jenny. 2001. "Opinion on asylum seeker integration remains mixed." *Guardian*, June 27.

Polman, Linda and Robert L. Bland. 2004. *We Did Nothing*. London: Viking.

Porter, Andrew. 2006. "Labour: Rights Act is mess." *The Sun*, 15 May.

Porter, Henry. 2006. "Blair gets away with his assault on liberty, because we let him." *The Observer*, 16 Apr.
———. 2006. "How we move ever closer to becoming a totalitarian state " *The Observer*, 05 Mar.
———. 2006. "Only a constitution can save us from this abuse of power." *The Observer*, 02 Apr.

Pound, Stephen. 2003. "Judge Makes Tackling Asylum Even Tougher." *Sunday Express*, 23 Feb

Press Release. 2006. *New Labour: Government policy to leave thousands homeless and hungry*. AsylumSupport.info 2002 [cited 30 Oct 2006]. Available from http://www.asylumsupport.info/thousandstobeleftdestitute.htm.
———. 2006. *Refugee Council's AGM hears evidence of Government action that has left victims of torture sleeping rough on the streets* AsylumSupport.info 2003 [cited 30 Oct 2006]. Available from http://www.asylumsupport.info/victimsoftorture.htm.
———. 2004. "Refugee Council welcomes Court of Appeal decision to uphold asylum seekers' right to shelter."

Prince, Rosa. 2005. "Our Terror Laws are Flawed, Our Asylum Rules Verge on Racist." *Daily Mirror*, 09 June.

Prosser, Tony. 1983. *Test Cases for the Poor: Legal Techniques in the Politics of Social Welfare*. London: Child Poverty Action Group.

Puttick, Keith. 2005. "Strangers at the welfare gate: asylum seekers, welfare and Convention rights after Adam." *Immigration, Asylum and Nationality Law* 19 (4):214-34.

Randall, Colin. 2005. "Ghost of Sangatte back to haunt Calais." *Daily Telegraph*, 28 Oct.

Refugee Action. 2006. "The Destitution Trap." London: Refugee Action.

Refugee Council. *High Court rules Home Office in breach of Human Rights Convention* [Press Release] 2003 [cited. Available from http://www.refugeecouncil.org.uk/news/press/2003/august/20030801high.htm.

———. 2006. *High Court ruling restores food and shelter to destitute asylum seekers* 2003 [cited 25 May 2006]. Available from http://www.refugeecouncil.org.uk/news/press/2003/february/20030219high.htm

———. *Home Secretary announces policy change regarding Section 55* [Press Release] 2003 [cited. Available from http://www.refugeecouncil.org.uk/news/press/2003/december/20031218home.htm.

———. *UK Asylum: new Bill endangers refugee protection in UK* 2003 [cited. Available from http://www.refugeecouncil.org.uk/news/press/2003/december/20031217ukas.htm.

———. 2003. "Update: Withdrawal of in-country asylum support." London: Refugee Council.

———. *Asylum seekers win back their rights to basic food and shelter* 2004 [cited. Available from http://www.refugeecouncil.org.uk/news/press/2004/june/20040625asylu.htm.

———. 2004. "Hungry and Homeless: The Impact of the Withdrawal of State Support on Asylum Seekers, Refugee Communities and the Voluntary Sector." London: Refugee Council.

———. *House of Lords backs judgment restoring support to destitute asylum seekers* 2005 [cited. Available from http://www.refugeecouncil.org.uk/news/press/2005/november/20051103house.htm.

———. 2005. "The Refugee Council's submission to the Campaign Against Legal Aid Cuts (CALAC) about the impact of changes to legal aid." London: Refugee Council.

———. *Section 9 is a question of morality, not law, says the Refugee Council* 2005 [cited. Available from http://www.refugeecouncil.org.uk/news/press/2006/january/20060131secti.htm.

————. 2008. "A briefing on the Draft (partial) Immigration and Citizenship Bill 2008." London: Refugee Council.

Richardson, G and David Machin. 2000. "Judicial Review and Tribunal Decision Making: A Study of the Mental Health Review Tribunal." *Public Law* Autumn: 494-514.

Richardson, G and Maurice Sunkin. 1996. "Judicial Review: Questions of Impact." *Public Law* Spring: 79-103.

Rippert, Ulrich. 2006. *EU summit steps up attack on refugees and foreigners.* World Socialist Web Site 2002 [cited 16 Oct 2006]. Available from http://www.wsws.org/articles/2002/jul2002/eu-j05.shtml.

Rosenberg, Gerald N. 1991. *The Hollow Hope: Can Courts Bring About Social Change?* Chicago: University of Chicago.

Rozenberg, Gabriel and Greg Hurst. 2004. "Backbench revolt over asylum shake-up." *The Times*, 02 March.

Rozenberg, Joshua. 2003. "Judges prepare for battle with Blunkett." *Daily Telegraph*, 26 Feb.

Sales, Rosemary. 2002. "The deserving and the undeserving? Refugees, asylum seekers and welfare in Britain." *Critical Social Policy* 22 (3):456-78.

Sarat, Austin. 2004. *The Blackwell companion to law and society.* Oxford: Blackwell.

Sawer, Patrick. 2008. "Asylum refugees' treatment 'inhuman'." *Daily Telegraph*, 29 Jun.

Scheingold, Stuart A. 1974. *The Politics of Rights: Lawyers, Public Policy, and Political Change.* London: Yale University Press.
————. 2004. *The Politics of Rights: Lawyers, Public Policy, and Political Change.* 2nd ed. Ann Arbor: University of Michigan Press.

Schultz, David A. 1998. *Leveraging the law: using the courts to achieve social change.* New York: P. Lang.

Sedley, Stephen. 2005. "The Rocks or the Open Sea: Where is the Human Rights Act Heading?" *Journal of Law and Society* 32 (1):3-17.

Semyonov, Moshe and Rebeca Raijman. 2006. "The Rise of Anti-foreigner Sentiment in European Societies, 1988-2000." *American Sociological Review* 71 (June):426-49.

Shapiro, Martin M. and Alec Stone Sweet. 2002. *On Law, Politics, and Judicialization.* Oxford: Oxford University Press.

Sharma, Parnesh. 1998. *Aboriginal Fishing Rights: Laws, Courts, Politics.* Halifax, N.S.: Fernwood.

Shelter. 2004. "Briefing: Section 55 of the Nationality, Immigration and Asylum Act 2002. Independent Review." London: Shelter.
———. 2004. "Press Release: Shelter is a basic human right, says Court of Appeal." Shelter.
———. 2004. Submissions (The Queen on Application of Limbuela, Tesema, and Adam).

Sherlock, Maeve. 2005. Asylum seeker destitution. Paper read at Church Action on Poverty, 03 Dec, at Manchester.

Shifrin, Tash. 2004. "Lords threaten to vote against asylum benefits ban" *Guardian*, 20 May.

Smith, Adrain A. 2005. "Legal Consciousness and Resistance in Caribbean Seasonal Agricultural Workers." *Canadian Journal of Law and Society* 20 (2):95-122.

Smith, Christopher E. 1991. *Courts and the Poor*. Chicago: Nelson-Hall.

Smith, Iain Duncan. 2002. "Why the French are laughing at us this morning." *Daily Mail*, 24 May 4.

Smith, Liz. *Britain: New government attack on asylum seekers.* World Socialist Web Site 2003 [cited. Available from http://www.wsws.org/articles/2003/nov2003/asyl-n15.shtml.

————. 2006. *Britain: Government steps up attacks on asylum seekers.* World Socialist Web Site 2004 [cited 16 Oct 2006]. Available from http://www.wsws.org/articles/2004/jan2004.bak/asyl-j05.shtml.

Smith, Roger. 2005. Speech: Five years of a Human Rights Act and the impact of terrorism. Paper read at Australian Human Rights Centre, at Sydney.

Smith-Spark, Laura. *'Vigilantes' set for Mexico border patrol* (March 28). BBC News 2005 [cited.

Sontag, Susan. 2004. 'Regarding the Torture of Others' *New York Times*, 23 May

Southworth, Ann. 2000. "The Rights Revolution and Support Structure for Rights Advocacy." *Law and Society Review* 34(4) 1203-19

Spencer, Sarah. 2003. *The Politics of Migration: Managing Opportunity, Conflict and Change.* Malden, Mass.: Blackwell.
————. 2008. "Equality and Human Rights Commission: A Decade in the Making." *Political Quarterly* 79 (1):6-16.

Stanley, Alison. 2004. "A knee-jerk immigration policy." *New Law Journal* 154 (7127):673.

Stevens, Dallal. 1998. "The Asylum and Immigration Act 1996: Erosion of the Right to Seek Asylum." *Modern Law Review* 61 (2):207-22.
————. 2001. "The Immigration and Asylum Act 1996: A Missed Opportunity?" *Modern Law Review* 64 (3):413-38.
————. 2004. "The Nationality, Immigration and Asylum Act 2002: Secure Borders, Safe Haven?" *Modern Law Review* 67 (4):616-31.

Stone Sweet, Alec. 2000. *Governing with judges: constitutional politics in Europe.* Oxford: Oxford University Press.

Sunkin, Maurice and Kathyrn Pick. 2001. "The Changing Impact of Judicial Review: The Independent Review Service of the Social Fund." *Public Law* Winter: 736-62.

Swedlow, Brendon. 2009. 'Reason For Hope? The Spotted Owl Injunctions and Policy Change' Law & Social Inquiry 34 (4): 825-67

Sylvester, Rachel. 2003. "Blunkett accuses judges of damaging democracy." *Daily Telegraph*, 21 Feb.

Tamanaha, Brian Z. 1997. *Realistic Socio-Legal Theory: Pragmatism and a Social Theory of Law*. Oxford: Clarendon Press.

Taylor, Matthew. 2004. "Asylum policies 'make 10,000 people destitute a year' " *Guardian*, 09 February.

Telegraph Speaker's Corner. 2006. "Time for a rethink on human rights?" *Daily Telegraph*, 11 May.

Tempest, Matthew. 2002. "Duncan Smith: keep Sangatte refugees out " *Guardian*, 24 May.

Tendler, Stewart. 2004. "'Unachievable' asylum policy led to detention centre riot." *The Times*, 17 Nov.

The Joseph Rowntree Charitable Trust. 2008. "More Destitution in Leeds." ed. D. Brown. London: The Joseph Rowntree Charitable Trust.

Thomas, Mark. 2002. "Mark Thomas considers the colour of Blunkett's dog." *New Statesman*, 13 May.

Thomas, Robert. 2003. "The Impact of Judicial Review on Asylum." *Public Law* AUT: 479-510.

Thompson, E. P. 1975. *Whigs and hunters: the origin of the Black Act*. London: Allen Lane.

Tickle, Louise. 2006. "Refugees in the front line of the fight for human rights." *Guardian*, 04 July.

Townsend, Mark and Jamie Doward. 2006. "Cash for asylum scandal hits Reid." *Guardian*, 04 June.

Townsend, Mark and Gaby Hinsliff. 2005. "Truth about Calais 'immigrant menace'." *The Observer*, 17 Apr.

Travis, Alan. 2001. "Blunkett fury at asylum camp defeat." *Guardian*, Sep 8.

———. 2003. "Asylum Policy Degrading, High Court Rules." *Guardian*, 01 Aug.

———. 2003. "Asylum test case fast tracks to high court." *Guardian*, 10 Feb.

———. 2003. "Benefits cuts stay for asylum seekers." *Guardian*, 09 Feb, 4.

———. 2003. "Blunkett aims to axe asylum legal aid" *Guardian*, 25 November.

———. 2003. "Blunkett asylum law 'will face court battle'." *Guardian*, 01 Dec.

———. 2003. "Judge orders urgent asylum case hearings" *Guardian*, 17 Jan.

———. 2004. "Asylum operation racist, say law lords." *Guardian*, 10 Dec.

———. 2004. "Blunkett backs down on aid for asylum seekers" *Guardian*, 26 June.

———. 2004. "Failed asylum seekers must work for no pay" *Guardian*, 09 June.

———. 2005. "Asylum centres plagued by racism and abuse, says report" *Guardian*, 22 July.

———. 2006. "Ministers accused of fuelling myths on human rights." *Guardian*, 14 Nov

Tremlett, Giles. 2005. "Under fire at Europe's border" *The Observer*, 02 Oct.

Tunstall, Kate E. 2006. *Displacement, Asylum, Migration: the Oxford Amnesty Lectures 2004*. Oxford: Oxford University Press.

Tyler, Richard. 2006. *Audit Commission report critical of Britain's compulsory dispersal of refugees*. World Socialist Web Site 2000 [cited 20 Oct 2006]. Available from http://www.wsws.org/articles/2000/jun2000/asyl-j06.shtml.

———. 2006. *Britain: Government and media conspire to whip-up anti-immigrant hysteria*. World Socialist Web Site 2003 [cited 04 Dec 2006]. Available from http://www.wsws.org/articles/2003/feb2003/brit-f10.shtml.

University of Essex. 2005 *The 2005 General Election in Great Britain*. BBC, 'Election issues: Immigration' (2005) April 05 <http://news.bbc.co.uk/1/hi/uk_politics/vote_2005/issues/4352373.stm>

U.S. Committee for Refugees and Immigrants. 2005. "World Refugee Survey." U.S. Committee for Refugees and Immigrants.

UNHCR. 2003. "Sofia Judicial Round Table on Refugee Protection." Sofia: UN.

———. *UN Refugee agency has grave concerns over tabloid reporting of asylum* 2003 [cited. Available from http://www.unhcr.org.uk/press/press_releases2003/pr23Oct03.htm.

————. 2003. "The Wall Behind Which Refugees Can Shelter." *Refugees Magazine* (123).

————. 2003. "UNHCR criticises Australia for turning boat people away." *UNHCR News Stories*. Geneva: UNHCR.

————. 2006. *The State of the World's Refugees*. New York, N.Y.: Penguin Books.

————. 2007. "Internally-displaced Persons: Questions and Answers." Geneva: United Nations High Commissioner for Refugees

Verkaik, Robert. 2003. "Asylum system flawed, rules High Court." *The Independent*, 20 Feb.

————. 2004. "Immigration lawyers facing campaign of fire-bombing and death threats." *The Independent*, 12 April.

————. 2004. "Race-hate crimes reach record levels - and experts say asylum policy may be to blame." *The Independent*, 07 April, 12.

————. 2005. "Britain in the dock for human rights failures after more than 100 'guilty' judgments filed." *The Independent*, 03 Oct, 6.

————. 2005. "Britain in the dock for human rights failures after more than 100 'guilty' judgments filed." *Independent*, 03 Oct.

————. 2006. "UN criticises Home Office over refugees." *Independent*, 28 June, 4.

————. 2008. "Asylum-seekers put at risk by law, warns top judge." *The Independent*, 02 Jul.

————. 2008. "How 'Independent' story was denied – then accepted." *The Independent*, 30 Sept.

————. 2008. "Investigation into claims of abuse on asylum-seekers." *The Independent*, 30 Sept.

Wadham, John. 2006. *The Human Rights Act: One year on*. Legal Action Group 2001 [cited 10 Oct 2006].

Walter, Natasha. 2006. "The asylum process is failing too many women." *Guardian*, 23 May.

Ward, David. 2005. "Asylum measure inhuman and disastrous, says report." *Guardian*, 07 Nov.

————. 2005. "Councils call for review of asylum law that strips families of benefits" *Guardian*, 09 Aug.

Waugh, Paul. 2003. "Think-Tank Distorts Asylum Facts, says Former Minister." *The Independent*, 19 November, 9.

———. 2004. "Crackdown on asylum leaving genuine refugees homeless and destitute, MPs say." *The Independent*, 26 January, 4.

Wazir, Burhan. 2004. "Inter-racial hatred pits local migrants against 'dirty' newcomers." *The Times*, 27 Nov.

Webber, Frances. *NASS: Chronicle of Failure*. Institute of Race Relations 2003 [cited. Available from http://www.irr.org.uk/2003/july/ak000010.html.

———. 2004. "Asylum: From Deterrence to Destitution." *Race and Class* 45 (77).

———. 2006. *The impact of the Asylum Bill*. Independent Race and Refugee News Network 2004 [cited 9 October 2006]. Available from http://www.irr.org. uk/2004/may/ha000011.html.

———. 2006. *Two landmark asylum judgments*. Institute of Race Relations 2006 [cited 30 Oct 2006]. Available from http://www.irr.org.uk/2006/october/ha000025. html.

White, Ben. 2008. "New Labour's bare-knuckle fight against asylum seekers." *Guardian*, July 25.

William MacPherson and Home Office. 1999. *The Stephen Lawrence Inquiry: Report of an Inquiry*. 2 vols. London: Stationery Office.

Willman, Sue. 2003. "Everyone's a winner?" *New Law Journal* 153:696.

Winnett, Robert and David Leppard. 2004. "Shires buckle under migrant tension." *Sunday Times*, 29 August.

Wintour, Patrick, Stratton, A. and Afua Hirsch. 2008. "Brown Advisor: Labour's Rights Record Dismal." *Guardian,* Dec 11

Yarde, R. 2001. "Demon of the Day." *Guardian*, November 12.

Young, James. 1999. "The Politics of the Human Rights Act" *Journal of Law and Society* 26 (1):27-37.

Younge, Gary. 2001. "The Waiting Game." *Guardian*, May 22

INDEX